Gender and C

Gender and Catastrophe

Edited by Ronit Lentin

ZED BOOKS
London & New York

To Alana and Miki

This project owes its birth to two ideational midwives whose work has inspired me to explore the link between catastrophes and the construction of gender. My compatriot Nira Yuval-Davis of the University of Greenwich has opened my eyes to the intersection of gender, ethnicity, nation and class. Joan Ringelheim's seminal work on women and the Shoah has also been inspirational in linking major catastrophes with women's experiences and the construction of gender. Thanks to both of them for doing the important work they do. Thanks also to all at Zed Books, especially my editor Louise Murray and Julian Hosie; to the production team, especially Lucy Morton and the copyeditor Helen Sniadek; and to the cover designer Andrew Corbett.

Gender and Catastrophe was first published in 1997 by
Zed Books Ltd, 7 Cynthia Street, London N1 9JF, UK, and
Room 400, 175 Fifth Avenue, New York, NY 10010, USA

Distributed in the USA exclusively by St Martin's Press Inc.,
175 Fifth Avenue, New York, NY 10010, USA

Typeset in Monotype Garamond by Lucy Morton, London SE12
Cover designed by Andrew Corbett
Printed and bound in the United Kingdom
by Biddles Ltd, Guildford and King's Lynn.

A catalogue record for this book is available from the British Library

A catalogue record for this book has been applied for
from the Library of Congress

ISBN 1 85649 445 4 (Hb)
ISBN 1 85649 446 2 (Pb)

Contents

Part I

Genders and Genocides

1

Introduction:
(En)gendering Genocides

Ronit Lentin

Although an ancient phenomenon, the term 'genocide' was first coined in 1944 by the Polish jurist Raphael Lemkin, a leading lobbyist for the 1948 United Nations Convention on the Prevention and Punishment of Genocide (UNGC). Racism's 'logic' often ultimately entails genocide, or slavery. The major issue in the definition of genocide is intentionality: ethnocide (the destruction of culture) and the failure to protect indigenous peoples from famine and disease are as foreseeable and intended as genocidal massacres. Helen Fein (1993) broadened, and thus (en)gendered, Lemkin's definition of genocide (1944) to include 'the sustained purposeful action by a perpetrator to physically destroy a collectivity directly or indirectly, through interdiction of the biological and social reproduction of group members'. Because women bear the next generation of a collectivity, they are put uniquely at risk as members of a group targeted as 'racially inferior'. Taking into account the construction of women as ethnic and national subjects, the definition of genocide must be gendered, to include political projects involving slavery, sexual slavery, mass rape, mass sterilization, aimed, through women, at 'ethnic cleansing' and the elimination or alteration of a future ethnic group. Catastrophes, genocidal or otherwise, as this collection illustrates, target women in very specific ways due to their social, ethnic and national construction.

In the last hundred years many millions of people were the casualties of genocides and catastrophes. In 1894–96, 200,000 Armenians were massacred, thousands were exiled and hundreds of settlements were burnt and looted by the Ottomans. In 1915, the post-Ottoman Turkish regime massacred the remaining Armenian male population and deported the women and children to the deserts of Syria and Mesopotamia, thus eliminating an entire nation from its homeland of several millennia. Refugees died of starvation, epidemics and exposure, and the memory of their nation was obliterated as churches and cultural monuments were desecrated (Hovannisian, 1988).

The Nazi regime systematically murdered over six million Jews. Condemned to death as a people, the Jews were ghettoized, starved, tortured and killed. Those who did not die in the ghettoes were shot by regular police units and mobile killing squads (*Einsatzgruppen*). To fulfil Hitler's promise that 'the result of [the] war will be the total annihilation of the Jewish people' (Brietman, 1992: 19), Jews had to be worked to death or deported to extermination camps, mostly in Poland. In the camps, the able-bodied were selected for slave labour; the rest were killed in gas chambers, on assembly-line principles, their bodies cremated or buried in mass graves (Rittner and Roth, 1993: 11–12). The Shoah, or Holocaust,[1] was based not merely on anti-Semitism, but on racist state ideology. There was a direct ideological and organizational link between the Nazis killing the retarded and mentally ill, the *Lebensborn* programme (kidnapping children of 'Aryan' appearance in Poland and inducing Aryans to propagate) and the Final Solution. The Nazi genocidal campaign – the encounter between factors themselves quite ordinary and common such as rationality, technology, bureaucracy and state violence (Bauman, 1989) – also destroyed millions of non-Jewish civilians, including a quarter to a half of the Roma and Sinti (estimates vary between 200,000 and 600,000 Gypsy victims); homosexual men (between 50,000 and 500,000 homosexual victims) (Laska, 1983: 261–2), Poles, Russians, POWs, the handicapped, Jehovah's Witnesses, Communists, Socialists, 'asocials' – 20 million in all, although only the Jews were marked for total destruction (Bauman, 1989: x).

There is a difference between genocide aimed at ethnic, racial and national collectivities, where membership is reproduced genealogically, and systematic extermination of ideological and sexual minorities in which people become members on an individual basis, even if their numbers reach millions. The labelling of Stalin's victims as 'enemies of the people' was used to attempt to legitimate the Communist regime. Soviet and Communist genocide and mass state killings, sometimes termed politicide, occurred in the Soviet Union, Cambodia and the People's Republic of China. The total number of victims of genocide, mass terror, slave labour, Stalin's 1933 engineered famine, and deportations in the Soviet Union between 1917 and 1987 is estimated at 62 million (Rummel, 1990). In Cambodia, Marxism served as an ideological justification for the massacre of one third of the Cambodians by the Khmer Rouge between 1975 and 1979.

Colonization entailed the destruction of native peoples in continents and states settled by Europeans: North and South America, Australia, New Zealand, Africa. The settlement process itself within the colonialist project is often seen as an act of genocide against the native people through violence accompanying the appropriation of land, diseases imported by the settlers, alcoholism, wars and slaughter by the colonists (Barta, 1987). Ethnocide (also called assimilating or 'civilizing' the Indians) was the principal US policy towards American Indians in the nineteenth century. The main forms of genocide were through famine, deportation, failure to provide food supplies, kidnapping Indian women and children and denying Indians protection from settlers, but also genocidal massacres. Among the Indian tribes targeted for genocide were the Cherokee, the Yuki and the Cheyennes (Chalk and Jonassohn, 1990).

Post-1945 genocides include: the Soviet Union (1943–68), Tibet and the People's Republic of China (1950–77), Rwanda/Tutsi (1962–3 and 1994), Burundi/Hutu (1972 and 1995), Indonesia/Communist Chinese (1956–66), Sudan (1955–72), Pakistan/Bengalis (1971–2), Uganda (1972–85), Paraguay/Ache (1960s–1970s), Cambodia (1975–9), Indonesia/East Timor (1975–date), Iran/Baha'is (1979–date), Guatemala/Indians (1980–87), Afghanistan (1980–89), Sri Lanka/Tamils (1983–7), Ethiopia/Tigray and Eritrea (1984–5), Iraq/Kurds (1959–75 and 1987–9). Between 1945 and 1980 genocides have caused twice as many deaths as have wars in the same period (Fein, 1993).

Additionally, in the twenty-five years from 1970 to 1995, some 134 million people were killed, injured or made homeless by catastrophes with a natural trigger (earthquakes, droughts and famines, high winds, landslides, volcanoes) or a non-natural trigger (accidents and fires). In 1995 alone, some 14.4 million people were refugees and asylum seekers, and 21.6 million people were internally displaced, having fled their homes for the same reasons as refugees, but without crossing international borders. Some 15,000 Africans died battle-related deaths in 1995, more than in the more 'publicized' wars in the Middle East and the former Yugoslavia (World Disaster Report, 1996: 124–37).

Since the female-to-male ratio is 1, or just over 1,[2] this means that half of the casualties of what is termed 'catastrophe' by organizations such as the International Federation of Red Cross and Red Crescent Societies, are women. Women, according to the International Federation of Red Cross and Red Crescent Societies, together with children, are particularly vulnerable to food deprivation, particularly when, in warfare, they stay behind while men migrate in search of food or are conscripted into armies. Women suffer disproportionately from disease such as respiratory and gastrointestinal disorders and cholera, as a combination of malnutrition and the lack of sanitation and water puts them more at risk. Women are often the victims of violence and hunger, especially in refugee situations (International Federation of Red Cross and Red Crescent Societies, 1996: 27–8), although, as Margaret Kelleher, in this volume, cites Amartya Sen (1981) as arguing, food deprivation often has to do with unequal and gendered food divisions within households. Considering the construction of women as ethnic and national subjects (Yuval-Davis and Anthias, 1989: 7), this introduction aims to theorize the ways women are targeted by major catastrophic situations.

To do this, I attempt to define 'catastrophe', and argue that in order to understand the full impact of extreme situations such as genocides, wars, famines, slavery, the Shoah, 'ethnic cleansing', and projects of mass rape and population control, definitions of catastrophe, and of genocide itself, must be gendered. They must be gendered well beyond the discursive level. Despite the 'linguistic turn' in the social sciences which has driven theorists to express social phenomena as 'words,' or a set of discourses, women know full well the meaning of 'things' in their lives. 'Things' such as genocide, hunger, displacement, sexual exploitation, war and migration cannot be dismissed as mere 'words' or 'accounts' as certain postmodernisms would have us believe (cf. Barrett, 1992; Linden, 1996).

Privileging women's lived experiences, I argue that we must consider women's own accounts of their lives as primary documents for interpreting their lives. Young and Dickerson (1994: 3) cite de Lauretis as asserting that feminist theory – of the embodied female subject, the woman who lives at a particular historical junction – is 'theory of the relationship between experiences, social power and resistance' (de Lauretis, 1990: 260).

We must analyse the ways women are targeted by major political projects and catastrophes, natural or 'man-made' (Davis, 1993), beyond women's victimhood. All the chapters in this collection address victimhood and agency in tandem, charting the routes of resistance available to women even when they are most deeply jeopardized. This volume does not assume power as neatly locked into a binary structure of possessing power versus being powerless with women viewed almost always as a powerless, unified group. This view of women as a universally oppressed group is, Chandra Mohanty argues, a Western feminist colonialist move, whereby Third World women never rise above the debilitating generality of their 'object status' (Mohanty, 1991: 71). Indeed 'women' cannot be considered a category of analysis across contexts, regardless of class, race–ethnicity, nationality and sexual orientation, not only because the world is not neatly divided into the binary opposition of the powerful (men) versus powerless (women), but also because such a construction, of women struggling across class and culture, against a general notion of (male) oppression, would assume 'a unilateral and undifferentiated source of power and a cumulative reaction to power' (Mohanty, 1991: 71). Although gender must be seen as part of an 'intersection of subordinations' within historical, cultural, race–ethnic, national, class and sexuality contexts, patriarchal social relations are endemic and integral to social formations with regard to the distribution of material resources and power. Thus patriarchal and sexist gender relations and racism are not independent but are products of social relations of power and subordination along different constructions of difference and identity (Anthias and Yuval-Davis, 1992: 109).

Indeed, focusing exclusively on women as universal victims does not help the survivors of genocides and other catastrophes. Nor does it allow us to address women's participation as benefactors or perpetrators of genocidal processes, as has been the case, for instance, in the 1994 Rwandan genocide (African Rights, 1995: 4), or the Shoah (Rittner and Roth, 1993: 320–23; Milton, 1993: 224–5).

Positioning women's experiences at the centre of feminist theory and scholarship, I wish to locate myself. I am a Jewish woman, many of whose family are Shoah survivors and some Shoah victims, and an Israeli woman, whose state, in occupying Palestinian lands and dispossessing the indigenous Palestinian population in the process of establishing a 'national home' for the Jewish people, brought about catastrophes to many Palestinian women, children and men. I am also a voluntary migrant: for the past 27 years I have been living in Ireland, where I have had experiences of displacement and resettlement. My interest in the ways women are targeted by genocides and catastrophes arose out of my doctoral research, an autobiographical feminist exploration of the gendered relations between Israel and the Shoah, between a fighting, active, 'masculinized' Israel and a passive, 'feminized' Jewish diaspora, who had allegedly gone passively to its death during the Shoah (Lentin, 1996). In arguing for (en)gendering social and political projects and 'catastrophes', I also argue for reclaiming women's experiences of catastrophe as historiographic and analytical resources, in order to understand not only the targeting of women, but the overall nature of those very catastrophic projects.

Catastrophes – Man-made Disasters?

Trying to determine what constitutes a 'catastrophe' is not only definitionally complex, it is also a political minefield, particularly for women. Some writers (for example, Smith, 1992), argue that the definition of catastrophe depends on the depth of effect. While a localized windstorm, for instance, can seem 'catastrophic' for the people whose lives have been affected, disasters are termed catastrophes only when their effects are widespread and extreme. Some writers who list and catalogue disasters and catastrophes (for example, Smith, 1992; Davis, 1993) tend to separate them from genocides and population movements, while others (for example, World Disaster Report, 1996), categorize casualties of genocides, wars, refugee movements and internal displacement together with naturally and non-naturally triggered catastrophes.

That black slavery, the Shoah and other genocidal projects, colonization, the sexual enslavement of thousands of East Asian women by Japan, the African, Bengali and Irish famines, Asian floods, nuclear testing in the Pacific, or 'ethnic cleansing' in the former Yugoslavia were major catastrophes with disastrous consequences not only for women, is universally agreed. There is less clear cut agreement about wars, population movements and Islamization projects. Is the ongoing conflict in Northern Ireland a catastrophe? Is the Islamization of the Iranian or the Pakistani states catastrophic? And what about processes of refugee uprooting and resettling? Furthermore, to what extent is considering political processes such as war, Islamization or refugee settlement a catastrophe politically dangerous not only for the women targeted, but for the women researching these processes? How can we be sure that fundamentalist regimes which target women as repositories of national and familial shame and honour do not imagine themselves as so unquestionably dominant as not to tolerate critiques that tar them with a 'catastrophic' brush?

Trying to answer this definitional dilemma, the distinction some writers make between 'natural' and 'man-made' disasters can be used as a guiding yardstick, at least as far as women are concerned. I am not proposing to essentialize 'women' as either a unitary victim group, or as more peace-oriented than 'men', nor to accord 'men' the exclusive universal power to inflict catastrophes upon a civilian population of 'women and children'. However, the gendered nature of political processes such as war, religious and political fundamentalism, or population movements may elucidate the catastrophic consequences, for women, of such processes, which women almost never generate (if we discount female heads of state such as Israel's Golda Meir or Britain's Margaret Thatcher, who presided over their countries going to war).

Genocidal projects, wars and other political processes which result, among other things, in mass population movements are, I argue from the social constructionist position (cf. Sharoni, 1992), the consequence of the construction of masculinity and femininity in society (cf. Connell, 1987). Gender must be the explanation of the way the military reproduces the ideological structure of patriarchy 'because the notion of "combat" plays such a central role in the construction of "manhood" and justification of the superiority of maleness in the social order' (Enloe, 1983: 12). Neither masculinity nor femininity are universal propositions, nor is power-positioning common to all masculinities. Euan Hague argues in this volume, however, that the Serb and Bosnian Serb military policy of genocidal rape imagined and constructed a specific type of 'hetero-national masculinity', and a converse inferior, powerless 'femininity'. Similarly, Lorraine Dowler argues in this volume that the war in Northern Ireland constructs gender roles in oppositional terms: men are perceived as violent and action-oriented and women as compassionate and supportive of the male warriors. During the Nazi period, to cite another example, 'predicated on authority in the form of brutality, the concentration camp was an ultimate expression of the extreme masculinity and misogyny that undergirded Nazi ideology' (Goldenberg, 1990: 163), in that both Aryan and non-Aryan women were targeted on the basis of their 'biological destiny'.

That the world tends to turn to armed forces for assistance in humanitarian emergencies derives from the fact that, 'aside from natural disasters, humanitarian emergencies in the contemporary world frequently emerge from military engagements' (Gordenker and Weiss, 1991: 1). Thus, not only are catastrophes gendered, but also their resolution; they are both inflicted, and assuaged, by the military, based, Connell reminds us, on a 'hegemonic masculinity', and a military apparatus as a classic dominance-oriented masculine structure (Connell, 1994: 158).

Population movements and mass migration are often generated by what Urvashi Butalia calls, in this volume, 'political manoeuvres' such as the 1947 division of India, the break-up of the former Soviet Union, the break-up of the former Yugoslavia, the Zionist expropriation of Palestinian land, to cite but few examples. But also by political projects such as colonization with the attendant ideological and political domination of the colonized and the resultant enslavement, exploitation, expropriation and expulsion of indigenous populations. In the course of the ensuing mass population movements women are targeted by state and ethnic violence, as is demonstrated by Urvashi Butalia in this volume, and their needs are not being adequately catered for in resettlement projects, as argued by Roberta Julian, Natalya Kosmarskaya and Tovi Fenster.

As for the gendering of catastrophes not triggered by political and military manoeuvres, such as famines and 'natural' disasters, which cannot be simplistically linked to the construction of gender in society, we must look at the targeting of women as mothers, unpaid domestic labourers, chattels, sexual objects, repositories of family and national honour and the symbolic representational trope of the nation. Nation as beloved mother, 'the defeated nation being reborn as a triumphant woman' (Boland, 1989: 13), to be protected, fought for and liberated 'for the sake of the women and children back home'. The 'figure of woman' (in famine narratives, for instance), argues Margaret Kelleher in this volume, is clearly chosen to represent crisis or breakdown. But in whose realm and on whose authority? 'Nature' or political economy? And why is moral behaviour required of women in times of catastrophe, when familial, class, communal, religious and national politics affect the construction of women's familial roles, as argued by Santi Rozario in this volume? All this clearly means that catastrophes, no matter what their origins, are always gendered in moulding historically-specific social constructions of masculinities and femininities in the light of these very catastrophes.

Biological Destiny: Beyond the Double Burden

Anthias and Yuval-Davis (1992) reject earlier attempts to posit a specificity of women's position as women enduring a double burden, and in the case of black women, a triple burden (for example, Amos and Parmar,

1984). They regard these attempts as unsatisfactory because they tend to treat forms of subordination and oppression through race, sex and class as cumulative rather than as intersecting to produce specific effects. They posit instead an 'intersection of subordinations' and speak of the links between states and other political processes, and women and ethnic and national processes, as located in several major ways in which women are targeted by and participate in ethnic and national processes. These are: as biological producers of members of ethnic collectivities and of the boundaries of ethnic and national groups, as transmitters of culture, as signifiers of ethnic or national differences and symbols of ideological discourses, as participants in national, economic, political and military struggles, and as participants in the labour market (Yuval-Davis and Anthias, 1989: 7; Anthias and Yuval-Davis, 1992: 115).

At the symbolic level, Anthias and Yuval-Davis argue, women's 'biological destiny' – that is, motherhood – is central to the nation's view of itself. At the practical level, women are central subjects to the construction of social policies directly concerned with structuring and restructuring the family and the centrality of women within it. Similarly, population programmes target women in order to control, enlarge or alter existing demographic patterns in favour of dominant ethnic groups (Anthias and Yuval-Davis, 1992: 115).

One classic example of women's biological destiny shaping their targeting by genocidal projects is Nazi ideology, which, resting on the eugenic conviction of German racial superiority, inevitably discriminated against women as childbearers. The Nazis legalized race-hygiene sterilization in the 1930s when 400,000 people with varying degrees of mental illness were sterilized because they were judged 'unworthy to reproduce' (Burleigh, 1995). At the same time the Nazis encouraged German women to become mothers and to bear illegitimate children, fathered by SS men and other 'racially valuable' Germans. Elderly Jewish women (and men), useless to the Nazis, were sentenced to death; women of childbearing age, although useful as workers, posed a menace because they could bear Jewish children and ensure the continuity of Jewish life (Rittner and Roth, 1993). As surgical sterilization was slow and expensive, German doctors, serving genocidal interests, experimented with X-rays, injections and drugs as faster and more easily applicable procedures to control reproduction by 'racially inferior' women. Roma and Sinti women married to Germans were sterilized, as were their children after the age of twelve. Jewish and Gypsy women were forced to become guinea pigs in Nazi medical experiments (Laska, 1983).

Eugenistic policies were practised in Singapore in the 1980s. Prime Minister Lee Juan, worried about the shrinking Chinese majority, promised financial incentives to low-caste, mostly Malay and Indian mothers to undergo sterilizations while promising 'graduate mothers,' mostly Chinese, generous tax breaks and other privileges to increase their fertility (Heng and Devan, 1992: 347–8). Eugenics is also practised by the People's Republic of China in several Chinese provinces such as Inner Mongolia and Manchuria. Aiming to improve the 'population quality,' the Chinese authorities ban mentally handicapped people from marrying unless they are sterilized. Chinese state ideology, claiming superiority over annexed Tibet, as reported by Yangchen Kikhang in this volume, practises cultural genocide through brutally targeting women, mass sterilizations and population transfers into Tibet, thus reducing the Tibetan population to dangerously low levels.

Women Shoah survivors speak of sexual humiliation, rape, sexual exchange, pregnancy, abortion and vulnerability through their children – concerns male survivors tend not to describe. Female concentration camp survivors speak of the humiliation surrounding the entrance to the camp, being nude, being shaved all over in a sexual stance straddling two stools, being observed by men. Sex with the rulers can become a means of survival under occupation. Women often survived the Shoah through sex, used as a commodity in some ghettoes and camps. In some concentration camps there were brothels reserved for the SS and other selected privileged male inmates (Tillion, 1975). The Japanese military used a complex system of military sex slavery during World War II, when Philippine, Korean, Northeast Chinese, Indonesian and Malaysian women served as 'comfort women', as reported by Nelia Sancho in this volume. Fewer than a third of these comfort women survived: some were summarily executed or forced to commit suicide together with defeated Japanese soldiers.

The use of mass rape as a political instrument highlights and further (en)genders the link between racism, sexism and genocide. During the 1970–71 West Pakistani occupation of Bangladesh between 200,000 and 400,000 Bangladeshi women were raped by the Pakistani army, as reported by Santi Rozario in this volume. The claims that it was military policy consciously planned by West Pakistan in order to create a new ethnicity and dilute the Bangladeshi nation, resonates with the genetic warfare arguably employed by the Serb and Bosnian Serb policy of genocidal rape, particularly the version that uses forced pregnancy as a kind of biological warfare (Allen, 1996).

The Centrality of Experience: Between Victimhood and Agency

Insisting that no catastrophe is the same for everyone, even when it reaches genocidal proportions, Joan Ringelheim, arguing for studying the Shoah from a gender perspective, writes that a study of women and the Holocaust calls into question some of the claims about the uniqueness of the Holocaust and the sameness of the Jewish experience, and thus even the ways in which the Holocaust is remembered. But there are deeper effects and more difficult tasks: to enlarge our understanding of the event by reclaiming the hidden experiences of women. Even if we assume that women and men suffered equally at the hands of the Nazis, we find that, in one way or another, to one degree or another, they experienced their circumstances as women and men ... (Ringelheim, 1992: 21)

Intragender differences between women are as significant as intergender differences between women and men, as argued, for instance, by Yvonne Corcoran-Nantes in this volume, and by Linden (1996). Privileging women's lived experiences as primary resources not only militates against universalizing 'womanhood' across contexts. It also enlarges our understanding of any catastrophic event by reclaiming experiences of women, 'hidden' in malestream historiography and scholarship, shaped, among other things, by the gendered construction of knowledge itself.

In inscribing experience into feminist scholarship, simply speaking 'as a...' may runs the risk of 'speaking for', as Liz Stanley cautions (1995). The decision to elicit contributions for this collection from activists as well as academics is the result of a commitment to situated experience. It stems from the deconstruction of the supremacy of 'theory' in academic feminist writing, which, as Stanley and Wise (1990) argue, 'is theory with a capital T, one produced by theorists who are supposed experts on the relationships between categories and thus on the "real meaning" of social experience and behaviour'. Academic feminism, they stress, becomes 'the legitimation for a new form of expertise, that of feminist theoreticians over "mere women"' (Stanley and Wise, 1990: 24).

It is important to stress that beyond 'words' and 'discourse', 'a real world and real lives do exist, howsoever we interpret, construct and recycle accounts of these by a variety of symbolic means' (Stanley, 1993: 214). Some writers in this volume base their work on first-, second-, or third-hand experiences of women, whose lives and interactions form the basis for this collection. Gender cannot be universalized nor can gendered experiences be presented without context; but neither can the demand that 'we must learn to theorize without categories' (Traweek, 1995, cited by Linden, 1996) be sustained if we acknowledge the importance of 'things' in women's lives, and deaths.

Importantly, none of the chapters falls into the trap Mohanty (1991) cautions against of viewing women as a homogeneous powerless group located as implicit victims of particular socio-economic systems. Instead of viewing agents and victims in oppositional terms, victimhood and agency are theorized in tandem. Through the concept of the 'victimized self', Roberta Julian in this volume argues that by taking action against victimization, women diminish it. In the case of migrant women, they do it by instigating the decision to leave, and by resettlement processes. Women are often theorized as familial dependants as is implied in feminist critiques of citizenship (for example, Walby, 1996). However, analyses of migrant women's agency upon settlement, as described by Natalya Kosmarskaya and Roberta Julian in this volume, show that it is often women who construct the household's 'refugee experience' and negotiate public spaces, and who, in post-migration periods, become the actual, though not nominal, heads of households. Bibi Bakare-Yusuf embodies the experiences of black female slaves as existing in real bodies of slaves as gendered and racial subjects. Locating the female slave's body as a complex site of colonial and patriarchal inscriptions, Helen Thomas and Yvonne Corcoran-Nantes, in two separate chapters, depict, among other things, the slaves' defiant response to the oppressive slave systems of America, Brazil, and the West Indies. Impregnated by slave masters, female slaves became highly adept at self-induced abortions, thus keeping birth rates down and reducing the masters' future property. In the Philippines, and in Korea, women's organizations are beginning to make vociferous, and increasingly successful, demands for apology and compensations from the Japanese for their sexual enslavement during World War II, as Nelia Sancho reports. In the former Yugoslavia, Rada Boric writes, women activists organize against war victimhood with the co-operation of former war victims themselves, exposing the androcentrism of war and demanding the degendering of the peace process. In Iran, responding to the Islamization of women's lives, and despite the increasing presence of women in the public domains of paid employment and education, dictated by growing gender segregation, not by gender equality, women continue to struggle to secure their legal rights and fight oppression, as Haideh Moghissi reports. Zohl dé Ishtar records Pacific women's voices, breaking the silences about babies born with deformities due to nuclear testing, and about nuclear neo-colonialism the world would prefer to forget.

Viewing women as homogeneously powerless and as implicit victims, does not allow us to theorize women as the benefactors of oppression, or the perpetrators of catastrophes. Without theorizing women within what bell hooks (1989) calls a 'paradigm of domination', it would be impossible to understand, and challenge, the nature of domination itself, in which both women and men have the capacity 'to be either dominated or dominating' (hooks, 1989: 20).

Describing women and girls as the principal victims of the genocide, and of genocidal rapes, in Rwanda, for instance, obscured their roles as aggressors, according to African Rights (1995). Throughout the genocide, it was Tutsi men who were the primary target. The involvement of women in the genocide and murder of Hutu political opponents failed to attract national and international attention, precisely because of the construction of women as the universal victims of that particular catastrophe. In fact, African Rights argues, many women perpetrators enjoy impunity; many are living in a comfortable exile in Zaire, Kenya and Europe and some have been employed by international organizations in the refugee camps in Zaire, Tanzania and Burundi. Thousands more are living in Rwanda, confident that their crimes will never be revealed, many working in government service as nurses, teachers and civil servants, 'sometimes in the very institutions where they committed unspeakable crimes'. Some have been arrested and the detention of women, including nuns, elderly women and mothers with small children, on charges of genocide, has been used by the killers to deflect attention from the genocide (African Rights, 1995: 4–5).

Although there is no systematic study of the uniformed SS women attached to the Nazi concentration camps, Milton (1993) reports that women played their part in the camp system. Most of the 3,000 uniformed female camp guards were labour conscripts, not volunteers. Yet several are remembered by survivors for their legendary cruelty, engaging in a bizarre rivalry emulating the excess and brutalities of their male superiors while others tried to mitigate the worst extremes (Milton, 1993: 224–5).

Closing the 'Memory Gap'

Taking herself to task for merely recording the differences between the experiences of women and of men during the Shoah in her earlier research, Joan Ringelheim (1985, 1993) argues against a 'cultural feminism' stance (Alcoff, 1988), which shares with liberalism a belief in individual solutions and in humanism, and addresses a universal 'woman' while privileging some women over others. A cultural feminism stance, which tends to valorize women's oppression, damages not only our politics, but also our research. Excavating an 'archaeology of silence' (Foucault, 1967: xi), that is reclaiming women's experiences, hidden from history as they may be, is not sufficient without contextualizing these experiences within the gendered analysis of catastrophic events.

One aim of genocidal projects is to erase not only the physical presence of a collectivity but also its memory. Traumatic and catastrophic experiences, too horrific to remember and too difficult to find words to articulate, often result in the temptation to succumb to silence. Because genocides often have no witnesses, they do not 'exist' in the conventional form and thus signify their own death and reduction to silence. Their survival in memory inevitably implies the presence of informal discourses, a degree of unconscious witnessing that could not find its voice during the catastrophe itself. Grunfeld (1995) posits a 'memory gap' which separates the material, bodily, immediate knowledge of catastrophe and the discursive, mediated memories that follow. Joan Ringelheim, in this volume, writes of the split memory between genocide and gender, split between traditional versions of history and women's own experiences. Split memory is a metaphor that represents the barriers against the inclusion of gender in analyses of catastrophe. However, this introduction argues, we cannot keep ignoring the particular experiences of victimization and resistance of women in feminist analyses of catastrophe. Official discourses of memory of catastrophe often exclude the unofficial secret memories of women who, Judith Zur argues in this volume, by the act of remembering, often turn private memories of victimization into articulated political acts of resistance. The importance of memory in constructing official history, Urvashi Butalia argues in this volume, is not in claiming 'objectivity', but rather in helping to tell the past in the light of the present, in order to shape the future, by, among other things, including women's oral narratives, as diverse, contradictory and complex as these may be.

Beyond the double jeopardy, and beyond victimhood and universal subordination, the chapters in this collection theorize the multi-faceted ways women participate in and are targeted by catastrophic processes. Theorizing the construction of gender and perceptions of 'masculinity' and 'femininity', the collection offers a forum for women activists and scholars to break the silences and close the memory gap between catastrophic events and the discourses available to represent them, and thus embody experience, which is at the heart of feminist epistemological processes (cf. Stanley, 1995). By (en)gendering catastrophe, we not only enhance and deepen our knowledge, we also put women's claims to be heard, and be compensated for past injustices, firmly on the feminist political agenda.

Notes

1. I prefer using the Hebrew term 'Shoah' meaning catastrophe, or cataclysm, to the English term 'Holocaust', which derives from the Greek Holocauston and literally means 'whole burnt', and which many Jews, conscious of the implicit Christian notion of a Jewish sacrifice or Calvary, reject (Young, 1990: 87). However, other contributors to this book do use the term 'Holocaust'.

2. However, by the mid-1980s in China the ratio was 0.941, in Bangladesh 0.940, India 0.933, and Pakistan 0.905. Tens of millions of women are 'missing' in excess mortality due to a lower access to food and healthcare; neglected relative to their fathers, husbands, brothers, women also face male violence, especially amid extreme poverty (World Disasters Report, 1966: 27).

References

African Rights. 1995. *Rwanda. Not so Innocent: When Women Become Killers*. London: African Rights.

Alcoff, Linda. 1988. 'Cultural feminism versus post-structuralism: the identity crisis in feminist theory.' *Signs*, vol. 13, no. 3: 405–36.

Allen, Beverly. 1996. *Rape Warfare: The Hidden Genocide in Bosnia-Herzegovina and Croatia.* Minneapolis: University of Minnesota Press.

Amos, Valerie and Pratibha Parmar. 1984. 'Challenging imperial feminism.' *Feminist Review*, no. 17.

Anthias, Floya and Nira Yuval-Davis. 1992. *Racialized Boundaries: Race, Nation, Gender, Colour and Class and the Anti-Racist Struggle.* London: Routledge.

Barrett, Michele. 1992. 'Words and things: materialism and method in contemporary feminist analysis.' In Michele Barrett and Anne Phillips (eds), *Destabilizing Theory: Contemporary Feminist Debates.* Cambridge: Polity Press.

Barta, Tony. 1987. 'Relations of genocide: land and lives in the colonization of Australia.' In Isidor Wallinmann and Michael N. Dobkowski (eds), *Genocide and the Modern Age: Etiology and Case Studies of Mass Death.* New York: Greenwood.

Bauman, Zigmunt. 1989. *Modernity and the Holocaust.* Cambridge: Polity Press.

Boland, Eavan. 1989. *A Kind of Scar: The Woman Poet in a National Tradition.* Dublin: Attic Press.

Brietman, Richard. 1992. 'The Final Solution.' In *Fifty Years Ago: In the Depths of Darkness.* Washington DC: United States Holocaust Memorial Council.

Burleigh, Michael. 1995. *Death and Deliverance: 'Euthanasia' in Germany 1900–1945.* Cambridge: Cambridge University Press.

Chalk, Frank and Kurt Jonassohn. 1990. *The History and Sociology of Genocide: Analyses and Case Studies.* New Haven and London: Yale University Press.

Connell, Robert W. 1987. *Gender and Power.* Cambridge: Polity Press.

Connell, Robert W. 1994. 'The state, gender and sexual politics: theory and appraisal.' In L.H. Radtke and H.J. Stam (eds), *Power/Gender: Social Relations in Theory and Practice.* London: Sage Publications.

Davis, Lee. 1993. *Man-Made Catastrophes: From the Burning of Rome to the Lockerbie Crash.* New York: Facts on File.

de Lauretis, Teresa. 1990. 'Upping the anti (sic) in feminist theory.' In M. Hirsch and E. Fox Keller (eds), *Conflicts in Feminism.* New York and London: Routledge.

Enloe, Cynthia. 1983. *Does Khaki Become You? The Militarization of Women's Lives.* London: Pluto Press.

Fein, Helen. 1993. *Genocide: A Sociological Perspective.* London: Sage.

Foucault, Michel. 1967. *Madness and Civilization.* London: Tavistock.

Goldenberg, Myrna. 1990. 'Different horrors, same hell: women remembering the Holocaust.' In Roger S. Gottlieb (ed.), *Thinking the Unthinkable: Meanings of the Holocaust.* New York and Mawah: Paulist Press.

Gordenker, Leon and Thomas G. Weiss 1991. 'Introduction: the use of soldiers and peacekeepers in coping with disasters.' In Leon Gordenker and Thomas G. Weiss (eds), *Soldiers, Peacekeepers and Disasters.* London: MacMillan.

Grunfeld, Uriel. 1995. 'Holocaust, movies and remembrance: the pedagogical challenge.' Unpublished paper, Pennsylvania State University.

Heng, Geraldine and Janadas Devan. 1992. 'State fatherhood: the politics of nationalism, sexuality and race in Singapore.' In Andrew Parker, Mary Russo and Patricia Yaeger (eds), *Nationalisms and Sexualities.* New York and London: Routledge.

hooks, bell. 1989. 'feminism: a transformational politics.' In bell hooks, *talking back: thinking feminist, thinking black.* London: Sheba Feminist Publishers.

Hovannisian, Richard G. 1988. 'The Armenian genocide.' In Israel Charny (ed.),

Genocide: A Critical Bibliographic Review. London: Mansell.

International Federation of Red Cross and Red Crescent Societies. 1996. *World Disasters Report 1996*. Oxford: Oxford University Press.

Laska, Vera. 1983. *Women in the Resistance and in the Holocaust*. Westport, CT: Greenwood Press.

Lemkin, Raphael. 1944. *Axis Rule in Occupied Europe*. Washington DC: Carnegie Endowment for International Peace.

Lentin, Ronit. 1996. *Reoccupying the Territories of Silence: A Feminist Auto/Biographical Exploration of the Gendered Relationship between Israel and the Shoah*. Unpublished PhD dissertation, Trinity College, Dublin.

Linden, Ruth R. 1996. 'Troubling categories I can't think without: reflections on women in the Holocaust.' *Contemporary Jewry*, vol. 11.

Milton, Sybil. 1993. 'Women and the Holocaust: the case of German and German-Jewish women.' In Carol Rittner and John K. Roth (eds), *Different Voices: Women and the Holocaust*. New York: Paragon House.

Mohanty, Chandra Talpade. 1991. 'Introduction: cartographies of struggle: Third World women and the politics of feminism.' In Chandra T. Mohanty, Ann Russo and Lourdes Torres (eds), *Third World Women and the Politics of Feminism*. Bloomington and Indianapolis: Indiana University Press.

Ringelheim, Joan M. 1985. 'Women and the Holocaust: a reconsideration of research.' *Signs*, vol. 10, no. 4: 741–61.

Ringelheim, Joan M. 1992. 'The Holocaust: taking women into account.' *Jewish Quarterly*, vol. 39, no 3: 19–23.

Ringelheim, Joan M. 1993. 'Women and the Holocaust: a reconsideration of research.' In Carol Rittner and John K. Roth (eds), *Different Voices: Women and the Holocaust*. New York: Paragon House.

Rittner, Carol and John K. Roth (eds). 1993. *Different Voices: Women and the Holocaust*. New York: Paragon House.

Rummel, R.J. 1990. *Lethal Politics: Soviet Genocides and Mass Murder Since 1900*. New Brunswick, NJ: Transaction Books.

Sen, Amartya. 1981. *Poverty and Famines: An Essay on Entitlement and Deprivation*. Oxford: Oxford University Press.

Sharoni, Simona. 1992. 'Every woman is an occupied territory: the politics of militarism and sexism and the Israeli–Palestinian conflict.' *Journal of Gender Studies*, vol. 1, no. 4: 447–62.

Smith, Roger. 1992. *Catastrophes and Disasters*. Edinburgh and New York: Chambers.

Stanley, Liz and Sue Wise. 1990. 'Method, methodology and epistemology in feminist research processes.' In Liz Stanley (ed.), *Feminist Praxis: Research, Theory and Epistemology in Feminist Sociology*. London: Routledge.

Stanley, Liz. 1993. 'The knowing because experiencing subject: narratives, lives and autobiography.' *Women's Studies International Forum*, vol. 16, no. 3: 205–15.

Stanley, Liz. 1995. 'Speaking "as a...," speaking "for the...,": On the mis/uses of the category "experience" in recent feminist thought.' *University College Galway Women's Studies Centre Review*, vol. 3.

Tillion, Germaine. 1975. *Ravensbrük*. New York: Doubleday.

Traweek, Sharon. 1995. 'Acting on images: patiently exploring Ob/Gyn in Japan, England and the US.' Paper presented to the conference on 'Revisioning Women, Health and Healing: Feminist, Cultural and Technoscience Perspectives.' San Francisco, October 1995.

Walby, Sylvia. 1996. 'Women and citizenship: towards a comparative analysis.' In Ronit Lentin (ed.), *In from the Shadows: the UL Women's Studies Collection Vol. II.* Limerick: University of Limerick.

Young, Gay and Bette J. Dickerson. 1994. 'Introduction.' In Gay Young and Bette J. Dickerson (eds), *Color, Class and County: Experiences of Gender.* London: Zed Books.

Young, James E. 1990. *Writing and Re-writing the Holocaust: Narrative and the Consequence of Interpretation.* Bloomington and Indianapolis: Indiana University Press.

Yuval-Davis, Nira and Floya Anthias (eds). 1989. *Woman – Nation – State.* London: Macmillan.

2

Genocide and Gender: A Split Memory

Joan Ringelheim

The strands are all there: to the memory nothing is ever lost. (Welty, 1984: 90)

A person who has been wounded tends to block out the memory so as not to renew the pain; the person who has inflicted the wound pushes the memory deep down, to be rid of it, to alleviate the feeling of guilt. (Levi, 1986: 24)

Auschwitz is so deeply etched in my memory that I cannot forget one moment of it. – so you are living with Auschwitz? – No, I live next to it. Auschwitz is there, unalterable, precise, but enveloped in the skin of memory, an impermeable skin that isolates it from my present self. (Delbo, 1990: 2)

... we must know the right time to forget as well as the right time to remember, and instinctively see when it is necessary to feel historically and when unhistorically ... the unhistorical and the historical are equally necessary to the health of an individual, a community, and a system of culture. (Nietzsche, 1957: 8)

Introduction

A Jewish survivor (let's call her Pauline) testified to having been molested while in hiding by male relatives of the people hiding her. They threatened to denounce her if she said anything. Pauline took the threats seriously and never said a word. She didn't tell the young Jewish woman who checked on her periodically. She didn't tell her twin sister who had been in the same location for a time. After the war, she didn't tell her husband or her daughter. Pauline was eleven or twelve years old when she was first hidden.

We spoke in 1984. 'I must say,' she remarked, 'that this is the first time I ever admitted this.' She described the situation:

[I was] ... physically developed for my age ... Constantly afraid of men because I stayed with strangers. Men would try to touch me. I was even afraid of the family – the sons (as well as the cousins, uncles, brothers-in-law, and other male relatives of the family), because I was constantly [fondled] ... [except] when the father was there ... I was afraid of strange older men ... they would rub themselves [on me] ... It was more than just [touching] ... This happened even on trains. We used to travel. We were very packed in. And men would ... you know, I can still smell it. It was a tremendous fear ... but somehow it didn't affect my [sex life later]. When it was finished, it was over.

Boys were romantically pleasant. But you know older men. I didn't imagine it ... They were not young men ...They were rubbing me and pushing themselves [on me] ... I was scared. They were drunk, you know, the Poles ... They would expose themselves in front of me.... I remember I was always ... afraid that I am going to be raped ... First time I was scared to say no. Felt guilty. It was [a] very complicated situation. I tried to stay out of situations when I saw that I'm alone with any of those sons. I would rather not ... come in. I avoid. I would try to look if the parents should be there; if any of my girlfriends weren't there. All kinds of situations when I went to [my] girlfriend's house and [her] father would be alone and he would try something. [I] didn't run away, didn't scream. Didn't put attention to myself, ... I was scared. Very scared.

I can still feel the fear ... Sometimes I think it was equally as frightening as the Germans. It became within me a tremendous ... I don't know how [to deal with it] ... what to do with it. I had nobody to talk about it. Nobody to turn to ... I was lonely as it is probably [common] ... This was just another part.

You see, [with] a boyfriend I was in control or I felt that I am. But here I was a hopeless victim ... and it's different when you are liked; sex is different when you like someone. But when you are put upon, you hate it, it's awful.

[But] I have nobody to complain to. Everything has to be wonderful, because that's what they want to hear ... I am happy, everything is fine, I'm alive. They took me from hell. Have to be grateful. I felt guilty always. Somehow I was [guilty]; really thought that maybe, something about me ... even a child feels it's his fault if an adult does something. [The fondling and rubbing] went on for a year.

After telling me of this situation she asked a question:

In respect of what happened, [what we] suffered and saw – the humiliation in the ghetto, seeing our relatives dying and taken away [as well as] my friends, ... then seeing the ghetto ... burn and seeing people jumping out and burned – is this [molestation] important? It is only important to me at the moment. It is past, gone ... Funny that ... what I want to say is that it is not the most important part of my life. When the war was over ... this fear disappeared. And I again had boyfriends, gave pleasure. I had a special need for that ... I like sex. And I liked men. I wanted to be loved. It was very important.

Although she minimizes the significance of what were the specifically female aspects of her Holocaust experience, the pain and humiliation in her words and in the tone of voice were unmistakable. A few days after the interview we spoke on the phone. 'I don't like the feeling of panic,' Pauline said. She took Valium after the interview so she could sleep. She was worried about the use of the interview and wanted her identity to be completely hidden.

Pauline decided to talk with me when she found out that I was doing research on women and the Holocaust. 'This [set of incidents],' she told me, 'flashed through my mind. Everything else is the same. But there are certain things that are different.' Pauline knew that this story would interest me; she also knew that the description of her situation helped to understand how complicated and difficult it was to hide. But she also wondered: 'is this [molestation] important?' Was this part of her story also a part of the Holocaust story? Although Pauline recognized her experiences as different from men's, she did not know how or where to locate them in the history of the Holocaust. Pauline's memory is split between traditional versions of Holocaust history and her own experience.

For most researchers, it has been difficult to focus on a personal assault such as described by Pauline. It is more arduous to connect those experiences to the broader systematic persecution and murder that is the Holocaust. To many, such experiences either do not appear connected or appear connected in insignificant ways. Assaults against women are both minimized and difficult to face. It is an interesting and disturbing duality.

It is common to hear certain questions raised about those who hid children: for instance, did some rescuers try to convert Jewish children when these children were so vulnerable? But rarely have questions been raised about children's sexual vulnerability and actual sexual victimization in hiding. Rarely have serious questions been raised about the sexual vulnerabilities and victimization of Jewish women as a group. There is a split between genocide and gender in the memories of witnesses and the historical reconstruction of researchers.

Gender and the Holocaust

What is meant by the notion of a 'split memory'? First, gender is considered irrelevant to the Holocaust. This results in 'forgotten' memories; memories that are misunderstood by the survivors or not taken as Holocaust-related and thus split from the Holocaust. Second, there is a dividing line between what is considered personal and private to women, and what has been designated as the proper collective memory of the Holocaust. These private and personal experiences are known to have happened and are sometimes mentioned. But, they are usually severed from serious talk about the Holocaust. This results in 'ignored' memories which eventually turn into forgotten memories also. What is superficially clear is that it is not easy for a survivor or researcher – whether male or female – to make a connection between genocide and gender. It is also clear that our conception of who is and who is not a genuine victim is at issue, as well as what is or what is not part of genocidal policy or its effects.

The Nazis' 'Final Solution' was total genocide of the Jewish population. Every woman, man and child defined as a Jew was to die or be killed. That meant that neither geography, nationality, class, professional or economic status or gender would allow an escape for very long.

If any policy could be considered a 'victim equalizer', it is genocide. Therefore, the logical conclusion is that every Jew was equally a victim in the genocide of the Holocaust. Consequently, it is not surprising that most perspectives on the Holocaust have been gender-neutral or seemed to erase gender as a category of analysis. Likewise, it is no wonder that any emphasis on gender can seem irrelevant, even irreverent.

Then again, one might be incredulous that gender has not been of greater interest. Isn't there something unusual in the intention to kill every woman and child along with every male from a targeted community? The Nazi so-called 'Final Solution of the Jewish Question' was one of the first times in history that the female population was not treated primarily as 'spoils'. This was one of the rare historical moments when women and children were consciously and explicitly sentenced to death in at least equal measure to men. A more mundane view would acknowledge that together with age, sex and gender are universal categories or classifications in all cultures. And would admit that there are always consequences of being in one or another category, whether the category is age, sex, gender, ethnicity or class.

Legitimation for targeting Jewish men was plentiful in Nazi anti-Semitic and racist propaganda and, more to the point, in Nazi policy. The decision to kill every Jew did not seem to demand special justification to kill Jewish men. They were already identified as dangerous. This was not so for Jewish women and children. Himmler's words speak to this need for justification and legitimation:

> When I was forced somewhere in some village to act against partisans and Jewish Commissars ... then as a principle I gave the order to kill the women and children of those partisans and commissars too ... Believe you me, that order was not so easy to carry out as it was logically thought out and can be stated in this hall. But we must constantly recognize what kind of a primitive primordial, natural race struggle (*Rassenkampf*) we are involved in. (Smith and Peterson, 1974: 201)

> We came to the question: what about the women and children? I have decided to find a clear solution here too. In fact I did not regard myself as justified in exterminating the men – let us say killing them or having them killed – while letting avengers in the shape of children ... grow up. The difficult decision had to be taken to make this people disappear from the face of the earth. (Smith and Peterson, 1974: xxx)

Jewish women were connected to the 'race struggle' of National Socialism because they carried the next generation of Jews and hence had to become a specific target as women. Obviously then children could not be allowed to live because they would become either Jewish men or Jewish women; hence, future enemies or avengers.

If we take Himmler's remarks into consideration, and more importantly, the fact of total genocide and the actual circumstances of Jewish women and children during the Holocaust, it seems impossible not to give gender serious attention. We cannot understand what happened to Jewish women if we look to the sort of anti-Semitism and racism that turned Jewish men into enemies of the Third Reich. After all, women were only minor players in the so-called 'Jewish World Conspiracy', almost an afterthought. We must move to the 'race struggle' of National Socialism to see that Jewish women were not merely connected as an appendage to the fate of Jewish men. Jewish women were essential to the completion of the 'race struggle' because, potentially or actually, they carried the next generation of Jews.

All in all, the genocide perpetrated by the Nazis against the Jews was not neutral about gender. Gender and sexism were coordinates in the process of destroying the Jewish population, even if not at the same level as racism. Both anti-Semitism and racism are part of the typical analysis of the Holocaust; both reflect the breaks with the past as well as the continuities. Gender and sexism were not invented by the Nazis either; they too were elaborated just as surely as were anti-Semitism and racism. Yet, as we know, gender and sexism are not typically included in analyses of the Holocaust.

The 'Uniqueness' of the Holocaust

The fundamental question is how to connect what we have come to identify as the Holocaust with the experiences of women. The dilemma emerges partly because our understanding of the Holocaust as a break with the past conflicts with our knowledge of the continuities that are present in these events. That break, as Hannah Arendt describes it (quoting René Char), has something to do with 'our inheritance [being] left to us by no testament' (Arendt, 1966: 3). This has always been true of thought, for Arendt. However, in our century Arendt believes that we have seen it become 'a fact of political relevance' (Arendt, 1971: 14). With the Holocaust, a new quality seems to have entered our world. Together with the two world wars, it has created unprecedented homelessness and rootlessness, according to Arendt.

Working from such concepts as a 'break with the past', or a 'gap between past and future', some scholars went way beyond what would make sense to Arendt or what should make sense to us, and constructed the concept of 'uniqueness'. 'Uniqueness', as related to the Holocaust, poses general conceptual problems as well as particular problems for the discussion of gender. While all events are unique, the Holocaust is said to possess more than this ordinary attribution. The Holocaust assumes a quality that takes it beyond comparison of any kind. If the Holocaust is specially unique, it has no historical context. 'Uniqueness' then becomes a stumbling block rather than a helpful notion. How can we understand or identify what has no historical context but only a metaphysical one? It is clear that the continuities as well as the breaks have to be included in our understanding of the Holocaust. Unless we do this, the Holocaust will never be integrated into the grid of human history nor will we ever get to gender as a relevant concept for understanding.

Although my ultimate purpose is to connect gender and genocide with racism and anti-Semitism, the immediate aim in this chapter is smaller: to exemplify some of the ways in which the split between genocide and gender functions, show its powerful attraction, and argue against it. To return to Pauline for a moment: Jewish women or young girls could hide more easily than Jewish men or boys who could be identified by their circumcision. For the most part, during this period non-Jewish men in Europe were not circumcised. That may mean that more female Jews were saved in hiding. This is not an insignificant fact of biology. At the same time, we cannot ignore the particular vulnerability and victimization of these women and girls in these situations. Pauline's story may or may not be typical. But if we keep Anne Frank's diary as the paradigm of hiding, we will never know.

Hannah Arendt suggested that within the totalitarian state enemies were designated by the laws of Nature (Nazi state) or the laws of History (Communist state). Arendt thought that, in either case, these laws are applied 'directly to mankind [sic] without bothering with the behavior of men' (Arendt, 1966: 462). In other words, totalitarian regimes in general, and the Nazi state in particular, create objective enemies in which the behaviour of particular individuals is irrelevant. One is guilty simply by being a member of a designated objective enemy group. This means that guilt and innocence in the juridical sense of the terms are eliminated. Thus, according to Arendt, 'guilt and innocence become senseless notions' (Arendt, 1966: 465).

Listening to Jewish Women's Holocaust Experiences

The Nazis had many so-called 'objective enemies', of whom Jews were the most prominent after 1938–9. Jewish men were always considered an objective enemy of National Socialism; they were certainly the first Jewish victims of forced labour and, in the beginning, the primary targets of the *Einsatzgruppen*. Jewish women eventually became significant enemies, hence the necessity to include them in the plans for extermination. They became primary murder victims because they were often not considered valuable for work and because they were the carriers of the 'race'.

Jewish women were always portrayed differently from Jewish men in Nazi propaganda and 'theory'. After the Holocaust, Jewish women were not portrayed as 'objective enemies'; even their role as victims sometimes took a backseat to that of men.[1] Consequently, we are often unable to either ask about or deal with the side-effects of Nazi persecution such as the sexual abuse described by Pauline. Who is a victim during the Holocaust? What is considered Holocaust victimization? What is included as part of genocidal policy? We have seen these questions raised, and to some extent answered, with respect to the recent and ongoing war in the former Yugoslavia. In this war, it has been made clear that women have been specifically targeted as women. Rape, in some form and to some extent, has been part of the genocidal strategy of 'ethnic cleansing'. When we think about the war in the former Yugoslavia, we visualize male and female victims differently because of how gender functioned in that war. Women were enemies as well as men. At this moment it is an indelible image. It is an image we cannot seem to manage about the Holocaust.

There are patterns or similarities in the persecution of women and men during the Holocaust. There are also differences in the role and functions of women and men within the Jewish community, and further differences in the Nazi perspective of those roles and functions. Further, women and men do not necessarily respond in the same way to the Nazis' persecution.

Scholars have had greater difficulty than Pauline in making a connection between the personal experience and the historical experience of the Holocaust. A particular incident illuminates the problem. There was an informal discussion about the sexual fears of children of survivors at a Holocaust Conference in 1978 or 1979, I believe. Among those sitting together, drinking and talking at the Holiday Inn were Yael Danieli, Eva Fleischner, Henry Friedlander, Raul Hilberg, Sybil Milton, and myself. Danieli, a therapist working with children of survivors, raised a question: 'Why do children of survivors fear that their mothers had been raped?' She thought that this fear was fairly widespread and might represent a reality worth investigating. I did not know what to make of her question. But many of my colleagues around the table did.

Instantly, and without apparent hesitation, those who spoke claimed that the fears were merely fantasies. Similar to Freud's final theory about the sexual abuse of young girls, these scholars claimed that the children were not describing actual incidents of abuse but rather fantasies induced by the media's sexualization of the Holocaust. No one quoted any research; no one referred to any documentation or studies of interviews of survivors, male or female. There was just an immediate and resounding disregard of the question. On reflection, one might think that we didn't want to confront additional painful realities about the Holocaust, that perhaps Danieli's question was going too far for these scholars. Since I had just begun to think about the issues of women and the Holocaust, I may have found some comfort in their denials.

The impulse to neutralize the issue of sex by treating it as non-existent or insignificant is entirely understandable. The possible rape of mothers, grandmothers, sisters, friends, or lovers during the Holocaust is difficult to face. The further possibility that mothers or sisters or lovers 'voluntarily' used sex for food or protection is equally difficult to absorb. All the experiences connected with sex, whether negative or positive, are understandably troublesome. After all, these are delicate and intimate issues. But to dismiss situations that relate so specifically to women makes it impossible to begin to understand the victimization of women. It may even make it impossible to really see Jewish women as victims, or visualize their victimization.

Some might argue that rape, abortion, sexual exploitation and pregnancy are always part of women's lives. In addition, because of the ubiquity of these experiences, others might argue that they can bear no relationship to the so-called 'uniqueness' of the Holocaust. From this viewpoint sexism is simply too banal. Or, it is believed that discussions about sexuality desecrate the memory of the dead, or the living, or the Holocaust itself. With these arguments, women's lives are ignored and/ or forgotten.

The Holocaust is not about sex. Of course that is true. It is also true that the victimization of Jewish men did not usually include sexual exploitation. But men did oppress women sexually and women were conscious of that possibility. 'Male memory can confront women as victims, but cannot confront male oppression,' Irene Eber (a survivor) told me in a conversation in 1987. She continued: 'The same may be true for women survivors. They can see themselves as Nazi victims, but not as victims of Jewish men or even Nazi men, except perhaps as non-female victims.' It has been difficult to confront the fact that Jewish women were victims as Jewish women, not only because some Jewish men exploited women, but also because Jewish men could not protect women and children from the Nazis. It has clearly been too difficult to contemplate the extent to which gender counted in the exploitation and murder of Jewish women; and the extent to which the sexism of Nazi ideology and the sexism of the Jewish community met in a tragic and involuntary alliance. To ignore the plight of women is, in reality, to ignore more than half of the Jewish population. And this ignorance is what most of Holocaust history delivers.

Jewish women were often more than 50 per cent of the population of Jews that Nazis deported or murdered; sometimes as high as 70 per cent. It is curious then that Danieli's question ended the discussion about women. There were no other issues raised, no other questions posed. No one spoke about relationships of love. No one mentioned the relationship between women and children. No one mentioned work. No one wondered about the death and killing rates in ghettos and camps. No one talked about German women and their relationship to Nazism, or about women as perpetrators, or collaborators; or the structure of the women's camps, women in resistance, women political prisoners, or the relationships of men and women. The consensus was that sex during the Holocaust was only a media fantasy, thus there was nothing more to say. None of us knew what to do – there were no concepts readily available; there was no historical road map. Feminist theory would have helped, but no one at that time was prepared to apply it to the Holocaust.

Trying to make it from day to day involved many things for both men and women – a struggle for food, shelter, clothing, help; a struggle to escape the Nazis or to save children, parents, friends or to fight back. No matter what the situation, it was always a struggle. By no means does sex cover all that would define or describe a woman's struggle. But it is the most obvious place to begin if one wants to investigate women's experiences. If the obvious is avoided, it is easy to turn away from the more obscure or the more complicated aspects of the history of women during this period – the history of all victims who were women, as well as all women who were perpetrators.

The first interview I did for my project on women and the Holocaust was with Susan in 1979. Actually, it was the first interview I had ever done. In that interview she talked about the uses of sex in Theresienstadt where 'you survived as a woman through the [Jewish] male'. Of her experiences in Auschwitz-Birkenau, she spoke of an SS man's interest in her (whose interest she avoided) as well as 'dating' a Polish man from the men's camp at Birkenau.

In the summer of 1982 she revealed something new. I was visiting at her home. Susan was sitting in a small room in a comfortable chair. As I entered the room and began to sit down on the couch, she said: 'I was raped in Auschwitz.' I don't remember saying anything right away; I just looked at her. She immediately added that she wasn't gang raped, and that it was her fault anyway.

I began to counsel her. I told her that this was often what rape victims said and tried to convince her that it wasn't her fault. My remembrance is that I then said: 'When you are ready to speak about this, perhaps in six months, I would like to hear about it.' Not surprisingly, Susan didn't say anything more about the rape.

Clearly, I wasn't ready to hear what Susan had to say. When I came home I spoke with my friend Gladys, a sociologist who was an experienced interviewer. Gladys very quickly and simply told me what I could have said: 'What happened?' She pointed out to me that an interviewer must not show judgement or fear. An interviewer has to be easily and equally inquisitive about everything.

Although it was clear that I was a novice in the interviewing process, there was something more complicated going on. We began to talk about the ways in which an interviewer or a researcher has fears or finds some situations too difficult to confront; over time these can disappear and sometimes return in cyclical fashion. Our lives affect what we ask about and what we hear in interviews.

But was I really afraid? Or was it simply that I could not find the right question to pose? Did I just lack certain crucial techniques? Or did I really not want to hear? Was I befuddled because this was a personal encounter and not an interview situation? Was I the researcher or the friend when she began to talk? I think now that all the questions apply – I was afraid, unsure and inexperienced.

It is one thing to figure out ways to ask questions so that you can get at difficult material, it is still another to be able to listen. In spite of my conversation with Gladys, I didn't run to the phone to ask Susan what happened. I just retained the lesson. I then used this story repeatedly as an example of what not to do in an interview. Only a few people asked me what had happened. A few years ago, I finally decided to ask. I called Susan and this is what she told me.

Susan was deported to Auschwitz in 1943. She was 21 years old and rather quickly became one of the so-called 'privileged prisoners'. Susan's friends in Auschwitz characterized her as having a hole in her stomach – no matter what she ate, she was always hungry. A Polish male prisoner, tall and blond, approached her one day and offered her some food. She recalled that he offered sardines. She admitted to wanting to be noticed, needing attention, even affection. She said she was not looking for sex. Susan told me that she never suspected anything. He told her where and when to meet him. She went. 'He grabbed and raped me.' She did eat the sardines but added that she was never caught in such a situation again. Her naivety ran out. No one knows how often this kind of circumstance occurred. Who asks? Who tells? Whatever else it means, it is surely an indication that some Jewish women were victimized as women even within concentration and extermination camps.

If you know what sort of information you are seeking, it appears to be a simple process to listen. Although my example is elementary, I think the simplicity of the story reveals a good deal about how deeply we may not want to hear; and about the ways in which we avoid listening no matter how directly a survivor (male or female) may tell us what happened (for example, cannibalism, hiding in a latrine, killing newborn babies, sexual violence). Sometimes we avoid because we are afraid; sometimes we avoid because we don't understand the importance of what is being said and thus don't pursue. After I began my work on women and the Holocaust, the Holocaust historian Raul Hilberg told me that he had seen some dif-ferences between men and women in his research but had no idea what to do with the information. That was something he didn't share the evening when Danieli posed her question about the fears of children of survivors. I suspect that he didn't make the connection then. Something might seem worth pursuing or even significant, but without a language, without a nomenclature, without a place for the memory, it will not be pursued.

The Invisibility of Women Victims

Three examples have been mentioned: (1) the survivor who wonders about the relationship between her molestation during hiding and the Holocaust; (2) the scholars who thought that sex during the Holocaust is nothing more than a function of media hype; and (3) the interviewer who found it impossible to ask about the rape a survivor mentioned. All of these examples are old. In case you think that there are no significant contemporary examples because there is now some recognition of women and the Holocaust, let me mention some. The Research Institute of the United States Holocaust Memorial Museum had its opening conference in December 1993. It was a four-day event with 18 panels and 80 partici-pants. Of these 80 participants, 16 were women. There were panels on topics such as 'Anti-Semitism and Racism as Factors in Nazi Ideology', 'The Politics of Racial Health and Science', 'Multiple Voices: Ideology, Exclusion, and Coercion' and 'The Place of Survivors'. There were lectures concerning the disabled, homosexual men, blacks and the 'ordinary men' who became murderers; lectures on the rescuers, the churches, the by-standers. But not one lecture on women or gender. When asked why, the answer sheepishly offered was 'we forgot'.

Another example concerns the Permanent Exhibition of the United States Holocaust Memorial Museum. In an otherwise problematic piece on the Museum in *Ms* magazine, Andrea Dworkin wrote:

> In the museum, the story of women is missing. Women are conceptually invis-ible: in the design of the permanent exhibition, by which I mean its purpose, its fundamental meaning; in its conception of the Jewish people. Antisemites do not ignore the specific meaning or presence of women, nor how to stigma-tize or physically hurt women as such, nor do those who commit genocide forget that to destroy a people, one must destroy the women. So how can this museum, dedicated to memory, forget to say what happened to Jewish women? (Dworkin, 1994: 54)

She is correct. Although there are brief exhibition segments on non-Jewish victims of National Socialism, there isn't even a sentence that points out the particularity of women's experience. One can ponder Free-masons, Roma and Sinti, Homosexuals, Jehovah's Witnesses, Political Pris-oners. But not women.

Does this mean women are not present? Absolutely not. It was as-sumed by staff members of the Museum that Dworkin's article could pose no problem because women are not missing in the Permanent Exhibition. Women are everywhere: in photos of German civilians; in a segment on propaganda showing Leni Riefenstahl directing; in the representation of books burned; in the segments on refugees, exiles, Anne Frank; documentary footage and photos show women in the ghettos, as victims of massacres as well as women as rescuers and resisters. In addition, women were certainly represented in the Testimony film at the end of the exhibition and in the 'Voices from Auschwitz' audio theatre on the third floor. And women, although not necessarily all feminists, were very much part of the Permanent Exhibition team.

I worked on the Permanent Exhibition staff, but could not exert influence on this issue. Consequently, when the above argument was presented – that women were everywhere, hence gender was not an issue – I wrote the following:

> There are groups in the Permanent Exhibition whose victimization cannot compare even numerically with the particular victimization of women, yet there is no sentence to this effect anywhere in the P.E. [Permanent Exhibition]. The actions and the policies of the Nazis did not obscure the identification of women as victims.
>
> It is not a question of using gender as the defining characteristic for the P.E., but rather indicating somewhere, where appropriate (e.g. Arrival at Auschwitz) that women were victimized in particular ways. We say that children and the elderly were gassed upon arrival. That is hardly accurate – women and children made up a significant population in these first selections, often 60–70 per cent of those gassed. Such a sentence would not have been difficult or changed the P.E. very much. But it would have been important. Gender may not define the Holocaust, but it is not trivial either. Certainly not less significant than Roma and Sinti, homosexuals, political prisoners, etc. – and of course all of these groups include women. I had argued against the 'women's room' which had first been proposed for the P.E., because the lives and deaths and sufferings of women are too integrated into the entire picture to segregate their experiences. We integrate photos, footage, voices, testimony; however, we don't integrate a conception [about women]. (Ringelheim, 1993)

I think that one can say there is an implicit conception about women in the museum and that is: women, whether Jewish or non-Jewish victims, whether perpetrators, bystanders, rescuers or collaborators, are not considered a group like Jews, 'Gypsies', Jehovah's Witnesses, homosexual men, Russian male POWs, etc. Since women, when victimized, were targeted as a sub-group of their 'larger' group identity, they were not considered a class of victims in the museum conception. It may be that Nazis had a varied or vivid imagination concerning Jewish men and a limited one concerning Jewish women. In spite of this, women turn out to be very dangerous because they carry the race. Thus genocide could not be partial. What then is the answer? Is gender a category like Jews, Gypsies etc.; or a subcategory like the *Judenrat*,[2] children, etc.?

Whatever the answer, the same conclusion emerges: some conceptualization of gender is needed, even if small. I think most members of the Permanent Exhibition team believed (and still do) that since Jewish women were persecuted and killed because they were Jewish, there is no need to say anything particular about the history of that persecution and murder. Because photo and film documentation does not exist for many of the situations that involve women – there are few photos of women in Auschwitz, for instance – words have to be used to portray gender.

To be fair, it is also the case that we are talking about a museum, not an encyclopaedia – a museum that has many stories to tell and simply could not tell them all. There are all sorts of things omitted from the story line. It could not be otherwise. Nevertheless, this omission of women is too big to ignore. We would not have needed another exhibit space to conceptualize the issues, as you would with respect to the Vatican and Italian Fascism for instance. Let's look at two small examples. First, the Museum opens with American liberation of the camps, but the photos one sees of these scenes on the fourth floor of the Permanent Exhibition are of men: men from the US army and male inmates. There is a reason – these were men's camps. But the visitor is not told that Buchenwald was a men's camp. Such a reference would not offer a sophisticated conception of gender but at least a consciousness which might work its way into the visitor's thoughts about the segregation of the sexes in the camps. Second, right after this initial exhibit there is a kind of sculptural collage primarily of men's uniforms – however, the caption never mentions this. The term 'prisoner uniform' is used when it could easily have said 'men's or women's uniforms' from this or that camp. These are two small instances where a brief comment could have revealed something about gender without any ideological strain. There are other more explosive examples which could be cited (for example, the argument about whether or not to exhibit women's hair from Auschwitz-Birkenau), but I wanted to point to simple examples at this time.

As Dworkin ends her argument, she writes, 'But because the museum did not pay attention to women as a distinct constituency with distinct experience, what women cannot bear to remember will die with them; what happened will die with them' (Dworkin, 1994: 58).

Andrea Dworkin is giving too much power to the museum and too little credit. The Permanent Exhibition is not all there is to the museum. And certainly women's experiences are being represented in the Oral History Department of the US Holocaust Memorial Museum; and around the world, in over 190 oral history projects on the Holocaust, as well as in many published memoirs and in archival holdings. Saying this does not answer the question raised earlier about the problematic nature of getting these stories. Dworkin, as is her wont, is exaggerating. Yet the warning should be heeded – when Dworkin exaggerates, there is always enough truth to warrant attention.

I think that these examples point to one basic problem: we have not wanted to go into the world of sexual exploitation amidst the other horrors of the Holocaust. Sometimes because we think it is trivial in comparison with genocide per se or because we think it is so banal. Yet when it is banal, it is too close to what we know in everyday life. We can then make connections. When we think about the Holocaust, we understand that people had to resort to elemental needs and behaviours. At the same time, it is claimed that we cannot visualize this universe created by the Nazis if we weren't there. But this is true even for survivors – can Pauline really know Susan's life in Auschwitz? It is always difficult, and sometimes impossible, to visualize when you were not there. This understanding is too difficult to confront it seems – it may bring us closer than we can bear.

There is an even stronger reason that gender is avoided. The Holocaust is defined by death. Without the killing operations there is no Holocaust. It is to this place that we must always return whether or not we talk about gender. But in this domain of death, it is crude, if not obscene, to avoid talk about gender. And yet, in spite of the available documentation, no analysis had been done until very recently. Historians published the death rates in the ghettoes and the Lodz and Warsaw ghetto deportation lists by sex, printed the *Einsatzgruppen* reports which often identified the murdered by sex, and still did not focus on the possible meanings of those figures. When I began to do this work in the mid 1980s, there were no historical or sociological analyses of the documents from the point of view of gender.

The Nazis specifically legitimated the murder of Jewish women and children because it was central to the race struggle. Jewish women were not simply Jews; they were Jewish women and treated accordingly in the system of annihilation. The documents clearly reveal that Jewish women were often the largest population available for the killing operations against the Jews, after Jewish men had emigrated, been evacuated, or been taken into forced labour. Nazi deportations (even when the Jewish Councils were allowed to create the lists), and the selection at the ramps of extermination camps, indicate clear differences by gender as well as by age. More Jewish women were selected for death in the extermination camps. Mary Felstiner is correct to say: 'One sex was chosen disproportionately for death' (Felstiner, 1994: 205).

After you ponder the actual figures, it is an effort to remain sanguine about the avoidance of gender in the study of the Holocaust. Talk about sex or sexual exploitation may be too delicate or intimate for some; talk about the genocide of Jewish women (and children) too frightening in a deep sense. However, if we begin to look at the experiences specific to women, we must include the sexual and we must eventually come to the death and killing rates. Women were 'objective enemies' to the Nazis; our task is to make that clear and understandable.

Conclusion: A Split Memory

Genocide and gender: a split memory. Any description of the split in Holocaust studies is linked to one result – gender is on one side, either ignored or hidden; genocide is on the other, neither ignored nor hidden. We must journey beyond this split. In the first place, Jewish men did not stand in line for Jewish women when it came to the killing operations. Jewish women stood in their own lines, so to speak, and were killed as Jewish women. Secondly, Jewish men cannot stand in for Jewish women as we try to understand everyday life with its terror, fear, loss, escape, hope, humour, friendships, love, work, starvation, beatings, rape, abortion, and killing operations. However much we may want to discuss the Holocaust in apocalyptic terms, those who were confronted by terror and murder found it in their everyday lives, not in some metaphysical reality. Jewish women and men experienced unrelieved suffering during the Holocaust. Jewish women carried the extra burdens of sexual victimization, pregnancy, abortion, childbirth, killing newborn babies in the camps, care of children, and often decisions about separation from children. Jewish women's lives were endangered as Jewish women, as mothers, as caretakers of children. For Jewish women the Holocaust produced a set of experiences, responses, and memories that do not always parallel those of Jewish men. As Pauline said: 'Everything else is the same. But there are certain things that are different.' If in the gas chambers or before the firing squads all Jews seemed to be alike to the Nazis, the path to this end was not always the same. The end – namely, annihilation or death – does not describe or explain the process.

Notes

1. See, for instance, the relative absence of women in Claude Lanzmann's nine-hour film *Shoah* (Lanzmann, 1985).
2. Nazi-appointed Jewish councils in the ghettoes.

References

Arendt, Hannah. 1971. *Between Past and Future*. New York: Viking.

Arendt, Hannah. 1966. *The Origins of Totalitarianism*. New York/Cleveland: Meridian Books.

Bock, Gisela. 1991. '"Equality", "difference", and "inferiority": motherhood, antinationalism and gender relations in National Socialist racism.' In Gisela Bock and Pat Thane (eds), *Maternity and Gender Policies: Women and the Rise of the Welfare States*. New York/London: Routledge.

Delbo, Charlotte. 1990. *Days and Memory*. Marlboro, Vermont: The Marlboro Press.

Dworkin, Andrea. 1994. 'The Unremembered: Searching for Women at the Holocaust Memorial Museum.' *Ms* magazine, November/December, 1994.

Felstiner, Mary. 1994. *To Paint Her Life: Charlotte Solomon in the Nazi Era*. New York: HarperCollins.

Hilberg, Raul. 1992. 'Men and Women.' In Raul Hilberg, *Perpetrators, Victims, and Bystanders*. New York: Aaron Asher Books/HarperCollins.

Levi, Primo. 1986. *The Drowned and the Saved*. New York: Summit Books.

Nietzsche, Friedrich. 1957. *The Use and Abuse of History*. Indianapolis, IN: The Library of Liberal Arts.

Ringelheim, Joan. 1993. 'Women and the Holocaust: A Reconsideration of Research.' In Carol Rittner and John Roth (eds), *Different Voices: Women and the Holocaust*. New York: Paragon House.

Smith, Bradley F. and Agnes F. Peterson (eds). 1974. *Heinrich Himmler: Geheimreden 1933 bis 1945*. Frankfurt: Propylaen.

Welty, Eudora. 1984. *One Writer's Beginnings*. Cambridge, MA: Harvard University Press.

Part II

Women in a War Zone:
The Construction of Gendered Identities

3

Against the War: Women Organizing across the National Divide in the Countries of the Former Yugoslavia

Rada Boric

May, 1996. Banja Luka, Bosnia. The first meeting of women from the so-called Republika Srpska and women from the Federation, both known as the newly divided parts of Bosnia, women from Croatia and women from what is now known as SR Yugoslavia (Serbia, in fact). The first meeting in five years in a country so brutally divided into the Federation (composed of Muslim Bosnians and Croats) and the Serbian entity. The background is the cruel reality of devastated land and destroyed communities, families divided, scattered all over the world. Two million Bosnians (without a national prefix). Two hundred thousand dead, uncountable wounded, widowed, orphaned.

Women came to share their experiences and tell how the war affected them. Their fear was etched on their faces. 'I fear I would be wrongly understood,' many of them wrote on the 'tree of fears and expectations'. After years of isolation and hatred, they came with fear and prejudice. But their fear was countered by the atmosphere of trust and understanding the women created.

For five years women were trying to survive the war in their own communities, in their own way. The traumas were experienced mostly by women, as were the losses, of loved ones, of identity and of the history of living together. It was a meeting of women from Bosnia who, separated from each other, did not know how much they had in common.

They were meeting women from Croatia and Serbia, who managed, in spite of the war and the exclusivist national politics, the broken telecommunications and mass-media blockades, to maintain their contacts and prove that working across frontlines was possible. In spite of their differences, it was proved as soon as they met that no matter how different their personal experience of war was, it had the same core – all have lost their basic security and trust in their neighbours.

This was why it was so important for women to come and share their experiences, to understand themselves, the war, others. The war in the former Yugoslavia had achieved its aim: dividing territory and dividing people. But women recognized the pattern of male-dominated power, male-oriented power; recognized how politics divides gender roles. While men spoke about abstract things such as state or nation, fighting for ghostly historical rights of one nation over another, women, traditionally raised and socially constructed to accept and support men, started organizing themselves. At the beginning it was out of a need to support their own families, but it soon became support for the whole community. It was evident during the war that women took on the tasks of community care and healing, humanitarian aid and anti-war protest. Women always had in mind the differences in their own communities, and they focused their struggle on actions that found resonance in the community. It was obvious, not only in Banja Luka, that women share a strong attitude towards war. Incapable of preventing the logic of war, and rarely included in military actions, women were never involved in peace negotiations (except as translators for the 'men only' delegations). But they bore the guilt (reinforced by 'the other side') of being the enemy, just because they belonged to the Serb, Muslim or Croat 'genocide nation', and they shared the responsibility for survival.

In order to resist the spread of hatred, violence and destruction, women started to oppose and attack the logic of militant nationalism, although it often meant becoming the targets of official state politics. They did this by organizing public action (Zagreb's Women's Lobby; Women in Black, Belgrade) and by initiating specialized centres for women (Medica Zenica, Bosnia; Centre for Women War Victims, and Rosa House, Zagreb).

Feminist solidarity was seen as a threat to national patriotism, writes Svetlana Slapsak, a feminist from Ljubljana:

> A number of well-known non-conformist women writers were singled out as 'witches' by the media (among them the writers and academics Dubravka Ugresic, Rada Ivekovic and Slavenka Drakulic). Details of their private lives were publicized, such as their spouses' and parents' ethnic origins ... (Slapsak, 1995)

Feminist solidarity was proved not only by the support of individual women, attacked by their own nationalistic misogynist societies, but also by many new projects supported financially by other women's groups from outside the new state borders. This support survived the war. For example, women from the Autonomous Women's House Zagreb, Small Step, the Centre for Peace and Nonviolence of the Anti-War Campaign of Croatia, and the Centre for Women War Victims, met and trained Albanian women in Kosova, part of Serbia, in June 1996.

Women's work in the former Yugoslavia consisted mostly of direct work with women who, due to the war, suffered male violence. According to the UN High Commission for Refugees (UNHCR), 80 per cent of the refugees were women and children. Therefore, women worked directly with women refugees, in refugee camps and collective centres, and in private housing. Initially, the work consisted of first aid; the focus of the first women's organizations in 1992 in Croatia and in 1993 in Bosnia was humanitarian. Women's groups in Slovenia and in Serbia, on the other hand, dealt more with male domestic violence than with war-induced violence. Because of the absence of foreign financial and humanitarian aid, the strictly humanitarian organizations in Croatia and elsewhere had to disband or to change their objectives. However, in the most difficult period, when almost half a million displaced persons and refugees congregated in Croatia, in addition to the almost two million refugees already there, these organizations fulfilled their objectives by giving aid and shelter, and by dressing and feeding women, children and the elderly.

After the 1995 military operations by the Croatian army in Krajina, almost 200,000 Serbs left Croatia. With the new flow of refugees into Serbia, women's groups there faced problems similar to those encountered by Croatian groups when, in 1993 and 1994, they tried to deal with half a million displaced refugees. Women shared their experiences in whatever way they could – by email, or by telephoning through a third party. Women and women's groups in the 'enemy' country reached one another even when telephone lines between Serbia and Croatia were cut. To be able to work in the most efficient way to stop the spread of hatred was as important as keeping our contacts alive in order to prove that nationalistic politics could not break the links between women's groups formed earlier around the shared agenda of struggling against male violence.

However, many of the groups established in the wake of the war never overcame the 'humanitarian aid' position and the majority still serve that purpose. In war-devastated Bosnia, basic aid is still most sorely needed, and women in Bosnia did not have the time to develop a feminist approach towards war violence, nor did they have any pre-war history of feminism. The task of developing a feminist perspective of the causes and consequences of war is still facing women's groups in the former Yugoslavia.

In this chapter I would like to address the work of the organizations established with a clear vision of what women's independent organizations should do, combining the principles of feminism, anti-nationalism and women's solidarity.

Women and War

The similarities between our own personal experience of war and the experiences of the women we work with are more than coincidental. Some of us have suffered less directly. My own town, Zagreb, was attacked 'only' twice. There was material damage and several dead, including a woman from Sarajevo who, after two years in Sarajevo's basements under constant shelling, was killed by shrapnel in Zagreb. We spent several nights in shelters, more as training than due to any real danger. But my fear meant that, after the attack, my alerted body woke up to the sound of the early morning tram. Days of depression and helplessness mean a unique body of women's knowledge of what violence is about.

We knew, through theory and through the experiences of other women, that violence committed against women in wartime was a continuance of the violence committed in peacetime, and that the difference was only in quantity, intensity and visibility. We remember the stories of the rapes in Bosnia, used in political games and employing the symbolism of woman only when politically necessary. According to Vesna Kesic, a Zagreb journalist and leading feminist activist:

> A raped Croatian woman is a raped Croatia. Here was a mystic unity of woman and the country identified through her. Once again, the nation's identity is established through women's bodies. The consequence of equating the raped woman with the 'dishonoured' country is that all members of the 'enemy' army are viewed as rapists – not just those who started the war, the politicians, the generals and the exponents of systematic rape in aid of 'ethnic cleansing'. There are no individual culprits, but the whole nation, including its women, is culpable. (Kesic, 1995)

The visibility of the atrocities against women was misused many times. The media was bloodthirsty in relation to Bosnia: pale children from Sarajevo's basements followed by ghostly men from Manjaca and other detention camps, were 'spiced' by pictures and testimonies of raped women, all feeding the public's hunger for a day or two. Some of the women organized themselves just as the media was flooded with pictures and stories of the rapes in Bosnia, with the aim of opposing every manifestation of violence against women, including the violations by the media and the politicians.

As in any country polluted by a militaristic, nationalistic uprising, Croatia surrendered to similar outbursts of nationalism, threatened by Serbian nationalism and mobilizing 'ethnically conscious' people ready to serve the goal of founding 'ethnically clean states'. Slogans such as 'wherever there is one Serbian grave, there is Serbia', and 'Croatia to the Drina river' which swept our countries, used the same *raison d'être* – our own 'ethnically cleansed' territories.

Women Supporting the War

Let us not deceive ourselves, however: many women have been trapped into the same extreme nationalism, supporting the war option in and out of parliament. Vesna Kesic writes about changes within the 'new democratic states' that occurred with great speed, and with predictably catastrophic consequences for women and for the newly created societies. In Croatia, traditional patriarchal images of the static gender roles of mother, wife, Virgin (if possible), and whore (when needed), appeared simultaneously with political and cultural emphasis on ethnic and national exclusivity. (Kesic, 1995)

Many women accepted the role of 'mothers-heroes'. Some women's groups organized to 'support our own soldiers' by collecting food and clothes, baking cookies and visiting wounded soldiers. And, at the very beginning of the war in Croatia, women tried to pull their sons out of the Yugoslav army when the 'people's army' sided with Serbia. These women were guided by the basic, traditionally reinforced and expected urge to care for others. Organized to protect their families, women proved how the personal becomes the political. Their efforts were manipulated to serve the purpose of the nationalistic politics of the 'sacred state'. Many of these women's groups did serve their purpose and some are still serving it by caring for the children of killed soldiers or by searching for missing relatives; but by the end of the war, many of them are already forgotten.

Women Manipulated for Political 'Higher Goals'

In the gathering of more than 5,000 women in Tuzla on the anniversary of Srebrenica's genocide and the resulting disappearance of some 10,000 men, on 11 July 1996, I sensed, on the one hand, the courage and power of women and their sadness in mourning for their loved ones. I have talked to the gentlest, most courageous women. One of them lost two sons and three brothers, another lost her husband who had not seen his baby, born three days after she arrived in Zenica. On the other hand, I also sensed that women were being manipulated for political 'higher goals', in order to put political pressure on the international community, who did not care, but who shared the responsibility for the killings and for the failure of Bosnia. Meanwhile, the women's own suffering was overlooked.

The women themselves were often not aware how their efforts were being manipulated. Women in women's groups which existed before the war were at a certain advantage. Prior to the war there existed a small, but highly profiled women's movement in the former Yugoslavia, mostly organized around work opposing violence against women. Several groups in Zagreb, Ljubljana and Belgrade (such as SOS Hot Lines; Autonomous Women's House, Zagreb) cooperated by exchanging experience and support.

With the beginning of the war, however, the women's groups in Zagreb were split on the national issue. Both sides continued to work with women, both claiming to work with women regardless of their nationality, but each accused the other of being non-patriotic or of not naming the aggressor clearly enough. Many women believed that supporting the new national (military) politics was the way to achieve democratization. They simply joined those who advocated the 'now or never one-nation state', forgetting that this always means a process of 'ethnic cleansing', a state without 'the Other', without difference. An example of how women were manipulated dates back to the beginning of the war in 1991 when women members of the so-called Movement for Yugoslavia in Belgrade, who expressed their support for the Yugoslav People's Army, were used by the military.

But there were other women too, as Stasa Zajevic, from Women in Black in Belgrade, writes:

> While some women were used for whipping up support for the war, members of the independent women's movement worked to promote pacifism and the right to self-determination. Some of the members of the Belgrade Feminist Association 'Women and Society'[1] reacted against the political manipulation of women by attending meetings organized by the Movement for Yugoslavia, where they waved banners with messages countering nationalistic proclamations. The messages read: 'Feminists against the militarization of Yugoslavia'; 'We are not mistresses of the Supreme Commander'; 'Fathers of the nation agree among themselves, and they lie to us'. (Zajevic, 1995)

Women who recognize the importance of understanding the politics that oppose nationalistic chauvinism and the role of women, never fall into the trap of supporting nationalistic oligarchies. Rada Ivekovic, a leading feminist scholar, writes:

> In particular, the extreme cases of war and nationalism take over and adopt the models of gender difference to their advantage, and organize themselves along its lines. In this process the enemy, the other nation, is made to be the Other, as is the Female. The symbolic system of nationalism in fact needs the construction of 'the Other' as an indirect means for its domination; 'the Other' is thus its constituent part. (Ivekovic, 1993: 115)

Working with Women Refugees

Women in Zagreb began working with women refugees in reaction to the violence that overwhelmed women and peace activists. Feminists primarily aimed to support women who were the most brutally abused, with stories of mass rapes being predominant. Very soon, however, they realized that they did not want to follow the pattern of the media and the politicians who have used raped women for their political purposes. Reports of sexual abuse were used to spread war propaganda, to justify military actions and ethnic hatred. Once again, women's bodies were treated as a battlefield, this time one of political strategy.

But violence against women in this war took many forms, and many
women needed help and support. When we spoke abroad in a 'women's
political mission' in an attempt to draw attention to our work with women
in the former Yugoslavia, Martina Belic, from the Centre for Women
War Victims in Zagreb, argued that violence against women was

> physical and psychological, individual and structural, sporadic and systematic.
> Though the levels of intensity might vary, the consequences are not necessarily
> proportional: it can be one blow or many. Sometimes violence is inflicted on
> individuals, sometimes on a community of women. Most frequently, the vio-
> lence is systematic, with severe long-term repercussions. Both mind and body
> become the battlefield on which power is exercised. Women who are on the
> side of the opposing nation are rarely recognized as individuals; instead they
> are viewed as Albanian, Croat, Muslim or Serb. (Belic, 1995)

The Centre for Women War Victims, Zagreb

The rest of this chapter describes the work of the women at the Centre
for Women War Victims as an illustration of the many women's projects
in the former Yugoslavia, one which demonstrates how women did survive the war not only as victims, but also as restorers of life.

The Centre was founded in December 1992 when women came together under the auspices of the Anti-War Campaign Croatia, eager to
use their fledgling skills as counsellors and organizers to work with women
war victims. Women active in several pre-war women's projects decided
they would form a centre for refugee women. They would not divide
women by their nationality or by any other means. Biljana Kasic, one of
the co-founders of the Centre and coordinator of the Women's Studies
Centre in Zagreb, describes the decision to found the Centre:

> Each and every one of us who decided to undertake this women's project had
> her personal nightmare. From the very beginning, Autonomous Women's House
> Zagreb had experience in working with women victims of warriors' violence.
> Some of us had personal 'women's reasons', wishing to return to women their
> dignity and self confidence. (Kasic, 1994)

Croatia was flooded with refugees. The news media were increasingly
full of atrocities directed mostly, but not exclusively, at women. Being
female in this war clearly meant being used and attacked, without having
the power to determine or choose one's role. There was little conception
of how non-governmental organizations might work to support refugees,
even less how to specifically support women refugees. The idea of self-
help groups and psychosocial group counselling seemed a proper way of
empowering women to regain the control over their lives they had lost
in the war. Although our ideas were very new, and we were probably the

first to promote this type of approach, our feminist philosophy and our pre-war experiences were the key to our success.

Initially, our work involved many hours of sitting on crowded beds in cluttered barrack-type rooms holding women's hands and trying to make some sense of the violence and the confusion. We visited refugee camps, old railway cars holding families, basements more akin to dungeons, and we talked. We saw that the idea of working only with raped women would validate one type of war trauma over another, and understood that all women needed counselling and support. Women slowly began to articulate their fears, needs and desires, but it was clear that they kept the worst experiences to themselves, feeling unsafe and fearing stigmatization. Experience showed that a raped woman could not be certain of sympathy from the community, but instead became the object of shame. Often many months passed before rape victims had the opportunity of meeting a therapist, so they had to suppress their emotions. This was due to the difficulty of travelling from Bosnia, but also to their internalizing of their traumas in order to prevent the stigmatization of other family members, particularly children. When they did meet us, they often invested all their energies in dealing with the pressures of their new circumstances.

At the Centre we attempted to resist the dichotomies pushed upon us – nationalism versus internationalism, victims versus aggressors, guilty versus innocent, Croat versus Serb, and we built a small multi-ethnic community of our own, comprising local women, refugee and displaced women.

By February 1993, a team of 24 women activists trained in counselling started to work with women refugees. Using our previous contacts, we established a solidarity network with feminist groups from Germany, Austria, Ireland and Britain who organized training, humanitarian and financial aid. During the first two years, the emphasis was on financial help, but political and moral support was equally important. We began to run groups for refugees and displaced persons, each facilitated by one of us and one refugee or displaced woman. Most group meetings took place inside the 16 refugee camps organized in response to the influx of refugees, but not recognized by the government.

Later in 1993 the course of the war became more complicated when Croatian and Muslim forces began fighting in Bosnia. Muslim refugees found themselves in increasingly hostile and uncertain situations. While earlier they had sympathy as 'victims of the same enemy', now they were considered to be the enemy, and the Croatian media were full of xenophobic attacks. The Croatian authorities treated the Muslim refugees as hostages and threatened to force them back to Bosnia. The media attacks were supported by leading politicians who spread xenophobia and revenge: 'while we are feeding their women and children, they are killing our sons and brothers ...' The Centre opposed such attitudes by sending letters of protest to Parliament and the media.

But we have already learnt that women from Bosnia survived incredible traumas: rape, seeing family members tortured and killed in front of their eyes, separation, missing family members, the burning and destruction of property, and uprooting. Coming to Zagreb might have taken days of unsafe travel, but their arrival created new traumas of living in very poor conditions, unsure of their status as second-class citizens. The place they expected to be secure turned out to be one of further humiliation. They were alienated, scared to go out and be detected as non-Croats, without money or travel documents, blocked at every turn by bureaucracy, ashamed of feeling like a beggar; in short – refugees. Within a few months, during the Croat–Muslim conflict, the fear and uncertainty grew into panic in the camps, which were being searched in order to discover 'illegal refugees'.[2] When these deportations – exchanging Bosnian women for Croatian soldiers – were taking place, we acted quickly, using our already considerable skills as advocates, to bring these refugees back to Zagreb. This was a turning point for the Centre in protecting refugee women's rights. Due to poor provisions and protection, we were mainly dealing with problems of entitlement to healthcare, documentation, relocation to third countries (we helped 500 women and children to relocate), humanitarian aid, and provision of shelter. At the same time we opened the house for refugee women and children, and the first tenants moved into Rosa House in spring 1994. Support was provided in a variety of forms: psychosocial therapy to recover from the traumas of war, skill building to improve employment and education opportunities, and income generation programmes. 'The house really feels like home,' said one of the women residents.

In response to the great influx of refugees in autumn 1993, the Centre recruited 16 more women to work with refugee women. Among them were three women from Bosnia who were living in camps and were members of our self-help groups. Two of them were supported to continue their studies. When they felt grounded enough, they began to train as facilitators. In accordance with our politics, our facilitator teams were increasingly 'mixed' (refugee and local, different nationalities).

In 1994 our workloads increased dramatically with the increase of the refugee population to 12 per cent of Croatia's pre-war population. We provided counselling to over 1,000 women, and supported another 1,000 in practical terms. Our phone rang constantly, and women, including women journalists from abroad, crowded our office day and night. We were invited to embassies, political tours, international events and training courses. We established contacts with women's groups and many became our friends and supporters. Several foreign women worked with us as volunteers. Yet the programme faced many difficulties. Some of our activists are refugees or displaced persons and many have moved to third countries since they faced no future in Croatia. To be a refugee means having no right to work, and therefore little chance of covering your living expenses. In the interest of our own mental health, we organized the continuous supervision of a professional therapist. As a group, we experienced turbulent changes. Since we were in situations which required immediate response, planning, administration and systematization received lower priorities: when faced with issues of life and death, bureaucracy no longer seemed important.

The report by Centre workers Nela Pamukovic and Rachel Wareham describes how we worked and felt:

> Despite training in coping with stress, we are often drawn across our own personal boundaries, feeling obliged to fulfil all sorts of needs that were pushed on us – from offering home accommodation to women without refuge, to becoming involved on all political and social levels. This arose from our great desire to influence positive processes towards stopping the war, and to pressure our government to respect human rights as it changed and manipulated laws for its own ends. Our whole lives have become submerged in our work: we sacrifice our family relations, and our partners joke about forming support groups for neglected spouses. We work very long hours, often into the night (a donor might require a report at 12 hours' notice), usually seven days a week. Journalists tend to arrive at weekends and have only a few days to get their stories before leaving. It is hard to resist because we rely on the international community as the only force which can influence our government. (Pamukovic and Wareham, 1995)

By 1995 our work was influenced by the political and military actions of the state. Not only did our work with refugee women in and around Zagreb continue, it expanded to areas outside the city to meet the needs of women affected by military actions in Western Slavonia and the former UNPA Sector north of Krajina. The Centre, therefore, began to work in the region of Pakrac and Petrinja, an ethnically mixed area before the war. In 1991 and 1992 this area was 'ethnically cleansed' of local Croats and other non-Serb nationals (Czechs, Slovaks and Hungarians) by the Serbian paramilitary army. Heavy fighting took place, and the result of undeclared war between Serbia (SR Yugoslavia) and Croatia was the occupation of a third of the Croatian territory and the formation of Serbian-controlled Krajina. In May 1995 the area underwent a second 'ethnic cleansing' through military action. This time Serbs were put to flight, although some Serbs, namely women and the elderly, remained. Croats who had been displaced in 1991 and 1992 began returning to their destroyed villages and cities. As 200,000 Serbs left former Krajina, Croat refugees from Banja Luka and Vojvodina (a Croatian minority in SR Yugoslavia) also arrived in the abandoned Serbian houses. Women from the Centre began visiting the region two days after the military operations. Destruction, looting and some killings continued. Our aim was, firstly, to protect the remaining minority of Serbian women, the most vulnerable of the remaining population, by providing psychological support and practical assistance concerning human rights, and, later, to help promote the idea of reconciliation and reintegration.

Despite the desperate conditions in the area, there is little understanding on behalf of the social welfare services of the different needs and problems faced by either the returnees or the refugees. The problems faced by the local population further exacerbated the emotional traumas, which can resurface in a variety of ways ranging from anger, rage and hatred to insecurity, depression and sorrow. In some parts of the former Krajina, the Centre is the only NGO providing any assistance. We have learnt from the women we work with how important that assistance is as a bridge to rebuild broken relations between communities, and our group meetings were recognized as places for establishing lost safety.

The Dayton Peace Agreement signed in November 1995 has, on the one hand, stopped the war, but, on the other, it has frozen the shaping of the Bosnia-Herzegovina map in accordance with the division achieved through military action. Thus the Agreement has justified bloodshed. The process of normalization, not to mention reconciliation, will be long and painful. The international community was slow and hesitant in deciding to help end the conflict, blocking and blaming one another while war crimes go unpunished and war itself continues. This war has resulted in 200,000 deaths, made 250,000 people homeless and, over the past four years, created some two and a half million refugees.

To the outside world, however, the Dayton Agreement suggests a different reality, that the needs of the refugees no longer exist. Financial and humanitarian aid is decreasing. Many aid and relief organizations have left Croatia with the belief that all the refugees will now return to Bosnia, although many of them cannot return to their previous homes due to the ethnic division of the country. For example, Bosnian Muslim refugees from Banja Luka cannot return home as the city is now within the Serbian-controlled Republika Srpska. According to the official UNHCR report (no. 3–4, March–April, 1996), there are 686,533 Bosnian refugees outside the former Yugoslavia and 645,300 refugees in the other countries of the former Yugoslavia. In Slovenia, there are 19,000, in Macedonia 6,300, in Croatia 170,000 (of whom 72 per cent are Bosnian Croats, 26 per cent Muslims and one per cent Serbs), and in the Federal Republic of Yugoslavia 450,000 (mostly Bosnian Serbs). In SR Yugoslavia there are 200,000 Croatian Serbs who left Croatia after the military operations of May and August 1995.

Conclusion: Life after the War

The post-Dayton developments, and the slow process of return to Bosnia and to parts of Croatia, mean an increase in the Centre's activities. Returnees must face destroyed houses, damaged infrastructure, high unemployment and poor local economies. The state made considerable promises to reconstruct, communicated through the media. Better-paid jobs and apartments are promised in an attempt to attract Croats to replace the Serbs who had left regions such as the former Krajina. The reality, however, is very different. The de-mining of over two million landmines used in the war is a slow and expensive process. The politics of 'ethnic cleansing' has ensured that communities are territorially ethnically divided; hence many people are unable to return to their original homes and are directed instead to other areas according to their ethnicity.

Now that the war is officially over, there is little hope. People are faced with destroyed homes, missing family members, mass graves and other atrocities committed in the name of war. Men who fought in the war must return to face traumas, unemployment and poverty, and try to find new roles and identities. In 1995 960 former soldiers committed suicide in Croatia; in April 1996 16 more took their lives.

These societal problems have a clear impact on women who face unemployment and poverty, and increased domestic violence. The Centre offers psychosocial support to returnees and refugees. We work within refugee camps (though they are gradually closing down) and with women in private accommodation. We work with local Serbian and Croatian women, Croatian and Muslim women from Bosnia situated in former Serbian villages. Our programmes focus on rebuilding trust, resocialization and reintegration. New circumstances forced us to open a transit house as short-term emergency accommodation for women 'passing through' Zagreb (for example from Sarajevo, Zepa and Srebrenica). And people continue to leave the Balkan countries to third countries despite the peace agreement.

Due to lack of funds and lack of awareness by the international community, we are unable to continue to provide regular financial support and humanitarian aid to women as we did before, and we are limited to providing emergency financial assistance. We continue to offer psychosocial counselling and legal advice to refugee women as camps are being closed by the Croatian government, forcing Bosnian refugees to return to their often non-existent former homes. We have trained women's groups all over the former Yugoslavia, in Tuzla, Split, Osijek, Zenica and Krajina, and facilitate meetings of women whom the war separated. We have also facilitated training in non-violent communication for international NGOs such as the International Red Cross Committee, Oxfam, and trade unions.

Our work is as crucial as ever. War trauma did not end with the signing of the Dayton Agreement. The leaders who began the war, constructed its policies of destruction and ethnic cleansing, and went on to sign the Dayton Agreement, remain in power. Our political situation cannot be stabilized until these leaders are removed. Ethnic cleansing itself has not ended. The policies of all ruling parties and governments in the region continue to be geared towards creating 'ethnically pure' states. People are pawns of such policies; they are moved from one area to another according to one agreement, and then told to move back again when another agreement is reached. The freedom of movement guaranteed by Dayton is yet to be realized. Permission to travel requires many papers; many areas are difficult to enter freely, and entrance depends on a person's ethnic background. There are no guarantees of safety and within Bosnia the UNHCR continues to protect people who return to their former homes, or visit family members.

The 200,000 Croatian Serbs who fled to Serbia during the military operations in 1995 face refugee status in Serbia with the resultant uncertainty, hopelessness and fear about the future. Many hoped to return to Croatia,[3] to the homes they left behind, but despite official promises both Serbian and Croatian policies actively prevent their return. Together with human rights and peace groups from Serbia and Croatia, we endeavour to raise these issues and provide practical assistance.

People are beginning to return from third countries as the political and economic situation becomes more certain. It is estimated that 2.5 million Croats, Serbs and Bosnians are currently refugees in third countries across the world and within the former Yugoslavia. Some may be forced to leave their countries of asylum without knowing where to return, and whether their villages belong to another country. We hope to be able to assist them in finding transit accommodation in Zagreb. Many refugees currently living in Zagreb would lose their refugee status as a result of the agreement between the Croatian and Bosnian governments, but would not want to return to Bosnia. Some families managed to find employment (mostly illegal), their children attend school; widows do not want to return to places where their partners were lost. If they decide to stay in Croatia without documents, they will become illegal and risk deportation. As there is no legislation to address the issues of migrants and asylum seekers, it remains to be seen how such people are treated by Croatian law. The Centre is committed to protect the rights of women who are not willing to go back and to engage in advocacy for refugee women.

Despite our financial problems, particularly in relation to our work with refugee women, the work of the Centre is an example of how women organize, across the ethnic divide, in working with other women to counteract the effects of war and to empower each other in building a better society.

Notes

This chapter is dedicated to all the women with whom we worked and with whom we survived the war.

1. An organization of the same name has existed in Zagreb since 1979 and cooperated with the Belgrade group. The first feminist conference in Belgrade in 1978, named 'Comrade Women', had an impact on women organizing in the former Yugoslavia.

2. Like other European countries, Croatia reduced the number of refugees it was willing to allow in, although it was the first possible place of exile for Bosnian refugees.

3. According to the Croatian Helsinki Committee (*Feral Tribune*, 19 August 1996) 25,000 Serbs requested permission to return to Croatia.

References

Belic, Martina. 1995. 'The biggest victims of the war.' *War Report*, no. 36, September 1995.

Ivekovic, Rada. 1993. 'Women, nationalism and war: make love not war.' *Hypatia*, vol. 8, no. 4.

Kasic, Biljana. 1994. *Pocetak, Zbornik, Centar za Zene Zrtve Rata.* Zagreb: Centre for Women War Victims.

Kesic, Vesna. 1995. 'From respect to rape.' *War Report*, no. 36, September 1995.

Pamukovic, Nela and Rachel Wareham. 1995. *Our Story.* Zagreb: Centre for Women War Victims.

Slapsak, Svetlana. 1995. 'Silence kills, let's speak for peace.' *War Report*, no. 36, September 1995.

Zajevic, Stasa. 1995. 'The guardians of "national values" and biological reproduction.' *War Report*, no. 36, September 1995.

4

Rape, Power and Masculinity: The Construction of Gender and National Identities in the War in Bosnia-Herzegovina

Euan Hague

There is no greater power than that which grows out of the barrel of a gun. (Arendt, 1972)

The first order of business in being a man is: don't be a woman. (Stoller and Herdt, 1982)

The category 'man' is not neutral – it implies power and domination. (Brittan, 1989)

Some of the most shocking crimes perpetrated during the war in Bosnia-Herzegovina were those of extreme sexual violence and systematic rape. This has since become an important issue of analysis, particularly the policy of 'genocidal rape' followed by the military and paramilitary units of the Serb and Bosnian Serb nationalist forces.[1] The horrific events and practices of raping in the war in Bosnia-Herzegovina have been repeatedly described.[2] In this chapter I intend to examine genocidal rape in the war in Bosnia-Herzegovina to evaluate how rape, in whatever context, is founded upon assumptions of power, domination and gender identity.

The many other instances of mass rape committed by troops during wartime are all horrific crimes.[3] I am not suggesting that rapes can be put into a 'hierarchy' as Nordstrom (1994) fears can be an indirect result of an analysis that highlights 'genocidal rape' as somehow different from 'normal' rape. The fact that genocidal rape has a political aim does not change the rape victim's traumatic experience. Neither am I suggesting that these rapes in the war in Bosnia-Herzegovina are divorced from wider societal gender and power relations. Indeed, it is these wider assumptions about certain types of soldierly masculinities that provide the basis for the perpetration of these crimes in Bosnia-Herzegovina.

Masculinity and Masculinities – Rape and Power

The Serb and Bosnian Serb military policy of genocidal rape presented very particular relationships of power, subordination and masculinity. Critical connections between violence, gender and nationalism formed the foundations of the policy of genocidal rape. To examine these connections I shall use contemporary theories of masculinity developed by Chapman and Rutherford (1988), Rutherford (1988; 1992), Brittan (1989), Connell (1987; 1989; 1994; 1995), Boone and Cadden (1990), Jackson (1991), Clatterbaugh (1992), Glenn Gray, (1992), Harris (1992), May and Strikwerda (1992), Seidler (1992), Weeks (1993), Cornwall and Lindisfarne (1994a; 1994b), Dawson (1994), Grosz (1994), Kandiyoti (1994), Loizos (1994) and Radkte and Stam (1994).

Much of the theorization of rape comes from Western feminist thought. Critics such as Griffin (1979), Warshaw (1988) and Brownmiller (1993) repeatedly assert that the rapist's mentality operates from a masculine position, arguing that rape is an alliance of masculine sexuality's aggressive, violent and dominating position with respect to femininity's allegedly inherent passivity. It seems that many masculinities construct men who enjoy a position of sexual dominance where pleasure is gained from the act of humiliation, subjugation and submission of the rape victim to the rapist's own will (Arendt, 1972; Winkler, 1995). I now evaluate these contentions in relation to the gender identities that the Serb and Bosnian Serb military policy of genocidal rape imagined and subsequently constructed in its criminal perpetration.

All rape is an experience of power, domination, degradation and humiliation, wherever, whenever and whoever commits the crime. Whether raping a woman, girl, boy or man, the rapist takes a position of power, subjugating the rape victim. Power relations infuse the entire context and perpetration of rape. The rape victim is physically and/or psychologically coerced into sexual acts (Bal, 1988; Warshaw, 1988; Brownmiller, 1993; Seifert, 1994; Winkler, 1995). Warshaw (1988: 14) defines rape as 'the total loss of control by one person to the will of another'. The rapist controls the situation, dictates the procedure and makes all the decisions regarding the continuation and perpetration of the rape (Winkler, 1995).

Society constructs masculinity as a bearer of power and subjugates femininity to maintain the dominance of that power through patriarchy (Kitzinger, 1994). Dworkin maintains that

> Men are [raping], because of the kind of power that men have over women. That power is real, concrete, exercised from one body to another body, exercised by someone who feels he has a right to exercise it, exercised in public and exercised in private. (Dworkin, 1983: 14)

This means that the feminine, to maintain social relations based on male power, must be constructed as (sexually) subordinate to the masculine. An aggressive masculinity dehumanizes and debases the sexual object. The humiliation of the sexual object through her or his coercion into performing degrading acts is a common aspect of reported rapes in Bosnia-Herzegovina. Griffin (1979: 7) states that 'many men appear to take sexual pleasure from nearly all forms of violence. Whatever the motivation, male sexuality and violence in our culture seem to be inseparable.' Rape is an assertion of man's superior and triumphant manhood (Brownmiller, 1993: 14).

The problem with traditional feminist contentions like those above is their universal implication that the rape victim is always, in all places, a woman. Clearly not all men are rapists, or are likely to be, yet these traditional contentions seem to suggest that man's *raison d'être* is to rape. Hall argues that the traditional feminist approach to rape as a system for maintaining male supremacy and patriarchy may be outdated. She specifically targets Brownmiller, challenging 'the ahistory of her model – her view of rape as a timeless paradigm, unmodified by social circumstances, of male violence against women' (Hall, 1983: 328).

There is also the problematic evaluation that all that is female is feminine, and all that is male is masculine. Grosz problematizes such assumptions and argues that although the sex of the body is an important factor in influencing which gender identity the individual inhabiting that body develops, 'Masculine or feminine cannot be neutrally attributed to bodies of either sex' (Grosz, 1994: 58). Not all men fit the standard model of what it means to be masculine unequivocally. Indeed, rather than a single masculinity, there are multiple masculinities that vary across space, time and context. The same contention applies to femininities. These many gender identities are continuously renegotiated daily by individuals in their social lives (Jackson, 1991). Jackson remarks that the very plurality of these gender descriptions make them valuable tools for the analysis of multiple patterns of social relations, particularly, he states, in assessing 'complex patterns of domination and subordination' (Jackson, 1991: 200). In some cases a woman may be seen as masculine, or a man as feminine but 'the "masculinity" of the male body cannot be the same as the "masculinity" of the female body, because the kind of body inscribed makes a difference to the meanings and functioning of gender that emerges' (Grosz (1994: 58).

Contemporary debates about gender identity and construction challenge these terminological dualisms (male/female, man/woman, masculine/feminine). However, these dualisms have long been defined by society and its institutions and are thus highly resistant to re-evaluation or re-theorization (Brittan, 1989). The belief that man = male = masculine and woman = female = feminine continues to be subscribed to by the vast majority of people. I thus continue to use these terms, albeit critically, throughout this chapter.

Nordstrom criticizes traditional feminist evaluations of rape, arguing that they are over-simplifications of the structure of rape:

> Rape is a fundamentally gendered phenomenon. Men, in the vast majority of cases, are rapists. This fact, however, has led to a tendency to restrict rape to analyses of men as perpetrators and women as victims. While there is no doubt that women bear the brunt of rape, an accurate understanding of rape has to expand out from an exclusive focus on women. Women *and* men are raped; adults *and* children are raped. (Nordstrom, 1994: 7)

Similarly I maintain that men and boys could have been, indeed were being, raped in Bosnia-Herzegovina, albeit much less often than women and girls (Gutman, 1993; Mazowiecki Report, 1993; Bassiouni Report, 1994; Helsinki Watch, e.g. 1993).

Brittan (1989) highlights a further problem with such generalized contentions; masculinities are not unequivocally powerful or inherently violent: power relations depend on contextual and circumstantial factors. However, masculinities can generally be equated with power-holding and the subordination of femininities. Jackson (1991: 201) outlines a 'hegemonic masculinity' that operates under patriarchy. It includes the ability to control and make decisions, to act rationally, to control emotions and to exhibit physical courage and muscular prowess. This masculinity is the one that the Serb and Bosnian Serb nationalist (para)militaries valued. As Olujic (1995) and Sofos (1996) explain, this is a type of masculinity that Serb rhetoric commonly demonstrated.

Cultural and social production constantly recreates, at all social levels, from local to global, (most) masculinities as dominant and (most) femininities as subordinate. Neither femininity nor masculinity is a universal proposition, nor is a power-positioning common to all masculinities. However, the Serb and Bosnian Serb military policy of genocidal rape imagined and then constructed a specific type of masculinity, consistently aggressive, violent, powerful and dominating. In this situation, to assume that the masculine subject is the power-wielding one is entirely valid. This masculinity is what I now assess.

Power and Military Masculinity in Genocidal Rape

In the crime of genocidal rape in Bosnia-Herzegovina, traditional gender assumptions of which persons are 'masculine' and which 'feminine' came under attack, and in many cases were reasserted, through ascriptions of national identity. The qualities of power, domination and violent subjugation often associated with a hegemonic masculinity accrued, in this context, to the national identities known as 'Serb' and 'Bosnian Serb'.

Gender and Catastrophe

Power and domination are central structures of rape. The rapist takes the power-holding position that I have shown to be 'masculine'. Holding power allows the rapist consciously to torture, attack and brutalize a victim that the rapist, or the policy of genocidal rape, defines as inferior. Those in the powerless position were, the genocidal rape policy maintains, gendered 'feminine' identities that the policy asserts should not be allowed to exist. These divisions permit violence against other human beings: 'Not only do men oppress other women, they also oppress other men ... the end result is the same – the division of society into those who have power and authority, and those who do not' (Brittan, 1989: 17).

Hartsock summarizes: 'the sexual dimension of power implies a masculinity structured by violence and domination' (Hartsock, 1983: 166). The Serb and Bosnian Serb military policy of genocidal rape, in addition to the atrocities it promoted, also produced a violent and domineering masculinity that accrued to the Serb nationalist forces. Those opposing these powers had their national identities gendered 'feminine' and therefore powerless. Sofos argues that in the war in Bosnia-Herzegovina, 'the category "feminine" has been employed to include virtually everyone – men and women alike – not conforming to the accepted "nationalized" versions of masculinity, or to the "gendered" versions of national identity' (Sofos, 1996: 67).

In Bosnia-Herzegovina, the Serb nationalist forces waged war against enemy, that is non-Serb, military forces and civilians. The Serb and Bosnian Serb militaries devastated non-Serb territory, destroying villages, churches and cemeteries to render the territory without a history. By removing such buildings, the Serb forces could claim that the territory had always been 'Serbia' and annex it accordingly. The non-Serb, person or territory, was, in the eyes of the Bosnian Serb soldier or associated irregular, contemptible, unworthy of existence – unless it became 'Serb'. By enforcing pregnancies and asserting that all children born as a result of these were 'Serb' and by removing all traces of non-Serb inhabitation of territory, the only national identity of the Balkans would be 'Serb'.

Serb and Bosnian Serb army soldiers objectified the non-Serb 'enemy' to hold power over, intimidate and humiliate her or him. According to Hartsock (1983), for many masculinities, humiliation of the sex object is common. Stoller (1985: 7) states that many sexual actions contain 'the desire to hurt, harm, be cruel to, degrade, *humiliate* someone', usually the sex object, that is, that which the masculine, power-holding person considers 'feminine'. Winkler (1995: 70) states that rapists want to humiliate, forcing their victims into a position without agency, indeed, one of 'non-existence'.

In the war in Bosnia-Herzegovina 'genocidal rape' followed these descriptions of masculinity. By humiliating non-Serb persons through a systematic programme of raping women and girls, and by raping women,

girls, men and boys as torture in prison camps (Allen, 1996), Bosnian
Serb forces not only bolstered their own masculinities and identities as
'Serbs' but eroded the identities of the non-Serbs by the extreme humiliation associated with the rapes. Dawson (1994) argues that to humiliate
is to 'feminize'. The combination of these positions shows that subjugation of the enemy as 'feminine' is central to a masculinity the perpetrator
conceives as superior.

This powerful Serb masculinity that genocidal rape constructed operated through the feminization of the rape victim, regardless of the victim's
sex as male or female. Military discourse, the discourse that formulates
the policy of genocidal rape, is traditionally heterosexually masculine and
thus perceives 'homosexuality' not merely as a sexual condition or practice,
but as a lack of the 'aggressive characteristics that were thought to
comprise masculinity' (Levy, 1989: 201). Thus even if a rape could be
described as 'homosexual' on physical criteria, the Serb or Bosnian Serb
soldier, by holding the power position, gendered himself 'masculine', the
non-Serb who was raped or who was forced to rape another non-Serb
was gendered 'feminine'. Such a contention is best explained by an
example: a male Serb prison guard raping a Bosnian male prisoner.[4]

The reasoning of genocidal rape and act of raping by the Serb or
Bosnian Serb soldier asserts his *hetero-nationality* – a different national
identity from that of the rape victim. In turn the rape victim has her or
his national identity (as Bosnian) rejected and humiliated as it is forced,
by the rape, into an inferior position as feminine. In this scenario, gender
and national identities, as Sofos (1996) agrees, are totally intertwined.
The result of the rape scenario I outline above leaves the Serb or Bosnian
Serb soldier with a strong and visible masculinity, even though the rape
in question could possibly be deemed by observers as 'homosexual'. As
I mentioned above, to be a homosexual soldier stands in contradiction to
military discourses of the 'correct' masculinity – one that valorizes hetero-
sexuality and virility.

Loizos (1994) explains that the power-holding penetrator in a homosexual rape is not stigmatized as 'homosexual' or 'feminine':

> [A] man who acts as the active partner in homosexual intercourse can still
> retain his self-respect as conventionally male ... *men fuck* and this is a masculine
> and *dominant* thing to do, and whomever or whatever is so used is the subor-
> dinated and therefore inferior party ... Penetration can be as much about
> power, then, as intimacy ... [and] to have penetrative sex with someone is ...
> thus to feminize him. (Loizos, 1994: 72)

Genocidal rape asserted a masculinity that, by the reasoning of the policy,
is positive, powerful and hetero-national as it attests to being 'Serb', where
Serb identity is more powerful than any other of the Balkan identities.

In the prison camps operated by the Serb and Bosnian Serb armies in the war in Bosnia-Herzegovina, Serb regular and irregular troops coerced and watched non-Serb men and boys rape and sexually abuse each other (Gutman, 1993; Stiglmayer, 1994a; 1994c; Allen, 1996). How does this situation create a Serb and Bosnian Serb positioning as powerful and masculine?

The prisoner-to-prisoner rapes in Bosnia-Herzegovina constructed both non-Serb prisoners as 'feminine'. The overseeing Serb and Bosnian Serb soldiers reasserted their gender identities as masculine through their ability to exercise power over the situation. The watching soldiers could humiliate the non-Serb prisoners and coerce them to degrade each other. The soldiers forcing these prisoners to rape each other maintained *hetero-nationality*. The policy of genocidal rape created a system where Serb nationality always assumed the masculine, therefore powerful, position while the subjugated and coerced prisoners were similarly constructed hetero-nationally as non-Serb, therefore weak, powerless and feminine. The prisoner-to-prisoner rapes, through their identification by the Bosnian Serb and Serb military policy, marked the non-Serb, the 'enemy', as feminine, cowards, inadequate fighters and therefore incapable, and unworthy, of doing men's jobs like protecting their nation.

Weeks (1993: 190) explains that 'Masculinity ... is achieved by the constant process of warding off threats to it.' The non-Serb males feminized by genocidal rape no longer offered a strong military threat to the Serb nationalist forces. The lack of aggressive masculinity, constructed by this policy as typifying non-Serbs, assured the success and strength of the powerful masculinity, that is, the masculinity which the policy constructed as being wholly 'Serb'.

By raping and impregnating women and girls, watching men rape each other in prison camps, and assuming the power position of 'masculine' in all rapes, the Bosnian Serb military and its allied irregulars proved to themselves their own identities as powerful, manly and, crucially, Serbs. The policy equation of Serb national identity to the powerful masculine position in the perpetration of genocidal rape, asserted the dominance of Serb and Bosnian Serb men across the Balkans. This in turn, in the reasoning of the military policy of genocidal rape, justified the subjugation of those identities that the policy of genocidal rape constructed through its practice as feminine (and thus inferior). These are the identities called 'woman', 'Bosnian', 'Croat', 'Muslim'.

The Importance of the All-male Group in the Perpetration of Genocidal Rape

A feature of the sexual crimes of the Bosnian Serb army and its paramilitary allies was that they were most commonly gang and multiple rapes (Bassiouni Report, 1994; Stiglmayer, 1994a, 1994c; Allen, 1996).

Gang rape is, Warshaw (1988) explains, often more aggressive than individual rape. As each rapist takes his turn, the acts performed on the rape victim's body become increasingly violent and degrading. The all-male setting of the military and the perpetration of gang raping creates a 'bonding' experience: 'Men who rape in groups might never commit rape alone' (Warshaw, 1988: 101). The group gives the rapist protection through loyalty and support, but also puts pressure on the man to imitate his peers and to live up to or even exceed their expectations with his actions. War creates a 'community of males', and this is, as Mosse (1985), Connell (1994) and Hicks (1995) show, at the root of nationalistic and militaristic politics (Hague, forthcoming). There is a strong 'conflation of valorized male sexuality and militarism' (Brittan, 1989: 177).

In the war in Bosnia-Herzegovina, genocidal rape usually occurred within a group context when other soldiers were available to observe this performance of masculinity. According to Folnegovic-Smalc,

> The rapes in this war are not individual rapes but gang rapes. They represent not a primarily sexual act, but rather an aggressive act that has as its purpose the destruction of the person's human dignity, her injury and humiliation. (Folnegovic-Smalc, 1994: 174–5)

The context of group rape is particularly important in a war where failure to obey orders to rape was likely to result in death for the abstainer. There was no anonymity for the soldier coerced to gang rape. There was no choice. Every other soldier in the all-male raping group could, if necessary, have identified the individual who threatened group cohesion by refusing to rape. This could have resulted in the resistant individual facing disobedience charges in a military court or, more likely in the context of this war, simply being killed by other soldiers or officers of Bosnian Serb or Serb military or paramilitary units. Without absolving these rapists for their crimes, the following issues should be raised. Who are the most culpable criminals here, the ground troops following orders or the officials and military staff dictating policy? Can degrees of abhorrence even be debated in relation to this issue?[5]

The prime example of an all-male grouping is an army and in such a group context, collective ethics erode and replace individual ethics (Hartsock, 1983; Mosse, 1985; Theweleit, 1987; 1989; Glenn Gray, 1992; Rutherford, 1992; O'Sullivan, 1993; Dawson, 1994; Kinzer Stewart, 1994; Hicks, 1995). Camaraderie and competition between the group members, here soldiers, coupled with increased alcohol consumption (a common feature of many of the rapists in Bosnia-Herzegovina) and the loss of self-identity within the group, allows sexual aggression to escalate rapidly. In rape/death camps, groups of soldiers selected women to repeatedly gang rape both as a method of torture and to enforce pregnancy – a feature pertinent to the Serb military policy (Stiglmayer, 1994b; Allen,

1996). Evidence also shows that other all-male groups in this conflict, such as soldiers from the UN Peacekeeping Force (UNPROFOR) and the official Croatian and Bosnian militaries, committed rape and gang rape against women residing in Bosnia-Herzegovina (Mazowiecki, 1993; Bassiouni, 1994).

'War was [*and still is*] an invitation to manliness' and is still largely an all-male domain (Mosse, 1985: 14; Ehrenreich, 1987). The association of warfare with 'proving manliness' is widely agreed upon by writers on both masculinity and military theory. Holmes (1985), for example, states that many males believe that fighting a war is a step towards manliness. He quotes Christopher Isherwood: 'War ... meant the Test. The test of your courage, of your maturity, of your sexual prowess: "are you really a man?"' (Holmes, 1985: 59). Rutherford (1988) also evaluates the long-held association of war with a male's rite of passage into full manhood and Perrin (1979) recounts the association between war and manliness in historical Japan.

In military discourse and, therefore, genocidal rape policy, to participate in war is to be masculine and manly. In war there operates a 'masculine pleasure-culture' (Dawson, 1994). The soldier gains pleasure, sexual or otherwise, by participation in war and by camaraderie and association with other men (Mosse, 1985; Theweleit, 1987; 1989; Glenn Gray, 1992). Audoin-Rouzeau (1995) calls this inter-male feeling *esprit de corps*. Fantasy, and the idealization of inter-male relationships in a wartime context, replaces the real political bases of events and actions. The consequence of this sentiment is, in Dawson's terminology, a 'masculine pleasure-culture' of 'soldier males'.

This all-male community excludes women. Women, and specifically 'the feminine', according to this mentality, threaten to contaminate the all-male group and destroy its unity. The only way of avoiding this pollution of masculinity is to subjugate and exert power over the feminine to the point of eliminating it (Theweleit, 1987; 1989). However, in its total exclusion of the female, this masculinity faces the equally unnerving challenge of the feminine in the form of the 'homosexual'. Although a discussion of sexuality and sexual orientation is not within the scope of this chapter, the all-male group of strong, cooperative soldiers, with women excluded, is clearly homoerotic (Mosse, 1985; Theweleit, 1987; 1989; Brittan, 1989).

Soldierly masculinity intends to build an unquestionable heterosexual identity – a virile, bodily masculinity that rejects homosexuality. Military masculinity understands homosexuality not as a real masculinity, but as a weak, contaminating masculinity, indeed a femininity, and thus an identity that must be eradicated. Homosexuality, in this reasoning, weakens military unity and the strength of the national army. To this mentality, homosexuality threatens the male-ordered world and the strength of the male body.[6]

Conclusion

The power over the 'feminine' in the Serb military reasoning of genocidal rape offered the Serb nationalist forces 'the assurance of a clearly recognizable gender identity and, through this, the security of belonging to a gendered national collectivity that imagines itself to be superior in strength and virtue to others' (Dawson, 1994: 282). By imagining their masculinity to be superior to others, persons who do not fit into this standard of Serb military masculinities – such as women and the non-Serb enemy – are rendered inferior, or 'feminine', by the Serb masculine, national identity. The ascription of a dominant, powerful masculinity, through the policy of genocidal rape, to the all-male group of Serb and Bosnian Serb military units and associated paramilitaries such as the Chetniks and Tigers, necessarily reduces non-Serb persons, within this reasoning, to powerlessness. This, in turn, provided the masculine nation with the justification to ascribe other nations as inferior and unworthy of existence. To defeat them in war would establish a 'legitimate' rule of Serb military masculinity across the Balkan region.

Rape is always structured by relations of power and coercion, constructing a context of subjugation and powerlessness. I have shown how the reasoning of the Serb military policy of genocidal rape operates at this intersection of power relations, gender and national identities. I have also argued that military discourse and policy are a critical feature of producing a valorization of a certain type of masculinity – a powerful, dominating, violent one – and how this, in turn, constructs all those who do not meet this gender-national identity to be deemed inferior and 'feminized' (Condren, 1995). In Bosnia-Herzegovina, gender was an important part of how nationalist forces understood and fought the war.

Notes

I would like to thank Beverly Allen, Apolline Baudry, Lorraine Dowler and Ronit Lentin for their comments on earlier drafts of this chapter.

This chapter assesses the *military policy* of genocidal rape by Serb and Bosnian Serb nationalist forces. I do not intend to suggest that all Serbs and Bosnian Serbs are rapists. Nor do I suggest that these rapes were the only ones that occurred during the war. Soldiers on all sides committed rapes, including those soldiers of the United Nations UNPROFOR battalions. However, the authors listed and the United Nations reports on the conflict demonstrate, I suggest, that there was a systematic policy of raping that many Serb and Bosnian Serb soldiers were ordered to follow.

1. See Gutman, 1993; Bassiouni Report, 1994; MacKinnon, 1994a, 1994b; Condren, 1995; Olujic, 1995; Allen, 1996; Sofos, 1996.

2. There is much interview testimony available (for example – in no particular order – Gutman, 1993; Stiglmayer, 1994c; Folnegovic-Smalc, 1994; Mazowiecki Report, 1993; Bassiouni Report, 1994; Janekovic, 1994; Condren, 1995; Olujic,

1995; Allen, 1996; Sofos, 1996; and regularly published reports by Human Rights groups like Helsinki Watch e.g. 1993).

3. There are many studies of other examples. Brownmiller (1993) addresses a number: raping of Highland Scottish women by English soldiers after the 1746 Battle of Culloden; of Belgian women by German soldiers during World War I; of women in Nanking (China) by the Japanese army, 1937; of German women by Soviet troops in WWII; of Bengali women by Pakistani soldiers in 1971; and of Vietnamese women by US men during the Vietnam War; rapes committed as tortures by French troops in Algeria (1954–61); by the Portuguese in Angola and Mozambique; and by post-WWII military governments in Argentina and Brazil. Hicks (1995) and Sancho (this volume) assess the 'comfort women' forced into prostitution during the Second World War by the Japanese military. Copelon (1994) reviews raping of Yuracruz women in Ecuador and raping that occurred during civil wars in Peru, Liberia and Burma. Nordstrom (1992; 1994; 1995) studies Mozambique, and Seifert (1994) raping by Moroccan mercenaries during World War II. There are also allegations of forced impregnation policy, called 'Hanization' operated by the Chinese in Tibet (1950–60) made by Davidson (1962), the Dalai Lama (1962) and Coburn (1995).

4. See the Bassiouni Report, 1994: articles 223–53.

5. That soldiers were coerced into committing rape does not absolve them. It does, however, raise difficult questions about who should be prosecuted for these war crimes – the individual soldiers or those giving the orders, or both? How can the evidence be collected for such prosecution? Does the individual soldier testify against his officers and then is prosecuted himself for his own actions?

6. Homosexuality in the army is still a major issue in contemporary society. Recent debates about the topic have surfaced, for example, in the USA and UK.

References

Allen, Beverly. 1996. *Rape Warfare: The Hidden Genocide in Bosnia-Herzegovina and Croatia*. Minneapolis: University of Minnesota Press.

Arendt, Hannah. 1972. 'On Violence.' In Hannah Arendt, *Crisis of the Republic*. San Diego: Harvest/Harcourt Brace Jovanovich.

Audoin-Rouzeau, Stephane. 1995. *Men at War 1914–1918: National Sentiment and Trench Journalism in France During the First World War*. Oxford: Berg.

Bal, Mieke. 1988. 'The rape of narrative and the narrative of rape: speech acts and body language in judges.' In Elaine Scarry (ed.), *Literature and the Body: Essays on Populations and Persons*. Baltimore, MD: Johns Hopkins University Press.

Bassiouni Report. 1994. UN Transcript.

Boone, Joseph A. and Michael Cadden. 1990. *Engendering Men: The Question of Male Feminist Criticism*. New York: Routledge.

Brittan, Arthur. 1989. *Masculinity and Power*. Oxford: Basil Blackwell.

Brownmiller, Susan. 1989. 'When men are the victims of rape.' In Michael S. Kimmel and Michael A. Messner (eds), *Men's Lives*. New York: Macmillan.

Brownmiller, Susan. 1993. *Against Our Will: Men, Women and Rape*. New York: Fawcett Columbine Books.

Brownmiller, Susan. 1994. 'Making female bodies the battlefield.' In Alexandra Stiglmayer (ed.), *Mass Rape: The War Against Women in Bosnia-Herzegovina*. Lincoln: University of Nebraska Press.

Chapman, Rowena and Jonathan Rutherford. 1988. 'The forward march of men halted.' In Rowena Chapman and Jonathan Rutherford (eds), *Male Order: Unwrapping Masculinity*. London: Lawrence and Wishart.

Clatterbaugh, Kenneth. 1992. 'The oppression debate in sexual politics.' In Larry May and Robert Strikwerda (eds), *Rethinking Masculinity: Philosophical Explorations in Light of Feminism*. Lanham: Rowman and Littlefield Publishers.

Clausewitz, Karl von. 1956. *War*. London: Routledge and Kegan Paul.

Coburn, Broughton (with Galen Rowell). 1995. 'Paradise lost.' *Worldview*, vol. 18, no. 2.

Condren, Mary. 1995. 'Sacrifice and political legitimation: the production of a gendered social order.' *Journal of Women's History*, vol. 6/7: 160–89.

Connell, Robert William. 1987. *Gender and Power: Society, the Person and Sexual Politics*. Stanford: Stanford University Press.

Connell, Robert William. 1989. 'Masculinity, violence, war.' In Michael S. Kimmel and Michael A. Messner (eds), *Men's Lives*. New York: Macmillan.

Connell, Robert William. 1994. 'The State, Gender and Sexual Politics: Theory and Appraisal.' In H. Lorraine Radkte and Hendrikus J. Stam (eds), *Power/Gender: Social Relations in Theory and Practice*. London: Sage.

Connell, Robert William. 1995. *Masculinities*. Berkeley: University of California Press.

Copelon, Rhonda. 1994. 'Surfacing gender: reconceptualizing crimes against women in time of war.' In Alexandra Stiglmayer (ed.), *Mass Rape: The War Against Women in Bosnia-Herzegovina*. Lincoln: University of Nebraska Press.

Cornwall, Andrea and Nancy Lindisfarne (eds). 1994a. *Dislocating Masculinity: Comparative Ethnographies*. London: Routledge.

Cornwall, Andrea and Nancy Lindisfarne. 1994b. 'Dislocating masculinity: gender, power and anthropology.' In Andrea Cornwall and Nancy Lindisfarne (eds), *Dislocating Masculinity: Comparative Ethnographies*. London: Routledge.

Dalai Lama. 1962. *My Land and My People*. New York: McGraw-Hill.

Davidson, Lionel. 1962. *The Rose of Tibet*. London: Gollancz.

Dawson, Grahaem. 1994. *Soldier Heroes: British Adventure, Empire and the Imagining of Masculinities*. London: Routledge.

Dworkin, Andrea. 1993. 'I want a twenty-four-hour truce during which there is no rape.' In Emilie Buchwald, Pamela R. Fletcher and Martha Roth (eds), *Transforming a Rape Culture*. Minneapolis: Milkweed Editions.

Ehrenreich, Barbara. 1987. 'Foreword', to Klaus Theweleit, *Male Fantasies – Volume 1: Women, Floods, Bodies, History*. Minneapolis: University of Minnesota Press.

Folnegovic-Smalc, Vera. 1994. 'Psychiatric aspects of the rapes in the war against the republics of Croatia and Bosnia-Herzegovina.' In Alexandra Stiglmayer (ed.), *Mass Rape: The War Against Women in Bosnia-Herzegovina*. Lincoln: University of Nebraska Press.

Glenn Gray, J. 1992. 'The enduring appeals of battle.' In Larry May and Robert Strikwerda (eds), *Rethinking Masculinity: Philosophical Explorations in Light of Feminism*. Lanham: Rowman and Littlefield Publishers.

Griffin, Susan. 1979. *Rape – The Power of Consciousness*. San Francisco: Harper and Row.

Grosz, Elizabeth. 1994. *Volatile Bodies: Towards a Corporeal Feminism*. Bloomington: Indiana University Press.

Gutman, Roy. 1993. *A Witness to Genocide*. New York: Macmillan.

Hague, Euan. 1997. 'Nationalism, gender and genocidal rape: identities in the War in Bosnia-Herzegovina.' In *Proceedings of the 1996 Maxwell Colloquium*. Syracuse, New York: Maxwell School, Syracuse University.

Hall, Jacquelyn Dowd. 1983. 'The mind that burns in each body: women, rape, and racial violence.' In Ann Snitow, Christine Stansell and Sharon Thompson (eds), *Powers of Desire: The Politics of Sexuality*. New York: Monthly Review Press.

Harris, Leonard. 1992. 'Honor: emasculation and empowerment.' In Larry May and Robert Strikwerda (eds), *Rethinking Masculinity: Philosophical Explorations in Light of Feminism*. Lanham: Rowman and Littlefield Publishers.

Hartsock, Nancy. 1983. *Money, Sex, and Power: Toward a Feminist Historical Materialism*. New York: Longman.

Helsinki Watch. 1993. *Abuses Continue in the Former Yugoslavia: Serbia, Montenegro and Bosnia-Herzegovina*. Vol. 5, Issue 11 (July). New York: Human Rights Watch Publications.

Hicks, George. 1995. *The Comfort Women: Japan's Brutal Regime of Enforced Prostitution in the Second World War*. New York: W.W. Norton.

Holmes, Richard. 1985. *Acts of War: The Behavior of Men in Battle*. New York: The Free Press.

Jackson, Peter. 1991. 'The cultural politics of masculinity: towards a social geography.' *Transactions of the Institute of British Geographers New Series*, vol. 16.

Janekovic, Vanessa Vasic. 1994. 'Ethnic Cleansing in Bosnia, June 1992.' In Lawrence Freedman (ed), *War*. Oxford: Oxford University Press.

Kandiyoti, Deniz. 1994. 'The paradoxes of masculinity: some thoughts on segregated societies.' In Andrea Cornwall and Nancy Lindisfarne (eds), *Dislocating Masculinity: Comparative Ethnographies*. London: Routledge.

Kinzer Stewart, N. 1994. 'Military Cohesion.' In Lawrence Freedman (ed.), *War*. Oxford: Oxford University Press.

Kitzinger, Celia. 1994. 'Problematizing pleasure: radical feminist deconstructions of sexuality and power.' In H. Lorraine Radkte and Hendrikus J. Stam (eds), *Power/Gender: Social Relations in Theory and Practice*. London: Sage.

Levy, C.J. 1989 'ARVN as faggots: inverted warfare in Vietnam.' In Michael S. Kimmel and Michael A. Messner (eds), *Men's Lives*. New York: Macmillan.

Loizos, Peter. 1994. 'A broken mirror: masculine sexuality in Greek ethnography.' In Andrea Cornwall and Nancy Lindisfarne (eds), *Dislocating Masculinity: Comparative Ethnographies*. London: Routledge.

MacKinnon, Catherine A. 1994a. 'Turning rape into pornography: postmodern genocide.' In Alexandra Stiglmayer (ed.), *Mass Rape: The War against Women in Bosnia-Herzegovina*. Lincoln: University of Nebraska Press.

MacKinnon, Catherine A. 1994b. 'Rape, genocide, and women's human rights.' In Alexandra Stiglmayer (ed.), *Mass Rape: The War against Women in Bosnia-Herzegovina*. Lincoln: University of Nebraska Press.

May, Larry and Robert Strikwerda (eds). 1992. *Rethinking Masculinity: Philosophical Explorations in Light of Feminism*. Lanham: Rowman and Littlefield Publishers.

Mazowiecki Report. 1993. UN Transcript.

Mosse, George. 1985. *Nationalism and Sexuality: Respectability and Abnormal Sexuality in Modern Europe*. New York: Howard Fertig.

Nordstrom, Carolyn. 1992. 'The Backyard Front.' In Carolyn Nordstrom and Jo-Ann Martin (eds), *The Paths to Domination, Resistance, and Terror*. Berkeley: University of California Press.

Nordstrom, Carolyn. 1994. *Rape: Politics and Theory in War and Peace*. Canberra: Australian National University Peace Research Centre Working Paper No. 146.

Nordstrom, Carolyn. 1995. 'War on the front lines.' In Carolyn Nordstrom and Antonius Robben (eds), *Fieldwork under Fire: Contemporary Studies of Violence and Survival*. Berkeley: California University Press.

Olujic, Maria B. 1995. 'The Croatian war experience.' In Carolyn Nordstrom and Antonius Robben (eds), *Fieldwork under Fire: Contemporary Studies of Violence and Survival.* Berkeley: California University Press.

O'Sullivan, Chris. 1993. 'Fraternities and the rape culture.' In Emilie Buchwald, Pamela R. Fletcher and Martha Roth (eds), *Transforming a Rape Culture.* Minneapolis: Milkweed Editions.

Perrin, Noel. 1979. *Giving up the Gun: Japan's Reversion to the Sword, 1543–1879.* Boston: David R. Godine Publishers.

Radkte, H. Lorraine and Hendrikus J. Stam (eds). 1994. *Power/Gender: Social Relations in Theory and Practice.* London: Sage.

Rutherford, Jonathan. 1988. 'Who's that man.' In Rowena Chapman and Jonathan Rutherford (eds), *Male Order: Unwrapping Masculinity.* London: Lawrence and Wishart.

Rutherford, Jonathan. 1992. *Men's Silences: Predicaments in Masculinity.* London: Routledge.

Seidler, Victor J. 1992. 'Men, feminism, and power.' In Larry May and Robert Strikwerda (eds), *Rethinking Masculinity: Philosophical Explorations in Light of Feminism.* Lanham: Rowman and Littlefield Publishers.

Seifert, Ruth. 1994. 'War and rape: a preliminary analysis.' In Alexandra Stiglmayer (ed.), *Mass Rape: The War against Women in Bosnia-Herzegovina.* Lincoln: University of Nebraska Press.

Sofos, Spyros A. 1996. 'Inter-ethnic violence and gendered constructions of ethnicity in former Yugoslavia.' *Social Identities,* vol. 2, no. 1.

Stiglmayer, Alexandra. (ed.). 1994a. *Mass Rape: The War against Women in Bosnia-Herzegovina.* Lincoln: University of Nebraska Press.

Stiglmayer, Alexandra. 1994b. 'The war in former Yugoslavia.' In Alexandra Stiglmayer (ed.), *Mass Rape: The War against Women in Bosnia-Herzegovina.* Lincoln: University of Nebraska Press.

Stiglmayer, Alexandra. 1994c. 'The rapes in Bosnia-Herzegovina.' In Alexandra Stiglmayer (ed.), *Mass Rape: The War against Women in Bosnia-Herzegovina.* Lincoln: University of Nebraska Press.

Stoller, Robert J. and Gilbert H. Herdt 1982. 'The development of masculinity: a cross-cultural contribution.' *The Journal of the American Psychoanalytic Association,* vol. 30, no. 1.

Stoller, Robert. J. 1985. *Observing the Erotic Imagination.* New Haven: Yale University Press.

Theweleit, Klaus. 1987. *Male Fantasies – Volume 1: Women, Floods, Bodies, History.* Minneapolis: University of Minnesota Press.

Theweleit, Klaus. 1989. *Male Fantasies – Volume 2: Male Bodies – Psychoanalyzing the White Terror.* Minneapolis: University of Minnesota Press.

Warshaw, Robin. 1988. *I Never Called It Rape.* New York: Ms. Foundation/Sarah Lazin Books, Harper and Row Publishers.

Weeks, Jeffrey. 1993. *Sexuality and its Discontents: Meanings, Myths and Modern Sexualities.* London: Routledge.

Winkler, Cathy (with Penelope J. Hanke). 1995. 'Ethnography of the Ethnographer.' In Carolyn Nordstrom and Antonius Robben (eds), *Fieldwork under Fire: Contemporary Studies of Violence and Survival.* Berkeley: University of California Press.

Woodward, Susan L. 1995. *Balkan Tragedy: Chaos and Dissolution After the Cold War.* Washington DC: The Brookings Institution.

5

Reconstructing the Self through Memories of Violence among Mayan Indian War Widows

Judith Zur

When memory goes out to pick up dead wood, it brings back the faggot that it likes. (Mossi proverb)

The Quiche Maya widows, whose voices form the basis of this chapter, lived through and survived the Guatemalan government's counter-insurgency campaign of 1978–85, but they cannot escape it. Their village, which I have called Emol,[1] was bombed, bombarded and occupied by the army during this time, called *La Violencia*; houses, livestock and crops were destroyed; people were killed. Before withdrawing, the military instituted the civil patrols, inducing all village men to volunteer to police their own communities on the army's behalf; refusers were humiliated, imprisoned or sometimes killed. The military had a spy in every household – except those headed by widows.

Army-trained patrol chiefs marked their usurpation of power by choreographing the 1982 massacre of twelve Catholic Action supporters in front of the whole community. The public murder of village men by their erstwhile friends and neighbours demolished the fragile fiction of community solidarity which had sustained villagers through the initial stages of *La Violencia*. The massacre became the defining symbol of *La Violencia*, the moment when time stopped and everything changed. A few weeks later, the army 'disappeared' everyone at the Sunday market, leaving no witnesses to the loss of around a thousand people. Since then, people have been abducted in ones and twos; in return, death squads dump the mutilated corpses of strangers around the village in a grisly game of intimidation. By 1986, Emol had lost roughly one third of its inhabitants through murder, disappearance and flight.

Terrified villagers distance themselves from anything which could link them with 'subversives'. Most have opted for the 'new start' offered by

Evangelical Protestantism[2] which is associated with the military; conversion offers some protection from this dangerous label. Villagers who retain their Catholic or *Costumbrista* faith are in a vulnerable minority. War widows, that is, widows of men whose deaths are attributed to *La Violencia* (although women and children were also killed the vast majority of victims were men) are the most vulnerable to intimidation and abuse: many have experienced economic and sexual exploitation, rape or gang rape; some have been murdered.

Although *La Violencia* ended in 1985 following the election of a civilian president, the terror machinery remains intact. Fear is *La Violencia*'s most enduring legacy. It is against this background that the widows relate their narratives. This chapter explores the violence to their memories which, though intangible, is just as profound as the physical violence from which it is not entirely separate.

The *Ladino* (male) state uses public official discourse for political and rhetorical purposes. The Mayan Indian widows resist the official version of events producing an alternative unofficial discourse; within this they rewrite their gendered roles portraying themselves as heroines who sacrifice their menfolk, and reconstructing personhood in the process.

Assaults on Memory

The history of *La Violencia* can be read as a war against memory, an Orwellian falsification and negation of memory and reality. A Swedish representative to the United Nations remarked that the military government's rhetoric reminded him of Orwell's novel *1984*. 'When they mean war they speak of peace', he said, 'and when they mean repression, they speak of freedom ... Guatemala is the same' (Simon, 1987: 114). On national and local levels, the army and paramilitary leaders respectively deny people access to truth, contaminating morality and memory.

An official history of *La Violencia* had been fabricated by the military state which vilifies the dead as communists, rebels excised in a necessary national cleansing of 'impure elements'. Social control is exerted through the cultivation of historical amnesia, which suppresses the alternative voices of human rights groups and relatives of the dead (Williams, 1977). Negating people's personal history weakens their sense of personal identity, 'deprives them of a sense of efficacy and thus the capacity to organize and initiate actions' and so 'furnishes a base for [the] undisputed triumph of official ideology' (Pateman, 1980: 35). However, remembering in Emol, where leftist sympathies had been strong, contradicts the official 'truth' which blames the dead men for *La Violencia*; to their widows, the dead men are martyrs who, like the saints, died for no good reason. This is a private truth, articulated only between groups of trusted confidantes.[3]

Talking about *La Violencia* and even mentioning the names of the dead is forbidden. Fear drives most villagers not only to comply but to report anyone who disobeys; the widows are always wary of spies. Opportunities to talk are limited, although the traditional division of labour helps: women talk while grazing their animals or tending their gardens. Other female activities include bathing in their sweat baths or accompanying a female shaman to perform traditional rituals. In more public places, widows use coded language and gestures to disguise their conversation.

On an individual level, the widows' need to talk and their desire to place their memories within a known framework is often hampered by the fact that the memories they try to recall, organize and understand are of events which could not be integrated into cultural categories or codes of significance in the first instance. Unclassifiable memories can be transformed, remaining in mind in their altered state rather than as the original experience. Memories logged as chaos remain in the mind as chaos. Additional distortions can occur as a result of psychic stress, torment and other causes. *La Violencia* was just too overwhelming for individuals to absorb coherently.

Reworking Memories: The Construction of Narratives of the Past

As they uncover memories, the women rework, relive, make sense of, come to terms with and integrate the traumatic events which dramatically changed their lives, thus giving a boundary to their suffering. Together they attempt to construct a narrative of the past which makes sense to them. Reconstruction and reshaping take place both individually and collectively as widows remember events and recount them to each other. In doing this, they are not necessarily searching for the historicity of their experience or attempting to establish the chronology of events;[4] they are primarily concerned with how this past relates to their present lives. Elements from different periods are used to reconstruct and reshape events according to hindsight, for example:

> It was only when *La Violencia* was upon us that I remembered what my grandmother had spoken of years before. Then she had warned us that 'they will eat [kill] among us and we will fight among ourselves. It will be the end of the world.'

Recognition occurs in retrospect: the vision, the foretelling, is constructed retroactively and then retrospectively confirmed. People do not rue their failure to read these omens when they occurred. Rather, the reinterpretation of (real or imaginary) signs helps them to gain some sense of mastery over events: they have managed to place events in known categories of causation.

In the process of retelling, widows incorporate details of other women's memories into their own. Memory-narratives can become over-elaborated, only to be stripped down and built up again. This is an ongoing process; the women are concerned about the discrepancies between what actually happened and received narratives about the past. Here, the widows discuss their memories of the massacre:

> *Doña Eugenia*: The men were tied up. They had thrown them on the ground like pigs who are about to be slaughtered.[5]
>
> *Doña Candelaria*: They were on the ground with their faces bloodied. Some shouted, 'Please forgive us' out of devotion [to God] and because they were suffering so much.
>
> *Doña Flora*: They asked the patrols to forgive them. Many of the murderers were evangelicals. After the killings, they told people that those assassinated had begged them, asking 'our pardon and our help to convert to our religion'.
>
> *Doña Eugenia*: But I know everything that happened and they [the victims] didn't say anything like that … In fact, many didn't even utter a word. They couldn't even if they wanted to, because they were hurt so badly they couldn't talk at all.
>
> *Doña Candelaria*: Perhaps a few of them said a few things but nothing about that.
>
> *Doña Eugenia*: Only my child [her forty-year-old son] said something when they first captured him. He said, 'Mother, ask the chiefs of the patrols to get help to free me. Tell him I have not done anything wrong.' So I went to Mr Justice [a chief] and I asked him, 'What did he do to make you take him? Why not let him go?' But he didn't respond; he just ignored me. I then followed him until we reached the centre of the village. He didn't stop there, he just continued on a path which led to the ravine where they were digging the pits where the men would be buried. This is what happened. And, I tell you, I heard nothing about what you said, about conversion. That's all a big lie … Indeed, what they [the chiefs] shouted was that the men they had rounded up were to be slaughtered because they had left the village and become 'organized'. They accused them of being guerrillas.

Doña Eugenia had blamed the military for the death of her son but reconsidered her position when Doña Candelaria said:

> when they had buried them, they all returned to the school to threaten all of us. They warned us, 'None of you had better utter a word about what you have just seen. And if we should learn that one of you has, then what you have just seen will happen to you and you'll go with them!' … Because of this, I realized that the chiefs themselves decided to kill the men [i.e. the massacre was not ordered by the army].

In telling each other stories, women place order on this traumatic event. Although they had not witnessed the actual killings (patrollers had locked everyone inside the school before taking the victims to the ravine, where they were killed), the women discuss what happened next:

Doña Candelaria: I do not remember well, but they tell me that the first to die was Tin Roos, since they thought he was the *brujo* [witch] of the subversives [the implication is that he was considered the most dangerous].

Doña Ana: Ah! he was the first. You see, I don't remember because by the time we arrived [outside the school], we were no longer people [this refers to the loss of control women felt, a condition viewed as non-human].

Doña Candelaria: Oh God! But who wasn't like that on that day?

Together the women produce altered drafts of the past, discarding one in favour of the other. There is no final version. Their memories change as they change; they alter as the state of oppression fluctuates. The time of year, events in the present, which friends they are with and so on, all affect the relation of narratives, modifying memories of what is being told. This potential for change, for adding or discarding, emphasizing or ignoring elements of a narrative, exists in all conversations concerning shared experiences; however, in situations where people's memories are incomplete, damaged, suppressed or otherwise inaccessible, this ordinary social behaviour can assume a creative and healing function.

The Re-elaboration of Memories

In devastating circumstances, the process of re-elaborating the past overshadows the actual event to a greater extent than in more mundane situations. Intolerable truths may be rejected and less painful versions constructed. Pertinent detail (in terms of absolute truth) may be omitted, either consciously or as the result of memory fragmentation; certain aspects may be exaggerated or completely fabricated. Doña Flora's concern to establish her husband's (and, by extension, her own) innocence, for example, led her to 'forget' his alcoholism and to portray him as a good Christian and hardworking family man:

> My son had only left for the coast on the Monday and this [the abduction of her husband] happened Wednesday night. I had told him to go with my son but he said, 'What for? I have to look after the *milpita* [field of young corn] ... I have to look after the things, cut the wood and store the fire wood and the planks.' He had worked hard this day, taking care of the wood. At the end of the day, he finally sat down; he was hugging Sebastian and Manuel was sitting on his knee when he said, 'Oh, my knees are tired', because he had carried a lot that day; he told me, 'Sit down beside me for while.' Because of the tiredness, he ate and he went to bed; perhaps if he had left then, nothing would have happened to him ... But he didn't leave, perhaps ... it was his *suerte* [destiny].

Intolerable truths are sometimes replaced with narratives of the women's heroism, a quality usually attributed to men but now claimed by women. These are the most dramatic form of fabrication. The village massacre was a common topic for revision. Doña Eugenia, for example, presented herself as taking a leading role in countering this abomination. According to her account, she had stepped forward, mumbling, and offered the assassins money to stop them beating her son; they responded predictably by hitting her with their rifle butts, shouting 'Xo!', as if she was an unruly animal.

The danger implied in Doña Eugenia's narrative evoked fear in her listeners. Quiche women are ordinarily silent in the face of male authority; as a woman and an Indian, Doña Eugenia had 'broken the rules'. Her testimony represents an infraction of the code which regulates women's relationships with male patrol chiefs who are associated with the army and hence *Ladinos*.[6]

Doña Flora also recounted a memory of her own heroism. She returned to her home, risking confrontation with the most feared patrol chief just one week after he had kidnapped and killed her son. She had already lost her husband, so her bravery in facing the possibility of meeting this man was genuine:

> Then, after a while, I thought, I want to see my house and if Mario [the patrol chief] sees me, then he can kill me. I said to myself that I wasn't doing anything and it was my house. In the end I came and I looked for a worker to look after the house and I would return every so often to see how the house and the corn fields were doing ... I returned for good four years later.

On the other hand, it is doubtful whether the incident Doña Flora relates below happened as she describes:

> He [the chief] asked me if I had heard that they would come to the houses here. I told him that I had. He threatened me, saying that they were in process of deciding which houses they would visit. I replied, 'Let them come, let them come, because here is their father', moving the machete in my hands [in a threatening manner]. You see, they got used to killing ... they killed our men ... now they want to kill us. This is what I said. I was hardly aware of what I was saying. I believe that because of what I said, they did not come ... Perhaps it would have been possible to injure one of them ... If I had been there, when they came, I would have opened the door, quickly and –

Doña Flora fled the village shortly afterwards, later reframing the incident in a manner which allowed her to establish, at least temporarily, a positive image of herself. Narratives about defying the patrols help women maintain their integrity and a perception of autonomous action. Accounts of bravery, then, do not necessarily reflect events as they actually occurred; rather, they are narratives of the emotions and desires the women felt as they stood immobilized by fear. Discourses containing fantasy are simply a way of covering up terrible events.

Women portray themselves as having taken an active role in trying to prevent disaster, taking risks and dealing with the hostile external (and internal) world. This is expressed in their retrospective interpretations of their dreams, which the Quiche view as omens. Doña Josefina recalled:

> I had a dream about two weeks before they kidnapped my husband … In the dream he was abducted so, when I woke, I told him, 'Leave man! Go to the plantations! Go wherever you can so you will be spared. Then, once it is all over, come home.'

Despite the women's depiction of themselves as taking an active, heroic stance, they continue to suffer from the memories of their failure to protect their families. Women lament their unsuccessful attempts to persuade their husbands and sons to leave the village and their inability to prevent their deaths once the killers were active within the community. That women had no means of defending themselves and risked their own deaths if they tried to fend off the killers has no place in these narratives. Doña Flora describes the night her husband was abducted:

> We were sleeping when they arrived and they called us names, like 'bad people' [guerrillas]. Six or seven entered the house while the rest remained outside. The ones who came in took my radio and our watch; they looked for money but didn't find any. They remained silent until I cried out in protest, then they shouted at me, 'Shut up, you old bastard' and they beat me down on the bed. I hid under the covers after that.
>
> My son was on the coast and my daughter-in-law was pregnant. I still told them to be careful because there was a pregnant woman in the bed. They threatened me again and then began to take my husband. They wanted him to kneel down on the floor and pray before they took him away but he refused. So they tied one of our belts [a cloth sash] over his eyes and led him away in his underpants. He didn't say anything to me, only to them. He asked them what crime he had been guilty of. They responded by hitting him and pulling him away.

The public nature of the exposure and humiliation of their dead kin is a particularly painful memory. Doña Flora stresses that her husband was taken 'in his underpants … he was taken naked through the village'. That Emol is a face-to-face society in which reputation is of importance and value exacerbates surviving relatives' humiliation. Women's preoccupation with the violent removal of their traditional wraparound skirts reflects that this appalling indignity, the loss of ownership of the status of wife and mother, occurred in public.

A woman's unavoidable failure to protect her kin during *La Violencia* is built upon even up to the present, for she sees herself in the eyes of her surviving children (and bystanders) as continuously failing to consolidate her family following a period of national and personal trauma. Even among themselves, the widows' inability to fulfil the quintessentially female function of protection is referred to obliquely; their comments that they can no longer keep their animals alive (a female gendered task) are allegorical expressions of their self-perception as inadequate carers:

> *Doña Eugenia*: Now my pigs die on me. Since *La Violencia*, no sooner were they born than they would die, they would be born and would die, born and die.
>
> *Doña Flora*: They don't live any more?
>
> Doña Eugenia: No, none of my domestic animals do. Only a short while ago I bought four foreign chickens and they have already died.
>
> *Doña Flora*: They died?
>
> *Doña Eugenia*: Yes, and then I went to buy four more and they died too.
>
> *Doña Flora*: Oh, my child! ... It also seems that we have lost our power and our will.

The women suffer from overwhelming feelings of guilt, shame and anger. Theirs is a complicated, ambiguous guilt which is more than 'survivor guilt'; it arises from the paralysis which prevented women who witnessed the murder or abduction of their menfolk from acting to protect them. Women spoke of this paralysis although they did not acknowledge the fear which stopped them searching for their abducted offspring; instead, they said that someone, usually an older member of the family, had told them that they should not go. This relieved them from some of the responsibility of this added failure. Doña Flora's brother persuaded her not to go to the army base to search for her son. She expresses her guilt through recounting what he had to say:

> My brother told me that it was my fault for not bringing my son to the town. I didn't reply, I only cried and cried, I didn't eat, but just cried. At the time I was crying, I came across a man in the town and he asked me what I was doing. I told him that I was looking for my son and he replied that it was pointless, because they had already killed the men the night before.

Women's guilt about their behaviour contrasts with their portrayals of their dead menfolk as good Christians and martyrs. Doña Flora reflects on her failure to persuade her husband to leave for the coast with her son (who was abducted when he returned to the village):

> Sometimes I think that if we had left then, this would not have happened. I suggested that we leave for the coast or for Quiche [the departmental town] but he didn't want to leave, so we stayed. He would say to me, 'I am not a sinner, what should I run away for? Christ let himself be killed because of the rest of us' ... He was ready [for them]: 'If they kill us, they kill us.'
>
> But I tried to insist, saying, 'Let's get our beans and tortillas together and leave', but he was firm, he said, 'No, what am I going to leave my house for? If they kill us, they kill us.' He didn't want to go, he didn't want to go to the coast, even though we had a friend who was there. 'Let's go!' I said. But he didn't want to go. The friend was from another hamlet which is part of Emol ... but he didn't want to leave. 'If they kill us, they kill us,' he said.

In this version of her narrative, Doña Flora also blames her husband's obstinacy for his death whilst at the same time proclaiming that, like Christ in the Garden of Gethsemane, he accepted the unavoidable suffering inherent in his fate. This multi-layered ambivalence is typical of the women's narratives.

The Creation of Fictitious Identities

That their menfolk were killed by the 'same side' contributes to the feeling of camaraderie among the women, who offer each other care and empathy. For example, Doña Flora told a grieving widow that:

> it was better to cry otherwise her heart would swell. I said that it was because she doesn't cry that her heart swells and she could end up having an attack. I said, 'Cry and then take your remedy.' She thanked me and told me I was the only one with whom she speaks about such things. She has a lot of confidence in me because we were both 'organized'.

In sharing memories, widows create a shared identity and a feeling of trust. Paradoxically, one of the things that makes memories shared is that some are not articulated: there is tacit agreement about what is remembered and what is forgotten. Silence and forgetting are not necessarily lackings but absences or negative spaces which shape what is remembered.

Widows feel a disconcerting sense of disjuncture in themselves and their lives as a result of their experiences during *La Violencia*. This has alienated them from their own conception of personhood as it operates in the present and as it operated before they found themselves in the midst of *La Violencia*, when it was impossible to operate according to known codes of conduct. The surviving widow feels divided by the past and cannot forge an integrated vision of herself. Discontinuity damages the integrity of the 'self', leading to feelings of a diminished 'self'; recounting memories to each other acts to form an identity which works against these sensations. The women's 'self'-constructions and reconfigurations of themselves (especially as heroines) have the same effect – at least some of the time.

At other times, the women speak of their damaged personhood in terms of 'not being human'. Doña Ana's 'mind was dead' during *La Violencia*, she 'didn't think or feel', 'could not remember anything' and was afraid she 'was no longer a person'. The mental and emotional numbness endemic to the circumstances, the impaired thinking resulting from tremendous grief and an abrupt change in identity, took place in a totally foreign atmosphere that negated responses that, among the Quiche are the 'right thing to do' – including those things that define a human being. When Doña Flora remarked that a 'good Christian' would have denounced the atrocities, which she herself did not do, she was retrospectively condemning her own, unavoidable inaction. This self-judgement led to a diminished 'self'-perception with which her memory and her continuing 'self' has to contend in everyday life.

Doña Flora is not the only widow to judge behaviour dictated by the specific circumstances of *La Violencia* in terms of Quiche norms as they stand in 'ordinary' times. In condemning themselves and others for not acting in accordance with traditional mores, the widows are staking a claim for the continuity of Quiche values. Establishing continuity, a bridge over *La Violencia*, is an important, if only partially successful, activity which counters the women's disconcerting sensations of disjuncture.

Only Doña Eugenia claims to be able to acknowledge change and restore continuity within the chaos of her identity: she presents herself as a bit of a rebel but qualifies this by saying that her rebellious streak is consistent with the nonconformist tendencies of her family. Creating a sense of continuity is more important than acknowledging change: even Doña Eugenia reaffirms her conformity to the Quiche values of working hard and being a good wife. She perceives a persisting status quo in terms of hardship and poverty which 'one must endure'. This is a classic example of the need, in dire situations, to protect the 'self' by minimizing radical shifts in 'self-concept', thus providing a sense of continuity with the past.

To a certain extent, the reconstructed identities can be considered as fictional in so far as they are based more on remembered or reconstructed past actions and future identity claims than on present pursuits. The women are unable to locate themselves in unmitigated reality (the lived present) and can only locate themselves in managed, re-presented reality (fiction). Some women even gave the impression that their sense of themselves was no longer of someone real but of something 'other'. 'You see me as a person', said Doña Ana, 'but I no longer feel like a person.' Such feelings arise with constructions which protect the 'self' at a time of disruption, loss and failure.

Despite the women's efforts to re-establish continuity in terms of traditional values, they seem to gain most strength from representations of themselves as 'disorderly' women who are able to overturn accepted gender roles; they cultivate the very 'disorderliness' with which the patrol chiefs try to taunt them. They present themselves as speaking out not only against the (male) perpetrators of atrocity but also against male authority figures in their personal lives, such as husbands and fathers. When Doña Flora returned to Emol, 'my father said I should ask the patrols' permission to return to my land but I said, "No, it's my land, so why should I ask for their permission? I am the owner of my house, so why should I ask them?"'

Doña Ana had the final word in an argument with her husband, which she would not have admitted in 'normal' times:

My husband was the one who usually gave the orders but this situation was a little different, for I really did not want to leave the house. I was thinking of my animals because, you see, they are mine. If we left, then we would have had to sell the cows. But if I had sold them, then I would have no way to make money for myself. So I told him, 'The cows are mine, I will not sell them and no one orders me around.'

For Doña Ana, the importance of the representation she has constructed for herself outweighs her tacit admission that her husband was murdered as a result of her decision not to leave. Doña Flora found herself in a similar position when relating how she confronted her daughter-in-law's father. He had known that she, her husband and son had attended the nuns' awareness-raising courses but did not get involved himself:

he said that organizers were killing people's husbands and that they were bad people [guerrillas] … He said to me, 'You will see what happens when you get involved in such nonsense. They are bad people,' he repeated.

'How good it is that *you* are not a bad person,' I replied; 'you have your wings with God but we are among those who still eat,' I said, 'and perhaps we got involved with these bad people. But you, how good you are, an Evangelical, and God has your wings and you are flying above!'

Doña Flora's pleasure in scolding this man is in keeping with her pride in the fact that it was she who introduced her husband and son to liberation theology. At other times, however, she berates herself for having involved them in something which ultimately led to their deaths.

The importance of these 'self'-representations lie in their symbolic, rather than simply reflective, character and, at the same time, in the recognition of their potential influence on forms of behaviour. The changes in women's perceptions of their personal identity create new experiences and interpretations of the past although they still see themselves as adhering to the Quiche value system of being oriented towards the good. The widows firmly reject the label 'wives of the guerrilla' as harmful to their sense of self. But refutation of a metaphor is not enough to bolster their 'selves' and so the women look for new ways to define themselves.

Continuity with Women in the Historical Past

Almost since its inception in 1988, the human rights' group CONAVIGUA (National Coordinating Committee of Guatemalan Widows) has fostered the positive construction of identity through connections with history, religion and myth. One of its founders is a young Indian catechist named Petronila, whose charismatic but gentle oratory helped to allay the widows' feelings of guilt and shame. The women recognized themselves in Petronila's speech and a side of their personalities fragmented by the violence clung to the chance to be cleansed.

Petronila repeatedly told widows that they were 'like the heroines in the Bible, Ruth, Esther and Judith from the Old Testament and saints such as the Virgin Mary from the New Testament'.

By 'indigenizing' biblical figures – the Virgin Mary, for example, became a girl from the corn fields who, like the widows, never went to school and didn't speak Spanish – Petronila was able to link them with characters from the Mayan 'Counsel Book', Popol Vuh (Recinos 1987)[7] who had also sacrificed their men, such as the mother of the twins Hunahpu and Xbalanqu. She explained that it was not the men who sacrificed their lives but 'the women were those who made the sacrifices – they sacrificed the lives of their men'.

Petronila told women who tend to idealize their dead kin as martyrs that they themselves were heroines (which led some widows to portray both themselves and their dead men as heroes); she called them celibates and virgins, labels full of positive, sacred meaning. The widows were special people, whose suffering, 'like Christ's', protects others. Seeing themselves as worthy not only provides comfort but protection from the symbolic devaluation associated with being labelled 'wives of the guerrilla'.

Biblical and historical contexts aid the positive renewal of identity. Again, the critical element is the creation of a sense of continuity: characteristics and events shared by ancient and modern heroines link past, present and future. The women draw on analogies from their cultural lexicon which have not been taken over by the state. In this way they construct sense and continuity via alternative routes, bypassing the unacceptable or unavailable aspects of their own personal history.

Conclusion

From the margins of society, Quiche widows question the 'natural order of things' promoted through state discourse in which reality is unified and self-explanatory. They create a secret oral discourse which is condemned to remain unofficial, as 'public secrets'. Very few widows are aware of their engagement in what can be construed as a disguised form of resistance.

The women's popular memories, private discourses and 'self'-constructions indicate their rejection of the official 'truth' which effectively silences them. Whatever the women's intentions, their truth confronts the state's assumed agenda, turning private thoughts into unobtrusive political acts which reinterpret the political domain. Some women are aware of the power of their speech; unfortunately, so are the perpetrators of violence, and the harassment of widows continues to the present day. Private memories may be open secrets but they are anything but public facts. The widows must sometimes wonder if there is any escape from *La Violencia*.

Notes

1. This, and the names of the women, are pseudonyms.
2. In the 1980s Evangelical Protestantism was the fastest growing religion in Guatemala, accounting for 12.5% of the population. In Emol, however, 60% of the villagers were at least nominally Protestant at the time of this research (1988–90).
3. My position within the group meant that I could not talk to men (unless they were an accepted part of the widows' household) or even Protestant women.
4. I tried to do this without much success.
5. Treating people like animals is probably the worst insult one can offer the Quiche.
6. Guatemala's population is approximately 60% Indian and 40% *Ladino* or *Mestizo* (of mixed, basically, Spanish and Indian, blood).
7. An anthology of Mayan mayo-history compiled circa 1550 and translated by Recinos.

References

Orwell, George. 1949, 1990. *1984*. Oxford: Heinemann.
Pateman, Trevor. 1980. *Language, Truth and Politics*. Lewes: Jean Stroud.
Recinos Adrián. 1987. *Popol Vuh: las antiguas historias del Quiché*. Versin de Adrián Recinos. Guatemala: Piedra Santa.
Simon, Jean Marie. 1987. *Eternal Spring, Eternal Tyranny*. New York and London: Norton.
Williams, Raymond. 1977. *Marxism, Literature and Politics*. Oxford: Oxford University Press.

6

The Mother of All Warriors: Women in West Belfast, Northern Ireland

Lorraine Dowler

Where are the lads who stood with me
When history was made
Gradh Mo Chraidehe
I long to see the boys of the old brigade
From hill and farm the call to arm
Was heard by one and all
And from the glen came brave young men
to answer Ireland's call
Twas long ago we faced the foe
The old brigade and me
And by me side they fought and died
That Ireland might be free
And now my son I've told you why,
On Easter morn I sigh,
For I recall my comrades all
From dark old days gone by.
I think of them who fought in the glen
With rifles and grenades,
May heaven keep the men
Who sleep from the ranks of the old brigades
(Local folk song, *The Boys of the Old Brigade*)

War has traditionally been considered the quintessential proving ground for masculinity, as the words of this Irish ballad reflect. More importantly, this song points to the profound bond which develops between individuals who have faced a common enemy together. In this chapter, I will explore how the formation of wartime friendships becomes exclusionary of women as a result of the spatial designation of men to public arenas such as the battlefield.

In Western societies, war, which would normally be considered a catalyst of change, has become, in relation to gender identities, an agent of conservatism. This conservatism can be seen in the 'symbolic' spatial relegation of women to the private/domestic realm. When a society engages in armed conflict there is a predisposition to perceive men as violent and action-oriented, and women as compassionate and supportive to the male warrior. These gender tropes do not denote the actions of women and men in a time of war, but function instead to recreate and secure women's position as non-combatant and men's as warriors. Having said that, the battlefield has long been a proving ground of hyper-masculinity. In this public arena men are transformed into iconic warriors embodying such characteristics as bravery and loyalty. This public trans-formation of men into super-heroes renders them void of such emotions as empathy, sympathy and compassion. Those emotions, conversely, have been reserved for the guardians of the home front: women, who are portrayed as pacifists, or patriotic mothers, whereas men are essentially viewed as aggressive or humiliated by their lack of aggression.

The gendering of identities in Northern Ireland is the result of a profoundly antagonistic political relationship between Irish/Catholics and British/Protestants since the signing of the 1921 partition treaty. This treaty resulted in the division of Ireland into two separate states: the Republic of Ireland, which had earned the right to self-determination by way of a bloody revolution, and Northern Ireland, which would remain governed by Great Britain. However, the bitter resentment between (Irish) Nationalists and (British) Loyalists did not become violent until 1969, when a series of civil rights demonstrations and street riots sparked off a period of political violence which Northern Ireland has had to endure for almost thirty years.

My interest in this chapter is to look past the rigid borders of West Belfast, which have been reinforced by the media and academics alike, and search for the more fluid spaces, or the 'frontiers', which could be shared by the Catholic and Protestant communities of West Belfast. Since femin-ist issues are usually eclipsed in favour of a nationalist agenda, I surmised that a feminist critique of nationalism would in part reveal the commonality of the everyday experiences of conflict for *all* women, regardless of their ideological allegiance. I contend that the essential element in the construc-tion of the static borders of West Belfast is the elimination of the feminine for the construction of a hyper-masculine landscape of solidarity.

The Northern Ireland Political Arena as a Masculine Construction

In Northern Ireland today the primary role of women remains that of reproduction of the body politic. Protestants represent the majority of the population, 57 per cent, but demographers are currently predicting that by the year 2050, the voting populations will equalize, because the average size of a Catholic family in Northern Ireland is substantially larger than that of a Protestant one. One explanation for this is the ban on the use of birth control by the Catholic Church. This ban is not observed in full by the majority of contemporary Irish Catholics, but in Northern Ireland religion imbricates with politics so that it has become an Irish woman's nationalistic duty to produce and raise children for the next generation of Irish voters. More specifically, Catherine Nash argues that in the historical case of Irish Nationalism, the exclusion of (Catholic) women from the public arena promoted a gendered relationship to place whereby the political arena was defined as masculine:

> the discourses that confined women within the domestic sphere simultaneously conferred on them the responsibility of maintaining the national population. Women's function was to reproduce the bodies of the 'body politic' represented as masculine. (Nash, 1994: 237)

One of my respondents explained to me that at the age 25 she had already given birth and was caring for five children. She asked her doctor to sterilize her, but he refused, explaining that she was young and could bear many more children for Ireland. This reproductive role is so elevated that women's participation in any other wartime activity would be deemed inappropriate, thereby influencing the perceptions of women as either 'self-sacrificing or as radical militant icons' (Radcliffe and Westwood, 1993: 2).

Today in Northern Ireland Catholic women tend to marry young and start their families soon afterwards. Their primary duties are directed to 'keeping the family together, making ends meet, and servicing political campaigns largely determined by men' (Edgerton, 1987: 61). Lynda Edgerton argues that in Northern Ireland deviating from these accepted norms of femininity would be considered the grossest of betrayals to one's community.

> For Catholic women in Northern Ireland the options are motherhood or perpetual virginity: Roman Catholicism emphasizes the authority of the father and the gentleness of the mother. It dignifies the celibate and the virgin. It symbolizes motherhood as sacrifice and suffering in the greatest of its causes. (Edgerton, 1987: 61)

Irish/Catholic women's confinement to the home front has prevented a radical reappraisal of Irish nationalist politics which has been instrumental in keeping women's liberation at the bottom of any political agenda. However, Amanda Mitchison points to an ironic emancipatory element within this marginalized space that suggests there is the possibility of a shared space or a passageway between Catholic and Protestant women:

> The 'troubles'[1] circumscribe a very limited area of social, family-related issues which Catholic and Protestant women can fight together. And, ironically, it is

a measure of male protagonism in the sectarian war, and the strict sex-role division within the society, that women are able to cross the religious demarcation lines at all. (Mitchison, 1988)

Fighting for the Sanctity of the Hearth

While in Belfast I talked with two women whose primary role was to 'fight for the sanctity of the hearth' by participating in the resistance in the more traditional role of wife and mother. Roisin is a woman in her late fifties who has spent most of her married life separated from her husband because he is wanted by the police due to his paramilitary activity. Roisin's statement reinforces the notion that women resented their confinement to the home during this resistance.

> I haven't seen my husband in 14 years. He's on the run. He had to leave the North because he is wanted here and he is also wanted in the Free State.[2] He gets me messages through his brother. He's lived in Africa, Spain and Australia. I have to stay here and raise the children. We can't all be moving around the world. The Ra[3] used to send him money but they just told me they can't give him any more money. If he had just gone to prison he would have been out by now. My children could have gone to visit him. He didn't want to go to prison. Said it was his duty to stay on the outside. Well then, why do I feel like I'm in prison? I know it's hard for him, but at least he's free. I can't go anywhere because I send him all the money. They also watch me, so if I leave the country the Brits would follow me. *As long as he's on the run I will always be in prison.*

Although women in this society are relegated to the domestic arena and this is a place in which they usually dominate, Roisin does not speak of her home as her sanctuary. She discusses her domestic duties in terms of a prison sentence. Ironically she envies the freedom of her husband who has gone underground to escape incarceration.

Geraldine is a woman in her seventies who reflects on trying to keep her family together when most of them were in prison as a result of the conflict. Geraldine does not resent her domestic role; rather she claims it was more crucial and enduring than the roles the men played in this conflict:

> I've been going to that prison for my whole life, first to visit me da, then to visit my husband, then to see me daughter, that was hard because I had her young'uns while she was in Armagh.[4] Now my grandson is in The Kesh.[5] I've been in the prison for each generation of my family. I've done my whack five times over. I've done more whack than any of these men around. They just think I'm a nice old lady.

Geraldine's sentiments do not exalt the role of motherhood, rather they sully the image by equating it to a lifetime in prison. Suddenly the image of the Madonna, in the crisp white linen apron, is soiled by the suggestion that she too is a warrior. Geraldine and Roisin exemplify the virtues which are honoured by this society – wife, mother, and nurturer – and yet they compare these roles to prison sentences. [6] Why then are these women not considered warriors? Why is it not possible for Geraldine to be both a nice old lady and a soldier?

I suggest that one of the most powerful images of resistance is that of the 'triumph of the weak'. The image of the underdog rising to the battle is a powerful portrait for building public sympathy, and a very convincing display of strength to one's enemy. Images of women in solidarity are selected, manipulated, and moulded in time of war, where the representations of 'manhood' reach elevated levels, whereas 'womanhood' is entirely collapsed to serve the perceived needs of war (Condren, 1995).

A Casualty on Both Fronts

Representations of the roles of women in war are determined by broader perceptions of appropriate female behaviour (MacDonald et al., 1993; Ridd, 1987). Una Gillispe, Sinn Fein Councillor,[7] comments on femininity in war:

> I think there is the attitude in general society that you're different because you go against the idea of a feminine stereotype. I was in England last week. I was with another councillor who was a man and we were interviewed by the press, they covered him in the paper and not what I said. I think it is because their attitude was to say if you portray a woman you're portraying the softer side, and if you portray a man you can get the harder aspect of it across. I think society thinks that women have to harden their souls to be part of the struggle. [But] we have as much to lose as men in a struggle like this. We are not political innocents.

Ironically, when women abandon their political innocence, they often have to forfeit an ecumenical sense of innocence or purity. These women are often seen as being tainted. Illustrative of this are the words of Liam, who was once in the IRA and served a lengthy prison sentence for his participation. Liam details the paternalistic attitudes of the paramilitaries:

> There was a girl in the Ra, Bonnie, she met a man in one of these clubs in the city centre. She was married and had some children. The bastard she was involved with was British Special Intelligence. He had pictures taken of them in the hotel room he took her to. He offered her a deal to inform on the Ra or he would send her husband the pictures. Bonnie accepted the deal, and informed on the Ra. After a while the Ra figured out what she was doing. They sentenced her to death for being an informant. The sentence was commuted because she was a woman and, most importantly, a mother. A man most certainly would have been executed. But the Ra see being a mum as the most important role to the struggle.

In my discussion with Liam there was the sense that Bonnie was not only a failure as a soldier because she became a British informer, but also as an individual, because she had forsaken her primary duty as a wife and mother. Bonnie's choice to become an informer rather than to admit to an infidelity illustrates that, for a woman, a betrayal of one's country is more acceptable than of one's family. Sadly, Bonnie's husband divorced her and she had to leave Belfast without her children. Bonnie is a casualty on both fronts.

The concept of a woman as a mother/warrior is foreign to this Irish Catholic society. Women who become soldiers tend to lose their identities as mothers within this community. Maureen and Peggy are both in their forties. Both were members of the paramilitary and explained to me that they felt men treated them differently because of their more public involvement in this conflict.

> *Maureen*: The people here definitely view us differently than they do the men. For instance there is always a big party for a man when he gets out of prison. A hero's return. I didn't have such a welcome home. It was as if, 'Thank Jesus that's over, now I can get my dinner on the table.' They also look at us differently than other women. First off, if we were in prison we weren't having wee ones which is what we were supposed to be doing. I think if my husband could have got me pregnant in jail he would have, because that was what he was supposed to be doing. A lot of the men think I'm wild because I did my whack, because women aren't supposed to be doing the same thing that the men are in this war.

> *Peggy*: Aye men think I'm wild because I was in prison. My marriage broke up when I was in prison. When the men get out of prison women line up to welcome the man back from his years of celibacy. Those women, who would go off for the night with the men weren't wild, but I was, because I came back from prison just as horny as any of the men.[8]

Why is it that women paramilitaries are tainted for participating in this conflict in a more active and public way? Peter Jackson (1990), while exploring the visual culture of military recruiting posters, concludes that the construction of hegemonic masculinity draws yet greater power through its juxtaposition with selected images of femininity. Similar to Ridd's (1987) argument, he contends that there is an inter-dependent relationship between masculinity and femininity. Jackson argues that 'there is something peculiarly powerful about the complementarity of hegemonic (dominant) masculinities and compliant (subordinate) femininities' (Jackson, 1990: 202). He explains that the presentation of such feminine attributes as 'fragility, vulnerability and gentleness' encourages men to be protective towards women who display these appropriate signs of female behaviour, thereby promoting 'misogyny in the guise of chivalry'. When Maureen and Peggy rejected the British government's authority in Northern Ireland, via their 'public and active' roles in the paramilitary, they were also rejecting a dominant masculinity inherent in Irish Nationalism.

In a prisoners' club I was conversing with several women, some of whom were at one time members of the IRA, and had served prison sentences. I asked these women how they would like historians to remember the women political prisoners.

Peggy: You know we went on hunger strike in Armagh. We also had a no-wash strike. These men don't know what it is like not to be able to wash when you have your period. Lots of the girls got infections. It was very painful. We were also strip-searched and it was humiliating for us. We even planned an escape just like the men did. Ours wasn't as successful as the men's but we tried it all the same.[9]

Kathleen: Some of the bravest people I met were girls in prison. Many of us had wee ones on the outside, it was so hard. Women are expected to take care of the young'uns so you feel much guilt, guilt the men don't feel. To tell these stories would be a way for us to be together. The men all come to these clubs and relive their stories at The Kesh, but most of the women are too busy and don't get a chance to talk about what has happened to them. Look at us here. We are talking amongst ourselves [looking at the men]. You'd think they would like to have a wee yarn with us? As soon as we get here the girls sit to one side and the boys over there. Since we sit alone with the women and most of the women haven't had to go to prison, we usually don't talk about it.[10]

Peggy and Kathleen are not just rewriting women back into the history of this struggle, they are redefining their participation as that of mothers/warriors. While they were in prison, these women were torn apart by concern for their families on the one hand and their nationalist ideologies on the other. The women told me that even though participating in prison protests lengthened their sentences, they knew they could not back down; it was their duty to resist the British government any way they could, even if it meant more time spent away from their children. The stories of these women are also filled with resentment for the men's lack of participation on the domestic front. But even though these women have been guilt-ridden over their separation from their families, they are proud of their contributions and explained to me they would do it again if need be. It is important to mention that they long for a different life for their children. They desire that the cycle be broken within this generation. They do not wish for their children to suffer what they had to endure. I personally cannot think of a more appropriate legacy than for a mother/warrior to leave her children a world safer than it had been for her.

In addition to these women rewriting women back into the history of this resistance, Peggy's observation that the world was blind to the efforts of the female hunger strikers brings to question why were the efforts of the male hunger strikers honoured and not the females'. The obvious answer is that women did not die on hunger strike as did the men. Some of the women hunger strikers were released from prison for medical reasons; in this way the British government did not have to negotiate the potentially potent symbol of female martyrdom. However, Ellmann raises the question of 'What exactly is a hunger strike?' with the story of a woman who had been on hunger strike in Armagh. She had survived the hunger strike, and had even been released from prison, but died within the year of anorexia nervosa. No one, however, pays much heed to the numbers of women dying of anorexia nervosa each day (Ellmann, 1993: 1). Elaborating on Ellmann's interrogation of the relationship between these two forms of self-starvation, I ask what is the relationship between the gazes over these two forms of starvation? Is the anorexic woman really a hunger striker in disguise, starving herself to defy the 'patriarchal values that confine their sex as rigidly as walls of stone or bars of iron'? (Ellmann, 1993: 2). Do women starve themselves to try to get the world to notice their imprisonment?

A Shared Space for All Women in Northern Ireland

The confinement of women to the more docile roles in this resistance is not exclusive to Irish Nationalism. In August 1993 Chief Constable of Ulster Sir Hugh Annesley announced that from April 1994 all women officers will have to carry firearms (*Sunday Life*, 15 August 1993). Woman Constable Sandra Twigg has been a police officer for 16 years and was the first woman to be trained to carry weapons. She comments on women carrying arms:

> The 1300 female officers in Ulster will face problems from their male colleagues now that they are to carry weapons, RUC[11] officers will have to ride the storm of discrimination until their male colleagues come to terms with them being armed ... women officers in the RUC will undoubtedly face this male macho idea that women can't do the job. It is just something that men have been brought up with but they have just got to get used to it. It is like the old image of women drivers. (Interview with an RUC officer, Sandra Twigg, by John Cassidy, *Sunday Life*, 15 August 1993: 17)

Twigg's statement was printed in the *Belfast Telegraph* with the caption 'Beware the Macho Male'. This warning was directed to Twigg's fellow (male) officer who did not want women on the force to carry guns. In additional interviews with the BBC, Annesley blamed the necessity for this action on the ruthlessness of the IRA. He charged that women officers were being maimed and killed and now drastic measures had to be taken. Annesley's statements were not reflective of the equal opportunity suit that a group of women officers had filed against the constabulary because they were not permitted to carry firearms.

The media coverage of this event stimulated much discussion in West Belfast. The 15 Irish Catholic women I talked with were all in agreement that women RUC officers should be allowed to carry guns. The following reflects some of their feelings on the matter.

Aye, if the men are carrying them then why not the women ...

Look don't get me wrong, I don't trust the RUC and I wish none of them had guns but if the men have 'em then the women should too ...

I remember when the women peelers[12] would walk in the streets next to the men. Once I saw a woman using the radio which was attached to the lad's back. They were walking together with this long curly cord between them. He had his rifle at his side. He looked like he was walking his pup. I wish there was no need for all these guns, on both sides of this war, but women should be able to protect themselves ...

I have almost been killed because I'm a Sinn Fein councillor so I have applied for a permit to carry a gun. I need to protect myself; so do those women. The women can lose their lives in this war too ...

Of course they should, sometimes I wish I had a bloody gun.

The women were in agreement that as long as the men were carrying guns then why not the women? However, I also talked with twelve men, of whom only four felt as the women did. Five of the men thought it was wrong for a woman to be carrying a gun, and that they shouldn't be in the RUC at all. Three of the men discussed the symbolic impact of the women carrying guns.

> *Conner.* Ach, this is an awful thing. I don't want to shoot a woman. No man in the Ra wants to shoot a woman. Sometimes the women RUC officers would get shot because they're in the crossfire but it's just not done. But if a woman is shooting at me, I'll have to shoot back, but I don't want to do it. This is just the British government trying to make us look like a bunch of murderers because now we'll have to shoot their women.

> *Sean.* I'm glad I'm not in it any more if this is what it has come to. When I was in the Ra women were never targets on any side of the line. In the 70s there weren't any women RUC officers carrying guns, but if there had been and they were armed, I would have been a dead man, I would have delayed and ended up dead. That's probably what the Brits are thinking about when they did this.

> *Kevin.* They don't think much of their women, we've kept our women out of the line of fire and they're putting their women right into it. It is just propaganda to make us look bad. It will also weaken us; no one wants to shoot a woman, but we'll have to now.

Conner, Sean and Kevin's discussion of how the image of women carrying arms would have a negative affect on the image of the IRA reinforces Rosemary Ridd's hypothesis that a movement is empowered when the weakness of women is exploited (Ridd, 1987). In other words, the more docile women's bodies remain in this conflict, the more empowering it is for men.

Another instance of the rendering docile of women's bodies as a strategy of warfare is the anti-terrorism advertising campaign which was released in the summer of 1993. The campaign was a trilogy of television

commercials aimed at the protective and nurturing nature of women. The
first commercial, *Lady*, is the story of two women, one the wife of a
terrorist victim, the other the wife of a police officer. The message of
this advertisement is that women share a common identity in this conflict
– widowhood. However, these women are depicted as tender, soft and as
victims. They are portrayed as docile with only one course of action
available to stop this conflict which they must endure quietly, and that
option is to call the confidential line and have someone else take action.
The second advertisement, *The Cat's in the Cradle*, is the tale of a second-
generation terrorist. Once more the woman is viewed as submissive,
simply standing by while her husband sets such a 'murderous' example
for her son to follow. Her son follows in her husband's footsteps, joins
the paramilitary and is eventually killed. In this advertisement the woman
is portrayed as not having any political convictions; she is marginalized
from the body politic, and she is the bearer of guilt for not trying to stop
this man's war. Her innocence will be restored by contacting the confidential line. The final part of this trilogy depicts a father and his young
son narrowly escaping being gunned down by terrorists. Although the
advertisement features only a father with his four-year-old son, the
mother's absence is duly noted, since the father is portrayed as careless
and inept by momentarily taking his eye off his son. Thereby he is not
a proper caretaker, and now the mother must take action to protect her
child and call the confidential line.

The television ads are not the first to have been made in the battle
against terrorism. What is most interesting about them, however, is the
marketing strategy the government adopted with these advertisements.
The viewers in Northern Ireland were shocked by the campaign's domestic
nature. When the advertisements first appeared, the *Belfast Telegraph*'s
headline was 'Shocking a community into beating terrorism' (Lindsay
McDowell, *Belfast Telegraph*, 20 October 1992: 14). The viewers' startled
reaction was due to the British government specifically targeting women
with these ads. The following paragraph, quoted by a spokesperson at
the Northern Ireland bureau, explains the rationale behind targeting
women:

> Research shows that the woman is both the victim of the paramilitary and his
> greatest hope. In those instances where a man has been able to draw away from
> the clutches of paramilitary violence it is generally under the influence of family,
> in particular his wife or mother. It's that old line about 'the power of a good
> woman'. In every sense it is the woman who is brutalized by the paramilitaries.
> What the ads do is recognize that suffering. They're also saying to the man
> caught up in paramilitary violence, think what you're doing to this woman …
> These ads are not going to hit home with the hard core terrorist. Rather they're
> aimed at the softer outer layer of people around them. And at the community
> in general. (*Belfast Telegraph*, Wednesday, 20 October 1993)[13]

This statement demonstrates two assumptions about women in this conflict. The first presumption is that they are docile and it is men who have been action-oriented. The second assumption is that if women are to take action, it would be in the role of mothers and nurturers and that their action would be limited to calls for help. These advertisements show terrorists as the villains of this war by depicting women as its victims. All three scenarios are capitalizing on the symbolic image of women as the protectors of the family. The advertisements make the assumption that the role of mother would overshadow any support for the paramilitary. Interestingly, the twelve women I talked with were saddened by the commercials. However, there was a general consensus that although the breaking apart of families is an awful part of the war, it was simply a way of life in West Belfast.

Aye, I've seen 'em, they're desperate, I cried, reminded me of when me brother went off to the Kesh. But that's the way things are here ...

I turn 'em off when they come on the telly, all of a sudden they are worried about us being alone, then why did they intern all our men, they're the ones who have kept the women alone and now they want us to blame our men for what they have gone and done ...

Yes the adverts are very sad, but this is the way life is here, why is it suddenly so bad here for the women, it has always been bad. Men come and go and we are left here. Those adverts make it look like this is something new.

These advertisements target women directly, but because of their violent nature they only appear on television after 9 p.m. This time slot is viewed equally by men and women. Most of the twelve men I talked with dismissed the advertisements as British propaganda. However, the following two statements, provided by men who were in the IRA, demonstrate that these advertisements were not completely ineffective to men.

Conner: I hate those adverts. They're nothing but British propaganda. No good Republican is going to call the confidential line on the Ra and they certainly are not going to get any help from the line, the confidential line is useless for a Republican, it is just a way of catching the Ra ... Look, I killed men, I killed men who have families, I think of those families every day, children without fathers, wives without husbands, I have to take that to my grave. They're just trying to make us look like a bunch of ruthless mad men. A bunch of butchers. Well, we're not. Do they think we want to do this?

Kalum: Aye, they're propaganda all right, but this batch has been better than any other. All the other times I said this is shite nonsense, but this time it made me think about all the families. My war was never with the Protestant people, it has been with the British government. I know there is good and bad on both sides of the line. The adverts made me think what would my Roisin and my children do if I ended up on the wrong side of the gun.

The deliberate targeting of women by these advertisements presumes that the women would be more loyal to the family unit than to a military unit. This reinforces the idea that military strength is not an inherently feminine characteristic but is something that has been learned out of a desperate situation. The strategy of promoting the weakness of women to infuse a movement with strength, as we have seen, is not just a British ploy but rather a wartime strategy, shared by a patriarchal political leadership on both sides.

Conclusion: Borders or Frontiers?

In conclusion, the (re)constructions of the border lines of West Belfast by way of gender identities demonstrates a need for geographers to delineate common spaces of communities in conflict. In this particular case, the borders implemented within feminine space could be examined as a political frontier whereby all women, Catholic, Protestant, paramilitary or police, are redefining the roles of women in this conflict. Therefore true political solidarity does not lie within the borders of Irish Nationalism, rather it exists in the frontiers of Irish feminism. To be specific, the salience of gender divisions in warfare among Catholics in West Belfast is, from my own observations and from a close knowledge of the relevant literature, also quite evident among Protestants there. We must perhaps try to escape from a territorialized, hermetically sealed cell-like view of human communities. A progressive geography, as Duncan contends,

> would require deterritorialization – the creation of open-ended, proliferating, and inclusive sites of empowerment and resistance against exclusionary, re-territorializing process: place essentialism and homogenizing identity politics or coerced assimilation. These would be sites of 'radical openness' as bell hooks (1990) puts it – sites which may be nurturing – which may serve as havens ... (Duncan: 1996: 26)

The spaces of the 'troubles' in Northern Ireland have historically been viewed as impenetrable. Years of academic surveys and ethnographic studies have simply reinforced the entrenchment of the Catholics and the Protestants of Northern Ireland. While trying to remain realistic and not have my conclusions leap light years ahead of my data, I can nevertheless only wonder if a more 'progressive geography' – one which surmounts difference and instead uncovers spaces in concert with each other – could potentially make a valuable contribution to the peace effort.

Notes

1. The 'troubles' is the name given to the ongoing war in Northern Ireland.
2. The Republic of Ireland.
3. Slang for the Irish Republican Army (IRA).

4. A Northern Ireland women's prison.

5. The Kesh refers to Long Kesh, the prison located outside Belfast where the majority of male prisoners are incarcerated.

6. Fairweather, McDonough and McFadyean's (1984) respondents used terms such as 'serving time' as mother and 'emotional housework' referring to visiting men in prison.

7. Sinn Fein (Ourselves Alone) is the political wing of the IRA.

8. Fairweather, McDonough and McFadyean (1984) address the issue of the purity of Irish/Catholic women during war in chapter 1: 'When you're in the ghetto nobody cares.'

9. Fairweather, McDonough and McFadyean (1984), chapter 4, 'The Road to Armagh'; D'Arcy (1981), *Tell Them Everything*; and McCafferty (1981), *The Armagh Women* detail life for women Republican prisoners.

10. In the prisoners' club most of the former prisoners are men and are accompanied by women who never served official sentences.

11. Royal Ulster Constabulary – the local Northern Irish police force.

12. Local slang for police.

13. The research that was mentioned in this paragraph was restricted. In fact the identity of the advertising agency which produced the advertisement was not allowed to be disclosed. The reason given was that the agency feared paramilitary retaliation.

References

Cock, J. 1993. *Women and War in South Africa*, Cleveland: The Pilgrim Press.

Condren, Mary. 1995. 'Work in progress, sacrifice and political legitimation, the production of a gendered social order.' *Journal of Women's History*, vol. 6, no. 4/ vol. 7, no. 1: 160–89.

D'Arcy, Margaretta. 1981. *Tell Them Everything*. London: Pluto Press.

Duncan, Nancy. 1996 'Renegotiating gender and sexuality in public and private spaces.' In Nancy Duncan (ed.), *BodySpace: Destabilizing Geographies of Gender and Sexuality*. New York: Routledge.

Edgerton, Lynda. 1987. 'Public protest, domestic acquiescence: women in Northern Ireland.' In Rosemary Ridd and Helen Callaway (eds), *Women and Political Conflict, Portraits of Struggle in Times of Crisis*. New York: New York University Press.

Ellmann, Maud. 1993. *The Hunger Artists, Starving, Writing and Imprisonment*. Cambridge, MA: Harvard University Press.

Elshtain, Jean B. and Sheila Tobias. 1990. *Women, Militarism, and War*. Maryland: Rowman and Littlefield.

Elshtain, Jean B. 1987. *Women and War*. New York: Basic Books.

Fairweather, Eileen, Roisin McDonough and Melanie McFadyean. 1984. *Only The Rivers Run Free, Northern Ireland: The Women's War*. London: Pluto Press

Jackson, Peter. 1990. 'The cultural politics of masculinity: towards a social geography.' *Transactions, Institute of British Geographers*, 16: 199–213.

MacDonald, S., P. Holden, and S. Ardener. 1993. *Images of Women in Peace and War*. Madison: University of Wisconsin Press.

McCafferty, Nell. 1981. *The Armagh Women*. Dublin: Co-Op Books.

Mitchison, Amanda. 1988. 'Ulster's family feminists.' *New Society*, 19 February 1988: 17–19.

Nash, Catherine. 1994. 'Remapping the body/land: new cartographies of identity, gender and landscape in Ireland.' In Alison Blunt and Rose Gillian (eds), *Writing Women and Space, Colonial and Postcolonial Geographies.* New York: Guilford Press.

Radcliffe, S. and Sallie Westwood. 1993. 'Gender, racism and the politics of identities in Latin America.' In S. Radcliffe and Sallie Westwood (eds), *ViVa.* New York: Routledge.

Ridd, Rosemary. 1987. 'Powers of the powerless.' In Rosemary Ridd and Helen Callaway (eds), *Women and Political Conflict, Portraits of Struggle in Times of Crisis.* New York: New York University Press.

Part III

Captured Subjects:
Displacing Women's Bodies

7

A Question of Silence:
Partition, Women and the State

Urvashi Butalia

The political partition of India caused one of the great convulsions of history. Never before or since have so many people exchanged their homes and countries so quickly. In the space of a few months, about twelve million people moved between the new truncated India and the two wings, East and West, of the newly created Pakistan. By far the largest proportion of these refugees – more than ten million of them – crossed the western border which divided the historic state of Punjab, Muslims travelling west to Pakistan, Hindus and Sikhs east to India. Slaughter sometimes prompted and sometimes accompanied their movement; many others died from malnutrition, cold and contagious disease. Estimates of the number of dead vary from 200,000 (the contemporary British figure) to two million (a later Indian speculation), but that somewhere around a million people died is now widely accepted. As with all such man-made catastrophes, there was widespread sexual savagery. About 75,000 women are thought to have been raped and abducted by men of religions different to their own. Thousands of families were divided, homes were destroyed, crops left to rot, villages abandoned. Astonishingly, the new governments of India and Pakistan were unprepared for this convulsion – they had not anticipated that the fear and uncertainty created by the drawing of borders based on headcounts of religious identity – so many Hindus and Sikhs versus so many Muslims – would force people to flee to what they considered safer places, where they would be surrounded by their own kind. People travelled in buses, bullock carts and trains, but mostly on foot in great columns, called *kafilas*, which could stretch for dozens of miles. The longest of them, said to comprise 800,000 refugees, took eight days to pass any given spot on its route.

This is the generality of Partition. It exists publicly in books. The particular is harder to discover. For many of us, who are first and second generation children after Partition, the event lives on in our minds, not so much through historical record as through the tales that are told and retold, particularly in north Indian families, of the horror and brutality of the time, the friends and relatives who continue to live across the border, the visits to old ancestral homes, much of this creating a yearning for a – mostly mythical – harmonious past where Hindus and Sikhs and Muslims lived happily together, something that we continue to hold on to in the face of an increasingly communal present.

So major an event is Partition that it forms a kind of pivot around which memories are constructed: practically all communal strife is measured by it ('it was like Partition again', 'we thought we had seen the worst of it during Partition yet …'). But so inadequately recorded. What records we have look at Partition mostly in terms of its constitutional history, its intergovernmental debate, the agreements and disagreements between Nehru and Gandhi and Jinnah, the growing divide between the Congress and the Muslim League – all 'political' actors in this game. Hardly any attempt has been made to record what ordinary people on both sides of the border went through. If these experiences remain largely untouched, there are other, lesser known ones that lie beneath and need further excavation. These are the experiences of women and children, lower castes and others on the margins of society. In this chapter, I wish to pay close attention to the particular experiences of women at this time, and attempt to demonstrate what I have increasingly come to feel, that Partition was a deeply gendered process, one in which we cannot simply look at how women were 'also affected'. Instead, we need to deploy gender as an essential category if we are to begin to approach an understanding of this crucial time in our history.[1]

Unearthing the history of women is not, however, an easy task. Official documents say little about them and, by and large, their voices are absent from public spaces. In the particular case of rape or abduction, and often murder, the silence is even more profound, for while speech may help to fill historical gaps, its implications for the persons involved hardly bear thinking about. My sources here consist of interviews with people who experienced Partition in different ways, of the diaries and memoirs of those who have managed to record something of that painful time, and of official documents, particularly parliamentary debates, newspaper reports and some secondary sources. In using oral history as one of my key sources I do not mean to privilege the experiences of 'ordinary people' over a category called 'history', for both are problematic concepts. Clearly there is no way history can incorporate all experiences at all times for much depends on who writes history, when it is written, who is written about and so on. But in recovering histories of those who are relegated to the margins, we have little option but to look at sources other than the accepted ones, and in doing so to question, stretch and expand the notion of what we see as history. Further, in attempting to recover the past from the perspective of the present, my search is informed by another agenda: that of action for the future. How do we deal with the many ramifications of Partition that we still find in our lives today? We need, I think, to go back to the many narratives of the event.

But first, I do not want to simplistically attribute the historical silence on what I would like to term the 'underside', that is, the human dimension, of the history of Partition to simple historiographical neglect on the part of historians. Rather, I believe that this history has been particularly difficult to approach because of a fear, on the part of most historians, of opening wounds that are still fresh, of laying bare a trauma riven with pain and grief. Not only does this kind of research put an end, once and for all, to any notions of the 'objectivity' of writing history, but it also forces the historian to rely on that most elusive – yet most important – tool of research, memory, and in doing so, to confront its many contradictions and ambivalences.

I am deeply aware of these ambivalences and am therefore not claiming objectivity or what is generally understood as 'factuality' for the accounts which form the basis of my work here. But I do wish to make the point that how people choose to narrate and remember any event/incident/process is as important a part of historical knowledge and enquiry as the so-called 'facts' of the incident itself. Instead of casting back into the past and constructing a historical account based on these 'facts' alone, I attempt here to create a picture based on facts and memory. In doing so, I have a particular agenda. In recent years, the growing polarizations within Indian society around religious identities have forced many people to confront Partition again. In many ways, this is the defining event of communal/sectarian strife; looking back at it helps to explain much, and becomes an almost necessary exploration in order to look at how one must act in the present, or indeed how one may look to the future. It is this realization that has gradually opened up new and different kinds of explorations of Partition in the last few years. The larger study of oral narratives that I have been engaged in for some years now is part of the same corpus of work.[2] Here, however, I would like to attempt to untangle some of the many strands that make up the web of women's experiences of catastrophic incidents of such magnitude. How, I ask, do such events impact on women? How are women themselves implicated in them? How do they deal with them? How are their experiences represented, and, indeed, who represents them?

I

Let me start this section with a quotation from the *Statesman*, an English-language daily that is still published in India today. This quote is dated

15 March 1947 and refers to an incident that took place roughly a week before.

> The story of 90 women of the little village of Thoa Khalsa, Rawalpindi district ... who drowned themselves by jumping into a well during the recent disturbances has stirred the imagination of the people of Punjab. They revived the Rajput tradition of self-immolation when their menfolk were no longer able to defend them. They also followed Mr Gandhi's advice to Indian women that in certain circumstances even suicide was morally preferable to submission.
>
> About a month ago, a communal army armed with sticks, tommy guns and hand grenades surrounded the village. The villagers defended themselves as best they could ... but in the end they had to raise the white flag. Negotiations followed. A sum of Rs 10,000 was demanded ... it was promptly paid. The intruders gave solemn assurances that they would not come back.
>
> The promise was broken the next day. They returned to demand more money and in the process hacked to death 40 of the defenders. Heavily outnumbered, they were unable to resist the onslaught. Their women held a hurried meeting and concluded that all was lost but their honour. Ninety women jumped into the small well. Only three were saved – there was not enough water in the well to drown them all.

Communal violence in the Punjab actually began some months before Partition, in March 1947. Early in this month, a number of Sikh villages in Rawalpindi district were attacked over a period of nine days (6 to 13 March) by Muslim mobs. The attacks themselves were in retaliation for Hindu attacks on Muslims in Bihar. It is futile to speculate whose was the primary responsibility: the reality is that once it became clear that Partition would take place, both communities, Muslim and Hindu, started to attack members of the other. In Rawalpindi district, in the villages of Thamali, Thoa Khalsa, Mator, Nara, and many others, the attacks ended on 13 March, when the army moved in and rescued what survivors were left. In many villages the entire population was wiped out; in others, there were a few survivors. Much of the material I present below is gathered from the accounts of these survivors.[3]

Apparently the greatest danger that families, and indeed entire communities, perceived was of conversion to the other religion. The fear was not unfounded: mass and forcible conversions took place on both sides. Among the Sikhs particularly (and these few villages were strongly Sikh) the men felt they could protect themselves but they were convinced their women would be unable to do so. Their logic was that men could fight, die if necessary, escape by using their wits and their strength, but the women had no such strength to hand. They were therefore particularly vulnerable to conversion. Moreover, women could be raped, impregnated with the seed of the other religion, and in this way not only would they be rendered impure individually, but the entire community would be polluted and the purity of the race diluted. While the men could thus save themselves, it was imperative that the women be 'saved' by them.

One of the first people I spoke to when I began to conduct interviews was an old Sikh called Mangal Singh. In Amritsar bazaar, where Mangal Singh lived, he was considered something of a legend. People urged me to speak to him because, they said, between him and his two brothers they had killed 17 members of their family in order to save them from conversion. Overcoming his initial reluctance to speak at all ('What is the point? What will you gain by raking up all this?') Mangal Singh spoke of these people – mostly women and children – with both pride and grief in his voice. He refused to acknowledge that they had been killed. Instead, he said they had been 'martyred', that they had 'become martyrs', or *shaheeds*:

> After leaving home, we had to cross the surrounding boundary of water. And we were many family members, several women and children who would not have been able to cross the water, to survive the flight. So we killed – they became martyrs – seventeen of our family members, seventeen lives ... our hearts were heavy with grief for them, grief and sorrow, their grief, our own grief. So we travelled, laden with sorrow, not a paisa to call our own, not a bite of food to eat ... but we had to leave. Had we not done so, we would have been killed, the times were such ...

Over the years, as I spoke to more and more people, both men and women, I was to come across this response again. The tone adopted by the *Statesman* report above was similar to that adopted by families when they spoke of the hundreds of women they had 'martyred' in order to save the purity of the religion. In Thoa Khalsa, one of the villages that was attacked, two such incidents took place. At first, 26 women were killed by their families. Following on this 90 women are said to have committed mass suicide by throwing themselves into a well to drown themselves. Three women survived, the others died. Bir Bahadur Singh, one of the people from Thoa Khalsa I spoke to, described the incident thus:

> in Gulab Singh's *haveli* 26 girls had been put aside. First of all my father, Sant Raja Singh, when he brought his daughter, he brought her into the courtyard to kill her, first of all he prayed (he did *ardaas*) saying *sacche badshah*, we have not allowed your Sikhi to get stained, and in order to save it we are going to sacrifice our daughters, make them martyrs. Please forgive us ...
> Then there was one man who used to do coolie work in our village. He moved forward and ... caught his [the father's] feet and he said, *bhapaji* [elder brother], first you kill me because my knees are swollen and I won't be able to run away and the Musalmaans will catch hold of me and make me into a Musalmaan. So my father immediately hit him with his *kirpan* and took his head off ... [then] Nand Singh Dheer, he said to my father, Raja Singh, please martyr me first because my sons live in Lahore ... do you think I will allow the Musalmaans to cut this beard of mine and make me go to Lahore as a sheikh? For this reason, kill me. My father then killed him. He killed two, and the third was my sister, Maan Kaur ... my sister came, and sat in front of my father, and I stood there, right next to my father, clutching onto his *kurta* as children do,

I was clinging to him ... but when my father swung the *kirpan* perhaps some doubt or fear came into his mind, or perhaps the *kirpan* got stuck in her *dupatta* ... no one can say ... it was such a frightening, such a fearful scene. Then my sister, with her own hands, moved her *dupatta* aside and then swung the *kirpan* and her head and neck rolled off and fell ... there ... far away. I crept downstairs, weeping, sobbing and all the while I could hear the regular swing and hit of the *kirpans* ... twenty-five girls were killed, they were cut. One girl, my *taya*'s daughter-in-law, who was pregnant ... somehow she didn't get killed and later my *taya*'s son shot her with a pistol ... [but she] was saved. She told us, kill me, I will not survive ... I have a child in my womb ... she was wounded in the stomach, there was a large hole from which blood was flowing. Then my mother and my *phupad* sat together and Harnam Kaur said to them – her name was Harnam Kaur – she said, give me some opium. We arranged for opium, people used to eat it those days ... in a ladle we mixed opium with saliva ... She said the *japji sahib path* ... just as the *japji path bhog* took place so did her *bhog*. Completely as if she was prepared for death ... few people can do that ... she had death in her control and it was only when she wanted it that death took her. For nearly half an hour she did the *path* ... half an hour and then as she spoke her last *shlok*, she also ended. She knew she would die ... so much control ... over death.[4]

Bir Bahadur's pride in his sister's sacrifice was echoed by many other people from his village who had been present at this mass killing. Shortly after this, the well jumping incident took place. Bir Bahadur Singh describes it thus:

at the well Sardarni Gulab Kaur ... in my presence she said *sacche badshah*, let us be able to save our girls ... this incident of the 25 girls of our household had already taken place ... so she knew that Sant Raja Singh had killed his daughters and other women of his household ... those that are left we should not risk their lives and allow them to be taken away. So, at the well, after having talked among themselves and decided, they said, we are thirsty, we need water, so the Musalmaans took them to the well ... I was sitting with my mother, this incident of the 25 women had taken place ... so sitting at the well, Mata Lajwanti who was also called Sardarni Gulab Kaur, she said two words, she did *ardaas* in two words, saying *sacche badshah*, it is to save our Sikhi that we are offering up our lives ... forgive us and accept our martyrdom ... and saying these words, she jumped into the well and some eighty women followed her ... they also jumped in. The well filled up completely; one woman whose name is Basant Kaur, six children born of her womb died in that well, but she survived. She jumped in four times but the well had filled up ... she would jump in, then come out, then jump in again ... she would look at her children, at herself ... till today I think she is alive.[5]

Today, half a century later, these and other stories still survive and are held up, not only as examples of the bravery and manliness of the Sikh race (although it is the women who died, the decision to sacrifice their lives is seen as the defining act of bravery, for it also 'saves' them), but also as examples of the heroism of the Sikh women who gave up their lives 'willingly' for the sake of their religion. In the remembrance rituals that take place in gurudwaras, these incidents are recounted again and again each year to an audience comprising men, women and children, and the women are exhorted to remember the sacrifice and bravery of their sisters, and to cast themselves in the same mould. Should the *quam* (race) or the *dharam* (religion) ever be in danger, they are told, your duty is clear. The sacrifice of the many women who died such deaths during Partition is compared, as in the *Statesman* article, to the extreme sacrifice of Rajput women who undertook mass self-immolation when they lost their husbands in war. It is not unusual to draw a direct and almost linear link between that sacrifice and this. Talk of the martyrdom of women is almost always accompanied by talk of those women whose lives were saved, at the cost of those which were lost, and although there may not be any direct condemnation, it is clear that those who got away are in some ways seen as being inferior to those who offered themselves up to death to save their religion.

Because the men were prepared to fight, and indeed many did so in order to save their lives, their desire to cling on to life is not seen in the same terms as that of the women. Bir Bahadur Singh asserted: 'If the women in our family had not been killed and those who jumped into the well had not taken their own lives, those who were left alive would not have been alive today.' And within families these acts of mass killing – whether voluntary or otherwise – are not seen as violent acts. They are, rather, valorous ones, shorn of the violence, and indeed coercion, that must have sent so many young women to their death. I am aware that among the many who died there must have been a good number whose deaths were voluntary, who needed no coercion; but equally, many of those who died could not have voluntarily chosen such a death.

Most discussion on the violence of Partition focuses on the mass killing, looting and arson that took place between both the Hindu (and Sikh) and Muslim communities, sparing no attempt to inflict such violence on each other. Hardly any mention is made of this kind of familial violence, perpetrated by and large by men of particular communities on their own women. In most instances that I have found, the burden of death, indeed the burden of martyrdom, and that of bearing the so-called honour of the community, was put on women by the men of their community. Perhaps some of them did actively take on this burden, but we shall never know how many felt coerced into the extreme step of taking their own lives, or those of their children. Kulwant Singh, another survivor from the Rawalpindi area, remembers his mother throwing her infant children into a fire. And for many of the people that I spoke to, those women who managed to escape with their lives, or those who showed fear and reluctance to become martyrs were seen as somehow lacking in courage and responsibility.

Martyrdom was not the only burden women carried. In the following section I will explore a somewhat different dimension of the experiences of women.

II

The fact that thousands of women, Hindu, Sikh and Muslim, were raped by men of the other religion in the widespread violence of Partition, is now widely accepted. Often abduction followed or accompanied rape; untold numbers of women were sold into slavery and prostitution, and in many places their bodies were marked with deliberate, carefully chosen humiliations: tattoos of the symbols of the other religion, slogans of a similar nature, the cutting off of their breasts, parading them naked in the streets, something which must have represented the depths of humiliation for women who had hitherto lived in seclusion. Many of these histories will perforce remain untold: most of these women have, by now, lived out their lives, keeping silent on all they have gone through. Historians who wish to recover their experiences have a virtually impossible task before them. There are some 'facts' which are horrifying: in Doberan 70 women were abducted, in Kahuta this figure was as high as 500, in Harial 40, in Tainch 30, in Bamali 105, in Rajar 95 and it is said that in Rawalpindi alone between 400 and 500 women were abducted.[6] But there is much beyond these facts which we can only guess at. For example, abducted women were often sold from hand to hand and were ill used by their captors. Anis Kidwai, a social worker who worked in Muslim camps in Delhi, records:

> We have considerable evidence before us to show that 75 per cent of the girls are still [probably in 1949] being sold from one man to another. [These] girls of tender years have not been able to settle down anywhere, nor will they be able to settle down for many years. Their youth is being sold for a few thousand, and lustful men, having satisfied their lust for a while, begin to think of the monetary benefit that could come from their sale.[7]

For the most part, women were picked up as large caravans of people (called *kafilas*) attempted to flee on foot, or by bullock cart, train or coach. Often, they were bartered by their families in exchange for freedom for the other members. In the initial stages, after the announcement of the Hindustan/Pakistan plan in June 1947, while the two governments set up an elaborate machinery to divide up and share their assets, there was no official or formal plan to initiate an exchange of population. But as communal violence escalated and people began to fear for their lives, the migration of millions began. It was in this process of mass migration, and the violence and killing that accompanied it, that the abductions and rapes of women took place. For men of both communities (Hindu/Sikh and Muslim) the women were easy game. Usually unarmed, they were unable to defend themselves; many were left behind in foot convoys, or picked up from the fringes of these; records of refugees at railway stations are full of stories of women getting dragged off trains, or being picked up near stations.

When families began to file complaints about missing women, the state was obliged to set up a machinery for their recovery. As early as 6 December 1947 – a bare three and a half months after Partition – the two newly formed nations came to an agreement on the question of 'recovering' those women who had been abducted and 'rehabilitating' them in their 'native' places. This vocabulary of recovery, rehabilitation, homeland, was actually a euphemism for returning Hindu and Sikh women to the Hindu and Sikh fold, and Muslim women to the Muslim fold. On this point – that this was what was to be done – both countries were agreed.[8] Thus even for a self-defined secular nation (India), the natural place/ homeland for women was defined in religious, indeed communal terms, thereby pointing to a dissonance/disjunction between its professedly secular rhetoric (although secular was also really understood in religious terms) and its actively communal (that is, religious) identification of women. Women who had been taken away by the other community, had to be brought back to their own community, their own homeland; both concepts that were defined for women by the men of the respective countries.

A major effort was mounted to recover abducted women: the primary responsibility lay with the Women Recovery Organization. In November 1948 this organization handed over the work of recovery to the Ministry of External Affairs. Soon after, on 31 January 1949, this work was given legislative sanction with the promulgation of an Ordinance, the Abducted Persons Recovery and Restoration Ordinance, which was later replaced by the Abducted Persons Recovery and Restoration Act 1949. The legislation enabled Indian workers and officers to enter certain parts of Pakistan, and set up searches for abducted women. They had the right to recover these women and bring them into transit camps, where they were lodged until such time as their families came to take them back. The legislation also provided for the setting up of an Indo-Pakistan tribunal to decide any disputed cases: for example, some women did not want to return, for a variety of reasons. Several were fearful that they would not be accepted back into their original families. Others had actually chosen to live with partners of the other religion, but had become tarred with the brush of abduction because any mixed marriages/relationships contracted after a certain cut off date were denied legitimacy. The act applied only to areas which were seen to be 'affected' (that is, where abductions had taken place): UP, East Punjab, Delhi, PEPSU (Patiala and East Punjab States Union) and the United States of Rajasthan, and special provisions were made for the recovery of women from other states.[9]

The terms of the treaty (which were somewhat changed when the Act was passed) were clear: women on both sides of the border who had been abducted were to be tracked down, forcibly recovered and restored to their families. Although the terms of the agreement referred carefully and consistently (except in Clause 1) to 'persons', what was being discussed was the fate of women. This is quite clear from the activity that followed, where large-scale rescue efforts were mounted to locate and rehabilitate women. Little attention was paid to men in this regard, presumably because they were able to make their own decisions.

The key officers who were charged with the responsibility of rescuing abducted women were themselves women. Mridula Sarabhai was put in overall charge of the operation and assisting her, or otherwise involved in the operation, were a number of other women: Rameshwari Nehru, Sushila Nayyar, Premvati Thapar, Bhag Mehta, Damyanti Sahgal, Kamlaben Patel and others. Anis Kidwai was involved as a social worker in camps in Delhi. These women social workers were assisted by the police of the country they worked in, with as many as 34–5 police officers and men of different rank making up their staff. Every time a rescue operation had to be mounted, a woman social worker was required to go along, accompanied by the police and others. In the eyes of the state, the women were better placed to handle the delicacy of the situation and to 'persuade' those who were reluctant to give up their new homes to return to the national/parental fold. 'Persuasion' was clearly a euphemism, since the agreement had categorically stated that the women's wishes were of no consequence. The feeling that women would be better placed to handle such a 'delicate' task was shared by some key women (Padmini Sen, Mridula Sarabhai) who also insisted that women should be sent to rescue women. Kamlaben Patel said, 'It was necessary that those women who have been forcibly abducted should be taken away from the "paraya" men who have made them slaves in "paraya" houses and they should be brought to their "real" homes.' Damyanti Sahgal said, 'Of course we felt for the women we were flushing out – sometimes we had to use the police to bring them out. But what we were doing had to be done.'[10]

The state was fully aware of the delicacy of the task: the Sixteenth Meeting of the Partition Council had decided, in early 1948, that both dominions should take charge of refugees in their areas and had also said that no refugees should be forced to return to their own areas unless and until it was clear that complete security had been restored and the state was ready to resume responsibility for them. But for women they said:

> The Ministry of Relief and Rehabilitation has set up a Fact Finding Branch in consultation with the Red Cross, an Enquiry and Search Committee with the special objective of tracing abducted women. Already 23,000 names have been given to Pakistan. For the recovery of abducted women the government depends

at present on the active assistance of military authorities, district authorities, women and social workers and prominent persons.

Concerted efforts continue to be made for the recovery of abducted and forcibly converted persons. On 6 December a conference of both Dominions was held at Lahore and it was decided that both Dominions should make special efforts to recover these women. More than 25,000 enquiries about abducted women who are in Pakistan have been received by the Women's Section of the Ministry of Relief and Rehabilitation ... nearly 2,500 have already been rescued ... *the main obstruction facing our rescue parties today is the fear harboured by the majority of abducted Hindu women that they may not be received again into the fold of their society,* and the Muslims being aware of this misgiving have played upon the minds of these unfortunate women to such an extent that many of them are reluctant to come away from their captors back to India. It has been mutually agreed between the two Dominions that in such cases they should be forcibly evacuated. [my emphasis][11]

But forcible evacuation was not that easy. Some of the women resisted – out of fear of a second dislocation, a repeat of the trauma, another uprooting, or fear of non-acceptance, and equally because many of them were actually happy and settled in their new situations – while others were happy to return. Another reason for resisting was the fear that many women had that they would not be safe even in the hands of their own men, their supposed protectors, such as the police or army. If the experience of those who had been killed by their own families is anything to go by, this fear was not unfounded. Kirpal Singh, one of the major documentalists of Partition, quotes a woman as saying to the District Liaison Officer, Gujranwala: 'How can I believe that your military strength of two sepoys could safely take me across to India when a hundred sepoys failed to protect us and our people who were massacred?' Two other women asked: 'I have lost my husband and gone in for another. You want me to go to India where I have got nobody, and, of course, you don't expect me to change husbands every day,' and 'But why are you particular to take me to India? What is left in me now of religion or chastity?'[12] While the women officials charged with the task of rescuing abducted women were recruited because it was felt that they would be better able to persuade reluctant women to return, being women they also understood only too well the fear and dilemmas faced by those they were recovering.

The women's fear was real. Their non-acceptance by Hindu families became a major problem: suddenly the state, so quick to come forward with its 'recovery' was at a loss to know what to do for the reintegration of these women into the new nation, which became, in the eyes of the state, synonymous almost with their families. And because of this the state became in a sense the head of the family into which the abducted women – who were seen as having strayed away or been lured away – were to be replaced. In doing this, the state would have achieved two things: it would have performed its duty to its citizens (both those who had filed complaints and those who were being rescued) and made families whole again, thus performing a vital – at the time – function of trying to establish a stable core in a time of flux. Anis Kidwai, Kamlaben Patel, Damyanti Sahgal, all three women who worked with abducted women, point to this. Several things were at work here: families had filed complaints about missing relatives, particularly missing women, but between the filing of complaints and the actual recovery, months, sometimes years, would pass. In the interim the women would often have married, or become mothers, or simply settled in their new homes. Anis Kidwai says: 'But now a different problem arose. The majority of the girls did not want to go back.'[13] While this was true for some of the women, many of their families faced a different dilemma. Some of the women were now 'soiled', they had lived with, married, borne children to the men of the 'other' community; they had therefore 'diluted' the 'purity' of the community, so how could they now be taken back? And what was to be done with the visible results of their impurity, their sexuality, that is, their children?

So acute was the problem that both Gandhi and Nehru had to issue repeated appeals to Hindus, asking them not to refuse to take the women back into the family fold. In a public appeal made in January 1948 Nehru said: 'I am told that sometimes there is an unwillingness on the part of their relatives to accept those girls and women [who had been abducted] in their homes. This is a most objectionable and wrong attitude to take up. These girls and women require our tender and loving care and their relatives should be proud to take them back and give them every help.'[14]

And Gandhi said: 'I hear women have this objection that Hindus are not willing to accept back the recovered women because they say that they have become impure. I feel this is a matter of great shame. That woman is as pure as the girls who are sitting by my side. And if any one of those recovered women should come to me, then I will give them as much respect and honour as I accord to these young maidens.'[15]

For several years afterwards – indeed well into 1955 – the fate of these women was of considerable concern to the two governments. The Act continued to be renewed every year up to 30 November 1957. But in 1954, it was decided at an Indo-Pakistan conference held in Lahore that because by this time forcible recovery and restoration meant having to break apart the new families that had come into being, the state would not now coerce abducted persons to return. Rather, special homes would be set up in both countries where unwilling persons could stay and could freely meet their relatives in order to 'make up their minds without fear or pressure'. However, after a person had stayed for some length of time in such a camp, the tribunal still had the right to decide, and even though in theory women did have a choice, they were seldom able to muster the psychological courage to take a stand before the tribunal. The work of recovery was also discontinued because of the problem of 'post-abduction children'. For example, from 1 January 1954 to 30 September 1957, some 860 children were left behind by Muslim women returning to Pakistan, while 410 were taken by them. The former then became the responsibility of the state.

III

Why did the woman's body become so important at this time, both to the community (and the family) as well as the state? The question is important, for both the Indian and Pakistani states at this time were preoccupied with problems of unexpected magnitude. Millions of refugees needed to be housed, compensated and found jobs. The violence that accompanied and followed Partition needed somehow to be contained; rail and other transport services restored; international credibility gained; assets and liabilities divided and fought over ... the list is endless. Why did *women*, marginalized at the best of times, assume such importance at this time of catastrophe?

There is little doubt that the Indian state needed to regain some measure of legitimacy. Consider some of the problems it was facing: many more people flowed into India than had left from there. This created an imbalance in the amount of property that was available to be distributed to refugees in India, and the amount those refugees had left behind. Almost everyone had to be content with less than they had had. Many of those who poured into the country had been involved in somewhat 'higher' professions (moneylenders, teachers, doctors, farmers, shopkeepers) than those who left (barbers, tailors, shoemakers, ironsmiths and so on). There was little room to accommodate refugees in the same professions they had left behind, and many had to learn to declass themselves in order to be able to earn some sort of a livelihood. Thousands of women had been widowed – they had to be provided with housing and jobs. Orphaned children posed another problem. And then, there was a machinery to be set up so that people could come away safely, and, if necessary, return to their homes to settle their affairs. Much of this task was left to the army, considered a neutral institution. But, at this time, the army itself was communalized and divided, with soldiers and officers being asked to choose which country they wished to belong to. And so on.

These were not problems that had easy or quick solutions. And all of them needed to be judged on tangible results: if a certain number of refugees had been adequately housed, for example, the state could claim this operation a success. With women, however, the situation was different. The moment the rescue operation was mounted, the state assumed a moral legitimacy, for it took on itself the role of parent, and began the search for its 'daughters'. It is true that there was considerable criticism, both in the media, and within the Legislative Assembly in the debates that took place on the subject, of what was seen as the poor perform-ance of the government in not having rescued adequate numbers of women. Nonetheless, the fact that the operation had been mounted at all was of importance. The women became crucial to the legitimacy of the state: if they could be recovered, and indeed if they could be 'purified' and reabsorbed into the fold of the community, the state would have legitimized itself.

Communities and families too needed similar legitimacy. At its most crass, their actions in killing women and children, or exhorting the women to take their own lives, can be read as attempts to rid themselves of inconvenient encumbrances so that they could get away. For many of them, their getting away was equated in their minds with the preservation of the 'religion' – for once in India, they could marry again, procreate, and create a new line of pure believers. Once again, this burden had to be carried by women: their bodies became the pure terrain of religion, which could, of course, be guarded only through death. I do not wish to suggest here that the women were mere instruments in the hands of men, and that they had no feeling either for what one might call the homeland, or for religion. There must have been many cases where women took their own lives. Equally, there were many abducted women who wanted to return to India, just as there were others who did not. But we shall, in all likelihood, never know how these women felt. Those who are still alive have no wish to recount these histories again. And the only accounts we have of their experiences are those that have been written, largely by male historians (which in itself is not necessarily some-thing one should dismiss) and largely based on so-called facts and docu-ments. These tell only one kind of story.

But while there was a similarity in how the state and the family/ community saw women as carrying the honour of both, there were also differences in how both approached the question of women. For the community it was the woman's sexual purity that became important, as well as her community and/or religious identity. For the state, because the women it was rescuing were already sexually 'impure', having often lived with their captors, this problem had to be approached differently by making the religious identity paramount, and emphasizing how some states of impurity were less impure than others because the women had lived in these states involuntarily. It was this also that made it necessary to continue to emphasize abduction. Hence Gandhi's exhortations to families to take their sisters and daughters back. Gandhi's and Nehru's were not the only exhortations: the Ministry of Relief and Rehabilitation is said to have issued a pamphlet which quoted Manu to establish that a woman who had had sexual congress with someone other than her husband became purified after three menstrual cycles, and hence her family could accept her back. Similarly, we were told in one of our interviews that stories were published which openly accepted that Sita had had sexual congress with Ravana, despite which she remained pure.

The initial impetus to recover those family members who had been lost, most of whom happened to be women, was a natural reaction. Families had been torn apart and many wanted to be whole again. But the sheer practical difficulties made it impossible for individuals to mount recovery efforts so they then turned to the state. Other things underlay this: for men, who had justified the killing of women as 'protection', the fact that many of 'their' women, or indeed women belonging to their religion, had been abducted (no matter that some women may have chosen to go, they had to be seen as being forcibly abducted), meant a kind of collapse, almost an emasculation of their own agency. Unequal to this task, they now had to hand it over to the state, the new patriarch, the new national, family. As the central patriarch, the state now provided coercive backing for restoring and reinforcing patriarchy within the family.

For the post-colonial, deeply contested, fragile and vulnerable state, this was an exercise in restoring its legitimacy which, I would suggest, depended very much on recovering what had been lost: a part of itself, a piece, if you like, of its body, and with it, prestige, honour and property. The recovery of women became the recovery of all these, and symbolically of legitimacy and honour which rested on the backs of, and in the bodies of women. Thus the state acted on its own behalf and on behalf of those communities who invested it with agency on their behalf; and for its self-legitimation, the question of gender became crucial.

The state's rescue operation could be said to have been premised on the fact that the state had an obligation towards its subject citizens to whose plight it could not remain indifferent. But, being women, these subject citizens were treated unequally, and therefore could not be given a choice in where they could stay. So deep was the ambivalence between seeing the woman as a person and a citizen that an ordinary police officer had the right to decide whether a woman had been abducted or not and which was her proper homeland; he had the right to force her to go there, and to pull her out of a situation in which she may well have wanted to stay.

Within parliament, some members objected strongly to this denial of rights to women. One member, Mahavir Tyagi, pointed to the crux of the problem when (speaking of Muslim women recovered from India) he said that: 'these women are citizens of India ... they were born in India itself. In taking them to Pakistan without their consent ... shall we not contravene the fundamental rights sanctioned by the Constitution? ... The fact that their husbands have gone to Pakistan does not deprive the adult wife of her rights of citizenship. They have their own choice to make.' Nonetheless, this choice was denied to women.

It is against this backdrop that we need to look at the women who resisted. For, although there were many who did resettle back into their families, there were others who did not want to be uprooted and dislocated again, who did resist and who refused to come back. It was towards these women that the rescue effort was especially directed: these were the women who had, by marrying, consorting with, and having children by, the 'other', transgressed the bounds set for them. There is no doubt that resistance, of whatever kind, and however small, was an act of courage, especially when the dice were so heavily loaded against them. But not everyone was able to resist, and many stories that survive provide evidence of this.

I would like to end this account with the story of a young Muslim woman who was sold to a Sikh from Amritsar district. Buta Singh and Zainab fell in love and married, and had two children, both girls. For several years after her disappearance, the girl's relatives, who lived on lands contiguous to the family's, made attempts to trace her. Finally, six years after her 'abduction' she was traced to Amritsar where she was now married and living with Buta Singh. Zainab refused to return, but the family was also adamant as they wished to marry her into the family in order to keep the land which would otherwise be taken over by the state. She was taken away by force, but was allowed to bring her younger child with her. Buta Singh made desperate attempts to get to Pakistan, and all the while the two kept in touch by correspondence. Finally he converted to Islam and found his way to Zainab's village. There, Zainab had already been married off to her cousin. The case came up before the tribunal and Buta Singh was confident that Zainab would choose to come back to him, but so strong was the family pressure on her that in court she rejected Buta Singh and returned their child to him. The bereft man then committed suicide and the case was talked about widely in the media. If, in spite of everything, Zainab could submit to family pressure in such a way, one wonders how many women would actually have the courage to speak up before the tribunal.

The silence that has surrounded these issues is part of the general silence on the pain and trauma of Partition. At the same time the silence about women's experiences specifically suggests something different: for what are at stake here are not only questions of state, but also questions of identity, of agency, of religion and of sexuality. As far as the Indian state was concerned, women were defined in terms of their religious identities (an unusual stance for a supposedly secular state to take) – they were either Hindu or Muslim. And the children of mixed unions, apart from being visible reminders of these, did not fit easily into either category.

Whatever accounts I have also suggest that there was considerable difference in the attitude of the two countries to the question of abduction. While both signed the treaty, Pakistan did not bring in legislation as India did; also, it seems as if on the whole Muslim families were more willing to take Muslim women back than Hindu families were, perhaps because Islam does not have the same codes of purity and pollution that Hinduism does. Some expressed reluctance, but it seems they were few in number. The Indian state's identification of women as primarily belonging to their religion did not go without question among women social workers. There are many accounts of how people like Damyanti Sahgal, Kamlaben Patel and others helped women in their camps to go back to their abductors, often putting their own jobs at risk. Anis Kidwai questioned how much meaning religion had for Muslim and Hindu women:

> And what does she know of religion anyway? At least men have the opportunity to go to the mosque, and pray, but the women, Muslims have never allowed them to stand up. The moment they see young women their eyes become full of blood: run away, they tell them, go off. What are you doing here ... the culprit is within themselves, but it is the women they make run away – if they come into the *masjid* the whole *namaz* is ruined. If they try to listen to the last call of the month of *ramzan*, everyone's attention is distracted ... if they go into a *quawali*, the sufis will turn their attention from god to the world ...

It is difficult to begin to understand the experiences of these women for there is almost no way in which we can recover their voices – nor, if we can, is it really desirable to do so. They will, therefore, perforce have to remain silent. What happened with abducted women during Partition is in many ways similar to what we see today – that during communal strife and violence, it is often women who are the most talked about, but once such violence is over, a silence also seems to descend about women. The story of these women is by no means over. Today, more than ever, it is becoming important for us to examine how women are inscribed into communal situations, how they locate themselves there, what their relationship with religion is; also how the state constructs women, and indeed the kinds of responses that we need to direct at the state. For this it is as important to explore our history as it is to do some introspection into our present – informed, hopefully, and educated, by the perspective of the past.

Notes

1. This is a small part of an ongoing project of research into the oral history of Partition. In the course of my research, I have come to believe that gender must form an essential category of analysis in any study of Partition, and indeed much of my published work so far deals with this. This includes the following: 'Community, state and gender: on women's agency during Partition', *Economic and Social*

Weekly; Review of Womens Studies, Bombay, April 1993; 'Gender, community and the state: some reflections on women and Partition', in Suvir Kaul and Ania Loomba (eds), *Oxford Literary Review* (Special issue on India), London, January 1995; 'Muslims and Hindus: men and women, communal stereotypes and the Partition of India', in Tanika Sarkat and Urvashi Butalia (eds), *Women and the Hindu Right: A Collection of Essays*, Delhi: Kali for Women, 1995; 'On widows and abducted women: questions of sexuality and citizenship', in Meenakshi Thapan (ed.), *Gender and Sexuality* (working title). Delhi: Oxford University Press (forthcoming). The question of gender has also been looked at by Ritu Menon and Kamla Bhasin in 'Recovery, rupture, resistance: the state and women during Partition', *Economic and Social Weekly*, and Veena Das, in *Critical Events*. Delhi: Oxford University Press, 1996.

2. See Urvashi Butalia (forthcoming), *The Telling is Upon Us: Untold Stories of the Partition of India,* Delhi: Penguin Books.

3. Many of the survivors from these villages live in Delhi. These accounts have been collected through extensive interviews with them over several years.

4. Bir Bahadur Singh, personal interview.

5. Ibid.

6. These figures are taken from different sources, among which are G.D. Khosla, *Stern Reckoning: A Survey of the Events Leading up to and Following the Partition of India*, Delhi: Oxford University Press, 1949, reprint 1989; Kirpal Singh, *The Partition of the Punjab*, Publications Bureau, Punjab University, Patiala, 1972; *Recovery and Restoration of Abducted Persons,* Government of India Publications, Ministry of Foreign Affairs, 1952.

7. Anis Kidwai, *Azadi ki Chaon Mein* (Hindi), Delhi: National Book Trust, 1983.

8. These discussions took place at the Inter Dominion Conference held on 6 December 1947.

9. Kirpal Singh, *The Partition of the Punjab.*

10. Damyanti Saghal, personal interview.

11. Sixteenth meeting of the Partition Council, 1948.

12. Kirpal Singh, *The Partition of the Punjab*, pp. 172–3.

13. Anis Kidwai, *Azadi ki Chaon Mein.*

14. *Hindustan Times*, 17 January 1948.

15. Quoted in G.D. Khosla, *Stern Reckoning.*

8

Women Face Cultural Genocide on the Roof of the World

Yangchen Kikhang

Tibet has a unique culture stretching back several thousand years and has for most of its history enjoyed the rights and privileges of a sovereign state, having developed its own political, economic and religious system. With a distinct language and written script, Tibet has produced a rich catalogue of musical and artistic treasures. In addition to this legacy, an immense body of philosophical teachings has been maintained through Tibet's native religious tradition of Bon and, later, Buddhism. Throughout most of its history, Tibet has been a peaceful nation, providing a stabilizing influence on neighbouring India and Nepal. That tranquil lifestyle now lies in tatters following China's invasion and brutal military occupation in 1950, which cost the lives of over one million Tibetans, nearly one sixth of the population.

Since then Tibetan women have been prime targets of human rights abuse. As documented by Asia Watch and Amnesty International, political prisoners suffer systematic torture and sexual violations. Detailed reports of forcible extraction of blood from female prisoners continue to emerge. Due to the courage and sacrifice of the Chinese human rights activist Dr Harry Wu, the West now knows about China's system of forced labour camps. Some of the most notorious of these are in Eastern Tibet and house countless numbers of women, who are exploited as slave labour. For women not involved in political activity, daily life offers little better. Unless they are able to speak the language of the occupying regime, the chance of finding even the most menial employment is almost impossible. In order to receive grain, women must carry a ration card bearing their name, date of birth and 'class'. The amount awarded is determined by a system of 'work points'. It is not therefore uncommon for women to be seen working in the fields from 6 a.m. to 8 p.m. Half of their yield is often demanded by China through various taxes such as the 'Love of the Nation Tax' or the 'Surplus Grain Tax'. Healthcare facilities mostly benefit the forces of occupation and the ever-increasing numbers of Chinese 'settlers'. Tibetans must pay for services offered, and since this is beyond their means, the majority rely on 'barefoot doctors'. This poverty, which has blighted most families, is such that a once self-sufficient land is now one of the poorest regions on earth, with an annual per capita income of about £60. Not surprisingly, China always seeks to cover up the degree of social deprivation of women and children in Tibet. In an interview featured in a 1991 US television documentary, Mr Cheng Muhai, senior counsellor at the Chinese embassy in Washington, dumbfounded at the evidence before him, cut short the proceedings when shown film footage highlighting the poverty in Tibet with the words: 'It's no good. I think we had better shut up.'

Tibetan Women Targeted by China's Population Programme

Tibetan women struggle against China's male-dominated state, characterized by deeply held racist convictions that operate a system of apartheid, reducing them to second-class citizenship in their own land. A commonly used Chinese term describing occupied people is *shung-nu* – 'barbarian slave'.

It is within China's notorious population programme that women in Tibet face the most widespread human rights violations. Reports of this programme began emerging from Tibet in the early 1960s. It has resulted in unimaginable suffering for women across Tibet and China. Denied freedom of choice or control over their own bodies, women are forced, through a series of financial penalties, intimidation and other oppressive measures, to submit to population control.

Tashi Dolma was a former health worker from Amdo in Eastern Tibet. In 1988 she became pregnant for the second time. Resisting initial pressures from family planning officials to have an abortion, she was fined 1500 Yuan (an enormous amount of money for most Tibetans). On hearing of her pregnancy, a Chinese doctor at the hospital in which she worked, pressurized her by saying: 'If you insist on having the child, the financial punishment is a small matter compared with the political crime you are committing. From now on, you will only get 30 per cent of your salary. Your salary will never increase. Your child will not have the right to claim his ration card, and will not be admitted to school.' Some four months into the pregnancy, Tashi collapsed under incessant pressure and submitted to 'menstrual termination of pregnancy (MTP)'. Tashi Dolma says about her operation: 'The complications and pain I suffered in the course of this operation were so terrible that I can't talk about it. However, it was nothing compared to what women suffer when they are operated on during their sixth and seventh months of pregnancy, which happens quite often at this hospital. In such cases, 0.2 ml of a solution called *le xun nur* is injected into the foetal bag by using a 12-inch syringe. The foetus loses its blood and stops breathing. About 72 hours later the dead foetus is delivered. I know at least twelve women who underwent such operations' (Testimony of Tashi Dolma, *Tibetan Review*, 1990). As she recalled, the operation left serious emotional and physical damage. 'My menstrual flow is erratic. I have constant pain in my back and intestines. My health is such that I am ignorant if I shall ever be a mother again' (Testimony of Tashi Dolma, 27 April 1990, cited in Moss, 1992).

There are also numerous detailed accounts of physical force being used against women who are dragged from their homes and beaten in preparation for 'birth control operations'. A disturbing account, 'China's wanted children' (Yin, 1991) was compiled by Liu Yin, a Chinese who was allowed to accompany a birth control 'task force'. Liu Yin's report documents a raid on a village in which houses are stormed and women carried out in blankets to be taken for sterilizations and abortions. Liu Yin comments on conditions at the temporary clinic: 'I could not believe what I saw. Hundreds of women, some more than six months pregnant, were packed into dark corridors and makeshift tents, waiting to be operated on.' She describes toilets filled with blood-soaked toilet paper and waste bins full of aborted babies.

In a report presented to the United States Congressional Delegation, two Buddhist monks from Amdo (Eastern Tibet) gave a harrowing account of a mobile birth control team who arrived in their village during the autumn of 1987. They reported that all women in the area were ordered to have sterilizations and abortions and those who resisted were taken by force. According to the monks, all women of childbearing age were sterilized, and 30 to 40 women a day were operated on. When they finished, team members moved on to the next village. The monks described women crying as they awaited their turn for the operation, heard their screams and watched a growing pile of foetuses outside the tent (Testimony, 20 October 1988, cited in Moss, 1992).

It is such atrocities that have gained the attention of human rights groups such as Independent Tibet Network (formerly Campaign Free Tibet) and Optimus. More recently, Amnesty International has condemned the human rights abuse within China's population policies and has recommended that China 'ensure that women are not detained, restricted or otherwise physically coerced in order to force them to have abortions or to be sterilized' (*AI Index*, 1995).

It is not only Tibetans who have seen women taken by force. Valda Harding, an English nurse, describes how, during a visit to Tibet in 1987, she witnessed Tibetan women caged like animals in wicker baskets in the back of a truck. When she enquired what their crime was, she was informed they were 'being taken away because they were having too many children'. She recalls having the impression that 'it sounds strange, but in Tibet you get used to seeing people kicked, beaten and abused' (*Tibetan Bulletin,* September–October 1991).

Recent television documentaries have highlighted the human rights violations caused by China's population policies. Terrified at the brutal fate ahead of her, Bai was escorted to the local family planning clinic. Strapped onto a medical table, she was yet another 'volunteer' in China's birth control programme. In pain and crying for an anaesthetic, Bai was ordered by the surgeon to 'put up with it'. Immediately after the operation, traumatized, and in obvious agony, she was left unattended in a grimy dormitory. These harrowing scenes were documented in the film *Women of the Yellow Earth* (Bulmer, 1994) which revealed the coercive nature of China's population programme.

But these images were eclipsed by those of the documentaries *The Dying Rooms* (Woods and Blewitt, 1995) and *Return to the Dying Rooms* (Woods and Blewitt, 1996). Both films recorded the inhuman treatment of baby girls left to die in China's state orphanages as a result of China's one-child policy and Chinese traditional preference for boys. The misery and suffering recorded in the films resulted in public outrage in Europe and the US and an intense public debate in the British national media.

In the drive to implement China's population programme, such gross violations have the approval and support of the Chinese government who urge regional and local family planning officers to meet birth control quotas. In 1981 Deng Xiaoping advised family planning officers: 'In order to control the population use whatever means you must, but do it' (*China's Spring Digest,* 1987). In 1992 Cheng Bangzhu, Deputy Governor of Hunan province, ordered birth control teams: 'In the autumn family planning drive, urban and rural areas must closely cooperate with one another, and must comb every household for unscheduled pregnancies, for which remedial measures should be taken' (*Hunan People's Broadcasting Station,* 14 September 1992).

Eugenics Revisited

The scale of human rights violations and the suffering of Tibetan and Chinese women is staggering. Dr Jonathan Aird, former senior China specialist at the US Bureau of the Census, estimated that between 1971 and 1985 alone there have been some 100 million coercive 'birth control operations', involving forced sterilizations and abortions (Aird, 1992). For Tibetans these population policies not only violate human rights principles, but form a dangerous and potentially disastrous assault upon an already severely diminished Tibetan population.

Chinese population control abuses are now widely recognized, yet some demographers, presumably keen to maintain career links and/or research

opportunities with China, choose to ignore the evidence of such violations. Perhaps they share the view of a Chinese Agriculture Minister: 'Only
coercive measures can be effective in alleviating the problems caused by
population explosion' (*New China News Agency*, April 1989, cited in Aird,
1990). The population crisis scenario, once the controversial possession of
social geographers and population analysts, has now entered the public
domain. It has also become something of a sacred cow, and those who
suggest that it is flawed, are open to charges of blasphemy. While there are
indeed very real economic and human concerns regarding China's population growth, the problems, invested with a forbidding sense of urgency
by advocates of the 'explosion theory', cannot be allowed to justify the
violation of fundamental freedoms or of women's human rights.

In Tibet and China, however, this is exactly what is happening, as the
United Nations, governments and multilateral population agencies ignore
the wealth of evidence of these abuses, muttering absurd arguments about
China having a potential for change. This reasoning could equally have
been applied to Nazi SS units which forcibly sterilized countless numbers
of 'racially inferior' women across Europe. Those who defend China's
population control programmes are asking the world to accept something just as controversial and distasteful, to say nothing about the
atrocities, the traumas, the terror and devastation inflicted upon women
simply because 'there is potential for improvement'.

There are several important considerations which must be taken into
account when examining Chinese population control programmes in Tibet.
It must be remembered that these programmes are part of a system of
oppression forced upon a subject people of an independent nation under
illegal occupation. It is a policy imposed by a colonial power through the
act of military occupation. The resulting birth control programme has
had a devastating impact on the Tibetan population, which, it is widely
agreed, was around six million before China's invasion in 1950. Since
then, some 1.2 million Tibetans are thought to have perished through
famine, disease, and in the 'Twenty Year War' of resistance (1954–74). A
serious population low must thus have occurred in the 1960s, which
meant that China forced its population programme upon an already
dangerously reduced population level.

It is significant that the population of Tibet makes up less than 1 per
cent of China's population. According to Chinese figures, Tibetans from
the so-called Tibet Autonomous Region (a truncated region forming a
third of Tibet proper) are just 0.2 per cent of China's total population.
It has been calculated that if the Tibetan population experiences an annual
increase of 2.1 per cent (equivalent to the replacement rate), it would add
just 0.3 per cent of China's yearly population growth. Tibet has a land
surface comparable in size to that of Western Europe, yet its population
is less than that of Greater London. The Tibetan population has co-

existed in balance with a resource-rich environment for several millennia. Taken together these facts make it impossible to accept arguments for any form of population control in Tibet.

Apart from employing dubious economic arguments to justify its population control programme, such as linking apparent rises in living standards for Tibetans with birth control policies, China also stresses the importance of 'increasing the quality of the nation'. Since the Nazi obsession with eugenics, no state has attached so much importance to what has been comprehensively described as 'the management and breeding for the purpose of improving stock' (*Issues in Reproductive and Genetic Engineering*, 1991).

Socially and biologically based eugenics has played a major role in China's justification of its population programme, particularly since the official introduction of the one child policy in 1979. In 1989, China's Gansu province (which contains large parts of annexed Tibetan territory) issued a mandatory sterilization regulation 'prohibiting reproduction by the mentally retarded'. China's definition of what constitutes retardation includes having an IQ of less than 49, or 'handicaps' in 'language, memory, orientation and thinking'. One is reminded of those certified as insane by the Nazi Criminal Biology Institute and sterilized on the basis that they held thoughts not in accord with Nazi ideology. In 1991, similar eugenics laws were adopted by at least five other provinces and Madame Peng Peyin, State Family Planning Minister, defended the forced sterilization of all mentally handicapped people, whether or not their problem was hereditary (Kristof, 1991).

For Tibetans these laws are a chilling addition to the systematic assault upon their population. According to Xinhua (China's News Agency), there are some 100,000 'handicapped' people in Tibet who, under China's eugenics laws, are considered 'undesirable'. As with most Chinese euphemisms, the term 'handicapped' could mean many things and the interpretation is often left to family planning officials at regional and local levels. As a result, Tibetan women find themselves at the mercy of politically motivated decisions that result in mass sterilization campaigns. Gansu Radio reported on 7 May 1990 that some 65,000 women and men have been sterilized in just two months (Moss, 1992). Deng Bihai, in an article for *China's Population News* (1989) trumpeted in overtly racist tones the superiority of Han Chinese over 'minority nationalities'. The article claimed that people such as the Tibetans are commonly 'mentally retarded, short of stature, dwarves or insane' and on this basis, Deng urged no relaxation in the birth control programme.

Conclusion: Cultural Genocide

The recognition of the abuse involved in China's population programme, and its racist and eugenic rationale, together with the fact that it has been forced upon a population already blighted by the loss of a million people, make it difficult to escape the conclusion that China is engaged in cultural genocide in Tibet. This genocidal programme is waged on Tibetan women's bodies. It is impossible to see any other reason for population control other than the aim of reducing the Tibetan population to a dangerously low level. With the added pressure of China's population transfer strategy, which means that Tibetans are becoming a minority in many areas of Tibet, Tibet faces the gravest crisis of survival in its history. In order to achieve this 'Final Solution', the rights of Tibetan women have been abolished by central mandate and they have no choice but to accept a position which renders them servile to the Chinese state. As one Buddhist nun has commented: 'In Tibet we have no rights, not even over our bodies.'

Note

The Women's Section of *Independent Tibet Network* has a considerable database of information about coercion within China's population programme and related human rights issues in China and Tibet. It is happy to assist with research. Address: Women's Section, *Independent Tibet Network,* 62A Upper Hill Park, Tenby, Pembrokeshire, UK SA70 8JF.

References

Amnesty International Index. 1995. 'Women in China.' *Amnesty International, AI Index.* June 1995. ASA/17/29/95.

Aird, Jonathan. 1990. *Slaughter of the Innocents.* Washington DC: The American Enterprise Institute.

Aird, Jonathan. 1992. *Foreign Assistance to Coercive Family Planning in China.* Paper tabled in the Australian Senate by Senator Brian Harradine, May 1992.

Bulmer, John. 1994. *Women of the Yellow Earth.* Documentary film, screened by BBC2 as part of the series *Under the Sun*, 24 July 1994.

China's Spring Digest, vol. 1, February 1987.

Issues in Reproductive and Genetic Engineering, vol. 4. 1991.

Kristof, Nicholas D. 1991. 'Parts of China forcibly sterilising the retarded who wish to marry.' *The New York Times*, 15 August 1991.

Moss, Martin. 1992. *Children of Despair: An Analysis of Coercive Birth Control Policies in Chinese Occupied Tibet.* Pembrokeshire: Independent Tibet Network (Formerly Campaign Free Tibet).

Tibetan Bulletin, September–October, 1991.

Tibetan Review. 1990. 'China's forced abortion techniques in Tibet.' *Tibet Review*, October 1990.

Woods, David and Kate Blewitt. 1995. *The Dying Rooms.* Documentary film screened by Channel 4, 14 June 1995.

Woods, David and Kate Blewitt. 1996. *Return to the Dying Rooms.* Documentary film screened by Channel 4, 19 January 1996.

Yin, Liu. 1991. 'China's wanted children.' *The Independent*, 11 September 1991.

9

A Broken Rainbow:
Pacific Women and Nuclear Testing

Zohl dé Ishtar

> We have deformed babies here.
> I know some women who gave birth
> to children with no hands, no ears,
> the feet are not fully made.
> It is a crime against humanity!
>
> Roti Tehaevra

Nuclear testing has wrought havoc in Tahiti-Polynesia where Maohi women experience increasing cancer rates and give birth to babies so deformed that they have no human shape. Children suffer from malnutrition because precious land has been stolen and contaminated. Women's social, political and economic status has been undermined by an alien male-dominated society. Despite this, and more, indigenous Pacific women have stood strong. They are leading the way back to a world free from racism, colonization and violence. This chapter gives voice to those women. Their testimonies – a warning and a gift to us all – were given to me over the past 15 years as I campaigned beside them.

The tentacles of the Bomb know no boundary but weave their way into the most hidden, personal corners. Children are born deformed, if born at all. Women bear marks where their breasts once fed the babies they managed, against all odds, to carry full term. The legs and throats of their menfolk are scarred where blisters festered after they'd gone fishing. Too many people have died, shattering families. Ancestral land, stolen for military bases or contaminated by nuclear explosions, cannot provide food, so people go hungry. The best beaches and most fertile valleys are taken up by foreigners who claim the land as theirs, leaving only the steep mountain slopes for the homes of indigenous people. The foreigners run the government, imposing cultural structures which do not benefit the indigenous, or into which they simply do not fit, like round pegs in square holes. They can't get a decent education, a decent job. They live in slums where youth suicide is too common and children die from preventable illnesses.

> *'We are already dying from nuclear war while you are thinking how to prevent it.' (Chailang Palacios, Francke, 1985: 31)*

Tahiti-Polynesia's nuclear era began in 1963 when Algeria won its independence and the French government moved its Centre d'Experimentation du Pacifique (CEP) to Tahiti Island. Amid assurances that 'No tests will ever be made by France in the Pacific Ocean', Moruroa and Fangataufa were chosen as the ill-fated sites for 44 atmospheric and 131 underground nuclear detonations by 1992.

Protests by the Maohi people, supported by peoples throughout the Pacific and around the world, were violently suppressed. Their concerns were met with promises that 'not a single particle of radioactive fallout will ever reach an inhabited island' (Governor Grimald, 1963). These promises ignored the nomadic people of Tureia and Mangareva who lived within the designated official danger zone and used Moruroa and Fangataufa as part of their seasonal food-gathering cycle.

Equally disregarded was the Partial Test Ban Treaty signed by the other nuclear powers (the USA, Britain and Russia) that same year. This treaty limited nuclear tests underground. The treaty was a direct result of the contamination of the US nuclear test sites in the Marshall Islands where, between 1946 and 1958, the United States had tested 66 bombs at Bikini and Enewetak atolls. The most destructive of these was the 1954 'Bravo' hydrogen bomb detonated above Bikini. Hundreds of tons of material from Bikini's reef, islands and lagoon were lifted up into the air and carried over the Marshall Islands. Nearby Rongelap was covered in fallout two inches deep.

Lijon Eknilang played in that fallout:

> I woke up with a bright light in my eyes. I ran outside to see what had happened … Soon after we heard a big loud noise, just like a thunder and the earth started to move – the ground started to sway and sink … A little later we saw a big cloud moving to our islands. It covered the sky … Then came the fallout. It was white and to us kids we thought it was white soap powder. The kids were playing in the powder and having fun, but later on everyone was sick and we couldn't do anything … For many hours poison from the bomb kept falling on our islands. (WWNFIP, 1987: 15)

Three days later, when the Rongelap people were evacuated to nearby Kwajalein Atoll, they were suffering from radiological illnesses similar to those experienced after the bombs at Hiroshima and Nagasaki. Darlene Keju-Johnson, a child on Rongelap in 1954 and now a health worker, recalls, 'When the fallout came on their skins, it burnt them. People were vomiting ... Their hair was falling out, finger nails were falling out ... but they were never told why' (WWNFIP, 1987: 7). Three years later the evacuees were returned to Rongelap amid secret statements by the US Atomic Energy Commission that 'the habitation of these people on the islands will afford most valuable ecological data on human beings'. The Commission also returned people to Rongelap who had not been on the island at the time of the blast. These people were to be the control group in their experiment.

By 1957, Rongelap women were suffering from a rate of stillbirths and miscarriages twice that of other Marshallese women. Babies were being born deformed or without human shape. Darlene Keju-Johnson reports:

> Children are being deformed. I saw a child from Rongelap. Its feet are like clubs. And another child whose hands are like nothing at all. It is mentally retarded. Some of the children suffer growth retardation. Now we have this problem, what we call 'jellyfish babies'. These babies are born like jellyfish. They have no eyes. They have no heads. They have no arms. They have no legs. They do not shape like human beings at all. (dé Ishtar, 1994: 24)

Rongelap women became afraid to give birth; children exposed on Rongelap developed thyroid abnormalities; cancer rates increased dramatically, particularly for women and children.

> *'French Polynesia, which is said in the tourist brochures to*
> *have the closest islands to paradise, is nurturing the fire of death, the fire of*
> *the disaster of humanity.' (Louis Uregei,*
> *cited by dé Ishtar, 1994: 203)*

The nuclear age was heralded into Tahiti-Polynesia on 2 July 1966 with the first French nuclear detonation at Moruroa. In 1964 Moruroa and Fangataufa had been ceded to France for use by the CEP. The atolls will be returned when the CEP stops its activities, in the condition they are at the time.

On 11 September a 120kt bomb was triggered on Moruroa, this time with President de Gaulle as audience. The wind was blowing the wrong way but de Gaulle was impatient. Within hours, radioactive fallout covered the entire Tuamotu and Society Islands (including Tahiti). Days later radioactivity reached Western and American Samoa, the Cook Islands and Fiji.

As with their neighbours, the Marshallese, throughout Tahiti-Polynesia people began complaining that they were 'withering away', their hair was falling out, they had blisters on their arms and legs and problems with their digestion. Cancers became far too common. Marguerite Tetunaui's story is one among many:

My mother is dead from cancer of the stomach. My brother Paulo is dead from general cancer. My sister Celistine is dead from cancer of the lungs. My sister Leonie is dead from cancer of the lungs. My sister Liliane is dead from cancer of the breast and lungs. My sister Madeleine and myself have had cancer of the breast. (Marguerite Tetunaui, 1995)

Women began to experience increasing miscarriages and stillbirth or gave birth to children with disturbing physical deformities. Toimata relates how her children were affected:

Our first and eldest child was born in 1975. She always seemed to be sick with a chronic cough and stomach pains ... My second baby was born premature at seven and a half months and died the day he was born. My third baby was born at home full term but died two weeks later. She had a skin problem. Her skin would come off immediately if it was touched ... Eugene, my fourth baby, was born at full time but died when he was two months old. He had diarrhoea ... When it stopped, it was replaced by another condition. The baby became rigid, like wood. Every part of his body was racked by continuous muscular contractions and he had a high temperature ... Our fifth baby is alive and well. The sixth baby was born at full term ... she died the next day. The seventh is alive and well. My eighth was still-born prematurely at six and a half months. My ninth baby, a girl, was born at full term but she died when she was eight months old ... they said she had a blood infection. The tenth baby was born mid 1985. She has had an airway infection and a heart condition since birth. We were told that she had a hole in the heart. (Mills et al., 1990: 63)

Toimata blames the Bomb for her children's suffering – her husband was one of hundreds who worked on Moruroa as a labourer.

Many women suspect that they have given birth to jellyfish babies but no one knows for sure. Because, as Roti Tehaevra of Vahine To'a (Women Warriors) asserts, the truth is suppressed:

Maybe we have babies like in the Marshall Islands – jellyfish babies. We don't know. Why? Because we don't have scientific people here to tell us the truth. Never the French government give us official records. (Tahaevra, in conversation with Zohl dé Ishtar, Papeete, 1995)

Despite the absence of a comprehensive radiological survey and the laundering of the few inadequate statistics that do exist, France persists in claiming that nuclear testing is safe. They base their analysis on some rather irrational thinking. For example, when the government announced that a clinic would be open to check anyone who believed their health had been affected by nuclear testing, no one turned up. The authorities took this as proof that no one had been affected by the testing.

Marie-Therese Danielsson explains that the reluctance of Tahitian parents to parade their children in front of the authorities allows the French government to pretend that children are not being born deformed:

There is an association of parents of handicapped children because we have many handicapped children, since the atmospheric tests. But when the authorities looked for the children they didn't find any. Why? Because the Tahitians don't like to show their handicapped children to people. Then the French said that there wasn't any. (dé Ishtar, 1994: 193)

The number of Tahitians seeking cancer treatment is alarming. According to Clarisa Lucas of Kura Ora, the nuclear-victim support organization:

Every month we have almost forty persons who fly to France to be operated for cancers and other maladies associated with nuclear. And when some of them come back they die. Forty persons every month. I know this. (Lucas, in conversation with Zohl dé Ishtar, Papeete, 1995)

The French Ministry of Health reports that in 1987 (the latest figures available) 285 Tahitians accessed foreign hospitals. Given that, according to the Ministry's own Dr Laudon, only 70 per cent of cancers diagnosed at Mamao Hospital in Papeete in 1988 were recorded, the figure is probably much higher.

The difficulty in documenting the health violations is due, Clarisa Lucas insists, to a deliberately fostered climate of fear:

People are afraid because of the pressure of the French government. Most victims are dead or they are dying and even those who are dying don't want to speak. My friend worked on Moruroa and he was contaminated. He was almost dead. I said to him, 'What happened?' He says, 'No. I can't talk. I am in a military hospital. Maybe they can kill me.' I was with some doctors. They saw an old man. He had a scar on his neck – thyroid – and his legs are all blistered and scarred but he keep the silence. The doctor ask, 'Can I write this?' 'Oh, no. No. Don't do this. I don't want to go to jail.' It is crazy. He's dying! Some people are very afraid. (Lucas, in conversation with Zohl dé Ishtar, Papeete, 1995)

The full human cost of nuclear testing will take several generations to be felt. Marie-Therese Danielsson warns that it will be the unborn generations who will suffer most:

We are only beginning to see the effects of the atmospheric testing, only the tip of the iceberg. When will we begin to suffer from the underground tests? Ten years, twenty? The government says everything is safe for a thousand years. Even if that were true, which it isn't, what legacy do we leave the future generations? (dé Ishtar, 1994: 193)

Roti Tehaevra voices the outrage felt by her people when she accuses the French government:

They don't have human feelings for those people who live there. Nuclear tests is not respect for human life. Only the bomb is the important thing. If people die of cancer it doesn't matter because you need rats, guinea pigs. We are the experiment for France. They say to the people that there is no danger. Bullshit! (Tahaevra, in conversation with dé Ishtar, Papeete, 1995)

> *'They have also managed, with absolute disregard for all Pacific peoples, to arrogantly and callously damage the environmental safety of our large ocean region.' (Myron Mataoa, cited in Connelly et al., 1987: 40)*

Irreversible damage has been done to the environment in which the Maohi live. When a bomb is lowered down a shaft sunk into the coral between 600 to 1200 metres deep and detonated it creates a brilliant flash and sends shock waves through the surface of the lagoon causing a mild earthquake and the lagoon water to bubble and froth. The fireball deep in the ground melts 10,000 tonnes of rock changing the structure of the atoll itself.

Fangataufa Atoll was irreparably contaminated by France's first underground test, on 5 June 1975. All future tests until 1988 were restricted to Moruroa.

Explosions result in earthquakes and tidal waves. Huge chasms have been blasted into the side of Moruroa Atoll. Fractures and cracks are appearing above and below sea level – the largest is one kilometre long and 30 to 60 centimetres wide. Between 1975 and 1981 Moruroa sank 1.5 metres from its original three metres above sea level. Moruroa, pregnant with radioactive debris, is riddled with holes. Caesium 134 and 137 and plutonium have been detected in the lagoon and surrounding ocean.

France persists in announcing that the underground tests are safe. They ignore their own studies and refute or argue to their advantage against the few limited studies that have been done, by other nations, which indicate that the porous coral of the Polynesian atolls is the worse possible site for underground testing. Pretending that seepage into the ocean is not occurring, and does not threaten, they insist that the atolls will contain the radioactivity for a thousand years.

Nuclear contamination is not the only result of the detonations. In islands adjacent to the nuclear test site the simple act of eating fish can be fatal. Marine food poisoning – *ciguatera* – can result in vomiting, diarrhoea, physical weakness, miscarriages, premature births and neurological disease in the newly born. It flourishes where the reef ecology has been disturbed by natural causes, such as earthquakes, or human activities like construction, dredging and explosions.

It is not by coincidence that Tahiti-Polynesia has a *ciguatera* rating six times the Pacific average. Marie-Therese Danielsson blames the nuclear testing: 'Before testing began at Moruroa … [Mangareva's] lagoon teemed with fish. Only two years later, all fish in the lagoon were poisonous and many people sick from eating them, displaying all symptoms of *ciguatera*' (dé Ishtar, 1994: 194).

The first case of *ciguatera* was recorded in Hao Atoll in 1966. By mid 1968 43 per cent of the population of 650 had been affected. Hao was used as a support base to the test sites and its lagoon dredged to allow large ships to harbour there. On Mangareva, the closest atoll to Moruroa, almost all of the 528 locals have suffered symptoms, with a mortality rate of one in six annually.

With fish the main staple food of the Maohi people *ciguatera* has had a massive social impact on the community. Unable to eat their local fish the Maohi people are forced to subsist on imported tinned fish and other processed foods. As a result children suffer from malnutrition.

> '*Money from the bomb does not interest us. It is better to be poor and in good health than rich and sick.*' *(Ida Bordes-Teariki, cited in dé Ishtar, 1994: 199)*

Deteriorating health, miscarriages, deformed babies, contamination of the environment ... these are the more obvious costs of the nuclear testing programme. The impact on the social, economic and political life of the Maohi people is often overlooked.

Before 1963, Tahiti-Polynesia provided for its people, then the French government needed labourers to construct the airport and other military facilities. Marie-Therese Danielsson recalls how the Maohi economy, hitherto self-sufficient, was undermined:

> The outer Islanders were drawn to Papeete, to the big city. People came from the Austral Islands where there was plenty of food and abandoned their plantations. They settled in Papeete where the population just keeps growing, people just keep coming. The women ... come to work in the restaurants and bars and become prostitutes. (dé Ishtar, 1994: 200–201)

As the construction era came to an end the Maohi labourers were laid off, but French promises of rehabilitation were conveniently forgotten. Oscar Temaru, Mayor of Faa'a Commune in Papeete and leader of Tavini Huraatira, recalls:

> [They] would ask members of their family to come and join them. Later, when everything was built, there was no more work, everyone was laid off, but they stayed. They never went back home. Now they are living in the urban zone in a very precarious situation. We are twenty-five thousand people – just in Faa'a! (dé Ishtar, 1994: 189)

The Maohi population explosion was mirrored by a similar influx of French civilians following on the heels of the military. Today 70 per cent of the nation's people crowd onto Tahiti Island. The French citizens invariably adapted the social and political environment to suit their own needs, pushing the Tahitians to the periphery until they became fringe dwellers in their own island. According to Oscar Temaru:

French people are flooding into Papeete. They come and take jobs. All the best jobs are for the French. All the administration, business and education is in French, so it's easier for them ... They take up housing and land, they have all the land on the flat and own the beaches. They make money while our children starve, our children have nowhere to play. Our people are dying of diseases because the living conditions are so bad. (dé Ishtar, 1994: 189)

The Maohi's living standard is so low that William Tcheng accuses France of treachery:

You have come with your civilization and you got them to go to your schools. You promised them good work, good salaries. And now they have to leave their families to live in Tahiti which is more like a punishment than reward. Tahiti is like a double-edged sword – no house, no family, exploited as a worker, as a prostitute. (dé Ishtar, 1994: 187)

There is nothing unique in this. Colonizers always import their own culture and the French have been embedding theirs in Tahiti-Polynesia since the 1700s.

> *'Pacific women are losing their status because we have inherited the modern civilization from your society.' (Suliana Siwatibau, cited in dé Ishtar, 1994: 234)*

The imposition of French culture undermined the traditional status of women. Although Maohi civilization was a hierarchical system, within class divisions women and men were equal. Now Tahiti-Polynesia suffers under the yoke of an imported male-dominant society.

When Europeans first arrived in Tahiti in 1767, they found a people that respected and honoured women. The English explorer Captain Wallis, on the *Dolphin*, attempting to annex the island in the name of his king, found himself pitted against Queen Purea and 4000 warriors on 500 war canoes. In 1842, when the French imposed their rule on Tahiti, it was a woman, Queen Pomare IV, who led her people in armed resistance.

Traditional Polynesian attitudes towards women differed remarkably from those of Europe. Maohi women enjoyed a respect far outweighing the social standing of European women – then or since. It was acceptable for women to reject monogamy and choose the role of 'firebird', or 'free woman'. Women owned their bodies. Sexual activity was as natural as eating and sleeping. Mothers were honoured, children cherished. Bands of women and men, called *Arioi*, travelled from village to village performing sexually to encourage and honour the joys of the human body. They chose this role freely as others might choose to be farmers or fisherfolk. When the Europeans arrived, the Tahitian women, believing that any children born to the strangers would inherit their knowledge and skills, thus benefiting all their people, chose to trade their bodies to the sexually inhibited strangers.

Then the inevitable missionaries arrived to impose their culture on the Maohi and by 1820, when the Russian navigator Bellingshausen visited Tahiti, he found that:

> All those who could wore European clothes, and both men and women had their heads shaved ... Tattooing had been discouraged, liquor was banned, and no one danced any more or played Tahitian music. Even the weaving of garlands of flowers was forbidden ... the Tahitian religion had long since been swept away, and the *arioi*, those votaries of free love, were married. Morality police roamed the countryside by night pouncing on illicit lovers ... The *marae* had collapsed into heaps of stones, and were overrun by rats. (Moorehead, 1987: 111)

It was a time when, according to Roti Tehaevra, Maohi men, faced with the intruders' gynophobic fraternity, began to believe that they were superior: 'In the Western system man is power. When our men saw the soldier – man – coming to the island they said, "Oh, only man comes." So they say, "Man is power. Woman you are under, I am top." That was not tradition' (Tehaevra, in conversation with dé Ishtar, Papeete, 1995).

This imbalance has been maintained by French settlers and, more recently, by military personnel. So that, Marie-Therese Danielsson asserts, Maohi women now experience the hardships imposed on women in any gender-distorted culture:

> [T]hey have become French. And at the same time they are Tahitian women, *vahine*. It makes problems in their lives ... They have to work very hard. They have a lot of children. They are beaten by their husbands. They have to make money because there is no money because he has spent it drinking. (dé Ishtar, 1994: 196–7)

Finding themselves at the bottom of Tahiti-Polynesia's imposed social structure, Maohi women attempt to break the cycle of poverty by investing in their children the dream of a just society. But, Maea Tematua warns, they are too often thwarted because they do not have the skills to assist their children to live in both worlds:

> [T]here are Tahitian women who do not speak French very well ... These women are not able to give their children an appropriate education, they can't help the children – and it is the children who suffer the consequences of this. There is a growing rate of failure at school. (dé Ishtar, 1994: 198)

Nor are they always able to protect their children, particularly their daughters, from the many acts of violence that assault them daily. Sexual assault, rape and prostitution are just some examples. According to Marie-Therese Danielsson:

> You have parents taking their young daughters to the Korean ships, very young girls because Korean men like young girls. You have a lot of prostitution with

the fishing ships. No one speaks about it. But if you go to the quay at night you can see them. And rape. Rapes are terrible here, you can't imagine. (dé Ishtar, 1994: 197–8)

Likewise, Maohi women are attempting to protect their children from nuclear testing. They are, Roti Tehaevra explains, at the forefront of the campaign:

The man power government has made many mistakes because they are proud. Women are not so proud. They have a humility because she feels very strong for the children of tomorrow, for the new population of tomorrow. Jacques Chirac is a man and he has taken a man decision. It is not a woman decision. It is a man decision. It is war. Man think war. Women don't think war. Women think protection. To protect the children. Not to bring them to the war to be killed. Women don't do that because they love their children. (Tehaevra, in conversation with dé Ishtar, Papeete, 1995)

Conclusion

> '*We cannot separate the fight for nuclear-free and independence because we are still a colony.*' *(Vito Maamaatua, in conversation with dé Ishtar, Papeete, 1995)*

On 5 September 1995, the world shook and a small isolated atoll in the Southern Pacific turned white. Fish died, birds fell out of the sky. A broken rainbow framed an orange cloud. A deafening silence screamed out across the ocean.

France, under Jacques Chirac, had terminated its 1992 moratorium on nuclear testing. The Maohi responded with outrage. Taking to the streets they burnt the city of Papeete and its airport while around the world people gaped in horror at France's arrogance. Seven explosions followed in quick succession, spilling more radioactivity into Moruroa and Fanga-taufa, where it waits to seep out into the surrounding ocean.

How did France manage to get away with this? The answer is simple. Tahiti-Polynesia is a stolen land. In 1842 500 armed troops, under cover of four warships, marched through Tahiti, arrested the Maohi monarch Queen Pomare IV, hauled down the Tahitian flag and raised the French tricolour in its place. Led by their queen, the Maohi responded with armed resistance but faced defeat under France's greater firepower. In 1880, after the death of the ever defiant Queen Pomare, the French bribed her son to abdicate and the islands became a French possession.

Since then, Vito Maamaatua explains, France has done what it likes with the islands:

In our statute for internal autonomy it says that the French have sovereignty of the air, the soil, under the soil and all the sea. They can do what they want here. We just have to sit down and shut our mouth. (Maamaatua, in conversation with dé Ishtar, Papeete, 1995)

France holds the Maohi people hostage to their nuclear weapons programme through a deliberate policy of economic dependency. They have created a fear that political sovereignty will result in economic and social disaster. Certainly France pours millions of francs into Tahiti-Polynesia each year but, according to Oscar Temaru:

All the money that the French government is putting into this country goes towards the French administration, the French military presence, French enterprises. They are taking the money back to France. (Temaru, in conversation with dé Ishtar, Papeete, 1995)

Tahiti's development over the past thirty years benefits the French minority and tightens their hold over the nation, Oscar Temaru claims: 'The French ... have implanted an economic structure where the Maohi are at the bottom and the French and Chinese are at the top' (dé Ishtar, 1994: 202).

The resumption of the nuclear tests stirred increasing numbers of Maohi people to turn away from France and demand their sovereignty. Clarisa Lucas reflects the sentiments felt by many other Maohi:

Polynesians are beginning to talk big for France to go. I believe in that. The French are saying, 'You Polynesians can't govern your country. We French know how to do that.' So now I say, 'Go away French! Go away!' We don't need French. They can go back. If they want to think French, eat French, do French, then they can go back – quickly. If they say that this is a free country, that this is Polynesia, then they can stay. But we need to decide what we need for our country. (Lucas, in conversation with dé Ishtar, Papeete, 1995)

Drawing on their recent history as a self-sufficient society many Maohi believe that they can provide for themselves. Oscar Temaru explains that, while it will not be easy, it is possible:

We know we are going to have problems for the first few years but we are very hopeful. We are only 150,000 people, we have a hundred and thirty islands and the biggest ocean ... We can see what we can do with our ocean. We can build fisheries here. Our ocean is used by the Japanese and Koreans, we can sell our fish ourselves. We can educate our people in animal husbandry. We can farm. And we have tourism. At the moment the money goes to foreign investors but we can do it in a way that is good for our people. Bring in just enough foreign currency so we can develop our country. (dé Ishtar, 1994: 202)

Responding to the legacy of resistance left them by their ancestors, the Maohi people are prepared to fight for their freedom. They are keen to regain their human rights through peaceful means but France does not intend to give up the islands easily. Marguerite Tetunaui warns:

For every country France gives back there is always war before freedom. I am from a political party that says, 'No war.' We don't want war. Our Queen Pomare IV said she will never want Tahitian blood, never, and we want to keep that. No blood. Maybe they will kill us. We don't know. We try for peace. (Tetunaui, in conversation with dé Ishtar, Papeete, 1995)

France has announced that there will be no further nuclear tests at Moruroa and Fangataufa but it has broken this promise before. Only when the Maohi regain their inalienable right to govern their lives and their lands, can we rest assured that the fragile Tuamotu atolls will never again quake with a nuclear explosion. As Marguerite Tetunaui warns: 'There is one very simple way to stop the French nuclear testing in Moruroa. It is to ask for the independence of our country' (Tetunaui, in conversation with dé Ishtar, Papeete, 1995).

It is essential that those of us who live outside Tahiti-Polynesia continue our vigilance and active support for the Maohi people. For, as Roti Tehaevra says, we are all a part of this nightmare:

The nuclear test is not only for us here. It is for all the people all around the world. If one government should drop a nuclear bomb in the village it is not only that village that is contaminated, the atmosphere is contaminated. So the whole world will suffer from this contamination. So we don't have to sleep. We have to prevent that no more happens like in Hiroshima and Nagasaki. (Tehaevra, in conversation with dé Ishtar, Papeete, 1995)

Note

In memory and honour of Darlene Keju-Johnson of the Marshall Islands and Marguerite Tetunaui of Tahiti-Polynesia. Both women gave so much, inspiring people around the world in their demand for justice for their people and us all. Both died from cancer, a direct result of nuclear testing.

References

Connelly, F. Grant, S.J. Cohn and F. Willard. 1987. *Pacific Paradise Nuclear Nightmare.* London: Women for a Nuclear Free and Independent Pacific and Campaign for Nuclear Disarmament.
dé Ishtar, Zohl. 1994. *Daughters of the Pacific.* Melbourne: Spinifex Press.
Francke, L. 1985. 'The Pacific Need for Peace.' *Sanity, Voice of CND*, May, vol. 5: 28–31. London: Campaign for Nuclear Disarmament.
Mills, S., J. Miles, M. Helmer, and S. Kouwenberg. 1990. *Testimonies, Witnesses of French Nuclear Testing in the South Pacific.* Greenpeace International.
Moorehead, A.1987. *The Fatal Impact: The Brutal and Tragic Story of how the South Pacific was 'Civilized' 1767–1840.* Harmondsworth: Penguin Books.
Tetunaui, Marguerite. 1995. Unpublished paper to the Fourth World Conference on Women, Beijing, 1995.
Women Working for a Nuclear Free and Independent Pacific. 1987. *Pacific Women Speak: Why Haven't You Known?* Bristol: Greenline.

10

Women and Fundamentalism in Iran

Haideh Moghissi

There is much debate and disagreement among scholars in the field about the legitimacy of the use of the term fundamentalism to identify the Islamic populist political movements in the Middle East. Given the Western- and Christian-derived origins of the term, and the fact that the Islamists themselves do not refer to themselves as fundamentalists, some prefer to use terms such as Islamic revivalism, Islamic resurgence or, simply, Islamism. But I am convinced by the writings of such scholars as Henry Monson, Aziz Al-Azmeh and particularly Jalal Al-Azm, that we can use 'fundamentalism' to refer to religious and political movements which, in Jalal Al-Azm's words, proclaim 'their determination to subjugate all aspects and areas of human life – social, economic, political, cultural, scientific, aesthetic, domestic, personal, etc. – to the will of God as manifested either in Islam and Shari`a Law on the one hand, or in Christianity and Biblical Law on the other'.[1] When it comes to women's social status, fundamentalists of all shapes and creeds, despite their (sometimes much publicized) differences and incompatibilities, have set for themselves the same God-given mission to revitalize gendered religious dogma as prescribed by holy texts. This fact, in itself, makes the use of 'fundamentalism' in the Islamic context justified.

In Iran, the sharp edge of fundamentalism was pointed towards women. Women became the first target of Islamic law and order from the start; they have borne the brunt of the regime's heavy-handedness in its reislamization project. The situation of women in Iran, the political struggle for and over women's rights, have been the subject of much investigation since the 1980s.[2] More recent studies of gender relations and women's life under Islamic rule focus, characteristically, on the compromises made in favour of women by the Islamic regime, particularly in the areas of women's access to education, employment and Family Law.

Central to these studies are the activities of a group of Muslim women, both inside and outside the Islamic power bloc, as promoters of these changes.[3] These studies are one-sided. The situation of women in Iran cannot be analysed in isolation from the experience of the rest of society. The balance sheet on the Islamic state is not encouraging, be it in protecting the rights of religious minorities, promoting economic justice and the accountability of the state, fostering democratic participation and a free press, guarding civil liberties or in allowing the expression of cultural difference. These are things that many studies of women's rights in Iran have difficulty seeing. Hence, the celebratory accounts of what women have managed to regain from the state, by way of their educational and employment status are, at best, unwarranted. In any case, concessions were achieved only after a hard fight.

In this chapter, I will argue that when we look at reislamization in the area of women's rights, and women's responses to them, we see that changes in material conditions which sparked off the determined resistance of women have forced certain compromises on the Islamic state. However, by looking more closely at the gender politics of the Islamic government and its consequences for women, I will argue that the extent of changes favourable to women, and, particularly, the role of Muslim women within the power bloc in advancing women's rights and status in Iran, should not be exaggerated.

The Advent of Fundamentalism and Reislamization Policy

Only four weeks into the revolution, Ayatollah Khomeini's statement on the veil, ordering working women to cover up, came down on secular, unveiled women.[4] The aims of reveiling were clear: veiled women, as the symbolic representation of Islamic order, signified the establishment of the Islamic state and the sovereignty of the Muslim community, *ummat*. For the women who took to the streets to protest against the Ayatollah's order, this message only confirmed the rumours they had heard – that the fundamentalists planned to abrogate all legal and social reforms of the pre-Khomeini era. The rising tide of fundamentalism was to sweep away the hard-won achievements of the previous decades in women's legal and social status. It planned to enfeeble women's presence in public life, denying women access to education and employment.

In the face of women's forceful demonstrations, protests, sit-ins, and work stoppages the regime retreated on the issue of veiling; but this proved to be only a temporary retreat.[5] A year later, in the summer of 1980, when the Islamic regime had firmly established itself in power through intimidation, silencing and brutal suppression of the opposition, it started its march towards the desecularization of society.[6] This was to be achieved through reinstitution of Shari`a as the basis of the personal status laws and the enforcement of the Islamic moral code. Women were forcefully pushed under the veil, from which they had been forcefully pulled out by a modernizing state some forty years earlier. Reveiling was followed by an onslaught in all areas of women's personal, legal and social rights.

Combined with legal rulings, clerical decrees and statements, and state policies and practices to control the women's movement and limit life choices signalled the clerics' intention to make Iran the bastion of 'the true Islam'. The creation of 'Islamic' institutions such as the Morality Police and the cleric-run Marriage Institutions (designed particularly to facilitate temporary marriage, *Mut`a*),[7] left no room for doubt as to the pressing priorities and main preoccupations of fundamentalist rulers. Their priority was the moral purification of society via the purification of the mind and body of female citizens, removing women from the evils of modern values and autonomous modes of life. The preoccupation of the Islamists with women's personal morality and social conduct stemmed from the idea that women have a pernicious seductive power which endangers Muslim social order. Women's sexuality had to be confined and tamed, and their moral conduct controlled for the good of the community.

The consequences were immediate. Suspension of the Family Protection Act re-established men's control over women's lives in the family. The legal marriage age for girls was lowered to thirteen, later to nine. Technical and vocational schools were closed to girls. With their exclusion from mixed schools, girls in rural areas were deprived of even a few years of elementary schooling. Women were banned from certain fields of higher education, such as engineering, agriculture and mathematical science. By 1985, women were banned from 91 areas of specialization offered by institutions of higher education.[8] Women jurists were sacked. Women were removed from managerial positions. Hundreds of female professionals, teachers and government employees were purged, pressured into early retirement or coerced to quit their jobs.

The clutches of the clerics were soon felt on every aspect of the lives of women (and men). The Morality Police had the authority to check cars for signs of alcohol consumption or audiotapes of 'corrupting' music, and to control public places to search for violations of Islamic moral codes. The police arrested couples on the streets and in restaurants if they could not provide proof of marriage or kinship, or if the woman did not conform to the rules for *hejab* (veil or veiling). The police raided wedding celebrations or parties in private homes to ensure compliance with Islamic codes of dress and conduct.

Women, however, not only did not give in to the pressures, but found new ways to deal with them. In a sense, reislamization policies produced effects quite the opposite of what was hoped for by the Islamists. Rising to the challenge from the fundamentalists, Iranian women responded creatively to policies designed to enforce domesticity and male-defined Muslim womanhood.

Women's resistance against reislamization policies centred, above all, on holding out against pressures. Women struggled to hold on to their jobs, despite despicable new measures in the workplace. They fought to enter new professional and artistic activities that were not taken up before by women. The advent of a few female film-makers, television camera-women, and one or two female taxi-drivers in Tehran, are cases in point. The jealously won success of professional women, female artists, and female students in university entrance examinations speaks loudly of women's perseverance and resistance to fundamentalist Islamization projects.[9]

The outbreak of war with Iraq in September 1980 also produced contradictory influences on the state's gender politics and women's quest for their rights. War efforts silenced challenges to Khomeini's authority and gave the Islamic regime a new legitimacy and support, chilling open resistance by the opposition, including resistance from secular women. Khomeini's repeated reference to the war as God-given and a blessing must be understood in this light. However, war, and particularly the migration of hundreds of thousands of skilled workers and professionals, slowed the process of replacing women employees and professionals with men. Massive war efforts forced the use of women's volunteer and paid labour. For political and military expediency, rigid Islamic rules and ideals surrounding female domesticity and seclusion had to be relaxed.

At the same time, reislamization policies created coercive apparatuses which required female labour. To oversee adherence to Islamic codes of dress and conduct, a select group of Muslim women, recruited mostly from the households of war casualties and martyrs, were assigned to all-female morality squads and to the Islamic Associations of government and semi-government agencies. Women were required for the Pasdaran Corps, the Society for Islamic Propaganda (*Howzeh-ye Tablighat-e Eslami*), the Martyrs' Foundation (*Bonyaad-e Shahid*) and neighbourhood Mosques – all charged with a strong mandate to disseminate Islamic values through indoctrination and intimidation.

These realities are reflected in official statistics. Women's representation in public-sector employment increased from 16 per cent of total government employees in 1976 to 29.2 per cent in 1986, with 70 per cent of women workers concentrated in education.[10] The size of this increase is inflated since the first statistic dates from 1976, three years prior to the revolution. Also, the increased need for female teachers parallels the increase in school-age children, reflecting the post-revolutionary population explosion. Nevertheless it is clear that, demographics aside, the policy of sexual segregation in schools, the university, social services, and the healthcare system necessitated further education, training and employment of young women.

The state's educational and employment policies and their impact on women cannot be analysed in isolation from the long-term goals of the Islamists and their Islamization agenda. At the top on this agenda is sexual apartheid in the production and use of knowledge and the channelling of women's professional and paid activities towards occupations where women predominate and whose value, in consequence, is taken to be less. Intimately joined to this project is the use of educational institutions and the state bureaucracy to promote Islamic moral values and ideological concerns. Not seeing the ideological side of the state policy on women may lead to a misunderstanding of new developments in these areas.

For example, the number of female entrants to medical schools increased sharply, so that women came to constitute 50 per cent of students enrolled in medicine in institutions of higher education. The increase in numbers and the more balanced female/male ratio in medical schools reflect partly the expansion of existing medical schools and the creation of new ones, trebling the number from 8 in 1978 to 30 in 1992.[11] Despite the massive exodus of full-time faculty after the revolution, the number of medical students multiplied six-fold from 5,000 to 32,000 for the same period. Yet women's concentration in obstetrics-gynaecology (now closed to male students), pediatrics and family medicine, and women's virtual exclusion from medicine's technical frontiers such as neurology,[12] all exemplify the ideologization of female education and employment and the unremitting commitment to segregation in the workforce. The formation of the Unit of Sisters' Affairs (*Vahed-e Omour-e Khaharan*) in the much publicized Islamic Open University (*Daneshgah-e Azad-e eslami*) is one of the many examples of how the primary task of female-centred institutions and offices is to serve the gender politics of the state, rather than the promotion of higher education for women. The unit has representatives in 110 campuses established by the Open University. The goal of advancing the cause of women's education, however, does not seem to be the first priority of the unit. Among its major responsibilities are presenting Islamic role models to female students and establishing marriage centres (*Kanoon-e Ezdevaj*) for girls and boys who cannot find suitable partners to marry.[13]

This is not to deny that the increase in women's public presence at school and work will be in the interests of Iranian women in the long run. Despite its holy war against secular values, clerical gender politics pertaining to women embody unplanned and unsought for elements of change favourable to women. But these advances, selective as they are, are beset by contradictions, paradoxes and complications which became even more tenacious after 1988. In the wake of the Iraqi war and

Khomeini's death, further compromises were imposed on the Islamic state.

Tactical Changes in the Islamization Project

The war ended without the victory promised by the Ayatollah. The ensuing economic crisis, rising unemployment and factional strife within the power bloc heightened the general population's disenchantment with the Islamic regime. Postwar social, economic and political conditions increased popular demands which had been suppressed and silenced during the war under the pretext that all resources had to be channelled into the war effort. The continuing resistance of women and Iranian youth, expressed in their defiance of Islamic moral and dress codes, brought home to the clerical rulers and their advisers that they could no longer rely on physical and ideological coercion to mobilize support.

The reislamization of gender relations and the reshaping of women's rights according to a more uncompromising interpretation of the Shari`a also had to be revisited. The policies formulated and executed by the state since 1988 were primarily aimed at confining and controlling the demands for change which were expressed by Iranian women and youth in many different ways. Men of power in Iran were alarmed. Understanding 'anti-imperialism' as a cultural war against Western values, the ruling clerics were particularly unnerved by the defiance of women and youth, their disconcerting apathy towards 'Islamic principles and values'. For the speaker of the previous *Majlis* (parliament), the apathetic and the antagonistic attitude of women and youth was *the* major problem faced by Iranian society.[14] The resocialization policy was meant to complement coercive measures, to win back the youth, who, according to a report produced by the Social and Psychological Research Centre of the President's Office, 'had become morally vulnerable. Linking all political-social contradictions and shortcomings to religion', the report said, 'they demonstrate defiance and disobedience'.[15] The state launched an ideological offensive to eliminate subversive voices among women and to win the support of the younger female population.

The Islamists' new ideological onslaught took many forms, including a more extensive programme of indoctrination and resocialization, aiming at creating a new value system and aspirations for the young female population. The Islamists hoped to capture the young generation on the premise that, according to Khomeini, the older generation had been corrupted by the Shah's regime and his modernization programmes. The effort included regular discussions of gender issues and man/woman's relationships at Friday prayers, in both Tehran and in provincial towns, and the organization of seminars, congresses and conferences to diffuse Islamic values relating to women's personal and social lives. 'Islamic' traditions and special days were invented to celebrate and disseminate notions of Islamic womanhood, including Islamic Mother's Day and Women's Day. In the schools, Celebration of Puberty (*Jashn-e Taklif*), was introduced for nine-year-old girls. According to the Shari`a girls reach womanhood at nine and can be married off.

The education system was much used to help in political and cultural resocialization. The official school curriculum was restructured to include courses on Islamic morality at every level of schooling, from kindergarten to university – a policy which started immediately after the revolution. Now every field of higher education, from humanities and social sciences to mathematics and medicine, includes courses on Islamic principles and morality. The elementary and high-school textbooks were reviewed and rewritten in accordance with official state gender politics. This included, for instance, reducing the presence of female characters in the textbooks, emphasizing women's wifely and motherly roles and their domestic responsibilities.[16] Other practices accompanying this approach included the annual Competition for Citation of the Quran, and the organization of female militia (*basiji*) in schools to oversee compliance with the Islamic code.[17]

The reislamization and resocialization policy included the formation of a number of female-centred offices, committees and commissions within the state bureaucracy, such as the Bureau for Women's Affairs, Women's Cultural and Social Council, Women's Commissions in the Ministry of Internal Affairs and the Women's Bureau of International Propaganda in the Ministry of Foreign Affairs. Various non-governmental groups were funded by the state, including the Society of Women of the Islamic Republic and Women's Section of the Society for Islamic Propaganda (*Howzeh-ye Tablighat-e Eslami*). To carry the torch, a group of trusted Muslim women were recruited from the homes of powerful clergymen, such as the daughter and daughter-in law of Ayatollah Khomeini; the daughters of Ayatollah Yazdi, the Chief Justice, of the deceased Ayatollah Dastghaib, of Ayatollah Khazali, member of the powerful Guardianship Council, and of President Rafsanjani. To these were added widows or mothers of Martyrs of the Revolution, such as the deputy Maryam Behroozi, former deputy Aateghe Rajaii and Nafiseh Fayyazbakhsh. This group was to present a new role model to the Iranian female population and to reshape social consciousness in favour of the status quo ante.

We need to understand what the Islamic state was facing. The Islamization policy has come up against the forces of change, which, once set in motion, could not be reversed. This is one of the clearly observable paradoxes of the revolution. Modernization under the Shah disenchanted the Iranian people and helped instigate the revolution which brought the clergy to power. But the fact that the people had tasted the impact of modernization blocked the ruling clergy, obstructing their efforts to establish a utopian Islamic order and to reconstruct Islamic gender roles. Decades of capitalist development, industrialization, consumerism, and the associated impact of the market economy, had irreversibly altered the lives of many women (and men), and given rise to a more relaxed gender interaction. These changes could be lamented, assaulted, outlawed, prohibited; but they could not be undone.

The economic and social changes of the pre-revolutionary period provided many women, including those from the lower middle classes, with access to education and to some forms of paid work. The younger generation, growing up under 'Islamic' rule, expected the same. Economic conditions were even more compelling than women's aspirations. The Islamists could hope for the replacement of secular women with trusted, practising Muslims, ideologically 'transformed' women, or women who simply managed to pass the formal ideological tests necessary for entry into university or government employment. But 'cleansing' the public sphere and state institutions by expelling women and returning them to the home was no longer a plausible goal.

Having said all this, two points are important to note here. The mere presence of 'working' women in the state bureaucracy, educational institutions and industry can represent, perhaps, a partial defeat for the ultra-orthodox Islamists, who hoped for the establishment of gendered Islamic law and order through an absolute de-womanization of public life. By itself, however, women's presence in the workplace does not represent a fundamental retreat by the regime on those issues which might compromise Islamic principles pertaining to women's personal and social rights and obligations. The example of the new Family Law enacted by the Islamic regime should help clarify the limits (and possibilities) of the new situation. Timid and ineffectual as it is, the new Family Law demonstrates the impossibility of effecting meaningful change in women's status within the confines of the present Islamic state.

Woman's Non-personhood Status in the Family Law

After the Shah's downfall, one of the first 'revolutionary' decisions made by Ayatollah Khomeini was the abolition of the Family Protection Act (FPA). After years of campaigning by Iranian feminists, heated debates over various proposals, and long hesitation by the state, the FPA was finally passed by the *Majlis* in 1967; but it did not annul the most discriminatory articles of the civil code taken from the Shari`a, as had been proposed by the Association of Women Lawyers. The proposal which was defeated included, for example, the prohibition of polygamy and temporary marriage, equal rights in divorce, custody and the guardianship of children, equality of rights in inheritance and women's rights to sustenance after divorce and to work outside the home – all of which would have represented a break from the Shari`a on the issues of women's personal status. The draft passed by the *Majlis* tried to modify some of the articles of the civil code, but without removing men's authority and prerogatives over women. The highlights of the Act, which caused strong opposition from the clergy at the time, dealt with divorce and child custody. Under the FPA, divorce, previously a unilateral right of men, and the custody of children, previously the non-negotiable right of the father for boys over two and girls over seven, were now made conditional on the Family Courts' decision.[18] But even these modest reforms infuriated the Muslim clergy, particularly Khomeini, who condemned the Act as a ploy of foreigners and the government to interfere with the explicit words of God and the sacred Islamic texts.[19]

The suspension of the Family Protection Act, however, was perhaps the only demonstrably male-serving decision by the Islamic state which negatively affected women of all classes. The destructive consequences of this decision for women were primarily appreciated and first picked up by secular feminist activists and the left and liberal women's organizations who were active after the revolution. In a couple of years, however, when the devastating consequences of the Ayatollah's decision started to surface, the Muslim female elites, and particularly state-sponsored women's journals, started their campaign for fairer family legislation. Focusing on the destructive results of men's unrestricted and unconditional legal rights over women, they reported on specific cases, individual women's life histories and relevant news items, and interviewed Muslim women who had become more vocal on the subject, particularly after the Ayatollah's death. The activities of the Muslim female elite were fuelled also by the influx of complaints by war widows, who under Shari`a law were denied custody of their children, and by reports on the skyrocketing rate of divorce (up to 200 per cent in Tehran over only one decade), as discussed in the *Majlis*.[20] Particularly alarming was the increase in the number of violent crimes committed against women, further reducing their sense of security and self-worth, and the growth in suicides and the self-burning of mothers with three, four or eight children, in Tehran as well as in remote villages and provincial towns.[21]

Despite these alarming reports, political pressure and the imperative need for new legislation, enactment of new legislation took several years and did not materialize during the Ayatollah's lifetime. The new law eventually passed in 1992. Like the pre-revolutionary Family Protection Act, it made divorce subject to court approval, with both partners having the right to institute divorce proceedings. In cases where the husband's decision to divorce his wife was found to be unjustified and without acceptable excuse, he had to pay her for labour in the matrimonial home. But the new law kept silent about polygamy and temporary marriage; and a divorced wife still was not entitled to alimony beyond the three months and ten days waiting period (*Eddeh*) that she has to observe before re-marrying.[22]

The Islamic legislation is sometimes presented as a law offering 'women more protection than had been afforded by the Shah's Family Code'.[23] Such a statement, however, is at best uninformed. Enactment of the new legislation is a positive step in the context of the many backward steps taken after the Revolution. But Islamic family law also represents the limits of reforms that are achievable within an Islamic framework. The limits of the new law represent, in fact, the limits of social creativity that can be furnished by the guardians of Shari`a. It shows as nothing else their stubborn, and, indeed, self-defeating resistance in an area that most desperately requires change, that is women's rights (or lack of rights) in the family. Indeed, the conservative clergy in the Council of the Guardians (*Shouray-e Negahban*), which oversees the consistency of all the legislation ratified by the *Majlis* with the Islamic Shari`a, circumscribed meaningful reforms and the extent of effective change in favour of women in family law. The right of women to custody of children (*Hezant*), for example, if granted, does not include guardianship (*Velayat*), which remains the non-negotiable right of the father and the paternal grandfather in case of the father's death. This was a regression from the Family Protection Act, as amended in 1975, granting women guardianship of their children. The 1975 law also tried to limit polygamy by making it conditional on the first wife's permission. Moreover, the man's remarriage was one of the grounds that entitled the woman to institute divorce proceedings.[24]

Indeed, the new law, by keeping silent on polygamy and temporary marriage, encourages these practices. The encouragement of temporary marriage promotes the notion of women as a disposable commodity which can be discarded after consumption. The consequences for women from poor classes in rural areas has already been recorded. A report by the General Director of Imam Khomeini's Aid Committees (*Komitehay-e Emdad-e Emam Khomeini*), for example, gives accounts of thousands of girls from poor families who were sold in the Khorasan province for a cheap price, and many more thousands who were 'married' off to Afghan refugees, without registration or any proper criterion and who have been deserted by their 'husbands' in Mashhad and around the borders with Afghanistan.[25]

Other regressive legislation such as the Islamic Law of Retribution (*Qisas*), by setting a price on human life, giving women's life half the value of men's,[26] has boosted violence against women. The unprecedented increase in the number of women in Iran who have been murdered under the pretext of defending 'family honour' has alarmed even Iranian officials. According to a report, 'many women and girls live in constant fear for their lives', simply because, as stated by Chief Justice Ayatollah Yazdi, 'some men murder their wives or daughters on slight suspicion and then are easily set free by paying a very low sum of compensation [blood] money (*dieh*) to the family of the victim'.[27] These murders have caused so much concern, particularly in the Southern province of Khusistan, that the Chief Justice had to instruct the courts not to free the murderers without proper investigation.

What the Chief Justice is not prepared to admit, however, is that this situation cannot be blamed only on lower culture or the deviant character of the men who resort to these crimes. It is part and parcel of a value system, promoted by the Islamists who see women as men's possessions. In this view, purification of the woman's body and soul is a religious and political duty for the individual man, and, by extension, for the Islamic state. By the same token, when moral rules are perceived to have been broken, the man has the obligation (and therefore the justification) to punish the rule-breaker. The violent solution is bound up in the fundamental inequality assumed (and enforced) between women and men.

Conclusion

The rise of Islamic fundamentalism has had immediate and devastating consequences for women. By giving male-serving cultural practices a divine character, fundamentalist rule has removed further the possibility for women to enjoy full citizenship status in their own country, that is, equality before the law and equality in the law. By revitalizing misogynist, brutal medieval traditions, such as stoning women to death on charges of extra-marital relationships, fundamentalists celebrate and promote violence against women. The repercussions of the cultural and religious values promoted by the Islamists are felt in every area of women's personal and social life.

On the surface, and if only the day-to-day reality of women's life is taken into consideration, the prognosis for women may not look very promising. I would argue, however, that the most hopeful indication of change is women themselves – women who refuse to accept the clerical definition of womanhood and prescribed gender roles. The continued resistance of women to *Hejab*, leading to the humiliation, arrest and torture of hundreds of women each year – is a case in point. The unresolvable socio-cultural contradictions, economic demands and political conflicts which have engulfed the Islamic Republic of Iran multiply the potential effectiveness of women's resistance to fundamentalism. Amidst brutal and unmasked violations of women's basic human rights by the Islamists, women's determination to resist is the surest sign that despite the strongest obstacles put in the way, change must come eventually.

Notes

1. For an enlightening discussion of the subject see Sadik J. Al-Azm 1993 and 1994, 'Islamic fundamentalism reconsidered: a critical outline of problems, ideas and approaches', Part I and II, in *South Asia Bulletin*, vol. XIII, nos 1 & 2 and vol. XIV, no. 1 See also Aziz Al-Azmeh, *Islams and Modernities,* London: Verso, 1993; and Henry Munson, Jr, 'Intolerable tolerance: Western academia and Islamic fundamentalism', *Contention*, vol. 5, no. 3, Spring 1996.

2. Among many studies on the women's social and legal status in Iran, their participation in the revolution and the post-revolutionary events pertaining to women, see H. Afshar, 'Khomeini's teachings and their implications for women', *Feminist Review*, 12, October 1982; F. Azari (ed.), *Women of Iran: The Conflict with Fundamentalist Islam,* London: Ithaca Press, 1983; M. Afkhami, 'Iran: a future in the past; the pre-revolutionary women's movement', in R. Morgan (ed.), *Sisterhood is Global,* Garden City, NY: Anchor Press/Doubleday, 1984; B. Bamdad, *From Darkness into Light: Women's Emancipation in Iran,* Hicksville, NY: Exposition Press, 1977; M. Bayat-Philip, 'Women and revolution in Iran', in L. Beck and N. Keddie (eds), *Women in the Muslim World*, Boston, MA: Harvard University Press, 1978; F. Milani, *Veils and Words: The Emerging Voices of Iranian Women Writers*, Syracus: Syracus University Press, 1992; H. Moghissi, 'Women, modernization and revolution in Iran', *Review of Radical Political Economics*, vol. 23, nos 2 & 3, Fall and Winter 1991; E. Sanasarian, *The Women's Rights Movement in Iran; Mutiny, Appeasement, and Repression from 1900 to Khomeini,* New York: Praeger Publishers, 1983; A. Tabari and N. Yaganeh, *In the Shadow of Islam: The Women's Movement in Iran,* London: Zed Books, 1982.

3. For such analysis, for example, see Patricia Higgins, 'Women in the Islamic Republic of Iran: legal, social, and ideological changes', *Sign: Journal of Women in Cultures and Society*, vol. 10, no. 31, 1985; Valentine Moghadam, 'Women, work and ideology in the Islamic Republic of Iran', *International Journal of Middle East Studies*, vol. 20, 1988; Nesta Ramazani, 'Women in Iran: The revolutionary ebb and flow' *Middle East Journal*, vol. 47, no. 3, Summer 1993; Homa Hoodfar, 'The veil in their minds and on our heads: the resistance of colonial images of Muslim women', *Resources for Feminist Research,* vol. 22, no. 3/4, 1993; Shahla Haeri, 'On feminism and fundamentalism in Iran and Pakistan', *Contention*, vol. 4, no. 3, Spring 1995; Parvin Paidar, 'Feminism and Islam in Iran', in Deniz Kandiyoti (ed.), *Gendering the Middle East: Emerging Perspectives*, Syracuse: Syracuse University Press, 1996; Nayereh Tohidi, 'Modernity, Islamization, and women in Iran', in V. Moghadam (ed.), *Gender and National Identity: Women and Politics in Muslim Societies,* London: Zed Books, 1994; and Haleh Afshar, 'Women and politics of fundamentalism in Iran', *Women Against Fundamentalism*, vol.1, no. 5, 1994.

4. *Keyhan*, 16 Esfand 1357/February 1979.

5. For an account of the events following Ayatollah Khomeini's pronouncement on veiling, women's response to it and the position of various secular political parties on the issue see my book *Populism and Feminism in Iran: Women's Struggle in a Male-defined Revolutionary Movement,* London: Macmillan, 1996. See also A. Tabari and N. Yaganeh, *In the Shadow of Islam: The Women's Movement in Iran,* London: Zed Books, 1982.

6. For an illuminating account of political events in the first few months after the revolution see A. Rahnema and F. Nomani, *The Secular Miracle*, London: Zed Books, 1990.

7. *Mut`a* or temporary marriage, a pre-Islamic custom, is a verbal contract between a man and a woman, who is *hired* to be the man's wife, for a fixed pay and a fixed period. *Mut`a* contract does not require divorce procedures and the man and the woman part when the contract is expired or when the man so wishes, that is, if he relinquishes his rights to the remaining period of the contract. *Mut`a* was forbidden after the Prophet's death. The practice, however, has been carried on through centuries in Shiite Iran. While *Mut`a* is essentially an easy and cheap means for sexual gratification, and it is widely considered a form of legal prostitution in Iran, it has also served other purposes in the past. For example, since any close contact and socialization between men and women, outside marriage, was prohibited except among immediate family members, the *Mut`a* contract was sometimes used to make the non-sexual contact and friendship religiously and culturally acceptable. On the institution of *Mut`a* see S. Haeri, *Law of Desire; The Temporary Marriage in Shii Iran,* New York: Syracuse University Press, 1989.

8. See Shahrzad Mojab, 'Education and human rights: Iran', in John Daniel et al. (eds), *Academic Freedom 3; Education and Human Rights,* World University Service, London: Zed Books, 1995; Sahar Qahraman, 'Siyasat-e Hokumat-e Islami Piramune-e Zanan be Amusesh-e Aali' (The Policy of the Islamic Government on Women's Higher Education), *Nimeh Digar,* 7, Summer 1994.

9. I have discussed this in more detail in 'Women and public life', in Saeed Rahnema and Sohrab Behdad (eds), *Iran After the Revolution: Crisis of an Islamic State,* London: I.B. Tauris, 1995.

10. Statistical Centre of Iran, *The Statistical Yearbook,* 1369 (1990) pp. 71, 75.

11. Asghar Rastegar, 'Health policy and medical eduction', in Rahnema and Behdad (eds), *Iran After the Revolution,* pp. 222–3. Rastegar demonstrates that the Islamic government's policy of mass production of university graduates in the field of healthcare has been carried out without much regard for the quality of the education. For example, the massive increase in the number of medical students means a higher professor–student ratio and lower quality of teaching, where only half of the university faculty have doctoral degrees.

12. *Zan-e Rooz,* no. 1330, 22 September 1991.

13. *Zan-e Rooz,* no. 1136, 13 October 1994.

14. *Iran Times,* 19 August 1993.

15. *Iran Times,* no. 1043, 8 October 1991.

16. Golnar Mehran, 'The creation of the new Muslim women: female education in the Islamic Republic of Iran', *Convergence,* International Council for Adult Education, XXIV/4, 1991.

17. *Iran Times,* no. 1130, 28 September 1993.

18. On the FPA see F.R.C. Bagley, 'The Iranian Family Protection Law of 1967: A milestone in the advance of women's rights', in C.F. Bosworth (ed.), *Iran and Islam: in Memory of the Late Vladimir Minorsky,* Edinburgh: Edinburgh University Press, 1971.

19. Ministry of Culture and Islamic Guidance, *Simaay-e Zn dar Kalam-e Imam Khomeini* (Image of women in speeches of Imam Khomeini), Tehran: Ministry of Culture and Islamic Guidance, 1988, pp. 133, 169–70.

20. *Zan-e Rooz,* 15 December 1989. See also 'Women and personal status law in Iran: an interview with Mehrangiz Kar', *Middle East Report,* vol. 26, no. 198 (January–March 1996). Kar, an Iranian female lawyer and an advocate of women's rights in Iran, notes the role of the Martyrs' Foundation, which does advocacy work for the families of the war dead, in pushing for amendment in the Family Law. The

foundation's move was in support of its constituency, that is, young women who had lost their husbands in the Iran–Iraq war as well as the custody of their children.

21. *Zan-e Rooz*, no. 1351, 8 December 1991.

22. *Zan-e Rooz*, no. 1414, 25 June 1993.

23. See Hoodfar, 'The veil in their minds and on our heads: the persistence of colonial images of Muslim women', *Resources for Feminist Research,* vol. 22, no. 3/4, 1993, p. 12.

24. Mahnaz Afkhami, *Women and the Law in Iran (1967–1978)* (Hoquq-e Zan Dar Iran), Women's Center of the Foundation for Iranian Studies, 1994, pp. 351–60.

25. *Iran Times*, no. 1051, 23 December 1992.

26. G. Hojjati Ashrafi, 1375/1996. *The Law of Islamic Retribution* (Ghanoon-e Mojazat-e Eslami), Tehran: Ganj-e Danesh Publishing House, article 300, p. 41.

27. *Zan-e Rooz*, no. 1415, 3 July 1993.

Part IV

Sexualized Slaveries

11

The 'Comfort Women' System during World War II: Asian Women as Targets of Mass Rape and Sexual Slavery by Japan

Nelia Sancho

She hated for the night to come and started crying when Japanese soldiers came into her room, knowing they would rape her. Some of the soldiers visited and raped her repeatedly. Some were waiting on vacant beds for their turn while she was being raped by another. (Tomasa Salinog, Filipino comfort woman)

Twenty tents were set up to serve as comfort houses. In front of those tents, servicemen stood in lines ... We served 20 to 30 men a day in those tents. When they thought I was not obedient enough, they slashed me with a sword at my right eye, beneath my forehead, the back of my neck and on my head. Even now, the scars from these wounds remain. (Kang Soon-Ae, Korean comfort woman)

Women were divided into groups of two or three. Each group occupied one tent ... They were alternately raped after dinner, from about nine o'clock. She does not remember if all the five men raped her because she fell asleep at night. The Japanese raped them in the daytime as well. Sometimes Villegas would awaken to the sobbing of her sister. They would embrace each other and cry. (Sabine Villegas, comfort woman)

One by one, they came out of a past, buried for fifty years by a conspiracy of silence and denial, shame and fear. These are their names: Rosa, Soon-Ae, Rufina, Yong-Sil, Ai-Hua, Cheng-Tze, Felicidad. And these are their stories.

One day in 1943, while passing a Japanese sentry in occupied Magalang town in Pampanga, the Philippines, Maria Rosa Luna Henson was stopped by Japanese soldiers and brought to their garrison. There she was held captive for six months, during which time she and six other Filipino women were raped by as many as 24 soldiers a day. There she got pregnant, lost the baby, caught malaria, got beaten with a bayonet. She was 15 years old (Testimony of Maria Rosa Henson, cited in *War Victimization and Japan*, 1993: 38).

Two years earlier, in Masan, South Kyongsang Province in Korea, Kang Soon-Ae returned from the market with her grandmother to find three Japanese soldiers in their home. They ordered her to come with them, promising her work. She was put in a ship, with other women, and brought to Palau Island, where she was put to work 'servicing' 20 to 30 and later as many as 50 to 60 soldiers a day. She was 14 (Testimony of Kang Soon-Ae, cited in *War Victimization and Japan*: 16).

More than fifty years after the end of World War II, Rosa and Soon-Ae and several hundred other Asian women, all survivors of the same crime, are still fighting their war to have these crimes known.

The Secret Crime

Before and during World War II, the Japanese Imperial Army set up a vast network of military brothels called 'comfort stations' throughout Asia, for the exclusive use of its soldiers in the invading armies (LILA-Filipina, 1993: 5).

To service these comfort stations, the army forcibly recruited an estimated 200,000 Chinese, Korean, Filipino, Malaysian, Indonesian and Dutch women and girls. The army used many means – women were violently taken from their homes, some literally from the arms of their fathers and mothers. They were rounded up in village raids and massacred after being made to witness the murders of their families; threatened at knifepoint; deceived and lured by the promise of legitimate jobs; conscripted for manual labour and then raped and forced into prostitution; captured while washing clothes in the river, gathering firewood, or just walking in the street. One girl was dragged from her home weeping, after seeing her father beheaded in front of her (Testimony of Tomasa Salinog, cited in *Philippine 'Comfort Women'*, 1993: 17).

Their ages varied, some had husbands and children, some were pregnant, some were barely more than children who had not begun menstruating. They were rich and poor, daughters, wives, sisters, mothers, nurses, students, workers. They all came to be known as *jugun ianfu* – 'comfort women'.

Jugun Ianfu

The case of the comfort women is the first and only case of government-institutionalized sexual slavery in the world's history of war (Mi-Gyeong, 1993: 9). Until the late 1980s, however, their existence has been largely left untold. This is not an oversight or an accident. The realities of sexual and racial discrimination, colonization and Japan's active suppression of the facts made certain that these crimes remained hidden.

The International Military Tribunal for the Far East, or the Tokyo

Tribunal as it came to be known, held at the close of World War II, focused solely on war crimes against prisoners of war and citizens of the United States and European nations. Likewise, reparations negotiated between the victorious Allied Forces and defeated Japan never touched on the issue of 'military comfort women'. The US, eager to consolidate its capitalist hold on Asia, gave Japan lenient terms in exchange for control over the country. Subsequently, in all the treaties that Japan signed with the Asian countries victimized by its war of aggression, the issue was never acknowledged (Yoshimi, 1993: 87). Given this complicity of silence on the issue, it is not surprising that no comfort woman survivor dared speak.

However, towards the end of the 1980s, several documents were found which brought the issue to light, and which, in turn, prompted the women's movement in Korea to investigate. Encouraged by this turn of events, in 1991 a former Korean comfort woman came forward, and for the very first time, gave voice to this silent suffering.

One voice was all it took. Women's movements all over Asia took up the cause and started the process of identifying the victims. In 1992, Maria Rosa Luna Henson of the Philippines heard a woman on the radio in her home in Pampanga, saying that they were looking for comfort women. Lola Rosa (Grandmother Rosa) still remembers what the woman said: 'Don't be shy, stand up, fight for your rights.' After hearing the appeal, made by the Task Force on Filipino comfort women for the second time, Lola Rosa decided to tell her story, and she became the first Filipina to identify herself as a victim. Within two and a half months, after she appeared at a press conference, 29 other Filipino women came forward to share similar experiences (*War Victimization and Japan,* 1993: 27). Elsewhere, Chinese, Taiwanese, Korean, Dutch and Indonesian women also broke their silence. Each woman told a different story, and yet the stories were the same. All spoke of their capture and captivity, of hate and humiliation, of pain and torture at the hands of the Japanese army.

In the Hands of the Japanese Army: The Comfort System

Direct, systematic, large-scale and brutal. These were the characteristics of the Japanese army's planning, establishment and management of the comfort system, as shown by official documents discovered.

Japanese military papers showed that the drafting of women, by what-ever means, to provide sexual services and satisfy the needs of Japanese soldiers, was an integral part of Japan's wartime policy and strategy. In the early 1930s, during Japan's incursion into Manchuria, and through the ensuing war with China, the existence of military comfort houses was confirmed in the recovered diary of General Okabe Naosaburo, Japanese

Consul in Shanghai. In 1937, after the Nanking incident – the mass rapes committed by Japanese soldiers, the Japanese military found the need to systematize the comfort system. Their reasons: to control the soldiers' behaviour and lessen the incidence of rape that increases tensions and resistance in the occupied territory; 'comfort' the soldiers, satisfy their sexual needs and keep up their morale; and prevent the spread of venereal disease among the soldiers (*Philippine 'Comfort Women'*, 1993: 36).

These, however, were the declared reasons. The hidden motives of the Japanese military were more insidious: raping and enslaving women to crush the spirit of the occupied populations, and subjugate and annihilate the Asian peoples whom the Japanese clearly felt were racially inferior.

In 1941, when World War II spread to Asia, the comfort women system became even more widespread; comfort houses were set up in all the occupied territories: China, Hong Kong, French-occupied Indochina, Malaysia, Singapore, British-occupied Borneo, the Dutch-occupied islands of Java, Sumbawa and Surwesi, Burma, the Pacific Islands of new Britain and Trobriand, the Philippines, as well as Okinawa and Ogasawara Islands in Japan (Yoshimi, 1993: 82). Wherever Japanese soldiers made war, they took women to rape and use as sex slaves.

A top-secret wartime diary taken from the camp of the Independent Infantry 35th Battalion, stationed in Manila during the war, outlined the regulations on comfort women. The 'Regulations of Authorized Restaurants and Comfort Stations in Manila', published by Lieutenant General Oonishi of the quartermaster corps in Manila, stated that there were 17 comfort stations for officers and soldiers, and about 1,064 'comfort women'. Four clubs for military officers also contained 119 comfort women (*Philippine 'Comfort Women'*, 1993: 9).

These documents, which include 14 kinds of forms submitted to the officer of supplies in Manila, make clear that the Japanese military ordered comfort stations to report on how the stations were being run. The Japanese military strictly regulated and supervised the comfort houses. It provided the buildings and locations for use as comfort stations, and it set detailed rules, rates, service hours, schedules for each unit and regulations for hygiene control. Military doctors routinely examined the women for venereal diseases.

While these documents point to the existence of comfort stations, they do not necessarily point to the fact that the women were forced to serve in these houses. For this, we have to look at the testimonies of the women themselves.

> Three Japanese soldiers and one Filipino came to our house. The Japanese were in uniform and military caps and carried bayonets. As they found me, they shouted 'Dalaga, dalaga' [Filipino word for young unmarried woman], and one of them tried to pull me by the arm. I tried hard to run towards my parents. The soldier, grabbing my arm, kicked my father so severely in the chest that he

could not move. The Japanese soldiers dragged me about one kilometre to Emanuel Hospital (which had been turned into a Japanese garrison). (Estelita Salas, Filipino comfort woman)

One day when I was eighteen years old, a Japanese man in a suit approached me and asked me to go with him, promising me a lucrative job. Judging it would be better than begging, in spite of my ignorance of the job, I followed him to a place where a dozen girls were already gathered. From there, we were driven by truck to the Hoeryong railway station. We boarded a train at the station, and after travelling for some time, arrived at Chonkhak-Dong, Kyonghung County (now known as Undok County) in North Hamgyong Province. A half hour drive by truck brought us to a valley. There we found ten or more girls, aged 17 to 18. Also among them were young girls no more than 15 years old. I asked them 'What place is this?' They answered, 'Why did you come here when you are not allowed to get out alive?' (Kim Yong-Sil, Korean comfort woman)

At the end of the war, with the Japanese defeated and the soldiers on the run, women were simply abandoned. Some escaped during attacks by Allied troops, some were returned to their families after being found sick and no longer useful, some were forced to commit suicide along with the retreating soldiers. Many broke free and survived by their wits, courage and daring. One Filipino woman survivor escaped by playing dead under a pile of other victims massacred during a retreat (Testimony of Juanita Jamot, cited in *Philippine 'Comfort Women'*, 1993: 36).

Breaking the Silence: The Comfort Women Survivors in the Philippines

LILA-Filipina, formerly the Task Force on Filipino Comfort Women, has documented 169 testimonies of Filipino survivors of Japan's wartime sex slavery. Beginning in 1991, the group used telephone hotlines, radio and other mass media to reach out to the surviving victims, encourage them to come forward and testify. Later on, it helped them organize into a movement to demand justice from the Japanese government. Four of the survivors have died since the movement began.

The comfort women system in the Philippines was different from those that existed in Korea, Japan and other occupied territories. This makes the Philippine claim different from that of other survivors. In the Philippines, the comfort women system, while no less extensive, was not as regulated as elsewhere. Instead of being transported, the women were chosen and raped on the spot. For the most part, women were simply captured by soldiers where they could get them and kept wherever they could be housed: in garrisons, tents, abandoned houses, air-raid shelters (called tunnels by the Filipino women survivors), in Spanish-type houses owned by the Filipino elite. Some were chosen by one particular officer and kept for his exclusive use. Some were captured by groups of soldiers on the move. Mass rapes of women were also reported, whereby girls were gathered in school houses or cotton plantations. One report tells of the rape of religious nuns in a Carmelite monastery in Davao (*War Victimization and Japan*, 1993: 31).

And while there were doctors who examined them, these examinations were mostly sporadic. Many women testified that they did not receive medical check-ups. Even though the soldiers were told to use condoms to prevent the spread of venereal diseases, few complied. Many women suffered excessive bleeding due to relentless abuse, others got pregnant and suffered miscarriages due to lack of care and to beatings.

Despite this, the presence of official sanction for these crimes is clear. Unearthed Japanese war documents revealed the names of Filipino comfort women and locations of comfort houses in the Philippines. A medical report dated 19 March 1942, submitted by a Japanese army doctor to the Kempeitai, showed a sketch of a comfort house in Lloilo City and listed the names of 19 Filipino comfort women (*War Victimization and Japan,* 1993: 29). Other Japanese documents contained reports of comfort houses and comfort women in the provinces of Masbate, Cagayan Valley and Samar. Other areas reported included Antique, Mindoro, Nogros, Isabela, Leyte, Laguna and Manila.

Crime and Punishment: The Comfort Women's Claims in Court

In December 1991, Korean comfort women survivors filed the first court case against the Japanese government. Two years later, in April 1993, 46 Filipino survivors filed their own suit at the Tokyo District Court. Both the Korean and Filipino survivors' class action suits demanded that Japan officially acknowledge its wartime crime, apologize to the victims and offer individual state compensation. In both cases, the two sets of plaintiffs charged that the crimes of rape, sex slavery and other forms of wartime sexual violence committed against them by the Japanese Imperial Army are war crimes against humanity.

Several international laws support this position. The Hague Convention of 1907 provides for the protection of civilians in occupied territories, and prohibits the violation of the basic rights to life and honour of individuals as well as families (*Philippine 'Comfort Women'*, 1993: 57). Clearly, rape and sexual abuse of women are a breach of this provision. Article 3 of the Convention provides that any party responsible for violating these provisions is liable to pay compensation to the victims. Japan ratified the Convention in 1912 and was thus bound by it in 1941 when it joined the Axis in World War II. But while the Hague Convention was used to judge the crimes against prisoners of war, it was not acknowledged with regard to the comfort women.

After World War II, 'crimes against humanity' were given a technical identity and defined in Article 6 of the International Military Tribunals Charter. Since then, the concept of crimes against humanity has been repeatedly adopted in such international laws as the Convention on Genocide of 1948 and the Convention on Apartheid (*Philippine 'Comfort Women'*, 1993: 58).

A new concept of war reparation was introduced by the peace treaty of World War I, when Germany was held liable for damages inflicted on individuals, in addition to those of the state. This is based on the principle that an individual's right to claim from a state should remain unaffected even when the state does not recognize diplomatic protection, or abandons individual claims through a reparation agreement.

More recently, these views have been supported by international human rights experts. The International Commission of Jurists based in Geneva concluded in its July 1995 Seminar that the Japanese army's action amounted to war crimes and crimes against humanity. It urged the Japanese government to take legal responsibility by admitting its guilt and apologizing, and by compensating the victims (Final Statement, International Commission of Jurists [ICJ] Seminar on Sexual Slavery and Slavery-like Practices in World War II, 1995).

In April 1996, human rights expert and UN-appointed Special Rapporteur on Violence Against Women Radhika Coomaraswamy, submitted a report to the 52nd Session of the United Nations Commission on Human Rights in Geneva. Contained in her report was an explicit condemnation of Japan's comfort system as a 'war crime' and a 'clear case of sex slavery' (Coomaraswamy, 1996: 4). Not only this, she also echoed the ICJ's recommendations of state compensation and official apology to the victims. Fifty-eight organizations from Japan, Korea, the Philippines, Taiwan and other countries converged in Geneva to lobby, successfully, for the acceptance of Dr Coomaraswamy's report by the UN Human Rights Commission. The support groups decided to formalize their alliance, named the International Alliance, to sustain the momentum achieved in Geneva.

Meanwhile, in Japan's Diet, 26 Japanese parliamentarians sponsored a landmark bill calling for the creation of a government committee that would investigate the entire comfort women issue, determine the role of the Japanese military, and identify the victims. This legislation, if passed, can pave the way for official action on the issue.

Insult and Injury: The Japanese Government's Position and the Asian Women's Fund

However, this initiative in the Diet does not characterize the Japanese government's reaction to the issue. On the contrary, the Japanese government has consistently upheld its view that all war reparations have been settled with the postwar treaties it signed with the countries it occupied. It has also repeatedly refused to release official documents that might shed light on the issue.

However, unable to ignore the claims of the survivors which have gained international attention, and more importantly, engendered an international movement supporting their claims, the Japanese Prime Minister Klichi Miyazawa issued a statement of regret and sympathy to the survivors. But while it expressed sadness over the tragedy, and acknowledged the involvement of the Japanese military, the statement did not admit the crucial point that the Japanese military were not merely involved, but were actually the instigators and main culprits (Yoshimi, 1993: 88).

These expressions of regret were echoed by successive Japanese leaders, including Prime Ministers Tomiichi Murayama and, now, Ryutaro Hashimoto. Murayama's and Hashimoto's statements acknowledged that Japanese soldiers may have been involved in the rapes and sexual slavery, but continued to deny Japan's accountability and rejected the possibility of any compensation for the victims.

In 1995, however, the Japanese government initiated the founding of the Asian Women's Fund, which aims to give 2 to 3 million yen to each survivor. Set for release in July or August 1996, the Asian Women's Fund was controversial from the start. While the sincerity of individual contributors could not be doubted, the fund's motives were not quite so clear. While initiated and overseen by the government, the Asian Women's Fund will not use government money. The money it aims to give the survivors will come from donations by private individuals and corporations in Japan. It is the classic attempt of trying to kill two birds with one stone. By distributing the Asian Women's Fund, the Japanese government hopes to silence the claims for individual compensation while at the same time successfully avoiding admission of guilt and punishment, since it would not use state funds.

This motive was made apparent with the announcement of the Fund's imminent release. Working behind the scenes, the Japanese government is trying to persuade individual women to accept the fund money, on condition that they will drop all further claims to state compensation.

Survivors reacted angrily: 'The Asian Women's Fund is without honour and dignity for us' (Oral intervention by Dalajadia Amonita, Filipino comfort woman survivor at 21st session of the UN Working Group on Contemporary Forms of Slavery, 1996). 'The amount means nothing' (Mitsuko Sugawara, Old Ladies Support Group, Kanagawa, Japan, cited in *Philippine Star*, 1996: 1). 'What does it mean, 2 million yen, 3 million yen? I don't even want to talk about it' (Kim Sang Hee, Korean former comfort woman, cited in *Philippine Daily Inquirer*, 1996: 1).

The International Alliance of Support Groups for the survivors rejected the Asian Women's Fund unanimously, arguing that the Fund reduces the entire issue of justice to a question of money alone. The Asian Women's Fund seeks to measure the suffering the women endured, the violations committed against their honour, their dignity and their human rights, and their struggle for justice in monetary terms. But can honour and dignity be translated into currency? Can pain and anguish, humiliation and torture be quantified? Can a lifetime of shame, dishonour and suffering be paid for? What the Asian Women's Fund does is to get the Japanese government off the hook. No more, no less. Except, perhaps, to reveal the Japanese government's contempt for the women its soldiers violated fifty years ago and who, the Japanese government thinks, are now too old and poor, and willing to settle for the money.

Japan and Militarism

However, contempt for the women it victimized is not the only thing Japan unmasks by its actions on the issue. It also reveals Japan's unwillingness to come to terms with its militaristic past, and the resurgence of this militaristic outlook.

In 1990 Japan passed the Peacekeeping Operations (PKO) Law, which, after fifty years, once again allows the deployment of Japanese troops in foreign countries to intervene in foreign disputes. The PKO Law contradicts the unique provision in Japan's Constitution which renounces the nation's right to bear arms, and raises the possibility that Japan might once again be more than willing to make use of these arms. This, in turn, awakens fears among Asian people who felt the brunt of Japan's aggression during World War II (*War Victimization and Japan*, 1993: 35).

Equally significant, two leading members of the ruling Liberal Democratic Party in Japan, Seisuke Okuno and Tadashi Itagaki, have openly questioned the veracity of the comfort women survivors' claim, saying they were 'exaggerated'.

Japan's reluctance to face up to the crimes it committed fifty years ago becomes entirely logical when seen in the context of Japan's resurgent militarism. If Japan is unwilling to apologize for the atrocities it inflicted on women fifty years ago, it is entirely possible that it is willing to commit such atrocities again.

Seen from this perspective, the significance of the comfort women cause cannot be underestimated. By demanding that Japan recognizes its wartime crimes and makes reparations for them, these comfort women are not fighting only for their own human rights. They are saying, let us not allow Japan to get away with its crimes, because if we do, then we open the door to Japan committing these crimes again. Japan must get the message that it cannot make war and violate women with impunity.

Conclusion: Women and War

The case of the comfort women is the most convincing argument against war. By telling their stories, these women survivors tell in the clearest terms possible the brutality and inhumanity that wars wreak on people, but most especially women. The oppression that women in Asia and the Third World confront in their lives, the inequality, the poverty, the discrimination, the gender violence, increase a hundredfold during times of war and armed conflict, when the 'normal' fabric of society is torn asunder.

Women, who are seen as weak and vulnerable, and at the same time bear their collectivities' honour and tradition, inevitably become the main targets of armies bent on destruction and annihilation of the 'enemy' (Burke, 1994: 10). This is the reason why wherever there is war, there are rapes and other forms of violence against women. In the war equation, men do the dirty work – they sell arms, they buy arms, they use arms – and women are the victims.

The testimonies of the comfort women survivors demonstrate this claim. However, the survivors also demonstrate that women are not only the victims of war, they can also be the voices that oppose wars, simply by bearing witness to the horrors unleashed by wars. By fighting to reclaim their honour and dignity and their human rights, the comfort women survivors are fighting the cause of all women victims of war, and show the way towards ending all wars.

References

Burke, Colleen. 1994. 'Women and militarism.' *Women's International League for Peace and Freedom (WILPF) Essays.* no. 1, December 1994.

Coomaraswamy, Radhika. 1996. *Report on Violence Against Women: Its Causes and Consequences.* Submitted to the 52nd Session of the UN Commission on Human Rights, Geneva.

International Commission of Jurists (ICJ). 1995. *Seminar on Sexual Slavery and Slavery-like Practices in World War II.* UN-University of Tokyo: July 1995.

LILA-Filipina. 1993. *Update on Filipina Victims of Sexual Enslavement by Japanese Armed Forces During World War II.* Manila: LILA-Filipina.

Mi-Gyeong, Mi. 1993. 'Realities of the 'comfort women' in South Korea.' In *War Victimization and Japan: Proceedings of the International Public Hearing Concerning Post-War Compensation of Japan.* Japan: Toho Shuppan Inc.

Philippine Star. 1996. 'Sex slaves pay: too little.' AFP wire report, published in *Philippine Star,* 6 June 1996: 1.

Philippine 'Comfort Women' Compensation Suit, Excerpts of the Complaint. 1993. Manila: Task Force on the Filipino Comfort Women.

Philippine Daily Inquirer, 1996. 'Sex slaves offered $18,500 each.' *Philippine Daily Inquirer,* 6 June 1996: 1.

UN Working Group on Contemporary Forms of Slavery, Sub-Commission on Prevention of Discrimination and Protection of Minorities. 1996. Geneva: UN Commission on Human Rights.

War Victimization and Japan: Proceedings of the International Public Hearing Concerning Post-War Compensation of Japan. 1993. Japan: Toho Shuppan Inc.

Yoshimi, Yoshiaki. 1993. 'Historical understandings on the "military comfort women" issue.' In *War Victimization and Japan: Proceedings of the International Public Hearing Concerning Post-War Compensation of Japan.* 1993. Japan: Toho Shuppan Inc.

12

Chattels and Concubines: Women and Slavery in Brazil

Yvonne Corcoran-Nantes

> As the nurse the slave girl suckled every Brazilian generation, as the personal servant (*mucama*) she lulled them all to sleep; as a man the slave toiled for every generation; as a woman, she surrendered herself to all of them. (Conrad, 1983: 223)

One often gets the impression that the twentieth century is the great epoch of catastrophes such as genocide, war and the abuse of human rights; but one of the greatest catastrophes yet perpetrated is that produced by the Atlantic slave trade over three hundred years from the early sixteenth to the middle of the nineteenth century. A trade that counted on the involvement, implicitly or explicitly, of most nations of the so-called civilized world, it removed millions of Africans from their homelands to be subjected to the vagaries of the slavocratic system that enriched the economies of the Americas and the Caribbean. While much has been written about the Atlantic slave trade, little has focused explicitly on the question of gender relations or the experience of women.

From the early days of Portuguese colonization and settlement in Brazil the socio-economic demarcation of the population based on race, gender and class was apparent. Wars of extermination, enslavement and the abuse of the indigenous Indian population claimed the land which would produce the lucrative export crops of coffee and sugar. In their wake came the Jesuit orders with a policy of 'detribalization' which effectively isolated entire Indian nations and undermined the specificity of their culture and ethnic identity (Marcilio, 1984: 43–4). The introduction of new diseases such as smallpox, measles and syphilis to a vulnerable population completed the annihilation of entire indigenous nations. As a consequence of all these factors the Brazilian Indian population was reduced to less than a third of its original size by 1570 (Marcilio, 1984: 41). If the predominantly male European settlers had little respect for indigenous property rights or cultural mores, they had even less for Indian women whom they took as slaves and concubines; they thus initiated a process of miscegenation that created a racial hierarchy which has persisted in contemporary Brazil and inextricably links race and class.

The early, although generally unsuccessful, attempt by the Portuguese settlers to enslave the Brazilian Indian population set a precedent for socio-economic relations based on gender and class, between white Europeans and the non-white population. Relations were structured, on the one hand, by the system of economic production and, on the other, by the initial scarcity of white women in the colony. Racism dominated European imperialism; there were few Europeans who considered slavery to be a bad thing. The general consensus was that the non-white population was inferior and needed civilizing, thus the condition of slavery was extremely beneficial to them (Greer, 1985: 404–5). These preconceptions which dominated race relations in Brazil also determined the nature of gender relations, whereby the social mores of a Latin culture based on family honour and male virility were translated into a stereotyped bifurcation based on gender and class. It was here that the basic tenets of what is referred to as Machismo and Marianismo were founded.

Machismo and Marianismo represent a total ideology of male and female behaviour in Latin American society and continue to have a significant impact on women's daily lives. The Chilean feminist Ximena Bunster describes Machismo and Marianismo as the bipolar gender concepts that underlie the socialization of men and women in Latin America:

> Machismo, as the cult of virility, is a Latin American manifestation of global patriarchy whereby the male enjoys special privileges within the society and within the family and is considered to be superior to women. Marianismo, Maryology or the cult of the Virgin Mother is the cult of feminine spiritual superiority – she who embodies simultaneously the ideal of nurturance/motherhood and chastity. (Bunster, 1986: 299)

In that Machismo means to show courage and strength and sexual prowess, this was frequently expressed by way of control over female kin, authoritarian behaviour and even violence. Marianismo was equated with submission, dependence and exclusive devotion to home and family (Stevens, 1973: 90–94). This image of what constitutes a 'perfect' woman was principally adhered to by the Portuguese middle and upper classes, and white women were expected to conform. Moreover, as Stevens argues, 'The ideal dictates not only pre-marital chastity for all women, but postnuptial frigidity' (1973: 96). Yet within this ideal type a good woman/bad woman dichotomy comes to the fore in which the non-white female population could not possibly aspire to the state of 'sainthood' proscribed for white women. They were the Other, women whose 'strange' social and cultural mores consolidated their racial inferiority and legitimized their sexual exploitation and abuse. 'It was their bodies – at times, tiny ten-year-old bodies – that, in the moral architecture of Brazilian Patriachalism, constituted a formidable block of defence against bold attacks by Don Juans on the virtue of white ladies' (Freyre, 1963: 455).

The exacerbation of Portuguese cultural mores in this way was on the one hand due to an androcentric frontiership which chose to revere European women as a scarce and important resource, while on the other hand undermining women of other cultures to support a social and cultural anathema which would shape the lives not only of those reconstructing Brazilian culture, but of men and women in the centuries that followed. The early colonization of Brazil was predominantly undertaken by men and created a powerful patriarchal system in which European family life, politics and economic imperatives were paramount. Within this system the polarization of the population on the basis of race and class was compounded by the construction of a specific set of relations between genders. This militated against an intra-gender solidarity that might have challenged a ubiquitous political imperialism shaped by androcentrism.

With the importation of African slaves, the control over women within the Brazilian slavocratic system was the principal source of power, and in this way both 'mistress' and 'slave' made very specific contributions to both its success and longevity. Subordinated within a patriarchal society, they became the means by which European men achieved and maintained their economic and political power. The interrelationship of exploitation by gender and class clearly demarcated the socio-economic relations between white and black women. Through the ownership and control of the means of production (land and slaves) and the means of reproduction (white women) the dominance of plantation owners, and later merchants and financiers, was assured.

Within this social milieu it was women at the very top and very bottom of the class hierarchy who were subject to the strictest social control. Female black slaves were classed as property, could be bought and sold, had few rights and little control over their destiny. Women of the upper classes were subject to the constraints of familial tutelage which was, in most cases, as repressive as the bonds of slavery. This chapter focuses on gender relations and the question of the empowerment and disempowerment of women under colonialism. At the same time, it offers an insight into the lives of women in this period and considers the dialectics of race and class at this historical juncture.

Life and Labour: The Disempowerment of Women

Many books have been written on the conditions of slavery, but it is gender relations within and between the most powerful elites in Brazilian society and the slave classes that is most illustrative of the antagonistic yet symbiotic relationship between the two. Women not only bore the brunt of colonization, development and patriarchy, but served to sustain and reproduce a system that militated against race, gender or class equality. Whether upper-class mistresses of households or slaves, women were subject to male domination and control and this was evident in the gender division of labour, marriage, family and legal rights. By considering the experiences of women within the slavocratic system, it is possible to identify similarity and difference in gender relations within and between slave and slave-owning classes.

For members of the slave class, the gender division of labour was less circumscribed than that of their owners. Women and men were bought for both agricultural and domestic work and a European gender division of labour was apparent in certain areas. Agricultural work was undertaken by both, although men, the majority of the slave population, outnumbered women in the fields. Gender preference was apparent, however, depending on the type of export crop that was produced. For example, planters preferred male agricultural labour for sugar and women for coffee. Even in the second half of the nineteenth century 57 per cent of the female labour force was engaged in agricultural activities (Merrick and Graham, 1979: 74). Agricultural tasks were the same for both men and women, the only concession to gender difference being that women were given a lighter hoe, although women were excluded from all tasks that involved the use of machinery such as sugar milling. On coffee and sugar plantations women were involved in planting, weeding and harvesting, excluded from the final processing of the sugar crop but actively involved in the process of drying, sorting and packing of coffee beans (Schwartz, 1984: 432–4).

Domestic labour was far more clearly demarcated: women were the tailors, nurses and laundry workers, while cooks, personal slaves and cleaners could be either male or female. While domestic service was considered to be less arduous than agricultural work, in the former women were required to perform the 'filthiest of tasks' in connection with household sanitation (see Stein, 1985; Cardoso, 1976; Dean, 1976). They also worked under much closer supervision and often only ventured outside the house on public holidays and to accompany the family to church once a week (Karasch, 1987: 59).

The slave population worked between seventeen and twenty hours a day, six days a week. Sunday was considered a day of rest except during the harvest period, and only religious holidays alleviated the unremitting work cycle (Conrad, 1983: 73–4). Free time was used to serve the subsistence needs of the slave population and engage in income-generating activities through which they could save to buy their freedom. On many plantations slaves were given small plots of land on which they could grow basic foodstuffs to supplement the meagre diet offered by their 'patrons'. Those who had no such access spent their free time engaging in handicraft production and clothing to sell in the Sunday markets (Stein, 1985: 162–70). As the cities grew in the late eighteenth and early nineteenth centuries both male and female slaves were expected to undertake domestic service and income-generating activities that should not only provide a steady income for their owners but also allowed the slave classes to accumulate money (Karasch, 1987: 205). Both male and female owners expected their slaves to produce a set daily income for the household; those who failed to do so were subject to physical violence and all forms of retribution (Goulart, 1971: 58). Nevertheless, urbanization brought much greater personal freedom for both male and female slaves and they managed to gain manumission at a far higher rate than those working in rural areas. The experience of African slave women, monopolizing trading and commerce in urban West Africa especially, enabled them to gain manumission at a rate disproportionate to their number in the slave population (Karasch, 1987: 20; Merrick and Graham, 1979: 53).

Female slaves were also expected to engage in sexual labour. From an early age pubescent females were given to young males in the household and were subject to all manner of abuse (Stevens, 1973: 97).[1] The master of the household would expect to have the female slave of his choosing wherever, however and whenever it pleased him. It was also customary to offer slave women to male house guests. As urbanization increased and many families migrated from rural areas, female slaves would be forced into prostitution. They might be street sellers or domestic servants during the day and prostitutes at night. It was not only the masters of the household who engaged in this practice but also their spouses, who would often use their maids to acquire an independent income for themselves (Freyre, 1963: 454). Mistresses would dress their female slaves in gold and silks to attract customers. Some female slaves would have to sit in the windows of the homes calling to male passersby, closely watched by their mistresses (Conrad, 1983: 132). The widespread sexual abuse of female slaves in both rural and urban areas exacerbated the spread of venereal disease; young syphilitic female slaves suffered from spontaneous abortions and sterility and eventually died from the disease. This, without doubt, contributed to the fact that in Rio de Janeiro in the mid-nineteenth century, four-fifths of all female slaves died before the age of thirty, as opposed to two-thirds of male slaves (Karasch, 1987: 95).[2]

Marriage and family life were generally denied to the slave population. Neither the Church nor slave-owners encouraged either slave marriage or slave reproduction. Marriage was impractical in an economic system based on the buying and selling of slaves and so *amazias* or passing unions were far more common among slaves. This made it much easier for owners to break up 'families' and sell them separately (Karasch, 1987: 287–91). Furthermore, the association of male and female slaves was restricted, especially on the plantations where they were housed separately and only allowed one or two hours' association at night. Consequently, little family stability existed and women were responsible for the care and socialization of the children they bore. Slave children were considered unproductive by their owners until the age of eight when they could undertake light work, but 75 per cent of slave children died before that age (Conrad, 1983: 100). Children who did survive were frequently removed from their mothers and sold or given as wedding presents or gifts to relatives (Dean, 1976: 74). Slave women, denied an opportunity to bond with and nurture their offspring, became the wet nurses of successive generations of the privileged white classes. The black mother or *mae preta* was highly regarded in the family, looking after the children as if they were her own and given reverential status in the annals of Brazilian history (Stein, 1985: 150). Unfortunately there is scant recognition of these women's personal tragedy.

Slaves had few if any legal rights and those that existed were generally unenforceable. For example, a 1824 law prohibited the torture and physical punishment of slaves although 'moderate' punishment was allowed. Yet slaves were considered to be property and therefore they could not testify against their owners. Female slaves were placed in the stocks, whipped, tortured, raped and sexually assaulted with impunity (Goulart, 1971: 50–68; Karasch, 1987: 115–24). Even legal action taken by the police against individual owners for rape, murder or assault were dismissed on the grounds that slaves were property and therefore this constituted legal behaviour until abolition (Conrad, 1983: 274). Moreover, a slave-owner had rights not only over the body of the female slave but also over her progeny. Even after the 1871 law which legally freed all children born to slaves, they were enslaved or sold illegally (Stein, 1985: 67). Before that date there was no law which required an owner to manumit his or her slaves, although slaves could buy their freedom or be given freedom by their owner on their death. Women gained manumission at a higher rate than men and this was especially the case in the cities where slave women dominated trading activities. Yet for most slaves this freedom was conditional upon serving a specified number of years or upon the death of their owner. Karasch calculated that even for women who were able to purchase their freedom, it could take up to forty years to obtain it (Karasch, 1987: 336–7). Nevertheless for those who gained manumission, as members of the non-white population, their legal status remained ambiguous until slavery was abolished in 1888.

The gender division of labour among the men and women of the middle and upper classes was more clearly defined than that of their slaves. The men of the household controlled and supervised all commercial, agricultural and business activities in the 'public' sphere on the plantations and in the cities. Until the nineteenth century women were confined within the walls of the home and rarely went out except to attend church and even then they did so in a sedan chair or hammock hidden behind curtains

(Goulart, 1971: 47). The role of the mistress of the household was considered by travellers and observers of the time to be insignificant but there is considerable evidence to show that they were much more influential than generally believed (Russell-Wood, 1968: 183). 'They supervised the production of clothing, food, domestic utensils and other necessities of a largely self-sufficient household and were responsible for the family's healthcare, numerous religious obligations and the training of dependents' (Hahner, 1990: 5). The mistress of the household exercised considerable control over all forms of domestic labour and both male and female slaves were expected to give unquestioning loyalty and service. Like their male partners, mistresses were not averse to subjecting their charges to severe punishment and physical abuse. Newspapers and police records of the time bore testimony to the maltreatment of slaves by their mistresses right across the country (Goulart, 1971: 50). By the nineteenth century, as the towns grew and business and social life expanded, women began to develop a far more visible social role, organizing parties, social gatherings and formal events, and engaging in philanthropic activities (Hahner, 1990: 9).

As opposed to the matrifocal family unit of social organization among the slave population, a strong patriarchal family unit was the core of existence of the white upper classes. The socialization of women reflected European attitudes of the time whereby women were to be 'moulded into passive creatures' who would become household managers and the mothers of legitimate children (Stein, 1985: 151). Young women were kept in virtual seclusion; education was not considered a priority until the early nineteenth century, when they were allowed to read and write, learn French, play the piano and in some cases help keep the household accounts. Marriages were more like mergers to consolidate wealth or property, and it was not uncommon for young women to be married to partners ten to fifteen years their senior at the tender age of thirteen, and in some cases to uncles or cousins (Freyre, 1963: 353). It was this social group that dominated the power structures of Brazilian society and therefore intermarriage within and between families led to a 'coincidence of interest' which reinforced their political power and influence. Women were expected to accept the partners chosen for them by their families and while escaping from the domination of one man, her father, a woman would be subject to the rule of another, her husband. On the plantations, the mistress of the household remained secluded, unseen by male visitors and rarely leaving the home. Successive pregnancies and isolation led to their physical deterioration; tired and worn by the age of twenty, many were physically incapable of feeding their newborn infants, hence the importance of the black wet nurse (Freyre, 1968: 91). The production of heirs was of considerable importance to the white ruling class: 'the white woman was seen as the instrument for populating the vast expanses of Portuguese America, offsetting to some extent countless numbers of slaves and free

blacks' (Russell-Wood, 1977: 7). Furthermore, like female slaves, matrilin-
eal descent was the custom, ensuring that children retained the status and
privileges commensurate with the political and economic dominance of
their families (Saffioti, 1979: 126).

In law, women were considered minors and subject to the control of
their spouses or fathers. Women had the legal right to own property and
conduct trade and commerce in their own right but could not actively
administer them without male consent. Moreover, the law operated dual
moral standards concerning marital fidelity. The question of family honour
was of utmost importance: female chastity and fidelity were inviolable for
women of the middle and upper classes. Conversely, the liberal sexual
mores of the Portuguese male were both accepted and sanctioned in law.
Adultery laws, therefore, treated male and female infidelity differently. A
man could divorce his wife for adultery while a woman often had to cite
a secondary cause such as cruelty. It was quite common for a man to
take the law into his own hands, severely beating or even killing his wife
on the mere suspicion of adultery. Others could solicit assistance from
the police, provided that the expenses were paid, to remove their wives
to a convent or retirement house: convent life was held out as a constant
threat to disobedient daughters and 'wayward' wives. In such instances,
the courts were inclined to uphold the actions of the husband while the
wife was unable to leave her cloistered confinement, and it was lenient
towards husbands who committed what was termed a 'crime of passion'
(Russell-Wood, 1977: 7; Freyre, 1968: 97–8; Degler, 1971: 232). Brazilian
law did little to protect women of any class from assault, murder or
maltreatment by men who either owned or had authority over them.
Female slaves in some ways enjoyed greater freedom than their mistresses
to accumulate sufficient earnings to purchase their freedom. Such liberty
could only be achieved by upper-class women through widowhood or
divorce when they could assume the role of full citizens exercising their
rights over property and taking control of their lives (Stein, 1985: 151).

Despite their shared oppression by men, class and race differences
divided the mistress from the slave. Relations between women were quite
complex. Women of the privileged classes not only supervised and controlled female slaves but also owned slaves themselves. The intra-class
relations that ensued would often counter any empathy that might exist
between them. Their attitude towards their female charges would vary
from acts of genuine Christian charity to abject cruelty. This was especially true in the case of female domestic slaves. Fathers and spouses
actively discouraged any familiarity between *their* women and female slaves
even though this was both expected and encouraged with relation to
male members of the household. 'While it was accepted that the white
woman was sexually unassailable, and that sexual promiscuity on her part
could result in death at the hand of her husband or father, for the black

slave, it was conceded that she was in no position to repel sexual advances by an owner' (Russell-Wood, 1977: 68). It was the sexual services demanded of female slaves by their spouses and sons that created the greatest antagonism between upper-class and slave women.

Upper-class women were expected to tolerate their spouses' relationships with female slaves. Often badly treated themselves, many women vented their frustration and anger on any slave who was the focus of their husband's attention. Female slaves had no choice: obedience was expected at all times and any demands made on them by their masters could not be repudiated. Diaries and journals of the time depict

> tales of *sinha mocas* who had the eyes of pretty *mucamas* gouged out and then had them served to their husbands for dessert, in a jelly dish, floating in blood that was still fresh. Tales of young baronesses of adult age who out of jealousy or spite had fifteen year old mulatto girls sold off to old libertines. There were others who kicked out the teeth of their women slaves with their boots, or had their breasts cut off, their nails drawn, or their faces and ears burned. (Freyre 1968: 305)

By damaging their spouses' property in this way, upper-class women were able to express their frustration at being confined within a marriage that they merely tolerated rather than enjoyed. On the other hand, many mistresses grew very attached to their personal slaves and on their death bequeathed household linen, jewellery, furniture, as well as a dowry to be married, and some even granted female slaves their freedom (Russell-Wood, 1977: 33). It was not uncommon for upper-class women to deliver the babies of their female charges, care for sick slaves, suckle slave children whose mothers had died or to become godparents to the children of personal slaves (Stein, 1985: 149–51; Freyre, 1963: 456).

Historical accounts tend to highlight the best and worst features of intra-gender relations principally because the day-to-day interaction between mistresses and slaves was rarely recorded. Subordinated within a patriarchal society, all women had few legal rights and they became the means by which white men maintained their economic and political power. The interplay of gender, race and class clearly demarcated the economic and social roles undertaken by free white women and black slaves in Brazilian society. Under such circumstances we might speculate that if intra-gender or inter-class solidarity existed between women, this could be considered the exception rather than the rule.

Women in Our Own Right: Empowerment, Individuality and Freedom

Until the nineteenth century the lives of upper-class women and female slaves were circumscribed within a slavocratic system in which few legal rights and scant social justice were enjoyed by either. Portuguese women who emigrated to Brazil with their families or spouses in the colonial period had to face considerable hardship, social and intellectual repression and virtual seclusion. The journey was not necessarily one of choice. Under the Portuguese Philippine Code of 1603, men were the legal heads of the household and exercised total control over their spouses and dependants, and that included deciding where they should live.[3]

African women too were unwilling participants in the development and occupation of Brazil. Kidnapped from their homes, removed from a way of life in which they had social status, economic independence and full participation in the political system, they were brought to Brazil as slaves to be worked to death, abused and denied any legal rights. Individual women of both classes justifiably rebelled against the strict social control under which they were placed. That women within the same social group pursued similar means to liberate themselves from the excesses of patriarchal tyranny which dominated their lives is under-investigated in the literature on slavery. Nevertheless, women chose the only avenues open to them to engage in passive resistance, subversion of family and societal power structures and sometimes open confrontation.

Female slaves throughout the slavocratic period became extremely adept at both passive and active resistance to their subjugation and abuse. The most adept form of passive resistance was that of limiting their reproduction by actively preventing the birth of slave children. Throughout the period there was a low birth rate and an inordinately high mortality rate among children under five[4] registered for the slave population up to abolition, and this has been attributed to two major causes. First, arduous working conditions, inadequate nourishment and sexually transmitted diseases caused low fertility and sterility in slave women. Second, and most important for our purpose here, almost every account of Brazilian slavery mentions the fact that slave women executed self-inflicted abortions and practised infanticide rather than commit their offspring to a life of slavery (Cardoso, 1976: 240). African women were knowledgeable about abortion techniques and this form of resistance was a source of considerable frustration to their owners (Dean, 1976: 64).

Many slave women were well versed in the use of herbal remedies and poisons that they often sold at local Sunday markets. Some earned considerable status as specialist healers and were in demand among wealthy families to treat and cure a wide range of ailments. At the same time these women would use their skill with poisons to seek revenge on their owners by committing covert acts of violence. They used snake venom, herbal poisons and ground glass to contaminate the food and medicines of their owners, some of whom became seriously ill or died. This practice was sufficiently commonplace that pharmacists introduced the practice of sealing medicines so it would be more difficult to tamper with them (Dean, 1976: 84).

Most slave women devoted their energies to the pursuit of emancipation. For slaves whose owners lived in the cities the opportunity to buy their freedom was three to four times greater than for their peers who worked on the plantations. The expense of living in the city for the upper classes was such that most were dependent on the income of slaves from free enterprise or hiring out their labour.[5] Female slaves engaged in domestic work and worked outside their home several days a week as well as working at night. In most cities they dominated the marketing of consumer goods and the sale of prepared foods, and many were forced by their owners to engage in prostitution. The success of all manner of enterprise in which these women engaged was verified by the fact that two-thirds of slaves buying their freedom in Rio de Janeiro, for example, were women. Many of these were successful market women who could also afford to obtain manumission for their children (Karasch, 1987: 336–47).

On the plantations, certainly up until the middle of the nineteenth century, the demands on the slave population to produce lucrative export crops as well as providing a full range of services on the plantations left little time or opportunity to engage in income-generating activities other than subsistence production on small plots allocated to them. The misery of slave existence exacerbated by physical abuse and the slim chance that their owners might consider them worthy of granting them freedom on their death left plantation slaves with two options – 'resist or run' (Stein, 1975: 177). Both forms of rebellion were punishable by death and women actively engaged in both slave rebellions and slave flight at a level commensurate with their numbers in the slave population.[6]

Slave flight was a sufficiently frequent occurrence to justify the creation of what were called bush captaincies in the early seventeenth century to 'hunt down' runaway slaves. One estimate places the average number of slaves 'absent' at any point at 3 per cent and only half of this number were ever found. Consequently, for slaves in rural areas, this form of emancipation was far more attractive than the chance of being given their freedom by owners (Dean, 1976: 84). The illegal settlements, called *quilombos,* formed by runaway slaves in the Brazilian bushlands and forests, achieved considerable notoriety in Brazilian history. These communities survived through subsistence agriculture and the organization of raids on local towns and plantations. The most famous of these was called Palmares, situated in the northeast of Brazil. It consisted of thousands of slaves, approximately one third of whom were women, housed in several villages and two towns. As the largest and most influential slave community it was subject to constant attack by the military and was finally destroyed in 1695 and its leaders executed.[7] The *quilombos* were a symbol of hope for slaves all over Brazil and many smaller communities in remote regions continued to exist even after abolition. One such community in

Salvador was led by a famous female slave called Zeferina, who led assaults
on plantations and townships in the region (Pescatello, 1975: 218)

Slave rebellions were frequent in the northeast of Brazil until the early
nineteenth century and women were also active participants in this form
of resistance. These rebellions, which involved hundreds of slaves,
occurred in the main agricultural regions of northeast and central Brazil
and in most cases needed to be suppressed by military troops. Evidence
shows that those involved in the rebellions were predominantly newly
imported slaves. These rebellions reached a peak in the nineteenth century
in regions where the conditions on plantations were particularly severe,
and this was especially the case in the state of Bahia from 1807 to 1835
(Degler, 1971: 51). One of the most violent rebellions occurred in 1827
when hundreds of slaves fought against the military; fifty men and twenty
women were captured, whipped in public and sentenced to death.

Familial tutelage for upper-class women was no less restrictive than
that of slavery but the avenues of resistance open to them were far fewer
than for female slaves. As members of an economically and politically
powerful social group, they risked social isolation and even violent reprisal
if they engaged in overt acts of rebellion or resistance. Consequently
women of this social group tended to engage in passive resistance and,
in some cases, used any legal means available to them to gain their independence. As we have seen, these women were not averse to resorting
to acts of revenge against slave women whom they felt to be a threat to
their position in the household. In the final instance it was the social
changes commensurate with urbanization that offered the greatest
opportunity for some women to assert themselves and pioneer change in
existing gender relations.

Up to the nineteenth century, upper-class women could only engage in
passive resistance to challenge the authority of their husbands; obedience
was imposed upon them. But women would rebel at the first opportunity.
Mindful of their husbands' and sons' propensity to buy extremely attractive
female slaves for their purposes, many women would deliberately buy
older or less attractive slaves in their absence much to the annoyance of
male members of the family. Moreover, the violence that mistresses might
inflict on favoured female slaves forced planters to hide them on the
plantation at a safe distance from the house (Stein, 1985: 157–7). Such
incidents indicate that upper-class women were not without some influence over their spouses, but the nature and extent of such influence remains
a matter for speculation. Nevertheless, a not insignificant number of women
from this social class were unwilling to tolerate the sexual promiscuity of
their spouses and separated from them. When upper-class men would
publicly flout their relationships with slave women, this was sufficient
grounds for women to obtain a divorce from the Church for the 'serious
infraction' of their marriage vows (Stein, 1985: 158).

Only separation and widowhood liberated women of the privileged classes from familial tutelage. As women of independent means, they gained financial power and control over their property. They successfully managed plantations and commercial enterprises and gave political and economic direction to their families (Pescatello, 1976: 147–9). Public records indicate that such women were not necessarily exceptional in colonial society. By the mid-eighteenth century, for example, 9 per cent of sugar mills were owned by women, in 1834 there were 87 female landowners registered in Rio de Janeiro; in the state of Bahia, of nine large legacies left to its most important charitable institution, the Santa Casa da Misericordia, two were from women (Pescatello, 1976: 149; Karasch, 1987: 7; Russell-Wood, 1968: 186).

By the beginning of the nineteenth century the migration of planter families to the cities and the expansion of their activities in business and commerce relaxed the social constraints on women. Upper-class women appeared on the streets unescorted, enjoyed a more active social life and supervised the income-generating activities of their female slaves. This created an environment whereby social pressures demanded that young women receive an education and they were given the opportunity to have some say in the choice of a husband (Pescatello, 1976: 174). Although initially the education of women only served to raise their standard of literacy, in some cases they were able to pursue a professional career.[8] It was from this new generation of women that the first political activists and protagonists for women's emancipation in Brazilian society came.

By the 1850s a 'women's rights press' was beginning to emerge whereby female newspaper editors began to criticize the patriarchal nature of Brazilian society and the oppression of women within it. The first of many journals to be published was called *O Jornal das Senhoras* (the Ladies' Journal), which advocated the education of women and a reconsideration of women's role and contribution in marriage and society. The female newspaper publishers, who chose what was a controversial and radical departure from the traditional view of women's contribution to public life, became the objects of ridicule and criticism by both men and women. Yet a significant minority of females and males chose to make written contributions to the newspapers, albeit anonymously in the case of many women, and this represented an important step in gaining the confidence to publicly decry the nature of gender relations in Brazilian society (Hahner, 1990: 26–7). From this beginning, 'Brazilian women's rights advocates demonstrated concern with a number of major issues, including the legal status of women, family relationships, access to higher education and careers and finally, political questions such as the abolition of slavery and the vote for women' (Hahner, 1990: 36).

Ironically, it was the promotion of a voice for the most privileged women in Brazil which encouraged women to become part of a political cause to liberate the slave population. While their role may have been confined to fundraising rather than public speech-making, their behind-the-scenes support for the cause even extended to sheltering runaway slaves in their homes (Hahner, 1990: 39). Men dominated the abolition movement, but the participation of women and their active support for what they believed to be a 'noble cause' was a radical departure from a previously apolitical existence (Hahner, 1990: 39–40). For a few upper-class women it also offered a clearer insight into the suffering and oppression of slave women who they believed were there to serve their interests and those of their families. This did not, however, represent a major shift from the, at best, detached intra-gender relations that existed up to abolition.

Conclusion: Moving Forwards, Going Backwards

Abolition brought few major changes to the lives of ex-slaves because the class and racial barriers to social mobility remained firmly in place. Freedom in practice often meant that women undertook the same work for their previous owners in return for a subsistence wage. Hence, the only change was one of status – free rather than slave labour – and in many cases they were materially worse off. Nevertheless, the change in circumstances did give them the chance, for the first time, to select their employers and compete for wages. The burden of sexual exploitation endured under the slave system was considerable for a woman because as a member of the most disadvantaged class she was in 'a weak, unprotected and "inferior" position [and] … considered by white males to be easy prey; this view of her has lasted, through succeeding generations, to include her descendants even today' (Dzidzienyo and Casal, 1971: 5).

For women of the upper classes, the increased opportunities that came with access to education and an increased participation in the social and economic life of Brazil strengthened their position of privilege *vis-à-vis* that of ex-slaves. By the end of the century there were a few white women who, by virtue of their social position and wealth, managed to receive a university education and enter the male-dominated professions such as law and medicine. Nevertheless, such women were still exceptional in an androcentric society which continued to believe that white women should and could be fulfilled through marriage and the family. 'In the final analysis, women remained far removed from the currents of social and political change, and their isolation was deliberately fostered by the men who remained openly hostile to women's participation in any and every activity that went beyond the bounds of the family' (Saffioti, 1979: 127).

It would be true to say, however, that after the abolition of slavery, urbanization and industrialization slowly changed the roles of women in Brazilian society, offering opportunities which gave their lives a new dimension and began to erode an autocratic patriarchy which had controlled the lives of women both at the very top and the very bottom of the class hierarchy throughout the period of slavery. In spite of their shared oppression and suffering, it was the dialectics of race and class that demarcated the socio-economic relations between white and black women. Their personal struggles, rebellion and resistance under the previous system gave women of both classes considerable strength to offer new challenges to the persistence of the cultural mores of Machismo and Marianismo after the demise of the slavocratic system. Yet the lives of white and black women were to remain socially and economically distinct, while the weight of tradition left its mark on the life and mentality of Brazilian women. Gender solidarity between the different social classes remains the major challenge to a unified gender politics even at the present time.

Notes

1. This practice was so widespread that some observers of the time accused black and mulatto female slaves of being the 'corrupters' of young males. See, for example, Cardoso, 1976: 228; Freyre, 1963: 395–6.
2. On marriage many women took their nurses and personal body slaves with them. They would also select and purchase the female slaves who would provide services for the women of the household.
3. This code remained in operation in Brazil until the introduction of a Civil Code in 1916.
4. Conrad reveals that even up until 1850 95 per cent of slave children died before reaching the age of eight (1974: 152)
5. This dependence, for many, was related to the expense of maintaining a large slave contingent providing necessary services for the family and the expense of providing food and clothing in an environment which did not offer the same resources for such households to remain self-sufficient.
6. It is important to note here that male and female slaves were imported into Brazil at a ratio of 2:1 and therefore there would necessarily be fewer women than men engaged in this form of resistance.
7. In 1996, for the first time, the public festivities were organized in the northeast of Brazil to commemorate the fall of Palmares, still recognized as the fulcrum of black resistance in Brazil. The commemorations bore testimony to the growing power and influence of the Black Movement in Brazil over the last ten years.
8. Hahner argues that this change in attitude toward women's education was not aimed at the intellectual liberation of women but rather that the declining fortunes of many plantation owners meant that they wanted their sons to train for the professions and therefore they could no longer allow the early education of their sons 'to remain in the hands of ignorant and illiterate women' (1990: 88–93).

References

Bunster, Ximena. 1986. 'Surviving Beyond Fear: women and torture in Latin America.' In H. Safa and J. Nash (eds), *Women and Change in Latin America.* South Hadley, MA: Bergin and Harvey.

Bradford-Burns, Edward. 1980. *A History of Brazil*. New York: Columbia University Press.

Cardoso, Geraldo da Silva. 1976. *Negro Slavery in the Sugar Plantations of Veracruz and Pernambuco, 1550–1680*. Lincoln: University of Nebraska, Unpublished PhD thesis [mimeo].

Conrad, Robert Edgar. 1974. 'Nineteenth century Brazilian slavery.' In R.B. Toplin (ed.), *Slavery and Race Relations in Latin America*. London: Greenwood Press.

Conrad, Robert Edgar. 1983. *Children of God's Fire: A Documentary History of Black Slavery*. New Jersey : Princeton University Press.

Dean, Warren. 1976. *Rio Claro: A Brazilian Plantation System*. Stanford: Stanford University Press.

Degler, Carl N. 1971. *Neither Black Nor White: Slavery and Race Relations in Brazil and United States*. New York and London : Macmillan.

Dzidzienyo, Anani and Lourdes Casal. 1971. *The Position of Blacks in Brazilian Society*. London: Minority Rights Group Report, no. 7.

Freyre. Gilberto. 1963. *The Masters and the Slaves*. New York: Alfred A. Knopf.

Freyre, Gilberto. 1968. *Mansions and Shanti*. New York: Alfred A. Knopf.

Goulart. Jose Alipio. 1971. *Da Palmatoria Ao Patibulo*. Rio de Janeiro: Conquista.

Greer, Germaine. 1985. *Sex and Destiny: the Politics of Human Fertility*. London: Pan Books.

Hahner, June Edith. 1990. *Emancipation of the Female Sex: The Struggle for Women's Rights in Brazil*. Durham NC and London: Duke University Press.

Karasch, Mary C. 1987. *Slave Life in Rio de Janeiro 1808–1850*. Princeton, NJ: Princeton University Press.

Marcilio, Maria Luiza. 1984. 'The population of colonial Brazil', in L. Bethell (ed.), *The Cambridge History of Latin America*, Vol. II. Cambridge: Cambridge University Press.

Merrick, Thomas William and Douglas H. Graham. 1979. *Population and Economic Development in Brazil: 1800 to the Present*. Baltimore, MD: Johns Hopkins University Press.

Pescatello, Anne M. 1975. *The African in Latin America*. New York: Alfred A. Knopf.

Pescatello, Anne M. 1976. *Power and Pawn*. London: Greenwood Press.

Rodrigues, Jose Honorio. 1965. *Brazil and Africa*. Berkeley: University of California Press.

Russell-Wood, Anthony J.R. 1968. *Fidalgos and Philanthropists: The Santa Casa da Misericordia of Bahia, 1550–1755*. London: Macmillan.

Russell-Wood, Anthony J.R. 1977. 'Women and society in colonial Brazil.' *Journal of Latin American Studies*, vol. 9, May.

Saffioti, Heleieth I.B. 1979. 'Women, mode of production and social formations.' *Latin American Perspectives*, vol. IV, nos 1 & 2.

Schwartz, Stuart B. 1984. 'Colonial Brazil, c. 1580–1750: plantations and peripheries.' In L. Bethell (ed.), *The Cambridge History of Latin America*, Vol. 2. Cambridge: Cambridge University Press.

Stevens, Evelyn. 1973. 'Marianismo: the other face of Machismo in Latin America.' In A. Pescatello (ed.), *Female and Male in Latin America*. Pittsburgh: University of Pittsburgh Press.

Stein, Stanley J. 1975. 'A nineteenth century plantation.' In A. Pescatello (ed.), *The African in Latin America*. New York: Alfred A. Knopf.

Stein, Stanley J. 1985. *Vassouras: A Brazilian Coffee County 1850–1900*. Princeton, NJ: Princeton University Press.

13

The Economy of Violence: Black Bodies and the Unspeakable Terror

Bibi Bakare-Yusuf

In this chapter I want to explore the relationship between the notion that physical brutality and force transformed the African body from a liberated body to a captive one, and Elaine Scarry's idea that the infliction of physical pain unmakes and deconstructs the body, while simultaneously making and reconstructing the world of the perpetrator. I wish to link these two ideas by proposing that under the slave economy and colonization two kinds of bodies were produced: the body of knowledge and the body of labour. These two bodies are missing from Scarry's discourse of the body in pain. They are also absent from most contemporary discourses about the body. Paying attention to the body of labour in particular, I wish to show how I find some of Scarry's arguments useful in relation to reading the slave narrative, *Mary Prince*. I am inspired by the connection Scarry makes between the infliction of pain, embodiment, voice and subjectivity and the ruination of the subject – and certainly *Mary Prince* bears this out. However, I suggest that the economy of violence which characterized the middle passage and the epoch of slavery had as its primary motive the extraction of capital and wealth through slave labour. Following Hortense Spillers's idea in her essay 'Mama's baby, papa's maybe: an American grammar book' that the middle passage and slavery was a brutal disruption of the African kinship system which denied the captive female a gendered position, I suggest that this degendering also entailed a deconstruction and unmaking of the captive's subjectivity. In their different ways both Scarry and Spillers address the intersection of bodily damage, objectification and assault on the flesh and the difficulty of expressing that assault. Both address the unspeakability of the terror of torture but Spillers actively focuses on the deconstruction of the African captive.

The Body of Theory

The body has become the most celebrated site for addressing a wide range of cultural configurations; for articulating contemporary experiences among feminists with divergent interests as well as social and cultural theorists. The privileging of the body is evident in the spate of books published with the word 'body' in their title. Among these are Elaine Scarry's *The Body in Pain* (1985), Elizabeth Grosz's *Volatile Bodies* (1995), Judith Butler's *Bodies that Matter* (1993), Moria Gatens's *The Imaginary Body* (1996), Bryan Turner's *The Body and Society* (1984). Many of these studies address the numerous ways of using the human body and embodiment as a conceptual tool for rethinking an array of issues: the problematic nature of sex, sexuality and gender; of ageing and aesthetics (Featherstone and Hepworth, 1991); of disease and illness (Turner, 1984; Bordo, 1990), pain and self-alienation (Scarry, 1985); of deconstructing the dualism in Western metaphysics. The body has replaced such categories as subjects, social agents, and individuals. It is, as Grosz points out, the 'very "stuff" of subjectivity' [and] ... all significant facets and complexities of subjects can be adequately explained using the subject's corporeality as a framework'. Like many current theorists of the body, Grosz calls for the need to fuse the historical specificity of bodies with the biological concreteness of the body since 'there is no body as such: there are only bodies – male and female, black, brown, white, large or small and gradations in between'(19). Much of this 'corporeal feminism' (Grosz, 1995) is grounded in linguistics and psychoanalysis where the body is read as discursive or textual (Butler, 1993), even as it claims to be 'concerned with the *lived body*, the body in so far as it is represented and used in specific ways in particular culture' (Grosz, 1995: 18). This attention to the body sometimes seems a mere flirtation with the idea of the lived body where the experience of lived bodies is constituted as a metaphor that is 'good to think with'.

But what of the dying body; the weeping, living, hurting body; the body as flesh that 'does not escape concealment under the brush of discourse or the reflexes of iconography' (Spillers, 1987: 67)? The body that is a site of physical and psychological trauma; enforced sexual practices and that 'Sadian imgination' (Carter, 1979), with its self-announcing presence on newsstands, in popular literature and medicine. The body that has served and continues to serve a heuristic purpose for the European (male) construction of subjectivity on the one hand and on the other the 'source of an irresistible, destructive sexuality' (Spillers, 1987: 67). The body at whose breasts white males suckle as they spread the expanse of their fluid around the globe. The body that enables certain categories of white women to retain fine, delicate, sickly hands. The body on which black men can at will unleash their rage and frustration. The body whose physical health will determine whether it will become the body of labour or the body of scientific knowledge. The body that nineteenth-century Europeans found so riveting that it became a prized attraction at fashionable Parisian balls and would later be subjected to the surgical instrument of the physician (Gilman, 1985; Schiebinger, 1994). What of the body that is always under the seduction of death, white racist violence, diseases, perverse heterosexism, pervasive addictions and unemployment? I am talking about the body that is marked by racial, sexual and class configurations. It is this body, this fleshy materiality that seems to disappear from much of the current proliferation of discourses on the body.

It is not enough to show the body as a discursive entity without addressing how different material practices are interwoven with the discursive to affect and shape the materiality of the body. The French theorist Michel Foucault understood the interdependency between the fleshy materiality of the body and its functioning, representation and regulation in discursive fields when he inaugurated, along with the effort of second-wave feminism in the seventies, the topic of the body in contemporary theory. In his numerous philosophical studies, Foucault described in great detail the historical specificities which produce the body in discourses and in everyday practices structure the way experiences of the body are organized. Accordingly the body is always in a political field where 'power relations have an immediate hold upon it; they invest it, mark it, train it, torture it, for it to carry out tasks, to perform ceremonies, to emit signs' (Foucault, 1991: 173). These inscriptions and incorporations of power onto the body mark the ending of one type of body and the beginning of a new kind of body: a useful body. But this body comes into being through new modes of subjection. Such a body, Foucault contends, also produces power that facilitates resistance, rebellion, evasions and disruptions. In other words, where there is power, there is resistance; where there is discourse, there is material; and both power and discourse are interconnected. Discourse then becomes just one of the modes in which political power manifests itself.

If current discourse analysis is to be useful for a black feminist project, we need to make connections with matters of the flesh on the lived body. For it is through the corporeal inscription of the black man as uncivilized savage and the black woman as embodying a hyperbolic sexuality which marked her as sexualized animal in the New World (Gilman, 1985; Jordan, 1982). As Fanon notes in his book *Black Skin, White Mask*, it is the 'corporeal schema' of the black (man) that structures how black people are perceived and 'the fact of blackness' is established: 'I am overdetermined from without. I am the slave not of the "idea" that others have of me but of my own appearance ... I strive for anonymity, for invisibility' (1992: 224). It is the visible physical difference that marked the African as inherently non-human.

By becoming aware of the slave experience as an embodied phenomenon, we can better understand: (1) the relationship between embodiment
and subjectivity; (2) the body as a surface, a surface that can experience
and be inflicted with pain, tortured and terrorized, but also a surface that
can be pleasured and is pleasuring; and (3) how bodies are linked in
distinctive ways through capitalist modes of production. Thus the history
of the middle passage and slavery is a history of endless assaults on
bodies; of bodies forcibly subjugated, in order to be transformed into
productive and reproductive bodies.

The Unspeakable Terror

One way to approach the issue of unspeakable terror is to ask: what is
the unspeakable? The answer will of course be: the experience of violence
against human flesh wherein the body-surface registers and transmits
nothing but pain, a pain that produces nothing but horror, a horror
which reads, according to Spillers, like a laboratory prose of festering
flesh, of limbs torn from sockets, of breasts branded with hot iron, of
severed tendons, bruises, exposed nerves, swollen limbs, of missing teeth
as the technology of iron, whips, chains, bullets, knives, and canine patrol
went to work (Spillers, 1987: 67). It is the struggle, the longing to speak
these horrors and the inability, the near impossibility of doing so that
confers on slave history the experience of horror and what Gilroy has
termed the 'Slave Sublime' (1993).

The conflation of the body and the unspeakable draws us into an
awareness of our physical mortality and the erasure of the human voice.
In her influential book *The Body in Pain: The Making and Unmaking of the
World* (1985), Scarry argues poignantly that the presence of physical pain
is difficult to express, and also has the capacity to destroy the sufferer's
language because it has no referential content in the external world. Unlike
other states of consciousness such as psychological and somatic states of
being which have referentiality to the external world – love of x, fear of
y, hatred for, being hungry for, and so on – physical pain has no such
referentiality. Its non-referentiality prevents and inhibits the transformation
of the felt experience of pain, leaving it to reside in the body, where the
sufferer reverts back to a pre-linguistic state of incomprehensible wailing,
inaudible whisper, inarticulate screeching, primal whispering which
destroys language and all that is associated with language: subjectivity,
civilization, culture, meaning and understanding (Sa'ez, 1992: 137).

While Scarry's model is plausible it is still based on a conception of
what the appropriate function of the body is and the appropriate function of the mind. Thus, for as long as we conceive of pain as an activity
of the body, and language as the function of the mind, pain will continue
to be resistance to language, and its sedimentation in the body will con-

tinue to confirm the notion that the body is always outside of culture and pre-language. I suggest that we view pain as not necessarily resisting language, but rather as resisting everyday speech. Pain has its own morphology and its own logic which govern its expression and representation and which produce its own meaning. The body writhing on the ground in agony communicates to the spectator the presence of pain (even if unshareable), using the body as a resource to do so. What cannot be spoken in language is evoked through other cultural representation such as dance.

Gilroy has argued that, while the experience of the middle passage and the diasporic plight might be resistant to (verbal) language, it is not resistant to representation (1993). The cultures of the black diaspora he notes have been an attempt to bring that scene of 'pure physical experience of negation' (Scarry, 1985: 52) into the realms of representation. The most elemental expression of this can be found in the music and dance of the black diaspora which produced new cultural meanings of the African past, present and future. Although pain has no referential content in the external world it is not unrepresentable.

Because physical pain is so nearly inexpressible and 'flatly invisible', its presence is often relegated to the status of non-existence. According to Scarry, that which is expressible is often made visible and thus elicits more attention. The mechanisms of torture and war, she argues, establish the presence of intense pain as absence as the regimes translate the infliction of pain into a language of political power. For Scarry torture is language-destroying; therefore, to elicit information from the tortured while fully aware of his/her powerlessness is to deconstruct his/her world:

> Intense pain is world-destroying. In compelling confession, the torturer compels the prisoner to record and objectify the fact that intense pain is world-destroying. It is for this reason that while the content of the prisoner's answer is only sometimes important to the regime, the form of the answer, the fact of his answering, is always crucial. (1985: 29)

Of course not all forms of torture fall under the interrogational mode in the way Scarry describes. During slavery the use of torture was not to elicit information, but was used instead to inspire terror and confirm to the enslaved the incontestable power of their masters and mistresses (Patterson, 1982). It also facilitated the extraction of subsistence labour for the development of the mercantile and industrial economy. Scarry's claims for an internal structure of torture, however, have implications for these arguments.

As theorized by Lacan, we become social subjects through our subjection to the laws of language and our capacity to understand and articulate language. But, as Scarry suggests, the body in pain is not able to participate fully in civic life, because pain destroys the capacity of language;

the body is denied the facilities that make subjectivity possible. It should, however, be noted that the formative role of language in subject formation is not the only means of constituting subjectivity. However, the ability to verbally express the presence of pain is unavailable to the person in pain. The (near) impossibility of constituting pain in language initiates a splitting, a splitting between the speaking subject (voice) and corporeal subject (body). This separation between the tortured (powerless) and torturer (powerful) means that the torturers are able to circumvent material representation, and are represented and describable through the making present of their voice while corporeality is displaced onto the person in pain. Thus, the person in pain becomes mere flesh and can only experience her own body as the agent of her own agony (Scarry, 1985: 47). This way of perceiving the body permits the one who is being inflicted with pain to shift from the position of sufferer to being the agent of his/her own annihilation; the cause of the pain is represented as outside those inflicting that pain. The possession of voice becomes significant for both torturer and tortured. For the torturer, the awareness of voice confirms his power, his existence, the presence of a world; for the sufferer, the absence of a world, the awareness of his/her corporeality, the limit of his/her extension in the world. 'Consequently, to be intensely embodied is the equivalent of being represented ... is almost always the condition of those without power' (Scarry, 1985: 207). This has been precisely the claim of feminists and black theorists, who have pointed out that the association of blacks and females with corporeality excludes and debars them from the public sphere that makes subjectivity possible (Gatens, 1996; Spelman, 1990; Fanon, 1992).

The Economy of Violence; The Violence of Economy

In the narrative of *The History of Mary Prince: A West Indian Slave. Related by Herself* (1987) we have a rare example of writing from the perspective of a black female in British anti-slavery discourse. Mary Prince's account provides insight into the atrocities and barbarity of the slave system, its absurdity and unrelenting commitment to brutalization and mutilation of the flesh. It shows the cool, calculated contempt for the flesh and the capacity of this barbaric system to rip apart and expose hidden tissues to the brazen gaze of the violator, violating human decency. As in most abolitionist material, while concern was to show the atrocities and catastrophic terror of the slave system, piety was far more important to the abolitionist than the desire to retell events as they really were. The detailing of atrocities in *Mary Prince* is somewhat circumscribed, especially as it relates to sexual violence. Nevertheless, Mary Prince's account succeeded in providing details of the atrocities, and the near triumph of the violator/enslaver over the flesh.

A persistent and poignant theme throughout the narrative is the grotesque and harrowing detailing of physical brutality, the physical torment which resulted in Mary's near blindness, and rheumatism, her mistress's noxious brutality, and the sadistic treatment of other slaves:

> Sarah, who was nearly past work ... was subject to several bodily infirmities, and was not quite right in her head, did not wheel the barrow fast enough to please him [the master]. He threw her down on the ground, and after beating her severely, he took her up in his arms and flung her among the prickly-pear bushes, which are all covered over with sharp venomous prickles. By this her naked flesh was so grievously wounded, that her body swelled and festered all over and she died in a few days after. (Prince, 1987: 65)

It is this flesh, this live tissue that registers 'these lacerations, woundings, fissures, tears, scars, openings, ruptures, lesions, rendings, punctures of the flesh' (Spillers, 1987: 67), that feels the hurt, the intense pain, that is continuously attacked, mutilated, that experiences the flesh as a burden – a venomous prickly pear. It is this flesh, so horribly lacerated, that is marked for enslavement, for raw violence and objectification, that serves others' will-to-power and their becoming beings. It is these ineffaceable markings that conveniently invalidate all claim of ownership to her flesh, because it is reserved for her master. Her flesh is the signification of her worth within a system whose organizing principle is premised on a proprietary conception of bodies; a system which deemed it its birthright to legislate on her very humanity, control her movements, her body. As Spillers notes, within this legal system, 'every feature of social and human differentiation disappears in public discourses regarding the African-American person' (Spillers, 1987: 78).

As a slave, she is perceived as having no soul, no human speech, no gendered subjectivity, no culture or language to speak of. Therefore, to devise and enact such elaborate mechanisms of torture, to send waves of terror down the spine of the tortured was the protocol of those who regarded themselves as having those attributes. As Taussig remarked of the colonial conquest of Latin America, it is 'terror as usual'. The use of terror was a national sport during the period of slavery and colonialism; it was the logic underpinning the creation of colonial reality and identity: 'it serves as the mediator *par excellence* of colonial hegemony' (Taussig, 1987: 5).

If, as Scarry points out, the infliction of violence on the body is also an assault on language, similarly, the insatiable and perpetual infliction of raw violence on the slaves is consolidated by the erasure of the human voice. All verbal forms of communication were severed. The only form of communication was to literally work upon/put to work the body of the enslaved. For Mary Prince, when her body was put to work in harsh conditions, her flesh began to give way to tears and to seizure, rheumatism, excruciating backaches and to a near-blindness. Her body became the site of ejaculatory orgasms that disfigured her 'while the powers that don't be join for a loving circle jerk' (Sapphire, 1994: 14). She is unable to speak these ejaculatory horrors even when she is permitted to do so because of Christian piety and the enormity of her pain. Unable to express the presence of her pain, Mary's masters and mistresses communicated their presence, confirmed the absence of pain.

The point of this grotesque torment was to inspire terror in the minds of the enslaved and ensure the absence of their world. It confirmed the presence of the violator, and, therefore, that the body of the enslaved will always be the property of her master and mistress. The enslaved could never claim ownership of her body. As a slave, her subjection is an act of de-subjectification. As Scarry describes, in the structure of torture, the infliction of bodily pain, the rupturing of tissues, the exposure of interior skin results for the sufferer in the dissolution of a world akin to the process of dying. This damage, so unalterable, leaves its mark – for example, her persistent lower back ache and rheumatism – long after the infliction ceased: 'what is remembered in the body is well remembered' (Scarry, 1985: 113). All trace of humanity, civilization is deconstructed in the infliction of bodily pain:

> The arms that had learned to gesture in a particular way are unmade; the hands that held within them not just blood and bone but the movements that made possible the playing of piano are unmade; the fingers and palms that knew in intricate detail the weight and feel of a particular tool are unmade; the feet that had within them 'by heart' (that is, as a matter of deep bodily habit) the knowledge of how to pedal a bicycle are unmade; the head and arms and back and legs that contained within them an elaborate sequence of steps in a certain dance are unmade; all are deconstructed along with the tissue itself, the sentient source and site of all learning. (Scarry, 1985: 123)

The horror of slavery was that it was an act of active and systematic deconstruction. To be sure, many bodies were destroyed in the process. However, unlike the Nazi atrocities where the aim was the total extermination of a so-called inferior race, the slave system needed the slaves to work. Although a labour system characterized the Jewish Holocaust, destruction was the ultimate aim. Slavery, on the other hand, was first and foremost a system of labour. The slavers did not intend the slaves to die; they were concerned to ensure the survival of the black body – albeit in a demoralized form. The black female body is a useful body because it is both a labouring, sexual and reproducing body and therefore it was necessary to preserve the health of the enslaved woman. The use of violence was therefore necessary to break them in, to fragment them, to destabilize them and to make them cease to be subjects, to transform them into 'docile bodies' (Foucault, 1977) that became bodies that labour.

Clearly, the purpose of torture during slavery was not to destroy, but to deconstruct the world of the body in pain. Torture is an imitation of death 'a sensory equivalent, substituting prolonged mock execution for execution' (Scarry, 1985: 27), an externalized violation of the body and psyche. To destroy the body in pain would have been tantamount to economic and ideological suicide. For how could the slave system perpetuate itself if the enslaved population was destroyed? The violent subjection of the slaves was a way of transforming their bodies into an entity that could produce and reproduce the property necessary for accumulating wealth. Thus, the enslaver/victimizer 'needs the victim to create truth, objectifying fantasy in the discourse of the other' (Taussig, 1987: 8). Destruction would have hampered a European expansionist programme. Therefore, to have deconstructed all traces of civilization, humanity and freedom encapsulated within the bodies of the enslaved assured both their subjection and the enslaver's subjectivity. Thus, Mary Prince was forced to bear witness to her worldlessness – the disintegration of her world, language, nation, voice, body – while being relegated to corporeality.

Imprisoned thus, Prince is able only to experience herself in the extremities of her body; the body literally and metaphorically caved-in, turned-back-onto-itself. There is no liberation from the body. In one episode she described the enormity of her pain as overwhelming her until she wished for death. This desire becomes pronounced during an event when her mistress noticed that she had broken an already cracked jar, and ordered her to strip naked. She whipped Mary's bare flesh with the cow-skin until her flesh gaped with blood: 'I lay there till morning, careless of what might happen, for life was very weak in me, and I wished more than ever to die' (1987: 59). The presence of such prolonged suffering according to Scarry, is what causes the person in pain to experience her world as no world and her body as the source of pain, deconstructing her world and notions of selfhood in the process:

> It is intense pain that destroys a person's self and world, a destruction experienced spatially as either the contraction of the universe down to the immediate vicinity of the body or as the body swelling to fill the entire universe. (Scarry, 1985: 35)

For Scarry then, the infliction of extreme physical violence is an attack, a destruction of subjectivity. This of course implies that the outcome of physical torment is the destruction of a pre-existing subject (Sa'ez, 1992). This is clearly not the case for the slaves. Their enslavement meant that all right to humanity and subjectivity was stripped at the moment of capture. According to Patterson, a slave had no claim to her person, no right to citizenship; she is the property of her master or mistress. Patterson quotes Henri Wallon:

> The slave was a dominated thing, an animated instrument, a body with natural movements, but without its own reason, an existence entirely absorbed in another. The proprietor of this thing, the mover of this instrument, the soul and the reason of this body, the source of this life was the master. The master was everything for him: his father and his god, which is to say, his authority and his duty. (Quoted in Patterson, 1982: 4)

The slave then ceases to be subject, all claims to personhood having been stripped at the time of capture, and she had no social existence: 'The slave was the ultimate human tool, as imprintable and as disposable as the master wished' (Patterson, 1982: 7). Thus the use of torture on the body of the enslaved suggests not a deconstruction of a pre-existing subject, but a radical desubjectification of a desubjectified subject. And in so far as the individual derives its subjectivity from the collective body, the absence of the apparatus that makes subjectivity possible means that the collective body also had to undergo a process of desubjectification.

Deconstructing Gender, Producing Property

If Scarry's thesis suggests that the infliction of extreme physical violence deconstructs and unmakes the world of the person in pain, Hortense Spillers's essay 'Mama's baby, papa's maybe: an American grammar book', provides an account of the way in which this deconstruction of the subject also entailed a deconstruction of gendered categories. Spillers contends that the transformation of the African captive into a commodified property deconstructed the African kinship structure, flesh and gendered subjectivity. As she sees it, in 'severing the captive body from its motive will, its active desire ... we lose at least gender difference in the outcome, and the female body and the male body become a territory of cultural and political maneuver, not at all gender-related, gender-specific' (1987: 67). Spillers notes that although the spatial organization of the slaver's hull revealed 'the application of the gender rule' (67), this was based on the logic of commodity, rather than on a conception of subjectivity constituted via gender difference. Using a Lacanian model, she argues that in so far as the captives were 'literally suspended in the "oceanic"' they cannot assume a gendered position because 'gendering' 'takes place within the confines of the domestic, an essential metaphor that then spreads its tentacles for male and female subject over a wider ground of human and social purposes' (1987: 72). Spillers's account of 'ungendering' is grounded within a legal discourse that marked the enslaved as non-human and consequently denied the rights accruing to the body that is considered to be human. Therefore, contrary to the arguments often mounted in second-wave feminism, which thought that gender deconstruction would lead to an androgynous utopia, Spillers's account suggests this is clearly not the case. In fact gender deconstruction results in a stripping away of any claims to personhood.

According to Spillers, in the slavers' hull enslaved women are prohibited from participating in the reproduction of mothering, which within 'this historical instance carries few of the benefits of a patriarchalized female gender, which, from one point of view, is the only female gender there is' (73). Therefore, the reproduction of mothering has radically different meanings for free white women and enslaved black women. For white women reproduction enables them to define themselves as human subjects since they are able to birth the next generation of the human subject even though they are excluded from full participation in the public realm of citizenship. For the enslaved woman, constituted as property, her reproductive capacity did not free her, in fact it reinstated her role as property. In this instance reproduction is not a reproduction of mothering but of property, because she transmits her unfreedom to her offspring. Spillers points to the way in which for the white enslavers descent is passed through the father's lineage, who then has ownership and control over his children and wife. But they were not regarded as non-human. For the enslaved descent was recognized through the mother and her children inherited their status from their mother. This means, according to Spillers, that the African male captive cannot participate in the social realm of the Law of the Father. Thus, gendered identity for the enslaved carries a double paternity. As Spillers writes, 'under the conditions of captivity, the offspring of the female does not "belong" to the Mother, nor is s/he "related" to the "owner", [but] "possesses" it, ... often fathered it, and, as often, without whatever benefit of patrimony' (74).

The destruction of kinship structure Spillers sees as a destruction of maternal rights and consequently a deconstruction of gendered subjectivity. The 'ungendering' process reduced the enslaved subject into a productive capital which denies the right to the claims subjectivity and humanity entails: citizenship, gender, name, language, family, marriage and rights to property: 'In this absence from a subject position, the captured sexualities provide a physical and biological expression of "otherness"' (67).

Reconstructing the Flesh

The fact that my focus on the body so far has fixed the experience of the body as a site of extreme physical violence for the purpose of utility is not to suggest that the body was always experienced in that manner, or that the captive body always relates to him/herself and the captive community solely as property. Rather, I am simply trying to capture the experience of the body from a single perspective in a given moment in its history. The body, as it were, is not what it is and it is not yet what it will become. Even though history has been terribly unkind to the

African body, the body was and still is capable of being something quite beautiful, quite sensuous, quite joyous. There is always a memory of the 'flesh', of the flesh that was once liberated. So, by way of summary, I want to return to the distinction Spillers makes between the flesh and the body to suggest an emancipatory reading of the body.

For Spillers the 'flesh' that is transformed to body as property is never totally wiped out in this transformation. Rather, it is hidden from the violation of the body. The flesh makes itself known to the body and in this visibility the captive male and female are carried to the frontiers of survival (Spillers, 1987: 67). This transformative return reunites the African captives to their ancestral body; it retrieves, recovers the memory of the body's capacity for resistance, for transformation, for healing. It is this somatic retrieval and recollection that facilitates the creation of what George Lipsitz calls 'counter-memory' (1991). Counter-memory enabled the slaves and their descendants to construct a different kind of history, a different kind of knowledge, a different kind of body that is outside the control of the dominant history and knowledge production. The body's return to the flesh is a central site for the production of that counter-memory. We see this in the expressive cultures of the people of the African diaspora. In her essay 'The Site of Memory', Toni Morrison expresses the way memories for diasporean Africans are stored in artifacts, stories and bodies:

> You know, they straightened out the Mississippi River in places, to make room for houses and livable acreage. Occasionally the river floods these places. 'Floods' is the word they use, but in fact it is not flooding; it is remembering. Remembering where it used to be. All water has a perfect memory and is forever trying to get back where it was. Writers are like that: remembering where we were, what valley we ran through, what the banks were like, the light that was there and the route back to our original place. It is emotional memory – where the nerves and the skin remember how it appeared. And a rush of imagination is our 'flooding'. (Morrison, 1990)

The terrorized body remembers the stories of the flesh and makes every effort to trace its step back to the feel of the flesh, the fecundity, the freedom and the dance of the flesh.

Note

I would like to thank Ekow Essuman, Jan Shinebourne and Bunmi Daramola for their stimulating and spirited dialogues, David Dibosa for bringing Toni Morrison's essay to my attention, and special thanks to Terry Lovell and Christine Battersby for their helpful critique.

References

Bordo, S. 1990. 'Reading the slender body.' In Mary Jacobus, Evelyn Fox Keller and Sally Shuttleworth (eds), *Body/Politics, Women and the Discourses of Science*. New York: Routledge.

Butler, J. 1993. *Bodies that Matter: On the Discursive Limits of Sex*. New York: Routledge.

Carter, A. 1979. *The Sadeian Woman*. London: Virago.

Fanon, F. 1992. 'The fact of blackness.' In James Donald and Ali Rattansi (eds), *'Race', Culture and Difference*. London: Sage.

Featherstone, M. and M. Hepworth (eds). 1991. 'The mask of ageing and the postmodern life course.' In M. Featherstone, M. Hepworth and B. Turner (eds), *The Body: Social Process and Cultural Theory*. London: Sage.

Foucault, Michel. 1977. *Discipline and Punish: The Birth of the Prison*. London: Allen Lane.

Foucault, Michel. 1991. *The Foucault Reader: An Introduction to Foucault's Thought*, ed. P. Rabinow. London: Penguin.

Gatens, Moira. 1996. *Imaginary Bodies: Ethics, Power and Corporeality*. London and New York: Routledge.

Gilman, S. 1985. *Difference and Pathology: Stereotypes of Sexuality, Race and Madness*. New York: Cornell University Press.

Gilroy, P. 1993. *The Black Atlantic: Modernity and Double Consciousness*, London: Verso.

Grosz, E. 1995. *Volatile Bodies: Toward a Corporeal Feminism*. Bloomington and Indianapolis: Indiana University Press.

Jordan, W.D. 1982. 'First impressions: initial English confrontations with Africans.' In C. Husband (ed.), *'Race' in Britain*. London: Hutchinson.

Lipsitz, G. 1991. *Time Passages*. Minneapolis: University of Minnesota Press.

Morrison, Toni. 1990. 'Site of memory.' In Russell Ferguson et al. (eds), *Out There: Marginalization and Contemporary Culture*. Cambridge, MA: MIT Press.

Patterson, O. 1982. *Slavery and Social Death: A Comparative Study*. Cambridge, MA: Harvard University Press.

Prince, Mary. 1987. *The History of Mary Prince: A West Indian Slave. Related by Herself*, ed. Moira Ferguson. Michigan: University of Michigan Press,

Sa'ez, N. 1992. 'Torture: a discourse on practice.' In F.E. Mascia-Lees and P. Sharpe (eds), *Tattoo, Torture, Mutilation and Adornment: The Denaturalization of the Body in Culture and Text*. Albany, NY: State University of New York Press.

Sapphire. 1994. *American Dreams*. London: Serpent's Tail.

Scarry, E. 1985. *The Body in Pain: The Making and Unmaking of the World*, New York: Oxford University Press.

Schiebinger, L. 1994. *Nature's Body: Sexual Politics and the Making of Modern Science*. London: Pandora.

Spelman, E. 1990. *Inessential Woman: Problems of Exclusion in Feminist Thought*. London: Women's Press.

Spillers, H. 1987. 'Mama's baby, papa's maybe: an American grammar book', *Diacritics*, vol. 17, no. 2, Summer.

Taussig, M. 1987. *Shamanism, Colonialism and The Wildmen: A Study in Terror and Healing*. Chicago: University of Chicago Press.

Turner, B. 1984. *The Body and Society: Explorations in Social Theory*. London: Sage.

14
Enslaved Black Women: The Politics of Reproduction and Infanticide

Helen Thomas

For Africa and its people, the practice of slavery during the seventeenth and eighteenth centuries was catastrophic in terms of its sudden over-turning of African culture and tradition, the disastrous effects of de-population upon the African continent and the innumerable physical and psychological tortures suffered by the slaves themselves. In their refusal to acknowledge Africans as fellow human beings on the basis of racial 'difference', proponents of slave ideology encouraged the unspeakable degradation of these slaves during their passage from Africa to the Americas. Thereafter, slaves were unrecognized by legislature and deprived of all human and formal rights. Following the cessation of the Royal African Company's monopoly over the trade in African slaves in 1698, the number of slave shipments in English vessels owned by private merchants rose dramatically and reached a total of 30–40,000 per year between 1750 and 1800. It has been estimated that the number of slaves shipped from Africa during the eighteenth century totalled approximately 6.7 million and that participating individuals and concerns may have generated as much as £300 million in profit. Since the statutory law of England accepted the slave system as a legal extension of the concept of property, the laws of the British colonies maintained this absolute erosion of slaves' subjectivity by means of common law principles. In 1637, the Government Council of Barbados decreed that those Africans and Indi-ans who arrived on the island as slaves would 'serve for life' unless a contract had been made to the contrary. Likewise, in 1672, the Antigua assembly ordered that a mulatto child produced by interracial sex would remain a slave for life (Cummins, 1994: 55).

The transmission of slave status through the mother created a particular problematic for the female slave and her reproductive rights: a child born to a female slave would remain a slave for life, even if its father were a freeman or, indeed, master. Apart from the handful of slaves who were granted their freedom by acts of manumission, the vast majority remained slaves until death.

'Institutionalized Sexism' and Racial Imperialism

In her authoritative and provocative analysis of black women and feminism, *Ain't I a Woman?*, bell hooks located 'institutionalized sexism' as the most significant factor informing racial imperialism and the American social structure (hooks, 1992: 115). According to hooks, sexism constituted an 'integral part of the social and political order' which white colonizers carried with them from Europe, a factor which was to have a 'grave impact on the fate of enslaved black women'. As a development of hooks's assessment of colonial ideology, this chapter seeks to examine the complex network of sexual 'contracts' between slave-owners and their slaves during the late eighteenth and early nineteenth centuries by means of an analysis of three main texts: the narrative by the male slave, Olaudah Equiano, published in 1789; the narrative by the female slave Harriet Jacobs, published in 1861; and the diaries of Thomas Thistlewood, the son of a Lincolnshire farmer who arrived in Jamaica in 1750 and lived there as a slave-owner until his death in 1786. In so doing, I seek to identify the complex sexual dynamics (including rape, pregnancy and infanticide) between slaves and their masters as a microcosm of the volatile colonial situation, itself a complex site of vulnerability, rebellion and autonomy, against the backdrop of colonial ideology and the corresponding legislature.

In the first of these texts, a two-volume work published in England in 1789 by the ex-slave Olaudah Equiano, the author presents a chilling account of the horrors to which enslaved black women were exposed on board the slave ships during their voyage from Africa across the Atlantic's middle passage:

> It was almost a constant practice with our clerks, and other whites, to commit violent *depredations on the chastity of the female slaves* … I have even known them [the clerks] gratify their brutal passion with females not yet ten years old; and these abominations some of them practised to such scandalous excess. (Equiano, 1789: 206)

Equiano's exposure of the slave traders' sadistic acts of sexual tyranny are, however, further complicated by his own complicity as a participant in the trade (working as a trader himself) and by his collusion (albeit as an observer) in his fellow shipmates' violations of his countrywomen: 'these [depredations] I was, though with reluctance, obliged to submit to at all times'. Yet his confessional 'eye-witness' account of these sexual plunderings highlights the complex dynamics between male and female Africans and their desperate attempts to counteract the effects of cultural dispossession via acts of non-compliance and/or collusion with the 'host' culture.

Given that rape was a common method used by slavers to subdue recalcitrant female slaves and that many African women were pregnant prior to their capture on board slave ships or transfer between slave plantations, a historical examination of the practices of fertility control, abortion and infanticide amongst slave women raises a plethora of important legal, social, economic and cultural issues (Morgan, 1994: 60–69). Significantly, it was during the seventeenth and eighteenth centuries that laws concerning infanticide in England and New England acquired their present form (Hoffer and Hull, 1981: ix). Prior to this and as a consequence of the Puritans' campaign against women's crimes, condemnations of child murder carried with them severe penalties. These interpreted concealment of death of a new-born as evidence of murder punishable by whipping, imprisonment or even death in the gallows. Subsequently, a more merciful toleration of illicit sexuality led to more lenient rulings.

Hence, whereas in 1562 George Parke (a clergyman), Jane Saway (a midwife) and Helena Millicent (the recipient of Parke's adulterous advances) were all hanged for their conspiracy to kill Millicent's child when it was born, eighteenth-century England and New England witnessed a significant decline in the number of indictments for infanticide. Yet despite this, between 1670 and 1780, blacks in New England were found guilty of these 'crimes' at one and a half times the rate of whites, even though they made up less than 4 per cent of the population. For instance, during the 1730s, an Indian female named Patience was tried twice in New England for infanticide: once for murdering her new-born child and later for strangling her master's neighbour's young son (Hoffer, 1981: 47–8).

Regardless of the number of indictments for infanticide, in the British Caribbean the significant decrease in the slave population was perceived as generating a permanent state of crisis. In Jamaica, for example, together with the low female to male ratio and the high risk of venereal disease amongst slaves, planters regarded induced abortions as one of the most significant factors in the slave population's failure to maintain its numbers (Higman, 1984: 304). Amongst free and enslaved women, incidents of miscarriage, abortion and infanticide were mainly unreported; deaths of infants aged five and under went unrecorded in the slave registration returns.

Amongst the slave populations of eighteenth-century North America and the nineteenth-century Caribbean, slave numbers had to be supplemented by the importation of newly enslaved Africans. Hence, apart from the pernicious effects of disease in slave societies, two of the most significant factors contributing to slave population decline were low birth rates amongst female slaves and high rates of infant mortality. Whilst the sexual exploitation of female slaves by male masters reveals a great deal about the sexual mores of eighteenth- and nineteenth-century society, the rape of such slaves must also be seen as a form of sexual and political violence, strategically set within an economic schema. In other words, rape was a method deliberately used by plantation owners and their overseers as a means of simultaneously maintaining their authority *and* enhancing the overall monetary value of the plantation by increasing the number of slaves. Only a small number of the children born to coloured creoles (slaves born in the Americas) in the Caribbean were fathered by blacks; most were fathered by whites, a fact which exposes the dominance of white physical and psychosocial compulsions (Higman, 1984: 359).

Apart from the slave masters' preference for lighter skinned women, they may have been influenced by the fact that creoles, unlike Africans, possessed a relatively sophisticated immunity to certain mortal diseases. Slave ideology therefore encouraged large-scale interference with the normal sexual habits of slaves in order to increase female fertility and rates of reproduction. As a consequence of this effort to increase slave reproduction and to safeguard against infanticide, female slaves in the British Caribbean were offered cash rewards for producing children, reduced working hours and varying degrees of medical care. For instance, the Newton Estate in Barbados gave slave-mothers 6s. 3d. if their children survived for more than one month. Likewise, since it was known to reduce fertility, slave-owners imposed limits on the time a slave woman could continue to breastfeed (Higman, 1984: 322, 348–9). As the role of the midwife became increasingly important in the slave plantations, it can be no coincidence that the wealthy Scottish plantation owner James Wedderburn was proud of his role as both slave-owner and male 'midwife' (Wedderburn, 1824: 6, 8).

The journal entries of the Jamaican slave-owner Thomas Thistlewood confirm the excessive nature of sexual desire directed towards female slaves, a desire informed by the slaves' limited means of self-defence and their infinite accessibility as legally determined forms of property:

Tuesday, 19th Feb. 1754: At night *Cum* Phibbah, Sup. me. lect.
Thursday, 21st Feb: p.m. *Cum* Phibbah. Illa habet menses.
Friday, 22nd Feb: At night *Cum* Phibbah.
Sunday, 24th Feb: At night *Cum* Phibbah ...
Friday, 1st March: p.m. *Cum* Phibbah and, in the evening, *Cum* Susanah in the curing-house, stans ...
Friday, 2nd July, 1767: Coming home, *Cum* Mirtilla *mea, sup. terr.* in the old Boiling House.
Fri. 13 Nov. 1767: *Cum* Franke [aged 15] *mea Sup* large cotton tree. (Hall, 1989: 62, 155)

Another of Thistlewood's female slaves was Damsel, a Chamboy slave purchased in 1765, aged 13, for £60. Damsel's original cultural markings of three long strokes down each cheek were effectively superseded by Thistlewood's ownership of her person as a form of property (her right shoulder was branded with his initials), as a sexual object and as a breeding machine. In his diary entry of Wednesday, 9 November 1774, Thistlewood recorded his sexual activities with her in his typical coded script, '*Cum Damsel (mea) Sup. Terr.*' On Sunday, 16 April 1775, Damsel went into labour and produced a son Quashe (valued in 1787 at £50), indicating that she was already five months pregnant at the time of Thistlewood's earlier advances (Hall, 1989: 315, 211). Damsel's other children (possibly fathered by Thistlewood) included Nelly (born September 1772), Viney (born July 1778) and Juno (born December 1785).

Resistance Strategies by Female Slaves

Yet, in spite of the significant extent of reproductive interference by planters as revealed by Thistlewood's journals, the low rate of slave re-production remained a crucial concern amongst West Indian slave-owners. This suggests that apart from those infants who died of whooping cough, diarrhoea or fever, many slave women aborted or miscarried their foe-tuses, or bore dead or dying infants. Using inherited knowledge from Africa, abortive techniques employed by female slaves included infusions from herbs, shrubs and bark and the use of sharp instruments inserted into the vaginal canal. As physicians in the slave-states of Tennessee and Georgia observed, despite slave masters' promises of special treatment for female slaves who became pregnant, self-induced abortions and con-traceptives devised from herbal formulae were frequently used by female slaves to prevent reproduction:

> They [female slaves] take it [camphor] just before or after menstruation, in quantities sufficient to produce a little nervousness for two or three days; when it has effect they consider themselves safe ... All country physicians are aware of the frequent complaint of planters of the *unnatural tendency in the African female population to destroy their offspring* ... Whole families of women fail to have any children. (Gutman, 1975: 70, 80, 393)

It has been estimated that in the British Caribbean approximately 50 per cent of infant deaths occurred in the first months. In St Kitts, the number of infants who died between 1817 and 1821 averaged 320 per 1000 live births, whilst in St Vincent this figure reached 360 per 1000, thus representing over one-third of the total number of births (Higman, 1984: 28).

Given the efforts made to advance contraceptive practices amongst the working class in England, it seems unlikely that knowledge of these methods failed to reach slave-owners and overseers in the colonies. As a result, their manipulation of their slaves' socio-sexual relations and reproductive systems must be seen within a strategic economic framework. Although the most significant breakthrough in the development of birth control coincided with the vulcanization of rubber by Hancock in England and Goodyear in America in 1844, the membranous condom (made from the dried gut of a sheep), or 'cundum', had been available for some decades (Hines, 1963: 187–92). In late-eighteenth-century England, hand-bills were distributed advertising the sale of 'cundums' such as that of 1776 which described the sheaths for sale at Mrs Philips's shop on London's Strand. In 1822, the founder of the Birth Control Movement, Francis Place, published his treatise on contraceptive measures, a work entitled *Illustrations and Proofs of the Principle of Population*. In this and other contraceptive handbills disseminated amongst the working classes, Place described the ways in which a 'sufficient check' might prevent the increase in population 'beyond the means of subsistence' by placing a piece of sponge into the vagina 'previous to coition' (Place, 1822: 165, 212–13). Similarly, in 1825 the editor of *The Republican* and *The Lion*, Richard Carlile (who spent time in jail on charges of blasphemy) published his *Every Woman's Book; or, What is Love?* In this text, which he claimed was not 'like one of those vile, mischievous, misleading, and fraudulent books … but a book of physical, philosophical and moral instruction', Carlile described the ways in which conception might be avoided:

> The important discovery is, that if, before sexual intercourse, the female introduces into her vagina a piece of sponge as large as can be pleasantly introduced, having previously attached a bobbin or bit of narrow riband to withdraw it, it will, in most cases, be found a preventive to conception, that shall neither lessen the pleasure of the female nor injure her health … One [other means] is, to wear the glove … Another is, not to inseminate the female, by observing a partial or complete withdrawing at the moment of seminal emission. (Carlile, 1826: 47–8, 38–9)

Yet decades before these publications, or the subsequent dissertations on 'coitus interruptus' and 'douching' by Robert Owen and Charles Knowlton between 1828 and 1832, female slaves were successfully controlling their own fertility and reproductive capacities on the slave plantations in America and the Caribbean.

As a consequence of this, slave testimonies, slave journals and slave-owners' diaries are filled with comments on the high frequency of abortions, miscarriages and the magico-medicinal remedies used to prevent or abort pregnancy. Enslaved black women's deliberate acts of induced abortion thus constituted a deliberate assertion of reproductive cognition and control. In so doing, they presented a significant challenge to the legislature both in England and the colonies, in particular sections 58 and 59 of the Offences Against the Person Act 1861 which prohibited (under criminal law) the procuring of miscarriage:

Every woman, being with child, who, with intent to procure her own miscarriage, shall unlawfully administer to herself any poison or other noxious thing, or shall unlawfully use any instrument or other means whatsoever with the like intent ... shall be guilty of an offence. (Mason, 1989: 45–79)

As the legal status of blacks at this time was practically non-existent, 'rape' (or 'raptus mulierum', the carnal knowledge of a woman taken forcibly and against her will) meant rape of white women, for 'no such crime as rape of a black woman existed at law' (Genovese, 1974: 33). The female slave's attempts to gain ownership of her own body by various methods of birth control, including abortion and infanticide, represented a complex challenge to a system of unlimited sexual access, maintained by the social structure and patriarchal ideologies of plantation society. In a sense, therefore, the preservation of colonial ideologies was significantly undermined by the slaves' voluntary acts of partial or lineal self-erasure. As an extreme example of this, the runaway slave Margaret Garner (the inspiration of Toni Morrison's acclaimed novel, *Beloved*), who escaped from Kentucky to Ohio in 1856, voluntarily murdered her own daughter rather than see her enslaved again (Davis, 1981: 21). These acts signified strategic negations of self-reproduction, wilful acts of biological and psychological self-forgetting or 'amnesia' which prescribed a complex reversion of plantocratic autonomy and which highlighted the complexity of the female slave's experience.

Six years after Margaret Garner's act of infanticide, the escaped slave Harriet Jacobs published her autobiographical account, *Incidents in the Life of a Slave Girl* (1861), in Boston, under the pseudonym Linda Brent and with the help of two female abolitionists, Amy Post and Lydia Maria Child. In its significant departure from the majority of male-centred slave narratives published around this time, Jacobs's narrative presents an explicit account of the experiences of a female slave. In so doing, it reveals the dynamics of racial and sexual abuse at work within the domestic scene of the plantation system. Yet Jacobs's careful exposure of what plantocratic society denied means that her text mediates awkwardly between the accepted dominant linguistic order and the silenced, hidden practices of early-nineteenth-century American society. Thus when she stridently declares, 'I willingly take the responsibility of presenting them [the public] with the veil withdrawn,' her allusion to the veil provides an appropriate euphemism for the hymen's location in the plantocratic world of sexual victimization.

I now entered on my fifteenth year – a sad epoch in the life of a slave girl. My master began to whisper foul words in my ear. Young as I was, I could not remain ignorant of their import ... He [Mr Flint] was a crafty man, and resorted to many means to accomplish his purposes. Sometimes he had stormy terrific ways, that made his victims tremble; sometimes he assumed a gentleness that he thought must surely subdue … He told me I was his property; that I must be subject to his will in all things. (Jacobs, 1861: 44–5)

Jacobs's own 'inter'-position as intermediary between her master and his wife, and between sexual and cultural 'knowledge' of the West and its antithesis, skilfully locates the dissolution between the boundaries of body and text, dominant narrative and subversive subtext. As she states in the chapter entitled 'The Jealous Mistress', the secrets of slavery are 'concealed like those of the Inquisition': 'My master was … the father of eleven slaves … [slave-owners] regard such children as property, as marketable as the pigs on the plantation' (Jacobs, 1861: 55–7). As she withdraws into an attic space (her 'loophole of retreat') for a period of seven years in order to escape her tyrannical master (even though this means that she must abandon her children), this complex form of rebellious 'self-erasure' enables her to re-establish a sense of physical and sexual autonomy. Thus her text articulates a form of self-inflicted marginalization which paradoxically empowers, a process not unlike the female slaves' conscious acts of non-reproduction.

As the slave interviews and testimonies collected by John Blassingame indicate, the threat of sexual violence by slave-owners functioned as a convenient means of control amidst the plantations and as a vent for their own private sexual frustrations. As one ex-slave reported, his slave master would 'use' a female slave whenever he saw fit: 'He generally carried a white oak cane, and if the woman did not submit, would make nothing of knocking her right down' (Blassingame, 1974: 400). Or, as another female slave testified, 'Dats my chile by him [the master] … I didnt want him but I couldnt do nothin. I uster say, what do yer want a woman all cut ter pieces like I is? But 'twant no use' (Blassingame, 1979: 540).

Harriet Jacobs transfers the scars of sexual violence onto text by reinflicting their mark on the American public and thereby reinscribes her claims for self-ownership through her confession of sexual victimization. She articulates her witness of sexual violence ('It pains me to tell you of it; but I have promised to tell you the truth') within a narrative structure which provides an alternative to the legislative arena from which she is denied entry (Jacobs, 1861: 83–4). Hence she is able to testify to her master's practice of psychological rape (as he 'peoples' her mind with unclean images) and excessive sexual abuse, as he forces her to witness his daily violations of the 'most sacred commands of nature' (Jacobs, 1861: 44–6) – presumably masturbation. Likewise, the crucial tenth chapter of her narrative, which is entitled 'A perilous passage in the slave girl's life', provides an appropriate duplicitous allusion to the slaves' transportation across the middle passage *and* the perils to which female slaves are exposed on their entrance into womanhood: 'The condition of a slave confuses all principles of morality, and, in fact, renders the practice of them impossible' (Jacobs, 1861: 85). Whilst exposing her own sexual vulnerability, Jacobs's text highlights the ambiguous triangular relationship between the slave-owner, his wife and his slaves and suggests that whilst Mr Flint's sexual advances are scarcely hidden from his wife's watchful gaze, Mrs Flint insists on identifying Jacobs as the sole threat to her conjugal sanctity:

> She [Mrs Flint] felt that her marriage vows were desecrated, her dignity insulted; but she had no compassion for the poor victim of her husband's perfidy. She pitied herself as the martyr; but she was incapable of feeling for the condition of shame and misery in which her unfortunate, helpless slave was placed. (Jacobs, 1861: 53)

Conclusion: 'My Story Ends with Freedom'

Jacobs's concluding declaration, 'Reader, my story ends with freedom; not in the usual way with marriage' typifies both a rejection of conventional narrative technique and an admission of her preference for illicit (non-sanctioned) sexual liaison, rather than the sexual victimization inherent in the slave system:

> It seems less degrading to give one's self, than to submit to compulsion. There is something akin to freedom in having a lover who has no control over you, except that which he gains by kindness and attachment ... I knew what I did, and I did it with deliberate meditation ... I feel that the slave woman ought not to be judged by the same standards as others. (Jacobs, 1861: 302, 84–6)

Her unorthodox bid for freedom and socio-sexual autonomy epitomizes, in a succinct form, the enslaved black woman's deliberate endeavours to preserve her sense of selfhood in spite of the catastrophic effects of slavery. In other words, as the texts of Equiano, Jacobs and Thistlewood demonstrate, through their efforts to maintain a significant level of resistance to the perpetrators of slave ideology, namely by the practices of abortion, birth control and infanticide, female slaves enacted their own dramatic subversion of the plantocratic order. In their strategic responses to the socio-sexual manipulation, sexual victimization and enforced reproduction of the plantation system, enslaved females continued to maintain a sense of autonomy. For many enslaved black women, therefore, alongside the conscious negation of slave ideology, the irrepressible momentum of liberty prescribed a preference for 'death' in terms of 'self-erasure', a conscious denial of self- and cultural-reproduction.

References

Blassingame, John. 1979. *Slave Testimony: Two Centuries of Letters, Speeches, Interviews and Autobiographies*. Baton Rouge: Louisiana State University Press.

Craton, Michael. 1974. *Sinews of Empire: A Short History of British Slavery*. London: Temple Smith.

Cummins, Alissandra. 1994. 'Caribbean slave society.' In Anthony Tibbles (ed.), *Transatlantic Slavery*. London: HMSO.

Davis, Angela. 1981. *Women, Race and Class*. London: Women's Press.

Equiano, Olaudah. 1789. *The Interesting Narrative of Olaudah Equiano, or Gustavus Vassa, the African, Written by Himself*. 2 vols. London: T. Wilkin.

Genovese, Eugene. 1974. *Roll, Jordan, Roll: The World the Slaves Made*. London: André Deutsch.

Grose, Francis (ed.). 1785. *The Classical Dictionary of the Vulgar Tongue*. London.

Gutman, H.G. 1975. *The Black Family in Slavery and Freedom, 1750–1925*. New York: Pantheon.

Hall, Douglas. 1989. *In Miserable Slavery: Thomas Thistlewood in Jamaica, 1750–86*. London: Macmillan.

Higman, B.W. 1984. *Slave Populations of the British Caribbean 1807–1834*. London: Johns Hopkins University Press.

Hines, Norman. 1963. *A Medical History of Contraception*. New York: Schoken Books.

Hoffer, Peter and N.E. Hull. 1981. *Murdering Mothers: Infanticide in England and New England*. New York: New York University Press.

hooks, bell. 1992. *Ain't I a Woman? Black Women and Feminism*. London: Pluto Press.

Jacobs, Harriet. 1861. *Incidents in the Life of a Slave Girl*. (Repr. Oxford: Oxford University Press, 1988).

Mason, Ken. 1989. 'Abortion and the law.' In Sheila McLean (ed.), *Legal Issues in Human Reproduction*. London: Gower.

Morgan, Jennifer Lyle. 1994. 'Women in Slavery and the transatlantic slave trade.' In Anthony Tibbles (ed.), *Transatlantic Slavery: Against Human Dignity*. London: HMSO.

Place, Francis. 1822. *Illustrations and Proofs of the Principle of Population*. (Repr. London: Longman, Hurst, Rees, Orme and Brown, 1823).

Richardson, David. 1994. 'Liverpool and the Caribbean slave trade.' In Anthony Tibbles (ed.), *Transatlantic Slavery: Against Human Dignity*. London: HMSO.

Smith, Valeri. 1960. *Self-Discovery and Authority in Afro-American Narratives*. Cambridge, MA: Harvard University Press.

Washington, Helen. 1897. *Invented Lives: Narratives of Black Women, 1860–1960*. (Repr. London: Virago, 1989).

Wedderburn, Robert. 1824. *The Horrors of Slavery Exemplified in the Life and History of the Rev. Robert Wedderburn*. London: Wedderburn.

Part V

Gendered Victimization:
Migration, Poverty, Famines

15

Invisible Subjects and the Victimized Self: Settlement Experiences of Refugee Women in Australia

Roberta Julian

At a BIMPR (Bureau of Immigration, Multicultural and Population Research) 'Women in Migration' conference held in Sydney, Australia, in June 1996, both participants and organizers acknowledged that refugee women were notably absent. A number of sessions had been organized with a focus on emerging communities in Australia but the presence and thus the 'voices' of recent arrivals, many of whom have entered the country as refugees, were missing. This highlighted one of the major ways in which refugee women differ from other migrant women in Australia; namely, their invisibility and their extreme powerlessness. While the conference was acknowledged as an overall success we left it with the feeling that we had achieved little by way of recognizing and/or representing the views of the most 'invisible' women in Australia.

In Australia, refugee women rarely represent themselves in any public forum. Typically they are spoken about and represented by others, such as feminist academics and migrant women of longer standing in Australia, most of whom are concerned to publicize the plight of refugee women. However, this political project depends in part upon a process of 'victimization'. Thus, in the public sphere refugee women are predominantly represented as victims: of war, of persecution, of tragedy and of state and patriarchal oppression. In this chapter I provide a critique of this public image of refugee women as invisible and powerless victims. I do this through an examination of the experiences of a sample of refugee women who have resettled in Australia since the mid 1970s.

The aims of this chapter are: to address the invisibility of refugee women in the sociological literature, particularly theories of migration and settlement; to critically examine the dominant representations of refugee women in this literature; and to disrupt the 'taken-for-grantedness' of these representations by presenting some empirical data on the settlement experiences of refugee women in Australia which contradict these over-simplifications. In particular, this material will disrupt the homogeneity of the representations by demonstrating diversity; adopt the conceptualization of identities as multiple and shifting as a framework to question the implicit essentializing which often takes place when referring to 'refugee women'; and finally, question the utility of conceptualizing 'victim' and 'agent' as oppositional subject positions in an analysis of the experiences of refugee women.

Methodologically, I will do this by drawing on the women's own experiences as presented in the context of household interviews conducted in 1995. Finally, I will suggest the need to recognize victim and agent as shifting subject positions and thus to acknowledge the confluence of victimization and agency under certain conditions. I will do this by adopting the concept of the 'victimized self' as presented by Johnson and Ferraro (1984) in their analysis of battered women.

The analysis has implications not only for our understanding of the lives of refugee women, but for the lives of other women for whom the discourse of modernity continues to legitimate stereotypical, essentializing images which serve to maintain Western hegemony: for example, 'Third World women' and 'migrant women'. Refugee women do not constitute a homogeneous category and thus should not be represented as an undifferentiated 'other'. Deconstructing the category to reveal difference(s) is an important step in identifying the multiple axes which shape women's lives and thus in recognizing the shifting, situated identities which unite women as well as divide them.

Theories of Migration

Historically, theories of population movement/migration have tended to make a qualitative distinction between refugee movements (defined as involuntary migration) and other population movements (defined as voluntary migration) (for overviews of the latter see Borowski et al., 1994; Hugo, 1994; Snowden, 1990; Papademetriou, 1988). Furthermore, migration theories focus almost exclusively on voluntary migration (Richmond, 1988). The legacy of this dichotomization has been a tendency to view refugee movements (and thus, I would argue, refugees) as 'abnormal', 'pathological' and 'deviant' phenomena. Theories of settlement, on the other hand, tend to be 'refugee-blind'. The tendency within these theories is to subsume refugee settlement experiences into analyses of migrant settlement (Richmond, 1988). The homogenization of a variety of migrants and refugees into the single category, 'migrant', reflects the politics of 'othering' which occurs for new arrivals.

The difficulties which occur in attempts to theorize refugee movements arise in large part from the false dichotomy constructed in defining refugee movements as involuntary and other migration as voluntary. This di-chotomy tends also to coincide with another false dichotomy; namely, that most migration is 'caused' by economic factors but that refugee movement is 'caused' by political factors. Richmond (1988) has argued the falsity of these distinctions. In arguing for a comprehensive theory of migration which can account for both types of movement, he emphasizes that in the context of contemporary global systems the interdependence of economic, social and political factors in all population movements must be recognized. He points out that 'it is no longer possible to treat "refugee" movements as completely independent of the state of the global economy' (Richmond, 1988: 12) and that 'so-called economic migrants are often responding as much to political repression as to material dep-rivation' (Dowty, 1987: 183 cited in Richmond, 1988: 12).

The distinction conventionally made between 'political' refugees and 'economic' migrants supports the representation of each category as homogeneous, distinctive and mutually exclusive. The definition of refugees as 'involuntary' or 'forced' migrants represents them as passive victims of political processes. Economic migrants, on the other hand, are repre-sented as decision-makers, in control of their lives, making choices within the context of largely economic constraints. These representations, I would argue, are extended into theories of settlement thereby suggesting that the settlement of economic migrants is more problematic, and thus worthy of more research and attention, than that of refugees.

Rather than viewing refugees as the passive victims of powerful forces which produce unpredictable population movements, it is more ap-propriate to examine refugee movements as empirically distinct popula-tion movements. In this way, it is possible to identify the unique characteristics of refugee movements *vis-à-vis* other migrations while at the same time allowing for the possibility of diverse types of refugee movements. Contextualizing refugee movements also avoids the tendency to homogenize refugees. Issues of control, agency and dependency/ independency are central to understanding refugee movements and should thus be problematized. Parsimony at a theoretical level, however, enables us to ask how refugees actively engage in the process of flight, exile and resettlement that characterizes their particular migration paths. Further-more, such an approach is crucial in providing a conceptual framework for examining the actions of refugee women in this process. Other approaches, as we have seen, represent refugees, and thus refugee women, as passive victims without agency.

Women in Migration and Settlement

In recent years, theories of migration and settlement have received criticism for their gender-blindness and limited applicability to female migrants

(Fincher, Foster & Wilmot, 1994; Julian, 1995; Vasta, 1991; Martin, 1984). At the same time the gendered nature of migrant selection policies in a number of countries has been acknowledged (Fincher et al., 1994; Madden and Young, 1993) as has the trend towards the feminization of international migration (Zlotnik, 1990; Castles and Miller, 1993; Kwitko, 1996; Battistella, 1996). Nearly half of all international migrants are women (Zlotnik, 1990: 372) and the UNHCR estimate that of the 17 million refugees currently recognized, two-thirds are women and children.

The invisibility of women in the international migration literature has been explained in part as a reflection of:

> the conventional wisdom that as females are not the initiators in the decision to migrate, their experience of migration can be adequately subsumed within that of males. There is a taken-for-granted view that women are the appendages of either protective males or the patriarchal state. (Fincher et al., 1994b: 150)

Once again, the predominance of the economic model of migration with its focus on the individual male labour migrant is apparent. The assumption has been that the male head of the household makes an independent rational decision with respect to migration, and that his wife and family follow him after the event.

The invisibility of migrant women is even more apparent in the Australian context than in other immigrant-receiving nations (see Fincher et al., 1994a; Alcorso, 1991). While a number of publications examine the relationships between class, gender and ethnicity (Bottomley and de Lepervanche, 1991; Bottomley et al., 1984; Misztal, 1991; Kalantzis, 1990) very few studies focus empirically on immigrant women (see, for example, Ram, 1996; Martin, 1984; Vasta, 1991). Studies which focus on refugee women are even sparser (Pittaway, 1991; MacIntyre, 1994; Rice, 1994).

Australia's postwar immigration programme had two major objectives: to provide unskilled and semi-skilled labour to aid the government's industrialization project and to contribute to population growth. Permanent settler migration was (and still is) fundamental to the programme. The 'populate or perish' objective has meant that postwar immigration to Australia has been characterized by family migration. It is this combination that established the socio-historical context of female migration to Australia. And it is within this context that migrant women have been conceptualized as dependants and/or victims in the migration process.

In one of the few analyses of migrant women in Australia, Martin (1984) noted government policy largely determined the representation of female migrants in Australia:

> The majority of non-English speaking migrant women who have arrived since 1945 have arrived as *dependants* (wives, daughters, sisters, mothers, and so on) of male migrants brought to Australia from non-English speaking countries to

work as semi- and unskilled workers ... They were to provide the emotional anchorage for settler migration schemes, by marrying their male compatriots and bearing their children, thereby securing appropriate nuclear family units for consumption and labour-force production. (1984: 111–12)

She goes on to argue that the reality of migrant women's settlement experiences differs dramatically from that described in policy and represented in cultural constructions of 'migrant women'. This difference has since been well analysed and documented by studies of migrant women's extensive involvement in the labour force (see Alcorso, 1991; ABS, 1993; Yeatman, 1992).

Refugee women experience many of the same tensions and contradictions as other migrant women. However, they face additional pressures as refugees and as recent arrivals, and are even more likely to be represented through the discourse of victimization. The 'refugee problem' is often represented as a Third World problem, a problem arising out of conflicts in other societies. Acceptance as a refugee is predicated on successfully presenting oneself as a victim of global economic and political processes. Within this context, refugee women are represented as the most powerless of the 'outsiders' accepted into the country. Like migrant women, they are viewed as dependants of their husbands, and like 'Third World' women they are represented as non-modern; that is, as oppressed, disempowered victims (Morokvasic, 1988).

This representation sits comfortably with the emancipatory discourse adopted by many who study and work with migrant and refugee women. This modernist hegemonic discourse, however, homogenizes and stereotypes all refugee women as victims. Defining these subjects as 'refugee women' denies, first, the relevance of their experiences prior to being accepted as 'refugees' and, second, the diversity of experiences which characterizes the members of the category. While 'refugee women' may share an on-arrival status as marginalized and powerless, the diversity of their life experiences prior to this point in their life histories is significant.

It is precisely because of the complex interplay of economic and sociopolitical factors which creates the context for the existence of refugees that 'refugee women' are even less likely to represent a homogeneous category than 'migrant women'. The experiences of refugee women in their homelands are clearly an important factor influencing their settlement strategies. Since the way in which they became refugees varies dramatically, the meanings they attach to their status as refugees will vary, as will the ways in which they respond. Settlement experiences for some can be read as emancipatory; however, for many the transition to 'refugee woman' can strip her of the power and freedom she enjoyed in her homeland. Furthermore, while the refugee status may be one of powerlessness and victimization, the ways in which women respond to this status and construct their own subject positions in relation to it, may equally indicate power and agency. Some recent Australian studies (Vasta, 1991; Thomas, 1994; Julian, 1995) have returned agency to migrant and refugee women as they have documented the resistances and negotiations which are part and parcel of their daily lives.

Refugee Women and the Victimized Self

The representation of refugee women as victims is problematic in three main ways. First, as discussed above, it homogenizes the experiences of a category of women constructed from an extremely diverse range of economic and socio-political backgrounds. Secondly, it assumes a binary opposition between victimization and agency. Thirdly, it legitimates an objective definition constructed by others and does not take into consideration the subjective interpretations of the refugee women themselves. My exploration of the subjective experiences of refugee women in Tasmania suggests the utility of the concept of the 'victimized self' (Johnson and Ferraro, 1984) in an analysis of refugee flight and resettlement. Importantly, this concept collapses the binary distinction between victim and agent by recognizing the redefinition of self as victim as a motivation for action.

Johnson and Ferraro (1984: 119) define the victimized self as:

a complex mixture of feelings and thoughts based on the individual's overriding feeling of having been violated, exploited, or wronged by another person, or persons. It develops when an individual feels a fundamental threat to his or her very being or existence. (1984: 119)

The victimized self typically leads to practical actions aimed at ending the victimization. It is often brought about by a turning point 'when the violence or abuse done to them (women) comes to be felt as a basic threat, whether to their physical or social self or to both' (1984: 120). Thus:

The victimized self emerges during moments of existential threat, and it dissolves when one takes actions to construct new, safer living conditions. The victimized self emerges when the rationalizations of violence and abuse begin to lose their power; it becomes the all-consuming basis for however long it takes to transcend this period of crisis and threat. It tends to dissolve, over time, for those who change their lives in new, creative ways, although the sense of victimization never disappears altogether. For all who experience it, it becomes incorporated into an individual's biography as lived experience. (1984: 121)

This concept of the victimized self is useful for analysing the position of refugee women. Refugee women in Australia, it can be argued, are those who have taken practical action to escape the violent conditions which contributed to their victimization. For many, the catalyst in the process was the perception of an immediate threat to their children. This typically brought about 'a penetrating fear'. Nevertheless, this is typically a temporary phenomenon since '[t]he very process of taking practical action inevitably diminishes the individual's sense of victimization' (1984: 129).

The decision to leave and the processes of flight, exile and resettlement are experiences which diminish the sense of victimization. The more involved the individual is in each of these processes, the more likely it is that the 'victimized self' will be a temporary condition. Thus, for many refugee women in Australia the application of the term 'victim' in an attempt to describe their subject position is inappropriate. The rejection of this label is clearly indicated in the words of a woman from Bosnia-Herzegovina who, when interviewed less than one year after her arrival in Australia, strongly asserted: 'I am not refugee any more ... Since we bought our house, I am not refugee.'

The Experiences of Refugee Women

The refugee experience is typically analysed in terms of a number of stages: flight, exile, resettlement and repatriation. However, it is argued here that any analysis of the settlement of refugee women must acknowledge that the lived experiences of refugee women begin in their home countries, long before the status of refugee has any relevance in their biographies. Thus a stage prior to flight must be added, a stage in which the decision to leave is made. Diverse social locations in their native countries provide the base for diverse biographical trajectories as women 'become' refugees. Furthermore, there will be wide variation in the degree to which women are actively involved in the making of decisions that will launch them into a refugee 'career'.

The refugee women whose lived experiences form the basis for this chapter are drawn from a wide range of societies: Vietnam, Chile, El Salvador, Laos, Iraq and Bosnia-Herzegovina. While all left their countries to escape violence, specific conditions varied dramatically from one country to another. The degree to which the lives of these women were directly affected by violence also varied, as did the strategies they chose to manage it. Furthermore, and most importantly, some are drawn from the middle classes and the elite in their home countries. They are very far removed from the images of Third World women which predominate in discussions of the plight of refugee women.

Deciding to leave

The majority of the women interviewed in this study had a significant role to play in the decision to become refugees. For many, this decision implicated the whole household and took place within its context. For others, however, it was the woman who made the decision *for the household*. It is in the latter context that the concept of the 'victimized self' is most powerful.

In Vietnam, household members often made a decision to flee in stages. Typically the husband and eldest son would leave first with the aim of sponsoring the rest of the household later. In recounting their flight from Vietnam a father of four highlighted the importance of his wife's role in shaping the refugee experience:

> I couldn't get work. We tried to get money. We didn't have enough money to bring my whole family here ... We thought if my son and I escaped from Vietnam we could sponsor our family later ...
>
> Most people were poor and had to divide the family. We were scared that the whole family would die. [This way] if we died at least half would remain alive.

Once at the refugee camp, 'choice' of country of destination also took into account the lives of all family members: 'I had the right to go to the USA but I refused because I heard in Vietnam that it was difficult to sponsor your family from there. That is why we decided on Australia.' While this meant that the wife remained in the homeland she typically found herself responsible for the family's survival in difficult economic circumstances. Sponsorship often took longer than expected:

> It took us about five and half years ... Australia and Vietnam were not talking together. I had to ask the Department of Immigration many times: 'What is the problem?' [In the meantime] my wife worked buying and selling things and the children went to school. She wasn't allowed to get a job in Vietnam.

For many families the stage of 'flight' thus took many years, during which time the wife became the active head of the household in the homeland.

In Chile and El Salvador, women often played an even more prominent role in the decision-making process. Many had lived as members of the households of political activists for many years, sometimes for a number of generations. For them, a way of life that encompassed street fighting, disappearances and torture had been established as 'normal'. Rationalizations in terms of their commitment to constructing a new future for their country were typically effective until a crisis occurred in their own families. For most, this revolved around a direct threat to their children, at which point they were motivated to flee. In this situation, women often made the decision for the household; the husband would comply but was typically left with feelings of guilt and shame for having abandoned 'the cause' and left others to continue to fight.

An interview with a young Chilean woman who recalls her mother's involvement in the decision to leave Chile tells one such story:

> My mum did all the work with the [Australian] embassy. Like she went and got forms ... and then she applies and this all happened within a month, you know,

four weeks. And she applied and we got accepted and we had to move next week sort of thing.

She goes on to describe the crisis that precipitated the decision to flee the country:

> Well, my father was never really clear until we got here as to what was actually going on but ... a couple of nights we found that his clothes were ripped, and later we found that he'd been shot. He was actually like attacked in a way, but my father carried a gun with him and we had a gun at home. And he'd been sent a letter to say that next time he was going to be killed. But at the time he was a very active man, you know, he was very fit ... so they couldn't catch him at the time. So they said that if they couldn't do anything to him or to stop him that they were going to hurt the more special things in his life. So that was me and my brother. So my mum was really worried. She started to take us to school, like waiting for us ...

Her mother's decision to approach the Australian Embassy for refugee status was influenced by her long association with Amnesty International: '[My mother] would go to Amnesty International straight away. She would try to find out like why he was being held ...' She goes on to comment on how little they knew of the country to which they were going and how little had been her father's involvement in the decision to leave:

> We had no idea. And he wasn't to know [anything]. Like he was very involved in his thing. We did all the paperwork. So we just told him, you know, we received a letter and we have to go there [to the embassy] quickly now ...
> We basically told our neighbours [but] we couldn't tell anybody when. It was a lot better just to go. Just because they were after my brother and I. We didn't go out visiting family and friends ... People were following us constantly.

For others the decision to flee was made after years of exile within their own homeland. An upper middle-class Salvadoran woman spent three years fearing for her life and that of her children as she tried to avoid the authorities in El Salvador. In her own words she recalls:

> I didn't leave my country for three years. Moved from one place to another ... I have to move, my children stay with my sisters ... I didn't work because I have to move. And also I didn't work in that time [because] it would be easy for them to find me.

Her decision to leave was prompted by fear for her children's safety:

> I heard from a friend that before they do anything to me they will hurt my children and then I decided to apply to come to Australia. Before I applied to come here I applied to go to Canada because my family, they asked me [to] because it was closer. I applied but nothing happened so I said to my family now I am going to apply to where I want to go. Because my feeling was to go far away ...

Flight

For many women the flight itself produced situations conducive to the development of the victimized self. The experiences they endured as they fled their homelands motivated them to continue their journey to a country where they could create a better life for themselves and their children.

Among Vietnamese refugees, flight typically involved an expensive and dangerous trip by boat. One man recalled the journey undertaken by himself and his wife:

> You don't know where you might end up. We left our waters at midnight. When we got to the big boat and the open sea, they started shooting. Fortunately no-one got shot. We were happy to get into international waters. At about four o'clock one morning we were attacked by Thai pirates. Two men jumped aboard. There was about seventeen people, a little girl and a boy. They raped three young women …

The women responded by deciding not to let anybody know of their ordeal as it would bring shame on themselves and those on board:

> We promised not to leak information not even to our families … I got a letter from my wife's mother asking about the journey. She heard about the pirates. My wife denied it but my mother-in-law didn't believe it.

Exile

After fleeing their homelands, the majority of these women and their families lived in a refugee camp in a foreign country. For many this was a temporary stay in a country very different from their own. The experience of camp life is typically recalled as unpleasant. An Iraqi woman with a medical degree who escaped to Turkey with her husband and young child recalls:

> After about three or four days we met a Turkish family and saw United Nations there. After a few days they moved us to another city and another city and then another boundary and then a camp. It was March 1990. Camp conditions were very difficult especially with a baby boy. He was not much older than six months and 900 grams. We reached the camp and stayed there for maybe two years … We were sent food from United Nations through the Turkish government. There was people from the village helping us by collecting money, sending food, clothing. It was hard living there. In one room were six families … First [we lived in] tents then we moved to the school. We were lucky because some people were in tents the whole time. If they had a baby they were put in the house. It was especially hard when my son was sick for ten days. It was very hard to buy medicine and antibiotics.

For the Hmong, life in the refugee camps took on a degree of permanency. Many lived in camps such as Ban Vinai on the Thai border for seven to fourteen years before being accepted as refugees in Australia or the United States. Many Hmong children were born in refugee camps and have no first-hand experience of life in their 'homeland'. While camp life differed dramatically from life in the mountains of Laos, the women typically responded to their new situation with initiative and fortitude. Many began to develop their own cash economy through the sale of handicrafts to tourists. The money would be used to bribe camp guards and to secure better food for their children.

Resettlement

Upon arrival in their new country many refugee women are immediately thrust into a new life. With high unemployment rates among refugees, many men retreat into the home and take refuge in each other's support. Women, on the other hand, often find themselves having to deal immediately with people in the hospitals, healthcare centres, schools and shops. This immediately places them as potential agents of change since, in many instances, the dominant institutional structures must deal with different cultural practices. This is apparent, for example, when refugee women confront the Australian healthcare system. As one Hmong woman explains:

> We tell them what's happening. Because some of our ladies have babies in the hospital … They want to kneel down on the ground … so they put the mattress on there for them to kneel down and have baby …
>
> Soon after you give birth to your child, you not allowed to do any housework, not allowed to do any cleaning, anything for the whole month … Everything has to be like hot drink, not cold drink … and warm showers … and allowed to have poached egg, steamed chicken and steamed rice … And we don't do exercise because after birth we just leave our tummy out and we use the long material to tie up the tummy … for the whole month … The hospital is very good … You can't really complain about them because I mean you can't expect them to do everything exactly as you ask them … The hospital try to do what it can … that's good enough I think.

Health problems were a common occurrence among refugee women in the study. For some this was exacerbated by the experience of downward social mobility. One Salvadoran woman recalls:

> Well, the beginning was really difficult, no friends, no family, no English … And then I get sick – from the weather. The doctor say it's because I used to work in an office and I didn't do anything at home. And then the change was so drastic … I have to take care of the kids, cook and clean … And also the stress … That year I was in bed three months, I think, from June to November. I couldn't go to [English] school because sometimes I couldn't walk.

For others, illness became a chronic problem associated with exile and resettlement. A young Chilean woman said of her parents: 'They're always sick ... which I think is part of the whole idea of feeling on your own ... of wanting attention I suppose.'

Post-traumatic stress disorder contributes to the health problems experienced by refugees during settlement. Eileen Pittaway's study of refugee women (1991: 21) cites evidence that 60 per cent of women seeking asylum in Australia have suffered from torture as defined by the United Nations. She further argues that sexual assault is a common feature of the female experience of refugee camps (Jupp, 1994: 60).

Other difficulties result from problems of domestic violence. Vietnamese communities in Australia increasingly recognize this as a problem for Vietnamese women. My own interviews with Vietnamese men elicited the following comments in response to a generic question about settlement problems:

> Domestic violence [is a problem] ... It's different in Australia. We keep it within the family and don't let outside people see what we are doing ... [S]ome have had the problems in Vietnam. Here they [the wives] have their freedom. The wives can say: 'I don't rely on you' ... In Vietnam you have to follow traditions. Men have more rights. That is maybe why men can hit their wives.

And a Vietnamese woman explains:

> Western ideas are different so some women when they come here pick up the ideas in this society. A lot of men don't want to change. They get angry. Most of the couples do everything. The man only works outside ... The men are like a bomb. They don't want to do anything. That is why the women get upset ... They have got to learn. The woman learns very quickly, the men don't want to change.

Recent studies in Australia (for example, Thomas, 1994) have begun to identify the ways in which refugee women develop collective strategies for addressing such problems. Rather than appearing to accept the position of victim in situations of violence, or of passive recipient of male authority, more generally Vietnamese women band together to produce positive outcomes for themselves while, at the same time, maintaining face for Vietnamese men. Since these strategies typically develop at the level of informal networks they may not appear highly visible and the women may be perceived as acquiescing. On the contrary, such studies illuminate the power mobilized by women in informal settings to achieve desired outcomes and implement change.

Conclusion

This brief excursion through the stages of a refugee career provide the basis for a number of significant conclusions with respect to the analysis of refugee women. Of greatest import is the clear indication that refugee women are often actively involved in constructing the household's 'refugee experience'. Far from being passive recipients of decisions made by male heads of households, it is often the women's lived experiences in the homeland which provide the impetus to embark on the career of refugee. Critical experiences in the home country, as well as during flight and exile, provide the catalyst for the development of the 'victimized self', a temporary subject position which motivates women to take action to escape.

Refugee women are those who have taken action to change their lives in new and creative ways. While the sense of victimization may never disappear entirely, the representation of refugee women as victims is clearly inappropriate. It would seem more appropriate to conceptualize victim and agent as alternatives within a framework of multiple, shifting subject positions. This points once again to the importance of conceptualizing the refugee experience as a 'career' characterized by distinct stages. With respect to the resettlement stage, in the new social context a refugee woman may find herself in a position of marginalization and powerlessness; under such conditions, she may be appropriately represented as a 'victim'. On the other hand, her experiences of escape and flight may have equipped her with the power to resist attempts at marginalization during resettlement in the new society. Universal claims that the overall experience of migration is empancipatory for migrant/refugee women are clearly inaccurate in that they do not take into account (a) heterogeneity within the category migrant/refugee woman, and (b) temporal variation in subject positions over the career of the refugee woman.

Finally, the analysis has demonstrated the need to engage in empirical investigations of the diverse experiences of 'women'. While feminist politics may depend on the construction of universalistic categories such as 'women', 'migrant women', 'refugee women', 'women of colour' and 'lesbian women', this leads to a tendency to essentialize women. While the contradictions between identity politics and empirical research pose a dilemma for feminist researchers (see Young, 1995) it is encumbent on us to examine critically the representations of women which are mobilized in our political projects and intellectual endeavours.

References

Australian Bureau of Statistics (ABS). 1993. *Women in Australia*. Canberra: Australian Bureau of Statistics.

Adelman, Howard, Allan Borowski, Meyer Burstein and Lois Foster (eds). 1994. *Immigration and Refugee Policy: Australia and Canada Compared*, volumes 1 and 2. Melbourne: Melbourne University Press.

Alcorso, Caroline. 1991. *Non-English Speaking Background Immigrant Women in the*

Workforce. Working Papers in Multiculturalism no. 4. Wollongong: The Centre for Multicultural Studies, University of Wollongong.

Battistella, Graziano. 1996. 'Migration and development in Asia: identifying issues that need attention.' Unpublished paper presented at the International Sociological Association Research Committees on Ethnic, Race and Minority Relations and Sociology of Migration Conference, Quezon City, Manila, 31 May.

Borowski, Allan, Anthony Richmond, Jing Shu and Alan Simmons. 1994. 'The international movements of people.' In Howard Adelman, Allan Borowski, Meyer Burstein and Lois Foster (eds), *Immigration and Refugee Policy: Australia and Canada Compared*, Volume 1. Melbourne: Melbourne University Press.

Bottomley, Gill and Marie de Lepervanche (eds). 1991. *Intersexions: Gender/Class/Culture/Ethnicity*. Sydney: Allen and Unwin.

Bottomley, Gill, Marie de Lepervanche and Jeannie Martin (eds). 1984. *Ethnicity, Class and Gender in Australia*. Sydney: Allen and Unwin.

Castles, Stephen and Mark J. Miller. 1993. *The Age of Migration: International Population Movements in the Modern World*. London: Macmillan.

Fincher, Ruth, Lois Foster and Rosemary Wilmot. 1994. *Gender Equity and Australian Immigration Policy*. Bureau of Immigration and Population Research, Canberra: Australian Government Publishing Service.

Fincher, Ruth, Lois Foster, Wenona Giles and Valerie Preston. 1994. 'Gender and migration policy.' In Howard Adelman, Allan Borowski, Meyer Burstein and Lois Foster (eds), *Immigration and Refugee Policy: Australia and Canada Compared*, Volume 1. Melbourne: Melbourne University Press.

Hugo, Graeme. 1994. *The Economic Implications of Emigration from Australia*. Bureau of Immigration and Population Research, Canberra: Australian Government Publishing Service.

Johnson, John M. and Kathleen J. Ferraro. 1984. 'The victimized self: the case of battered women.' In Joseph A. Kotarba and Andrea Fontana (eds), *The Existential Self in Society*. Chicago: University of Chicago Press.

Julian, Roberta. 1995. '"When the rain is white": power, conflict and change among Hmong refugee women in Australia.' Unpublished paper presented at the First Hmong National Education Conference, St Paul, Minnesota, USA, 6–8 April.

Jupp, James. 1994. *Exile or Refuge? The Settlement of Refugee, Humanitarian and Displaced Immigrants*. Canberra: Australian Government Publishing Service.

Kalantzis, Mary. 1990. 'Ethnicity meets gender meets class in Australia.' In Sophie Watson (ed.), *Playing the State: Australian Feminist Interventions*. Sydney: Allen and Unwin.

Kwitko, Ludmilla. 1996. 'Filipina domestic labour in Hong Kong.' Unpublished paper presented at the International Sociological Association Research Committees on Ethnic, Race and Minority Relations and Sociology of Migration Conference, Quezon City, Manila, 31 May.

MacIntyre, Martha. 1994. 'Migrant women from El Salvador and Vietnam in Australian hospitals.' In Charles Waddell and Alan R. Petersen (eds), *Just Health: Inequality in Illness, Care and Prevention*. Melbourne: Churchill Livingstone.

Madden, R. and S. Young. 1993. *Women and Men Immigrating to Australia: Their Characteristics and Immigration Decisions*. Canberra: Australian Government Publishing Service.

Martin, Jeannie. 1984. 'Non English-speaking women: production and social reproduction.' In Gill Bottomley and Marie de Lepervanche (eds), *Ethnicity, Class and Gender in Australia*. Sydney: Allen and Unwin.

Misztal, Barbara A. 1991. 'Migrant women in Australia.' *Journal of Intercultural Studies*, vol. 12, no. 2: 15–34.

Morokvasic, Mirjana. 1988. 'Cash in hand for the first time: the case of Yugoslav immigrant women in Western Europe.' In Charles Stahl (ed.), *International Migration Today, Volume 2: Emerging Issues*. Paris: Unesco and University of Western Australia, Centre for Migration and Development Studies.

Nicholson, Linda and Steven Seidman (eds). 1995. *Social Postmodernism: Beyond Identity Politics*. Cambridge: Cambridge University Press.

Papademetriou, Demetrios. 1988. 'International migration in a changing world.' In Charles Stahl (ed.) *International Migration Today, Volume 2: Emerging Issues*. Paris: Unesco and University of Western Australia, Centre for Migration and Development Studies.

Pittaway, Eileen. 1991. *Refugee Women – Still at Risk in Australia*. Canberra: Australian Government Publishing Service.

Ram, Kalpana. 1996. 'Liberal multiculturalism's "NESB Women": A South Asian post-colonial feminist perspective on the liberal impoverishment of "difference".' In Ellie Vasta and Stephen Castles (eds), *The Teeth are Smiling: The Persistence of Racism in Multicultural Australia*. Sydney: Allen and Unwin.

Richmond, Anthony H. 1988. 'Sociological theories of international migration: the case of refugees.' *Current Sociology*, vol. 36, no. 2: 7–25.

Rice, Pranee Liamputtong (ed.). 1994. *Asian Mothers, Australian Birth*. Melbourne: Ausmed Publications.

Snowden, L.L. 1990. 'Collective versus mass behaviour: a conceptual framework for temporary and permanent migration in Western Europe and the United States.' *International Migration Review*, vol. 24, no. 3: 577–90.

Thomas, Mandy. 1994. 'Balancing acts: problem solving in the informal networks of Vietnamese women in Australia.' Unpublished paper presented at the 'Linking Our Histories: Asian and Pacific Women as Migrants' Conference, Melbourne University, Melbourne, Australia, 30 September–2 October 1994.

Vasta, Ellie. 1991. 'Gender, class and ethnic relations: the domestic and work experiences of Italian migrant women in Australia.' In Gill Bottomley and Marie de Lepervanche (eds), *Intersexions: Gender/Class/Culture/Ethnicity*. Sydney: Allen and Unwin.

Yeatman, Anna (with Carol Bradley). 1992. *NESB Migrant Women and Award Restructuring*. Office of Multicultural Affairs, Canberra: Australian Government Publishing Service.

Young, Iris Marion. 1995. 'Gender as seriality: thinking about women as a social collective.' In Linda Nicholson and Steven Seidman (eds), *Social Postmodernism: Beyond Identity Politics*. Cambridge: Cambridge University Press.

Zlotnik, Hania. 1990. 'International migration policies and the status of female migrants.' *International Migration Review*, vol. 24, no. 2 (Summer): 372–81.

16

'I Have a Feeling of Being Exiled Here': Women Migrants in Central Russia

Natalya Kosmarskaya

The breakdown of the Soviet Union gave rise to a massive inflow of ethnic Russians and those who consider Russian to be their native tongue (including Ukrainians, Byelorussians, Jews, Germans) back to the Russian Federation. But this process has little in common with an idyllic return to the motherland. This chapter examines how women migrants settle down and adapt to new surroundings in one part of Central Russia. The specific roots of women's vulnerability and stress will be contextualized within the Russian-speakers' position in the societies of origin and women's role in Soviet and post-Soviet families.

These women's painful adaptation experiences in a dramatically and unexpectedly different socio-cultural environment seem unremarkable when compared with women's suffering in extreme situations such as war, famine or genocide, as depicted in other chapters. Yet, sometimes comparisons are odious, and, to paraphrase Leo Tolstoy's words, knowing about other people's sorrows cannot console.

Migration, irrespective of its course, causes and historical background, is inevitably a traumatic experience, though with specific implications for women and men. That is why it is important to present the 'gendered victimization' due to migration and resettlement. I have written this chapter for two reasons. First, I feel I must use every opportunity to make the voices of women migrants heard both in the West and the East to show the drama of people who, having moved to their historic motherland, found themselves 'in the other world where only the language is the same, everything else is different'. This is the only thing I can do for them besides talking to them and trying to understand their pains and sorrows.

The second consideration is of a scholarly nature and concerns the specificity of the current massive population movement from the former

Soviet republics to Russia. And here throwing some light on the new migration patterns in the former USSR might be relevant, including their quantitative and qualitative parameters.

Post-Soviet Migration: A General Overview

A change has taken place from the so-called 'normal' migration patterns, motivated by economic and personal considerations (job, marriage, study) to one motivated by stress. That is why the term 'forced migrants' has appeared, both in the academic lexicon and in the legislation,[1] to identify those ethnic Russians and Russian-speakers in the New Independent States (NIS) who, having found themselves in an environment no longer comfortable and friendly, decided to move to Russia. The forced character of people's displacement, provoked by the numerous ethno-political conflicts in the former USSR, is also evident.

This new feature of post-Soviet migration goes hand in hand with the fact that the ethnic component has become a key factor underlying the present population mobility, its roots and/or consequences. For this reason the term 'ethnically-based migration' as a new phenomenon resulting from specifically post-Soviet realities is gaining increasing academic recognition.

According to official estimates, about 6 million people from the NIS resettled in Russia in 1989–95 (*Population and Society*, 1995: 4; *Numbers of Population and Its Mobility in the Russian Federation*, 1995: 23). These are overall estimates of the State Statistical Committee whereas the only detailed data available concerning the ethnic, age, or gender structure of forced migrants are those which have been collected by the Federal Migration Service (FMS) since its creation in July 1992. It should be noted that not more than 27–30 per cent of migrants go through official FMS registration (974,428 people between 1 July 1992 and 1 January 1996, of which 53.2 per cent are women (*Numbers of Population and Its Mobility in the Russian Federation*, 1995: 62, 73)).

This is the outflow of Russian-speakers, helpless in the face of new ethno-political and social realities and disturbed by the discrimination against them, or what they feel as discrimination, on the part of the titular nationalities. But how can this be situated within the types of migrational processes?

What is taking place is the natural result of the collapse of the empire – repatriation or return to the metropolis of the empire's dominant ethnic group or groups. It was by the exertion of this group that the empire was sustained, developed, and functioning during the course of several centuries. Repatriation is none other than entry to one's own genetic society, and in this case no significant ethnic, linguistic or socio-cultural barriers are supposed to emerge between the repatriates and the host society of the imperial centre. All this dulled the vigilance of researchers in my country, who did not anticipate any serious ethno-cultural or socio-psychological complications of migrants' adaptation. It explains why much more attention has been paid to the material side of migrants' life (accommodation, jobs, social security, etc.) in the far from extensive study of post-Soviet ethnic migration already conducted by scholars and journalists.

In reality, however, a socio-psychological distance between newcomer and host communities does exist, creating an intriguing dilemma for a researcher. This was my second reason for agreeing to contribute to this book, as well as the gender dimension of the new migration patterns, which has also been seriously under-explored in present-day Russia.

In my opinion, with a vast diversity of socio-cultural settings both in the NIS and in Russia itself, what must be emphasized is the intricate combination of what is left by migrants' 'there' and what is faced 'here'. In relation to this, three characteristics of the forced migrants moving to Russia deserve special attention.

Who is Arriving in Russia?

The majority of the forced migrants, judging by the statistics of the FMS, as of 1 January 1996, reflecting a general tendency, are emigrants from Central Asia and Kazakhstan (57.9 per cent), and from Trans-Caucasia (23.6 per cent). Only 13.1 per cent migrated within the Russian Federation and a tiny number, 2.7 per cent, came from the Baltics (*Numbers of Population and its Mobility in the Russian Federation,* 1995: 62).

Despite all the differences between Central Asia and Kazakhstan, on the one hand, and Trans-Caucasia on the other, the position and psychology of Russian-speakers in these regions during the Soviet regime have a great deal in common. This separates them from their former compatriots living in such places as, say, the Ukraine or the Baltic states. I will provide a short description only of this phenomenon of 'Russians in the Orient', with cultural and civilizational distance between the titular ethnic groups and the Russians, perceived by the latter as grounds to justify their ethno-social superiority and 'senior brother' complex. The migrants' heightened realization of their belonging to what might be called 'Central Asian Russians', is a significant factor in the internal consolidation of the group. When in Russia it makes their entry to the new community more difficult. These points will be further developed below in relation to women's responses to resettlement.

Two further characteristics of the stream of forced migrants are also worth mentioning. The cultural and economic takeover of the southern regions of the Russian Empire developed historically in such a way that at the time of the collapse of the USSR, the Russian-speaking population concentrated in the large towns and industrial centres. According to the last All-Union Population Census of 1989, 70 per cent of the Russian inhabitants of Kirghizia were urban; in Kazakhstan this figure was 77 per cent, in Armenia, Georgia, and Azerbaijan 85–95 per cent, in Tajikistan, Uzbekistan and Turkmenia 94–97 per cent (*Russians. Ethno-Sociological Essays*, 1992: 25).

As the same census shows, around half of the Russian-speaking population of Central Asia and Trans-Caucasia were born in those territories, whereas another substantial part (27.8 per cent in Kirghizia, 29.5 in Azerbaijan, 31.7 in Georgia, 32.8 per cent in Kazakhstan, 33.3 in Turkmenia, 33.4 per cent in Uzbekistan, and 37.2 per cent in Tajikistan) had lived there for more than ten years (*Russians. Ethno-Sociological Essays*, 1992: 52).

In this way those who arrive in Russia are mainly people who have left behind specific oriental, albeit sovietized, socio-cultural and ethnic milieux. This was a society where they had lived their entire lives, or a significant part of them, where they had enjoyed many privileges as a ruling ethno-social group as well as the social advantages and living conditions of an urban and often capital city's way of life. What and who awaits them in the huge, multi-ethnic Russia, heterogeneous in many other respects?

Resettlement Destination: The Case of Central Russia

A significantly large share of the migrants has been forced to resettle in rural areas. The latest FMS data suggest that this share is 37.8 per cent for Russia as a whole, with lower percentages in the north and larger ones in the better climatic zones (*Forced Migrants in Russia*, 1995: 35–6). Officially this is voluntary, but actually migrants have no choice because of the housing crisis and growing unemployment in the towns.

Beside the urban/rural division, there is a regional dimension to what migrants face in Russia. The rural setting of the twelve *oblasts* (the main units of administrative division in Russia) of Central region and of the adjoining North-West and Central Black-Heath regions represents one example. What follow are some key regional socio-economic parameters to throw light on the hardships that migrants, and especially women, face in their everyday lives.

This is a vast zone of socio-economic depression, with poor soil and a very low level of agricultural production which has, for decades, been in need of state funding in order to keep the unprofitable collective and state farms (*kolkhozy* and *sovkhozy*) afloat. Hence, for many years, ever since Khrushchev gave the *kolkhozniks* passports, there has been considerable outflow of able-bodied inhabitants to urban areas. Things became so bad that a phenomenon known as 'dying villages' emerged, villages whose inhabitants consisted of only a few old women. This territory is characterized by extremely underdeveloped systems of communications, transportation, social infrastructure and services. The income of the population employed predominantly in agriculture is extremely low, and consumer demand is marginalized. Housing conditions are squalid (a stove, a well, no inside plumbing, no baths or bath-houses, outdoor latrines, etc.), entailing the backwardness of everyday culture.

This picture is in harsh contrast to the migrants' familiar patterns of everyday life. Even the villages, not to mention the towns, in those parts of Central Asia with a reasonable number of Russians are, as a rule, better equipped with public services and utilities. This was a result of Moscow's imperial policies: the colonization of the USSR peripheries in order to impose new cultures and ideologies implied the provision of reasonable living conditions to demonstrate the advantages of socialism.

Due to the gender differentiation still prevalent in post-Soviet families, childcare, housekeeping and the like are primarily in women's hands. So the new setting women migrants find themselves in adds substantially to their home chores, not only by extending their working hours but also by forcing them to master previously unfamiliar tasks, such as wading through mud all year round on a family plot, where potatoes and cabbages are cultivated, which is crucial for economic survival, and where the bulk of labour – pig and poultry breeding, milking cows and many other such tasks – is female manual labour.

It was in just such a typical Central Russia village located in Oryol *oblast* where I carried out my fieldwork on forced migrants' adaptation in August 1994, February and October 1995.[2] In this *oblast*, as in other parts of Central Russia, many migrants live in rural settlements.

Description of Research

The migrant community I studied is located about 450 km from Moscow and 135 km from the *oblast* centre. It comprises two villages, Retchitsa and Bezodnoye, where the migrant and resident population live and work together on a collective farm (the main sample). Data were also collected in three other migrant communities scattered around the *oblast*.

The main sample is made up of 50 respondents (34 women and 16 men), about 30 per cent of the working-age members of the migrant community, and the second sample consists of 31 women and 25 men (106 in total). Since pensioners and unmarried young people tend to follow their families in migration, and do not bear the basic load of adaptation, I chose to limit my respondents to married or divorced people of working age with dependants.

Most respondents arrived in Russia in 1992 (36.9 per cent) and 1993 (29.2 per cent), during the largest outflow of Russian-speakers from the NIS. They had already experienced the first shock of the move itself and had formed firm impressions of life in Russia. Based mainly on qualitative methodology, my study makes no claim to be representative in the strictest sense of the word. However, respondents do not deviate greatly from migrants registered both in Oryol *oblast* and Russia as a whole, as far as their ethnic composition, birth-places and regions of emigration are concerned.[3] In all five villages the respondents were given a detailed questionnaire. In Retchitsa and Bezodnoye questionnaires were completed by a researcher, and in most cases this procedure became a semi-structured interview, producing non-formalized qualitative information. An on-the-spot primary analysis of the questionnaire material made it possible to plan the basic reference points for in-depth, non-structured interviews with women which were basically oral histories describing migration and resettlement covering aspects of time, space, events and attitudes. Another useful source of qualitative information was my informal contacts with both female and male migrants whom I met in the streets or to whose homes I was invited, as well as correspondence and participant observation. The goal of each successive visit was not so much to extend the sample, but rather to pay visits to former respondents in order to follow up the adaptation process on community, family and individual levels.

Moods and Perceptions: A Gendered View

My research findings demonstrate that migrants are in a state of psychological stress, deeply dissatisfied and unhappy. As answers to the closed questions testify, the difference between men's and women's perceptions is not striking, although it does exist. Thus, 36.6 per cent of 41 men and 40.3 per cent of 62 women responding to the question: 'Were your expectations concerning the resettlement compatible with the realities?' have chosen the option 'all this brought nothing but disappointment', whereas the option 'our expectations were only partly met' has been selected by 31.7 per cent of men and 45.2 per cent of women.

Interview transcripts and people's numerous spontaneous comments, however, demonstrate women's more emotional responses:

> Here one needs strong nerves in order to survive. [m]
>
> Why was I born Russian? It would have been better to be an Uzbek. [m]
>
> Here I am rotting away. [w]
>
> I live only because I must for the children. [w]
>
> Before we did not live here [in Russia] and now we are not living here either; we are just existing. We lived in paradise, but have fallen into an inferno! [w]

The complex emotions of a so-called sense of exile also appear to be more typical for women than for men.

Psychologically, 'idealized perceptions of the society of origin or home-land', nostalgic reconstruction of the past, perspectives of and/or hopes for return provide an 'open-ended' character to migration and so 'generate increasing dilemmas and uncertainties'. All these elements of the ideology of exile, vividly described by Marita Eastmond (1993: 35–54) in her work on Chilean women exiles in the United States, and commented on by Gina Buijs (1993: 2–5), are consonant with my female respondents' moods and perceptions.

The uncertainties about the future are most eloquently expressed by a woman who said she had no particular problems 'here', but just 'pitch darkness ahead, no prospects for a better life'. There is a feeling that the stay 'here' is something of a temporary nature, like a short trip or a 'dream' ('it is like a bad dream, and I am waiting for the moment to wake up'); or the word 'exile' was used: 'I have a feeling of being exiled here …'

Idealized recollections of the past, of the familiar patterns of everyday life ('these memories will never die away'), were among the most persistent and most psychologically stressful for women respondents to produce and for the researcher to listen to. Thus, the most heartfelt and touching descriptions of what was left behind were provided by women (in their case it was Tajikistan, which the majority of the Russians abandoned under extreme circumstances):

> It was just a mere chance that I landed in that place in my childhood; during all the long time I lived there I did not like it, but when everything started to fall to pieces, I realized that it was my true Motherland.

> You ask what I like about Tajikistan and my town? There was nothing special there to like, just an ordinary small provincial town in a mountain valley; hot … difficult to breathe there … but for us it was home, our Motherland, where we knew every tree, every ditch.

The difficulties of rural life in a more severe climate or the necessity, especially for women, of mastering unaccustomed and unpleasant domestic labour do not seem to be the main reason for their depressed psychological state. Women's new household obligations are far from being a pleasure, but the overwhelming majority of female respondents did not touch upon this subject spontaneously. When asked, they noted serious difficulties but, with a few exceptions, did not consider them insurmountable. A review of several hundred explanatory comments by migrants, both spontaneous and in answer to my questions, suggests that the main issues were socio-psychological, concerning the relations with the host community.

Two Communities: Bones of Contention

The main lines along which tensions arise between the two sections of the population, can be structured as follows.

- The feudal nature of social relations, typical for the Soviet system of agricultural production and remaining practically intact, with its arbitrary rules and specific role of personal links:

  The farm manager talks to us as if we were slaves; he should not make himself out to be the lord of the manor, he should treat us as humans.

  This work is like penal servitude; we are here without any right to say a word, and all this because we have nowhere to go.

- Typical Soviet envy and enmity because of other people's material wealth fuelled here by a real or imaginary gap in living standards:

  They [the locals] all think that we arrived with millions.

  They are envious, they call us bourgeoisie.

  They think we should have arrived without anything, and then we would be on an equal footing with them.

  The migrants understand very well why they incite the locals' enmity: 'The Russians in Central Asia always lived materially better than in Russia. We had no envy, but here they do.' The problem is not only migrants' material possessions (furniture, carpets, electrical household goods which can hardly be called luxuries), but also in the way they use these things, in their domestic culture, in the way they equip the micro-environment of the home. These are all different from the way of life of the inhabitants of the ravaged Russian villages, who 'all their lives have been washing over a bowl'.

- Fear that there will be fewer goods due to the migrant inflow (the people in the Russian countryside remember too well the deficit of goods from which some of them are still suffering):

  They reproach us, say we eat their bread.

  They say that we have bought up everything here.

- Competition for jobs between the newcomers and the resident population:

  They say, in the past there were times when the farm-manager implored them to work; now he does not humble himself before them because we are ready to work for 20 hours a day for a minimum wage.

- Differences in labour ethics which are caused, on the one hand, by the low productivity of local agriculture that offers no incentive to work harder. On the other hand, production was more efficiently organized in the industrialized zones of the imperial periphery and, moreover, the ideology of ethnic subordination worked there as an additional incentive for the Russian-speakers.

- Differences in socio-cultural traditions and norms of community life (mutual aid, hospitality, funeral and wedding arrangements, women's domestic culture, upbringing traditions, speech mannerisms, etc.) which are deeply rooted in the differing ethno-cultural milieux the two population groups originate from. Theoretically, such differences can only be welcome in as much as this creates a good foundation for mutual enriching of both cultures. But things are not that simple because traditions are intimately bound up with ethics. This was a particularly sore point for the migrants. The tragic event that occurred in the village on my first visit – the death of a five-year-old son of migrants from Kazakhstan who drowned in a pond – was received with indifference by the local inhabitants. This remained in people's memories for a long time and often served as grounds for complaints:

> We were more united there; here, if something bad happens to someone and if they are not summoned specially, they don't come; even the neighbours don't help. They have savage customs.

> These are very wicked people – 'I am doing fine, just you make ends meet for yourself'; it is better for them to throw away leftover food or give it to the pigs than to share it with others.

> Here they do not respond to grief.

> In Central Asia turn to anyone and they will help, but here it is only for a bottle of vodka.

- And, finally, the new arrivals evoke ethnic associations for the locals. Ethno-cultural distances would not be expected since formally migrants are joining communities of the same ethnic affiliation, but they do exist. Newcomers are sometimes labelled '*nierusy*' in Central Russia (a slang derogatory expression deriving from the ancient name of the country and implying 'non-Russianness') and are very often called 'Kirghiz', 'Kazakhs', 'Uzbeks', etc., depending on the country they came from (see Kosmarskaya, 1996, for a more detailed analysis).

I have described the most sore spots in inter-community relations in order to demonstrate the variety of daily problems women migrants have to cope with. Why should women's experiences be specifically stressed here?

Women's Adaptation Problems: The Public/Private Dichotomy

In the Soviet and post-Soviet context, as far as the level of inter-community, inter-family and inter-personal communication is concerned, it is first of all women who find themselves in the demanding role of mediator and

contact person. This is due not only to the very high rate of economic
activity of Soviet women, but also to the pattern of family role distribution
outlined above. Women are extensively involved in everyday contacts
outside the house, such as standing in queues, visiting shops, hospitals,
marketplaces, taking the children to and from school, kindergartens, etc.
(where they usually deal with women as well). Women, therefore, are more
visible, more public than men. This is even more so in the specific village
atmosphere, where people's lives are usually open to public scrutiny. This
visibility is supported by popular conceptions of cultural gender stereotypes: for instance, people would find it very strange if a man were to seek
permission to leave his workplace in order to take his sick child to a
doctor.

In my study, it was mainly women rather than men who spoke of
problems in different spheres of inter-community relations. I heard a lot
of stories about women's strained contacts with their neighbours; about
bickering in public transport, in shops and in the street; about problems
at work springing, according to them, from their migration; about
incidents in their children's school life that evoked dissatisfaction. The
bulk of men's critical testimonies, far less abundant, concerned their professional activities. If they touched upon anything else, the men tended
to refer to their wives' experiences rather than to their own.

It should be pointed out that the rigid division between women's
position in the private sphere and men's in the public one has been
problematic for Soviet and post-Soviet society. Moreover, there seem to
be other noteworthy manifestations of women's being 'public' which go
far beyond their habitual responsibilities.

According to my observations, it is mostly women who leave no stone
unturned at local migration and other authorities' offices, trying to make
arrangements regarding citizenship and migration status, money allow-
ances, and other formalities. Men's visits to such places usually took place
only at the final stages of signing the documents. As a rule, it is women
who negotiate on behalf of the family with farm managers or other lower
bosses on matters such as the rate of wages, different kinds of aid and
informal permissions, fines and other punishments.

There are other specific examples that cannot be attributed to community life as they are individual family matters. In one family, for instance, it was the wife who searched for a house for sale; in another
family it was the wife who found a job in the town for her husband who
had been scandalously dismissed from the *kolkhoz*; it was another wife
who initiated the idea of emigration to Germany and went through all
the formalities. There are many similar examples.

However, women's 'publicness' and 'activism' should not be over-
estimated. To my mind, it is a compensatory reaction to men's passivity
resulting from long decades under the repressive totalitarian environ-

ment, rather than women's striving for personal self-realization in the public domain. In the context of the study, the mass hard drinking of male migrants following local village 'traditions', is another not insignificant factor promoting this behavioural mode in the women.

Women's important mediating functions can make them active and influential agents of everyday communication. At the same time, beside increasing women's responsibilities, the demands of such 'contact' obligations add to their psychological burdens. This is especially the case when host and migrant communities are obliged to coexist under pressure of disjoining factors. The frequency[4] of women's identification with 'other similar migrants' in answer to the question: 'Whom would I consider to be "one of us", part of "our own people"?' seems a psychologically grounded self-protective reaction.

Women migrants' communication preferences are also interesting in this respect. Only two women out of the 20 interviewed in a specific oral history format said that 'here' they preferred contact with women, but it was only because of men's drunkenness and rudeness, and three women expressed no special preferences. However, 15 of the interviewees expressed a strong preference for dealing with men in various everyday, social and professional activities ('in my life in general' and/or 'here, after the resettlement'). General ideas about women's nature and character based on respondents' bitter life experiences were presented as grounds for this bias.

My findings do not seem to support the idea that 'women refugees and other women migrants appear to show greater resilience and adaptability than do men,' typical of women's migration in other parts of the world (Colson, cited by Buijs, 1993: 4). This idea, widely accepted in the European debate on migrating women, and the way different scholars substantiate it, provides a good contrasting background for disentangling Russian women's adaptation experiences.

Women's Adaptation Problems: Shifts in Social Status

Two points are usually emphasized in the interpretations of men's and women's different adaptation modes. Gina Buijs argues that women appear more resilient than men 'because they have the responsibility for maintaining household routines which provide them with occupation, and also ... they are less conscious of status deprivation' (Buijs, 1993: 4). And that 'men and women appear to find different kinds of situations particularly stressful ... Men appeared more vulnerable to economic stress and the strain of trying to gain or hold social status when they lacked the required resources, while women were strongly affected by stress linked to family events' (Colson, cited by Buijs, 1993: 6).

The first point is linked to women's household responsibilities and their primary involvement in managing family life, which supposedly ease the hardships of migration. In many societies women are positioned within the private domain, and it is mainly from these distinctively patriarchal societies that flows of migrants are supplied to Western Europe. Nevertheless, this approach, to my mind, needs further empirical justification because it denotes a stereotypical idea about women's 'natural' pre-destination: family and household obligations are something innate and habitual, so they could serve as a kind of a lifebelt during the turmoil of migration.

I have argued above that in the post-Soviet migrational context things are different. The specific combination of women migrants' involvement in the private and public spheres is one of the crucial factors making their socio-cultural adaptation a painful and troublesome process, with gender playing a not insignificant role in determining people's perceptive and behavioural responses to resettlement.

The second point of the Western scholars' argumentation is related to the shifts in social status due to migration. Let us look, for instance, at how Marlie Hollands sums up her findings on refugees' integration into Dutch society:

> Refugee men tend to refer longer to a past in which they were *somebody*. Due to male dominance in most societies they more often than women had positions of power and status, in the field of work, in the field of politics and also as men … Refugee women on the other hand seem to refer sooner to the present and to a future in which they hope to become somebody … For women this might create some space to escape from oppressive social codes concerning female roles, female behaviour and female identity. Their position as women has not been that self-evident as it had been for men … This can be also a basis for solidarity, with other refugee women, migrant women, but also Dutch women. (Hollands, 1996: 11–12)

Russian women migrants demonstrate quite a different vector of social status dynamics, and this is another factor underlying their difficulties of coping with the 'present' and of their attraction to the 'past'. Here, ethno-social variables seem to outweigh gender as determinants of migrants' perceptions.

Similarly to men, women *were* somebody in the past, and so their position in the societies of origin was quite self-evident – that is a position of a privileged ethno-social group supported by the imperial centre. Though gender discrimination is an inalienable part of the marketization process, when most migrants left the Central Asian states, this process was just beginning and could not shake women's strong self-identification along ethno-social rather than gender lines. Even during my last visit to Kirghizia in October 1996, when Russian and Kirghiz women's marginalized position in the labour market had already become a concern for progressive journalists and scholars, all the Russian women I talked with treated their problems within the categories of inter-ethnic relations.

The move to Russia has certainly led to the loss of this kind of social status both for women and men, but the same cannot be said about the psychological heritage. The superiority complex and missionary ambitions can hardly be repudiated or restructured by the mere fact of migration. Female and male respondents' reaction to the question: 'How do the local Russians differ from those who live in Central Asia?' would be relevant here. In most cases this section of the questionnaire evoked a glib response, and was taken as one more opportunity to express dissatisfaction to a stranger. All the respondents, except one, answered 'yes' to the first part of the question, and then talked about the most striking differences. What is most important in the context of my argument is that all the respondents, again with one exception, depicted the local Russians' 'otherness' in negative terms only, within the rigid dichotomy: 'we are good, they are bad'.

For women, with their specific public obligations, this psychological heritage of the past can hardly ease the adaptation process and so let them 'refer to the present and to a future' by creating a 'basis for solidarity' with the local women and the host population in general.

In conclusion, I would like to re-emphasize the following points. On the level of the individual, stress and frustration appear to be common features of the Russian women's adaptation to the new surroundings in the historic motherland. Viewed as a socio-cultural process, adaptation is a complex interplay of gender and ethno-social factors. This complexity is exacerbated by a diversity of socio-cultural settings left by the migrants 'there' and faced 'here.' Viewed through the lens of the European debate on women in migration, the case presented here might suggest that known models of women's adaptation, in spite of their prevalence, do not fit the post-Soviet experience, nor should they be seen as universal.

Notes

1. In accordance with the legislation, 'forced migrants' are mainly Russian-speakers, citizens of the Russian Federation driven by ethno-political and social tensions in the former Soviet republics or within Russia and seeking new, permanent residence there in the latter territories.

2. I would like to thank Hilary Pilkington not only for her financial support which made possible my first field trips to Oryol *oblast* as a gender-related part of her own project, but also for sharing with me the joys and frustrations of our stay in the Russian countryside, especially in autumn 1993, the most critical days of my country's recent history.

Since June 1995 my research has become an integral part of the two-year international project 'Post-Soviet Migration and Ethno-Political Tension: Conceptualizing the Interaction' sponsored by the International Association for the Promotion of Co-operation with Scientists from the Independent States of the Former Soviet Union (INTAS).

3. Thus, 86.4 per cent of 106 respondents are Russians, 6.8 per cent are

Ukrainians, and the rest are Germans, Tatars, and Armenians. the FMS Oryol oblast data are, respectively, 86.3 per cent Russians, 5.7 per cent Ukrainians, followed by Tatars, Armenians and Germans. The majority of the respondents (72.8 per cent) were born in the republic from which they migrated, whereas 27.2 per cent were born in Russia; 66.9 per cent lived in urban areas, around half of them in capital cities, and the remainder lived in rural areas. As for the countries of exodus, 33.9 per cent of respondents came from Kazakhstan, 23.7 from Kirghizia, 20.3 from Tajikistan, 15.4 from Uzbekistan, 5.1 from Azerbaijan and 1.6 per cent from Abkhaziya thus reproducing the general migration pattern described above.

4. 54.5 per cent of women compared with 20.0 per cent of men in the main sample and 55.2 per cent and 24.0 per cent in the second sample.

References

Buijs, Gina. 1993. 'Introduction.' In Gina Buijs (ed.), *Migrant Women. Crossing Boundaries and Changing Identities*. Oxford: Berg Publishers.
Eastmond, Marita. 1993. 'Reconstructing life: Chilean refugee women and the dilemmas of exile.' In Gina Buijs (ed.), *Migrant Women. Crossing Boundaries and Changing Identities*. Oxford: Berg Publishers.
Forced Migrants in Russia. 1995. Moscow: Federal Migration Service of the Russian Federation, Statistical Bulletin no. 5.
Hollands, Marlie. 1996. *Of Crowbars and Other Tools to Tackle Dutch Society: The Integration of Refugees and the Multicultural Society*. Report presented to the Second International Conference 'New Migration in Europe: Social Constructions and Social Realities.' Utrecht, Netherlands, 18–20 April 1996.
Kosmarskaya, Natalya. 1996. *A Micro-Level Study of Forced Migrants: Adaptation in Central Russia*. Working report for the INTAS project seminar, Moscow, 1–5 June 1996.
Numbers of Population and Its Mobility in the Russian Federation. 1995. Moscow: State Statistical Committee of the Russian Federation. Statistical Bulletin.
Russians. Ethno-Sociological Essays. 1992. Moscow: Nauka Publishing House.

17

Ethiopian Women Immigrants into Israel: The Loss of Space and Body

Tovi Fenster

This chapter is an analysis of the expressions in space of the changes in lifestyle, traditions and gender relations undergone by Ethiopian immigrants during their absorption process into their new Israeli environment. The analysis is performed in two ways: first, by analysing the perceptions and use of space by immigrant men and women, and second, by analysing the state's perception of these changes, expressed in the subsequent development of planning projects for immigrant absorption.

The chapter deals with the experiences of immigration as a 'catastrophe' in the sense of losing values, norms, identities and spaces which were significant in an immigrant's former life. This loss is usually more traumatic for women, because cultural norms and values of their bodies and the use of space are more restricted and concrete. The chapter suggests planning procedures which can ease the process of integration and the trauma of immigration. It describes and analyses this process with regard to Ethiopian immigrant absorption in Israel during the 1980s and 1990s.

The chapter begins with a brief discussion of space as a factor of analysis in the comprehension of social relations. I then discuss the role of space as a component in planning, with particular regard to pluralist planning. The definition of pluralism used is the relationship between ethnicity and citizenship, and their different meanings for men and women. These dimensions are also used to analyse social change. The next section describes the process of social change, from the perspective of ethnicity and citizenship, undergone by Ethiopian immigrants in Israel, and its effect on their use of space. The following section evaluates the state's perceptions of the process as reflected in the two master plans formulated for the absorption of Ethiopians. I conclude with a brief discussion on whether the components of pluralism – ethnicity, citizenship and gender – work in conflict or coexistence in planning.

Social Change, Space and Planning

The role of space in social theory has become increasingly significant in the past two decades when it became clear that spatial relations can represent and reproduce social relations. One expression of this shift is the acknowledgement by Marxists that geographical, and especially spatial perspectives, are vital for understanding social theory. Crises of capitalism have their own geographers, who also recognize that spatial structures are intrinsic to the resolutions of these crises (Harvey, 1989). The process of 'spatialization of social theory' (Soja, 1989) was further reinforced by Giddens (1979, 1981), whose structuration theory disentangled the Marxist dialectic, separating 'structure' and 'human agency' in order to investigate their interrelationship (Smith, 1994). Another important change, which influenced the introduction of space into social theory, was the shift in attitudes towards modernity which began to dismantle in the 1960s. This, in turn, initiated significant shifts in the nature and interpretation of development and growth interpreted, in the light of modernity, as exploitation of marginalized groups such as blacks or other ethnic minorities, women, students, etc., all expressing discontent with their subordinate position within the modern order (Lefebre, 1992).

The spatialization of Marxist theory, together with the shift in approach towards modernity, is echoed in planning theories too. If planning is defined as a set of rational actions aimed at organizing the use of space according to principles and goals determined in advance, then the process of the actual planning of space may be viewed as one of the expressions of social relations within society. From the Marxist perspective, this means that planning can be viewed as an expression in space of the power relations between different social groups, while the goals for the planning of space are usually formulated by the dominant group controlling the resources.

The development of planning theories with regard to social relations and space may be viewed as the dichotomy between *procedural* and *progressive* planning theories. The former represents a modernist outlook of society, emphasizing a rational comprehensive approach to planning; a formal, top-down process which ignores the 'others' – the marginalized – and therefore pays little attention to social relations and their expressions in space. The latter represents a more open view of social structures and relations, and connects them directly to the use of space.

In Israel, *procedural* planning has invariably been favoured, precisely due to the multi-ethnic nature of Israeli society, and the need to foster a national consensus ideology. The result was that in certain areas, where specific planning of housing and infrastructure was required to meet ethnic needs, these needs have been ignored. Such planning is typified by the absorption of Mizrahi Jews (Jews immigrating from Arab and North African countries) during the 1950s. They were met by a cohesive and centralized Western-oriented socio-political system, controlled by Ashkenazi (European) Jews upon arrival in Israel. They were sent to live in 'development towns', mostly peripheral communities, sponsored by central government. Most of these immigrants, having no alternative, stayed on in these towns and remained dependent upon the government for the provision of employment, education, housing and social welfare services. They lived in inadequate accommodation which failed to cater for the ethnic needs of a traditional, religious, ethnic community (Ben Zadok, 1993). The government's approach to this immigrant community was uniform and functionalist, emphasizing national interests, as determined by policy-makers. It did not consider the process of social change that these groups were undergoing, a crucial omission when the target group consisted of immigrants with different social, cultural and economic needs. Unfortunately, these policies were repeated during the 1980s and 1990s with regard to the Ethiopians. This sudden mass influx presented highly complex issues, not least of which were logistical problems.

This chapter argues that a more pluralist view of planning, and a wider use of progressive planning theories, is needed in the absorption of such immigrant communities. Sandercock and Forsyth (1996) call this approach 'planning for multiple publics' at the centre of which is 'the acknowledgement and celebration of difference'. This requires deeper consideration of cultural expressions in space, which would ease the integration and adaptation of these immigrants into their new homes. This process can be described as a dialogue between the tendency to preserve cultural norms and the will to change and adopt new norms. It is also a dialogue between assimilationist and more pluralist approaches. This dialogue also raises the issue of whether cultural traditions which perpetuate women's subordination should be further perpetuated, and in what form?

This chapter aims to encourage pluralist planning, with particular attention to gender perceptions and needs in space. The planning of space for immigrants needs to take into consideration the fact that men and women clearly experience social change differently, due to their different social roles and spatial mobility.

Pluralism in Space and Planning: Perspectives on Ethnicity, Citizenship and Gender

Ethnicity and citizenship

Ethnicity is 'the feeling of belonging to, and of solidarity with, cultural units wider than families' (Horowitz, 1985). For society at large, this feeling creates the 'other', the 'different', the 'minority', which planning schemes and development programmes ignore.

Ethnicity in general emphasizes the different values, norms, language, religion, customs, clothes, food, festivals, ceremonies etc., formed and preserved by a particular group of people. Ethnicity is a highly complex form of collective identity, more complex than, for example, territorial, religious or gender identities. It is often born and perpetuated through conflict with a socially and culturally heterogeneous environment or as a response to civil discrimination (Smith, 1991).

Space is where ethnic values affect women. Cultural codes and a sense of ethnicity influence perceptions and meanings of space, especially prohibition and acceptability of the use of space. This is most relevant to women, as they play major roles in the construction and defence of cultural and ethnic collectivities. They are often the symbol of a national collectivity, its roots and spirit (Yuval-Davis, 1995). Therefore, their spatial mobility is very much dictated, if not controlled, by the cultural meaning attributed to space. Thus, cultural and ethnic norms create 'spaces of modesty and immodesty', 'spaces of purity and impurity'. The boundaries of these spaces are usually dictated by 'the cultural guards' of society, that is, men (Fenster, 1997b).

Citizenship is about equality, communality and homogeneity, almost the opposite of 'difference' or ethnicity. Citizenship is interpreted by Marshall (1950, 1975, 1981) as 'full membership in a community', encompassing civil, political and social rights. The discussion on citizenship during the past decade is probably the result of political and social crises, wherein the exercise of power is challenged and thus the widely used definition of citizenship has shifted to a more complex, sophisticated, less optimistic interpretation (Kofman, 1995). The idea of citizenship is now used analytically to expose differences in the de jure and de facto rights of different groups within and between nation states (Smith, 1994). The concept is also used normatively to determine how a society, sensitive to human rights, should appear. Three main models of citizenship can be identified (Kofman, 1995). First, the Civic Republican model, which focuses on the civic rights of the individual citizen, and which is associated with the American and French revolutions. Second, the ethnic model which preserves citizenship for those members of a nation whose status is defined by a community of descent. This model suits Germany and Israel. The third is the model of social citizenship which emphasizes social rights as part of citizenship and was mainly promoted by Marshall. A gendered, women-friendly conception of citizenship represents a synthesis between the last two models (Lister, 1995).

Expressions of citizenship in space have recently been coined as 'spaces of citizenship' (Painter and Philo, 1995), the expression in space of the relationship between the state and its citizens, that is, whether *all* citizens get *equal* treatment from the state in matters which involve equal access to natural resources such as land, water, or minerals, as well as equal access to government development facilities, for example, infrastructure, welfare services, education and employment.

A *pluralist perception of citizenship*

From the above statements on both ethnicity and citizenship, pluralist principles of citizenship can be deduced which, in turn, require respect on the part of the state for both the right to equality and the right to preserve cultural differences and the *different* or traditional uses of space (Fenster, 1997a). This interpretation of citizenship opposes the modernist view of citizenship which emphasizes equality, deliberately avoiding the different, ethnic components that may challenge this approach with traditional belief systems and different expressions in the use of space.

Just as pluralist citizenship includes both equality and difference, so should pluralist planning incorporate the components necessary for equality whilst serving ethnic needs. The ultimate goal of pluralist planning is to encompass the ethnic perspective.

The case-study related in this paper demonstrates the kind of adaptation immigrant communities were forced to undergo due to the modernist planning approach practised in Israel, and exposes the weaknesses of its over-simplified approach.

Gender, ethnicity and citizenship – *the private/public discourse*

The distinction between 'public' and 'private' space is an integral part of the definition of citizenship. Turner (1990) employs these terms to distinguish between his four typologies of citizenship, which differ, in varying degrees, in the extent to which the state interferes or abstains from involvement in the private domain. Jayasuriya (1990) also uses these terms to distinguish between needs, which are met by the state, and wants, which are satisfied by the private domain. Yuval-Davis (1991) argues that such distinctions are not only culture-specific but also gender-specific. It is the state which, for example, excludes women from certain citizen rights, by defining the man as the head of the family. Due to the fact that the state plays such a major role in the articulation of planning policies, and is ultimately responsible for ensuring the provision of civil rights to both men and women, extra caution is required in the case of immigrants, who are in any event vulnerable to discrimination, due to their legal status as 'not yet citizens'. Feminists have struggled to deconstruct the 'patriarchal separation' between the 'public' and the domestic 'private' because the public and private define each other and take meaning from each other. As Lister (1995) argues, we cannot understand the gendered patterns of entry to citizenship in the public sphere without taking into account the sexual division of labour within the private. This struggle to control the meaning and positioning of the divide is central to the project of engendering citizenship (Lister, 1995).

Engendering citizenship has many implications for space. Men and women experience differently the move in space due to their defined social roles. As these roles begin to change, so do perceptions and uses of space. These changes are reflected in the different patterns of spatial movement by women which are very much dictated by the definitions of 'public' and 'private' spaces as illustrated in the Ethiopian experience.

The Ethiopian Immigrants in Israel: Perspectives on Space and Planning

The process of social change in housing, employment, language acquisition and cultural identity

The 53,000 black, rural Ethiopian Jews now living in Israel have undergone dramatic changes in all aspects of their lives. As farmers and potters (Salamon, 1993), they lived in extended family structures (Doleve-Gandelman, 1990), retaining their own particular religious traditions. As immigrants, they faced totally unfamiliar social, economic and religious norms and values. For the majority, the process of change has proved difficult.[1] For many, their ethnic identity is still dominant. This is mainly expressed in differing norms regarding work habits (Doleve-Gandelman, 1990), and their need for specific spaces, expressed through their housing needs. Most Ethiopians were raised in large families and were used to living within an extended family space. Upon arrival in Israel they were forced to adapt to living in small government-provided apartments, at a higher density level than the average Israeli (1.47 per room, or 2 per room in temporary housing as compared with 1.1 per room in the majority population). In addition, they also had to adjust to the concept of living in a nuclear family space, often at a great distance from their relatives, an important break with their cultural norms.

This is particularly problematic for those who arrived later, wishing to be reunited with their families. The desire for communal space is still widespread, as revealed in the results of a survey carried out in three cities: Natanya, Afula, and Kiryat Gat (Benita, Noam and Levi, 1993). Even among veteran immigrants (who arrived in 1984), 48 per cent stated the proximity of relatives to be the main reason for choice of location. Of the Ethiopians in Kiryat Gat 60 per cent said it was important for them to have other Ethiopians in the same neighbourhood, and 57 per cent said it was important to have other Ethiopians in the same building. These figures are lower among veterans than among more recent arrivals from the 1991 wave, suggesting an adjustment over time.

The Israeli government has adopted a policy of 'cultural integration' which opposes ethnic separation. As a result, many mixed spaces were created, especially at the neighbourhood level. These are known as 'integrative neighbourhoods', where Ethiopians live together with Russian immigrants and Israeli-born families. The experience of integration is not easy. There are many reports of conflict over cultural and lifestyle differences. In these neighbourhoods there is a need for intensive community work in order to facilitate coexistence.

Patterns of employment have also undergone dramatic changes. In Kiryat Gat, only 46 per cent of the Ethiopians aged 22–64 are employed, while in Ethiopia almost all were employed.[2] The major reason is the type of employment offered. The majority are now employed in industry (66 per cent), or public services (24 per cent), while only 6 per cent are employed in agriculture, construction and commerce. In Ethiopia, the great majority (72 per cent) were farmers, the remainder either blacksmiths or soldiers (Benita et al., 1993). Only 53 per cent of the Ethiopians express satisfaction with their work, compared with 77 per cent among the Jewish Israeli-born population. Sixty per cent of the respondents claimed that their income was not sufficient to support a family. The majority of the Ethiopians surveyed indicated employment difficulties as the most severe problems in their integration into Israeli life.

Language is another indicator of integration. Although 75 per cent of those surveyed in Kiryat Gat attended *Ulpan* (a Hebrew language course), only 58 per cent were able to speak fluent Hebrew, and only 37 per cent were able to write a simple letter, with 43 per cent able to read a simple letter.

Perhaps the two harshest indicators, reflecting the traumatic process of social change and vindicating pluralist planning, are the relatively high number of suicides, and the rapid spread of Pentecostalism amongst the Ethiopian community. A survey carried out in 1992 (Arieli et al., 1994) indicated a level of suicide 137–667 per cent (depending on the area) above the average rate in Israel. Most of the suicides were men in their early twenties to late thirties. These rates are particularly high, even when compared to other immigrant communities in Israel, or to immigrant groups in the USA, Canada and France (Arieli et al., 1994). The reason for these high rates of suicide according to the above research, is 'acculturation stress' most probably related to lack of consideration for ethnic and cultural needs (Arieli et al., 1994).

The rapid spread of Pentecostalism is also a result of modernist planning and ignorance of ethnic needs. This missionary born-again Christian movement has gained great popularity around the world amongst uprooted communities (Rosen, 1995). Its spread and success in Israel is an expression of the lack of sense of belonging of this community, severe economic problems, and the indication that its ethnic and citizenship needs are not being met. Exact figures of the above phenomenon are, as yet, unknown, but it is estimated by the Ministry of Absorption that approximately twenty such centres exist in locations densely populated by Ethiopians (Rosen, 1995).

Gender relations in Ethiopia and Israel and their expressions in space

Women made up 49 per cent of the Ethiopian immigrants, of which 46 per cent were 16 and above. About 28 per cent of the families in the first wave of immigrants (1984) were single-parent families, of which 83 per cent were matriarchal households. This was due to the fact that there were many couples where one partner stayed behind in Ethiopia, or died on the journey to Israel. Long separation led to infidelity with no subsequent divorce, and this often created turmoil in the family structure.

Immigration to Israel had a tremendous effect on gender roles. While in Ethiopia the husband ruled the family, controlling finance and decision-making, in Israel he had to adapt to a more open sharing of responsibilities (Beitachin, 1994; Westheimer and Kaplan, 1992). In Ethiopia, the patriarchal structure of the family defined clear-cut divisions between gender roles, and private and public spaces. Men ruled the family and functioned in both private and public spaces, as they were the bread-winners, usually in traditional occupations. The woman's role in Ethiopia left her solely in the private spaces. Her traditional role was the typical triple role: childbearing, child-rearing and basket-weaving, always within the domestic domain (for details see: Moser, 1993). In addition, women were in charge of domestic management in general: collecting wood, carrying water from wells and taking care of the health and education of their children (Westheimer and Kaplan, 1992). The wife obeyed and respected her husband; she would feed him before the rest of the family, wash his feet when he returned from work, and honour him by keeping the traditional Jewish laws concerning family purity, moving during men-struation to a separate hut. This custom was considered a woman's right, not just an obligation to be honoured.

In Israel, these roles within the family have changed dramatically. The patriarchal structure of the family is breaking down due to unemployment among Ethiopian men and a growing independence among Ethiopian women, often as a result of their need to maintain the family financially, whether by working or receiving social security payments paid directly to them. This growing independence has propelled women further in the public domain and has decreased the authority of their husbands.

Changes in gender roles and norms have affected men and women differently, both in their roles and in their changing spatial mobilities (Ben Zvi, 1989; Elias, 1989; Litman, 1993). For women this has meant that more spaces have became 'public' whereas for men it has often resulted in the opposite situation, so that their lives have become concentrated in the 'private' spaces.

Four reasons explain the different effects of social change on men and women. First, the process of change has been somewhat easier for women, since they have been assisted by social workers, nurses, teachers, etc., most of whom are women themselves (Westheimer and Kaplan, 1992). The men have found it more difficult to open up to these professionals and identify with them. As a result, Ethiopian women are more likely to seek the help of the social services when they are in need. Men, on the other hand, tend to rely on the ethnic, religious, traditional Ethiopian establishment (the *Kessim*, religious leaders), whose authority maintains their superior position in the family (Betachin, 1993). Second, as mentioned above, Ethiopian women have become more independent due to their better employment opportunities, but more as a result of the necessity to provide for their families than of a conscious struggle for equality. Third, Ethiopian women in general are more open to change. In Ethiopia they were subordinated, uneducated and often illiterate. Interestingly, the subordination of women, on an ethnic basis, gave them the advantage of being more flexible in accepting new cultural patterns and a new citizen identity, while their men had been educated to adhere rigidly to old ethnic traditions (Master Plan, 1985). This made the women 'agents for change' in the eyes of the Israeli authorities, with a greater ability to absorb the concept of 'similarity' related to citizenship. As Ethiopian women are on average also much younger than their husbands, they are more open to change. Finally, in Israel, the legal system and society's norms provide women with mechanisms to defend their civil rights, for example, social security, prohibitions against domestic violence, and the active fight by women's organizations for women's rights. This has provided Ethiopian women with new means of defence and helped them to develop their self-esteem (Beitachin, 1994).

These changes have engendered increasing tension within families, particularly between husbands and wives (Beitachin, 1994). Living in a nuclear family, rather than as an extended family, has dismantled the traditional mechanisms of conflict resolution previously available.

Social Change as Expressed in the Use of Space and Body

One of the obvious expressions of these tensions is in the changing perceptions of family purity and the cultural meaning attributed to space, distinguishing between 'pure' and 'impure' spaces. Social change in this respect refers to the changing boundaries between these two kinds of spaces. How do 'pure' and 'impure' spaces interrelate to 'public ' and 'private' spaces? It seems that the notions of public and private have their own meanings in Ethiopian society because of principles of purity and impurity. Traditional customs in Ethiopia, among both Christians and Jews, view women's menstrual blood as impure, and therefore, for a certain period of the month, or after childbirth, women are not allowed to move in certain public and even private spaces, such as churches for Christians or even their own home in the case of Jewish Ethiopian women (Punkhurst, 1992). For these times, special spaces are allocated in the menstruation hut.

Pure and impure spaces: the menstruation hut

The separation of women during menstruation and after childbirth, when they lived in the 'impurity hut' – the *yamargam gogo* – was a symbol for pure and impure spaces. It also separated these women from their daily routine. This tradition adheres to a strict reading of biblical law which says that a Jewish woman is considered impure during her menstruation (for seven days), and after giving birth. The women's relatives would bring food to the 'impurity hut' on special plates. Located close to the village, these huts were partially surrounded by a stone semicircle which delineated the boundaries between the 'impure' and 'pure' spaces. These houses, preferably located near rivers, also emphasized the Jewish identity of these women in villages where Jews and Christians lived together (Salamon, 1993).

Changing perceptions of pure and impure spaces during the process of integration

In Israel, the meanings and uses of spaces have changed dramatically and these specific spaces have no parallel. Due to the fact that no space was found in modern Israeli building schemes, Ethiopian women have lost a space which permitted them to remain closely in touch with their bodies (Doleve-Gandelman, 1990). The consequence of this rapid change has led to increased tension among family members, and especially among women who have experienced feelings of guilt and shame. Many women have tried to use replacements for the hut, such as balconies, hotel corridors or even a closet (Zehavi, 1989; Halper, 1987; Westheimer and Kaplan, 1992). A small number seem to have found a solution to this problem in adopting the common Jewish rabbinical laws of *nida* (menstruation), and immersion in the *mikve* (a pool-like ritual bath) to replace the bodily purification in the running water of Ethiopia's rivers. Some women have tried to retain a modicum of separation in their home by allocating special rooms and building separate bathrooms for their menstrual period (Antebi, 1996), but for most women the loss of the ritual hut was the loss of an important social institution. Antebi (1996) claims that Ethiopian women have lost their social role in indicating, with their bodies, the boundaries between 'pure' and 'impure' spaces. In Ethiopia, this segregation between 'pure' and 'impure' spaces belonged to the public sphere. In Israel, with the lack of physical opportunities to maintain this segregation, it has become part of these women's 'private' space. During their menstruation periods women now sleep in separate rooms in their private homes. Due to the above, a large amount of non-verbal information regarding the community life itself in Ethiopia has been lost: by staying or not remaining in the hut, the Ethiopian community would know whether a woman was pregnant, an issue which would not then be discussed verbally.

Gender reactions to these changes among the Ethiopian community are mixed. Some women are happy to be relieved of the menstruation hut, whereas others have nostalgic memories of this tradition. Perhaps the most significant and painful expression of this loss, is expressed by the feelings of some Ethiopians that Ethiopia is a 'clean' place and their present living environment is 'dirty' (Antebi, 1996). Interestingly, Westheimer and Kaplan (1992) found that the fact that this custom has been preserved, even in a compromised form, while others are disappearing, should serve as a warning against any single interpretation of their meaning and function. Neither the feminist perspective, which attacks these customs as 'double subordination', nor the romantic approach, which defends them as a way of separating the woman from her daily routine, has really understood the rationale of this custom.

All this raises crucial questions about the desired rate of change necessary for an immigrant society to absorb new cultural norms. It also implies the need for planning policies to be more sensitive to the conflicting processes of preserving and changing cultural norms in a community returning to its 'homeland' so as to ensure smoother and less traumatic integration. An analysis of the state's perceptions of the above dilemmas, as expressed in the two master plans formulated for Ethiopian immigrant absorption, highlights the inadequacies of meeting the needs of this community.

The State's Perceptions: The Master Plans for the Ethiopian Community in Israel

The state of Israel prepared for the absorption of the Ethiopian Jews by preparing two master plans. The first was drafted in 1985, a year after the arrival of the first wave of immigrants; the second was formulated in 1992 and was an updated version of the first plan.

The master plans for the absorption of the Ethiopian Jews – a modernist perspective

The first master plan for the absorption of Ethiopian Jews was a very elaborate, detailed programme. The planning included housing, education, employment, organizational aspects of absorption, and policy guidelines regarding specific groups such as women, youth and single-parent families. No doubt the plan was formulated with the best intentions, but the results have been disappointing, suggesting that a pluralist approach to citizenship, and in particular closer attention to the immigrants' ethnicity, may have been necessary. As with each wave of immigration, emphasis on consensus, modernist thinking and national priorities has tended to outweigh these considerations.

The first master plan was formulated along the lines of a rational comprehensive approach, whereby immigrants are regarded as similar to the majority population. The second plan, which was formulated to absorb the 20,000 Ethiopians who arrived in 1991, adopted the same planning approach. This approach diminished the importance of ethnic differences and their space implications, which are on the contrary highlighted in pluralist planning, in order to integrate the immigrants into a new society as smoothly as possible. The plan did not recognize the necessity for different spaces: rather, this modernist, rational, comprehensive planning approach derived from an assimilationist view of society, which transformed the cultural meaning attributed to space on a gender basis into a unified pattern of the use of space.

This approach is illustrated in housing policies. These policies ignored the social and cultural needs of the Ethiopians in two important ways: the lack of consideration for family size and the extended family, and as mentioned earlier, the ignorance of the need for separate spaces for women and men. Instead, immigrants were housed far from their relatives, in conditions that were often too cramped to accommodate even the nuclear family.

Regarding gender issues, although the customs of family purity, as preserved in Ethiopia, were well known to the planners, they were not taken into consideration, probably because the planners assumed that this habit would quickly disappear with assimilation into the majority society, and perhaps because the planners thought it was important to emphasize similarities between the immigrant community and the host society, rather than highlight differences. As mentioned above, this has made relations between men and women in these immigrant households more volatile.

The plan did approach women and men differently with respect to their separate experience of social adjustment, although not with respect to their different needs in uses of space. At the outset, the women's ability to participate in activities such as the *Ulpan* (Hebrew School) and employment training was regarded as fairly unlikely, although the planners did recommend involving women as much as possible. Attendance was hindered due to the traditional perception of their triple role, their concentration in the private sphere, and the fact that there were not enough childcare facilities. However, the plan indicated great potential for these women's adjustment and they were further viewed as 'agents of change'. In contrast, as mentioned earlier, the men, due to their superior position in the ethnic community, were expected to have more difficulties in accepting changes in gender relations, and therefore they were not regarded as being good agents of socialization. The plan therefore suggested encouraging women to participate in activities, especially language acquisition, as a symbol of their new citizen identity, and employment training, providing adequate childcare facilities. Despite the positive intentions and correct observations regarding the effects of immigration on men and women, the plans did not tackle the delicate balance between ethnic and citizenship identities on the socio-economic and cultural-spatial levels, as discussed earlier.

An overview of the plan suggests that the approach to integration with regard to women did not result from a desire for equality, but rather from a functionalist approach towards the role of women in the process of social change. The authorities were actually more interested in training women as agents for re-educating the next generation of Israeli citizens than in improving their present status, or considering their ethnicity.

Conclusion

Israel's planning policies have predominantly been shaped by national, citizen, modernist trends, which ignore the 'other', whether on an ethnic or gender basis. Thus they turned the process of immigration into a 'catastrophe'. But it is the neglect of ethnic sensibilities which clearly needs to be addressed if future approaches to absorption are to ease the difficulties of transition for immigrant societies. In order that planning can learn from past failures, it is argued here that the appropriate planning procedure for immigrants must take a more pluralist view of citizenship.

The major questions raised in this chapter are: does a pluralist definition of citizenship work in harmony or conflict regarding gender relations? Are planners supposed to encourage such changes? And what type of plan is 'appropriate' in terms of the balance between equality and difference? All of them aim to ease the sense of trauma and catastrophe which are part of the process of immigration in Israel at present.

Such discussions are not usually part of the agenda of procedural planning in Israel. Planning is traditionally more concerned with the formal aspects, rather than the social, cultural and organizational perspectives, neglecting the spatial expression of different ethnic needs. The master plans for the Ethiopian Jews are an example of this neglect, and of the need for a more progressive and pluralist approach.

Such debates are usually part of the *raison d'être* of the progressive planning tradition, which regards the planning process as a dialogue between planners and beneficiaries. An important element in this process is consultation with the community at various stages of the planning process, in particular in deciding the speed of change, and the translation of the community's social and ethnic needs into space. Community participation is a tool for pluralist planning as beneficiary participation ensures the creation of diverse planning options. It is also the basic principle of citizenship and especially gendered citizenship, which means ensuring a full participation of women in the planning process and in determining their needs in space.

Many questions should be addressed as to the possible conflict between what is viewed as a pluralist perspective towards gender relations emphasizing equality, and the response of members of the ethnic community, especially the men. It may be argued that the separation of 'pure' and 'impure' spaces encourages women's subordination and therefore should be ignored. Notwithstanding the planners' personal view, it is obvious that social and cultural changes are time-consuming and planning should take this into consideration. A plan can only be decided upon after evaluating whether immigrant men and women can integrate sudden changes into their lifestyle. Equality cannot be reached at any price, and the transition is sometimes a slow process, which planning should respect. The case of the Ethiopians demonstrates that a call for equality sometimes creates unexpected conflicts for which planners have not provided adequate tools. The planning process should therefore involve consultation with the immigrants themselves, in order to set the rhythm of the process. The existing procedural planning traditions are inadequate, as they are based on consensus and do not include negotiations in the planning process. A new planning approach requires a methodology in which the political dimension of planner-beneficiary negotiation is central and the introduction of social relations in space is more clear cut.

Notes

1. Much has been written describing the difficulties faced by Ethiopian Jews in Israel. Among others, see Westheimer and Kaplan (1992), Ashkenazi and Weingrod (1987).
2. The figures appearing in this section are based on a census carried out among Ethiopian residents living in three towns: Kiryat Gat, Afula and Natanya. These figures are not representative of all Ethiopians in Israel but provide an indication of their situation.

References

Antebi, L. 1996. 'There's blood in the house: negotiating female rituals of purity among the Ethiopian Jews in Israel.' Unpublished manuscript.
Ashkenazi, M. and A. Weingrod (eds). 1987. *Ethiopian Jews and Israel.* New Brunswick: Transaction Books.

Arieli, A., I. Gilat and S. Izak. 1994. 'The suicide of the Ethiopian Jews.' *Journal of Israel Medical Association.* vol. 127, no. 3–4: 65–70.

Ben Zvi, N. 1989. 'The integration of Ethiopian Jews in the employment sector.' In *The Absorption of the Ethiopian Jews in Occupation Employment Agency.* Jerusalem: Ministry of Welfare, pp. 43–55 (Hebrew).

Beitachin Information and Counselling Centre on Family Affairs. 1993. *Women in the Ethiopian Community in Israel.* Jerusalem (Hebrew).

Beitachin Information and Counselling Centre on Family Affairs. 1994. *Ethiopian Jews in Cultural Transition: the Family and Life Cycle.* Jerusalem (Hebrew).

Benita, E., G. Noam and E. Levi. 1993. *The Absorption of Ethiopian Immigrants: Findings of a Survey in Kiryat Gat.* Joint (JDC), Israel (Hebrew).

Ben Zadok, E. 1993. 'Oriental Jews in the development towns: ethnicity, economic development, budgets, and politics.' In E. Ben Zadok (ed.), *Local Communities and the Israeli Policy.* New York: State University of New York Press.

Elias, J. 1989. 'Working life in Ethiopia.' In *The Absorption of the Ethiopian Jews in Occupation.* Jerusalem: Employment Agency (Ministry of Welfare) (Hebrew).

Doleve-Gandelman, T. 1990. 'Ethiopia as a lost imaginary space: The role of Ethiopian Jewish women in producing the ethnic identity of their immigrant group in Israel.' In F. MacCannell (ed.), *The Other Perspective in Gender and Culture.* New York: Columbia University Press.

Fenster, Tovi. 1997a. 'Gender and space: the case of Bedouin women in Israel.' *Studies in the Geography of Israel* (forthcoming, Hebrew).

Fenster, Tovi. 1997b. 'Spaces of citizenship: the Bedouin in the frontier development of the Negev – Israel.' *Progress in Planning* (forthcoming)

Giddens, Anthony. 1979. *Central Problems in Social Theory.* London: Macmillan.

Giddens, Anthony. 1981. *A Contemporary Critique of Historical Materialism.* London, Macmillan.

Halper, J. 1987. 'The absorption of the Ethiopian immigrants: a return to the fifties.' In M. Ashkenazi and A. Weingrod (eds), *Ethiopian Jews and Israel.* New Brunswick: Transaction Books.

Harvey, David. 1989. *The Conditions of Postmodernity: An Enquiry into the Origins of Cultural Change.* Oxford: Blackwell.

Horowitz, D.L. 1985. *Ethnic Groups in Conflict.* Berkeley: University of California Press.

Jayasuriya, L. 1990. 'Multiculturalism, citizenship and welfare: new directions for the 1990s.' Paper presented at the 50th Anniversary Lecture Series, Department of Social Work and Social Policy, University of Sydney.

Kofman, E. 1995. 'Citizenship for some but not for others: spaces of citizenship in contemporary Europe.' *Political Geography,* vol. 14, no. 2: 121–37.

Lefebvre, H . 1992. *The Production of Space.* Oxford: Blackwell.

Lister, Ruth. 1995. 'Dilemmas in engendering citizenship.' *Economy and Society,* vol. 24, no. 1: 2–40.

Litman, E.M. 1993. *Ethiopian Immigrant Women: Transition to a New Identity?* PhD dissertation, Ohio State University.

Marshall, T.H. 1950. *Citizenship and Social Class.* Cambridge: Cambridge University Press.

Marshall, T.H. 1975. *Social Policy in the Twentieth Century.* London: Hutchinson.

Marshall, T.H. 1981. *The Right and Welfare and Other Essays.* London: Heinemann Educational Books.

Ministry of Absorption. 1985. *The Absorption of the Ethiopian Jews – Master Plan,* Jerusalem.

Ministry of Absorption. 1991. *A Plan for the Absorption of the Ethiopian Jews – Second Wave*, Jerusalem.

Moser, C. 1993. *Gender Planning and Development: Theory, Practice and Training*. London: Routledge.

Painter, J. and O. Philo. 1995. 'Spaces of citizenship: an introduction.' *Political Geography*, vol. 14, no. 2: 107–20.

Punkhurst, H. 1992. *Gender, Development and Identity*. London: Zed Books.

Rosen, H. 1995. 'The Beita Israel and their missionary nemesis.' Paper presented at the second international conference of the Society for the Study of the Ethiopian Jewry, Jerusalem and Beer Sheva.

Salamon, H. 1993. 'Beta Israel and their Christian neighbours in Ethiopia: analysis of central perceptions at different levels of cultural articulation.' Unpublished PhD Thesis, Hebrew University, Jerusalem (Hebrew).

Sandercock, L. and A. Forsyth. 1996. 'Feminist theory and planning theory.' In S. Campbell and S. Fainstein (eds), *Reading in Planning Theory*. Oxford: Blackwell.

Smith, Anthony. 1991. *National Identity*. Harmondsworth: Penguin Books.

Smith, N. 1994. 'Marxist geography.' In R.J. Johnston (ed.), *The Dictionary of Human Geography*. Oxford: Blackwell.

Soja, E. 1989. *Postmodern Geographies: The Reassertion of Space in Critical Social Theory*. London: Verso.

Turner, Bryan. 1990. 'Outline of a theory of citizenship.' *Sociology*, vol. 24, no. 2: 189–217.

Westheimer, R. and S. Kaplan. 1992. *Surviving Salvation*. New York: New York University Press.

Yuval-Davis, Nira. 1991. 'The citizenship debate: women, ethnic processes and the state.' *Feminist Review* 39: 58–68.

Yuval-Davis, Nira. 1995. 'Ethnicity, gender relations and multiculturalism.' Paper presented at the Euroconference on Migration and Multiculturalism, London.

Zehavi, A. 1989. 'The integration of the Ethiopian immigrant women in the employment sector.' In *The Absorption of the Ethiopian Jews in Occupation*. Jerusalem: Employment Agency (Ministry of Welfare) (Hebrew).

18

Woman as Famine Victim: The Figure of Woman in Irish Famine Narratives

Margaret Kelleher

Contemporary media representations of famine and disaster, in seeking to convey individual experiences of victimization, continue to yield a striking prevalence of female images: emaciated and suffering figures, denoting passivity and despair. In recent years, the tendency to present the developing world mostly through images of powerlessness and helplessness, a trend familiar not only from media depictions but also from the advertising campaigns of some non-governmental agencies, has been sharply criticized and the adverse effects of such scenes, with regard to public opinion and policy-making, explored. This chapter offers a historical perspective to such debates on representations of crisis and catastrophe through a study of the literature of the Irish 'Great Famine' of the 1840s.[1] The function of female figures, specifically famine mothers, and their effect on audiences and readers will be explored. In examining the types of response thus generated, three possible analytical models will be suggested.

The Great Famine of 1845–51 was by far the most catastrophic of a number of famines which occurred in Ireland in the nineteenth century. It developed after the partial failure of the potato crop in autumn 1845 was succeeded by its almost complete failure the following year. By 1851, an estimated one million deaths had resulted from hunger and disease while, from 1847 to 1852, an estimated 1.3 million emigrated; thus the pre-famine population of eight million was reduced by over one quarter in six years (see Ó Gráda, 1993: 102–111). The causes of the famine and, more specifically, the responsibility of the British administration remain contentious questions. The prevailing government ideology of *laissez-faire*, coupled with an official declaration as early as summer 1847 that the crisis was past, would appear to have contributed significantly to the scale of the crisis. Questions as to the gendered nature of Irish famine mortality are only beginning to be raised but already prove to have important implications for the wider discussion of gender entitlements and deprivation during crisis and catastrophe. Thus a brief survey of recent historical findings regarding women and the Irish famine will be provided before turning to an analysis of the figure of women in narratives of the Great Famine, as a paradigm for representations of famine in general.

Women and Famine: The Irish Experience

The view that women are more resilient to famine is one which finds expression in many different historical and cultural contexts. The philanthropist and journalist Sidney Godolphin Osborne, writing in the *Times* on 9 July 1849 of conditions in Ireland, remarked that, in his view, 'the girls and women bear it better than the males'. A year later, in his volume *Gleanings in the West of Ireland*, Osborne commented on this phenomenon in more detail:

> No one has yet I believe been able to explain, why it is, that men and boys, sink sooner under famine, than the other sex; still, so it is; go where you will, every officer will tell you, it is so. In the same workhouse, in which you will find the girls and women looking well, you will find the men and boys, in a state of the lowest physical depression; equal care in every way being bestowed on both sexes. (Osborne, 1850: 19)

Arguments as to women's greater ability to withstand famine may also be found in other nineteenth-century famine situations. The observation by one Indian famine commissioner, Sir Charles Elliot, that 'all the authorities seem agreed that women succumb to famine less easily than men' is cited by economist Amartya Sen as representative of 'the general belief regarding nineteenth-century Indian famines' (Sen, 1981: 210–11). More recently, many commentators during the 1940s Bengal famine placed heavy emphasis on the higher rates of male mortality, Calcutta's Department of Anthropology calling this 'a very sinister and significant feature' of the famine (Sen, 1981: 211, n.29). Whether or not such general perceptions are accurate reflections of famine mortality is a more contentious question. In biological or physiological terms, women are usually considered to be 'less vulnerable to deprivation, having smaller needs for energy and most nutrients because they are smaller than men, have a lower metabolic rate and a higher body fat' (Rivers, 1988: 91). This would suggest a reduced vulnerability in times of famine. Yet, as Drèze and Sen (1989), David Arnold (1988) and Paul Greenough (1982) have argued, such a relative advantage needs to be set against patterns of exploitation and discrimination, especially within family situations, which may value less highly the needs of female members during periods of crisis. Consequently, in *Hunger and Public Action*, Drèze and Sen identify the existence of 'two – possibly opposite – tendencies' regarding female deprivation:

On the one hand, there is considerable evidence that the proportionate increase of mortality is typically *lower* for women than for men in famine situations … On the other hand, a number of studies also bring out the fact that, in many societies, the priorities of the family are often pro-male in distress situations. In so far as *greater* physical distress coexists with a *smaller* increase in mortality for females *vis-à-vis* males, the explanation may have to be sought, at least partly, in terms of greater female ability to survive nutritional stress. (Drèze and Sen, 1989: 55)

The heaviest mortality during the Irish Great Famine was experienced by the young and the very old who accounted, Phelim Boyle and Cormac Ó Gráda (1986: 555) estimate, for approximately one-third of the population but about 60 per cent of the excess deaths. In his study, *The Great Irish Famine*, Ó Gráda contemplates the personal horrors behind such statistics: 'the Famine presumably forced many families, like the occupants of an overloaded lifeboat, to make life-and-death choices: an equal sharing of the burden of hunger might have doomed all' (Ó Gráda, 1989: 50). Based on an estimate of one million excess deaths, that is, deaths directly attributable to famine, Boyle and Ó Gráda suggest that in absolute terms there were slightly more excess deaths among males, but with a very small differential (1986: 554–5).[2] This general picture, that 'women were less likely to succumb than men', is confirmed in a recent paper by David Fitzpatrick in which he analyses famine mortality in various age groups, in public institutions, towns and rural districts. Overall, Fitzpatrick suggests, 'Females accounted for 48.1 per cent of estimated excess mortality, being outnumbered by males in every reported age-band. The discrepancy was negligible for young children, but substantial among the elderly' (Fitzpatrick, 1997: 52). Many of these estimates are obviously very general in nature and are limited in the light they cast on individuals' experience. The more detailed and regional studies now under way promise more insights in the future.

To date, most of the explanations proffered for differences in mortality figures, specifically the possibility of female 'advantage', involve physiological factors such as the superior female capacity to store body-fat. Mary Daly, in her history of the 1840s famine, speculates that the greater vulnerability of men 'may be due to the pressure of relief works, particularly for bodies deprived of food, or may simply reflect the fact that men have higher calorie requirements than women and thus faced greater difficulties in coping with scarcity' (Daly, 1986: 100). Similarly, Margaret Crawford has noted that while the most vulnerable famine victims are young children, old people, and pregnant or lactating women, 'adolescents and adult women tend to survive better than men' (Crawford, 1989: 201). Fitzpatrick, on the other hand, turns to sociological factors to explain women's survival, and, more contentiously, challenges the arguments of Amartya Sen and others regarding women's relative deprivation. In his pioneering 1981 study, *Poverty and Famines*, Sen coined the term 'endowments' to include property, access to employment or production of resources, while 'entitlements' refers to the value of these endowments, as determined by prices and general market conditions. The revolutionary aspect of Sen's analysis, for famine studies, is his argument that famine may occur without a significant decline in food availability; instead what is significant is a person's 'entitlement' or ability to command food. Thus in the case of the Bengal famine of the 1940s, sharp changes in the distribution and price of food caused many to starve, although no significant change occurred in the overall amount of food produced in Bengal as a whole (see Sen, 1981: 195–216). Fitzpatrick's work provides a significant extension of Sen's theories in suggesting that women possessed other less material or non-monetary resources as 'reproducers and household managers' and as the providers of 'the unquantifiable services of affection and consolation' (Fitzpatrick, 1997: 64–9). Since famine clearly enhanced other family members' need for such services, particularly nursing care, the rise in value of this endowment may have safeguarded women's interests within a family situation.

These observations, perhaps inevitably, remain speculative and risk becoming expressions more of late-twentieth-century debates regarding gender than of the historical situation of the past. Conclusions as to the various experiences of famine's female victims are further hindered by the particular difficulties in tracing women's fates in the official record. As Fitzpatrick acknowledges, enumeration of deaths, made retrospectively and by heads of family, may have omitted many women who were widows and may have died alone (Fitzpatrick, 1997: 53, n.13). The 'layers of evasion and anonymity' that veiled local records of the time were, according to Robert Scally, compounded for women:

> In different ways, both the culture of the townland and that of the legal structure above it tended to separate women from any formal economic or political identity, especially while the male head of family lived … All of these circumstances tended to cast the women of the neighbourhood, apparently of all classes, into a formal passivity that may or may not have disguised a more powerful role in fact, in the silent economy, in the cabin councils, or in the pecking order of deference and respect. (Scally, 1995: 126)

Yet occasional glimpses of women's famine experience are possible. In *The End of Hidden Ireland*, Scally explores the fate of the females 'missing' from contemporary records. 'Some of the women missing in 1846, when the hunger was first felt', he suggests, 'may have found refuge as servants in households not yet severely affected or survived from day to day in the relief works' (Scally, 1995: 124). Women's special mobility is also indicated by the higher rate of single emigration by women in the first stages of the famine and the return of some female orphans and widowed dependants to the households of their birth 'as a way to relieve the families expecting eviction of an extra mouth to feed' (Scally, 1995: 125). In addition, women in poorer families 'were more accustomed than men to seasonal begging in the bad years' while 'others may have resorted to the workhouse sooner than the men, for whom it apparently carried a greater stigma' (Scally, 1995: 124). Similarly, Dympna McLoughlin's work on pauper women (1989) provides important insights into the survival strategies adopted by women including spurious claims of desertion in order to gain temporary admittance to the workhouses for themselves and their children.

The analysis offered by Scally, McLoughlin and others poses important challenges to simplistic views of women's passivity and victimization, and encourages students and researchers to examine the means through which many women sought to withstand the ongoing crisis. An examination of gender issues in famine mortality needs, therefore, to move beyond simplistic readings of survival/death rates in order to investigate the complexity of survival *within* the specific crisis. Furthermore, as Joan Ringelheim, historian of the Holocaust, has warned, arguments regarding the 'difference' between men and women's survival and the consequent emphasis on one group's 'better' resistance may be 'pernicious' if it causes us 'to forget the context of these supposed strengths' and 'to ignore the possibility that they may be only apparent' (Ringelheim, 1993: 387). The valorization of one group as victims may be replaced by an emphasis on their 'survivor' abilities which merely inverts, rather than challenges, overly general and reductive categories.

More complex insights into the famine period emerge from research such as Maria Luddy's study of prostitution and rescue work in nineteenth-century Ireland which indicates that arrests in Dublin for prostitution were high during the famine years, though these years also indicate a decline from a peak of 3,855 in 1844 to 3,754 in the following year, 3,407 in 1846 and 3,010 in 1847 (Luddy, 1989: 52–6). Famine also produced quite sharp declines in nuptiality and childbirth, the drop in fertility estimated at some 25 per cent or 300,000 averted births (Boyle and Ó Gráda, 1986: 553–5) as a consequence of malnutrition and consequent amenorrhoea. The desperate acts to which some families were driven, the sacrifice of younger members, specifically through acts of infanticide, are also mentioned by contemporary commentators. In May 1847, R.D. Webb, a member of the Society of Friends, writing from Belmullet, Co. Mayo, records 'instances of women wilfully neglecting their young children, so that they died' (Webb, 1847: 199).[3] The general breakdown in family structures occasioned by famine is memorably described, a year later, by Dr Daniel Donovan, a doctor in Skibbereen, Co. Cork: 'I have seen mothers snatch food from the hands of their starving children; known a son to engage in a fatal struggle with his father for a potato; and have seen parents look on the putrid bodies of their offspring without evincing a symptom of sorrow' (Donovan, 1848: 67).

The Figure of Woman

The studies of Irish famine discussed above suggest that mortality was relatively more severe among males, though with a very small differential. Yet representations of Irish famine, whether in contemporary eye-witness accounts or in literary narratives spanning the last hundred and fifty years, display, in the great majority of cases, images of women's victimization and deprivation. These scenes have a strong affective power yet, as will be shown in more detail later in the essay, may also serve to obscure the full implications of the famine experience. Over and over again, individualized depictions of victims are of women, usually mothers: a dry-breasted woman unable to feed her child, or a child suckling at the breast of its dead mother; a woman snatching food from her child or her 'heroic' opposite, a mother sacrificing her last food for her child. The spectacle of famine thus finds its most graphic form through the female body, objectified and exposed by the controlling gaze of the powerful spectator. In contemporary representations of Irish famine, the observer may be journalist, doctor, philanthropist, priest or minister, artist or engraver; later, in the Irish context, historian, poet, novelist, or dramatist; and more recently, in world famines, reporter, newsmaker or camera operator. Hidden within many of these observations, whether verbal or visual sketches, are the efforts by their subjects to withstand such scrutiny: women's attempts to cover their bodies with scanty and inadequate clothing, to hide their children from an intrusive gaze, or to obtain from the visitor or tourist the means to bury a dead child. Very often the focus of the scene soon changes to the dilemmas experienced by the observer – how to portray a scene which according to many visitors to Ireland in the 1840s was beyond the power of 'tongue' or 'pen' (for example, Bennett, 1847; Nicholson, 1851), how to convince readers of the veracity of scenes which defy belief, and how to respond to the needs and dignity of an individual in the midst of scenes of large-scale hunger and death.

The reasons why particular images recur throughout famine representations is a complex question; once such types are established, their familiar status means they generate an immediate response and this therefore further justifies their use. My interest in the remainder of this chapter is in the function of such female images, how the figures of woman which proliferate in representations of the Irish famine affect their readers. To that end, I suggest three models through which famine's female figures may be investigated: their affective dimension, their representational function and their socio-political dimensions; in each topic, theoretical analysis will be accompanied by more specific examples from writings of the Irish famine. Famine's significance as crisis is also a crucial factor: a crisis in authority, both economically and politically, and, for those who seek to depict this catastrophe, also a crisis in representation. Female figures emerge as a means through which the extent of catastrophe may be portrayed, in graphic and emotive terms, but also, and more troublingly, they are frequently the means through which other aspects of crisis may be avoided.

The affective dimension of maternal images has been suggestively explored by Julia Kristeva, in writings from her 1977 article 'Stabat Mater' to *Powers of Horror: An Essay in Abjection* (1980). In 'Stabat Mater' (1977: 163), her study of the figure of Mary standing at the foot of the cross on which her son is crucified, Kristeva asks:

> What is there, in the portrayal of the Maternal in general and particular in its Christian, virginal one, that reduces social anguish and gratifies a male being; what is there that also satisfies a woman so that a commonality of the sexes is set up, beyond and in spite of their glaring incompatibility and permanent warfare?

Later in the article, some answers are presented:

> Man overcomes the unthinkable of death by postulating maternal love in its place – in the place and stead of death and thought. This love, of which divine love is merely a not always convincing derivation, psychologically, is perhaps a recall, on the near side of early identifications, of the primal shelter that ensured the survival of the newborn. (Kristeva, 1977: 176)

If the figure of maternal love can offer a means of overcoming 'the unthinkable of death', then its role in representations of famine and catastrophe becomes crucial.

A famine novel published twenty years after the 1840s Irish famine confirms Kristeva's argument in uncanny detail. The novel, *Golden Hills*, was written by Elizabeth Hely Walshe, a native of Limerick city; in the course of the narrative, the dead bodies of a woman and child are found in a cabin by the seashore:

> On a table which some neighbour had lent, lay two bodies: one, that of an attenuated woman, wrapped in an old cloak; beside her, inclosed by her arm, was a dead baby. The coroner had arrived, and they were forming a jury in the presence of the poor dead ones, whose emaciated faces and lean limbs told enough of the cause of death. Frank felt cold as he looked on the hollow eyes and claw-like fingers of the wretched mother, and the pinched, oldened features of the hapless child, whose life had yielded to the slow torments of hunger. (Walshe, 1865: 203–4)

As the passage continues, the author directs the attention of her readers to what is to be read from the scene:

'The crathur! her arm was about him to the last,' said a by-stander. 'I'll be bound it's more of him than of herself' she was thinkin' even in the agony – poor weenoch, his little hand is round her finger.' The women were weeping; men could scarcely repress emotion. O love, stronger than even death! O mother's instinct, more imperative than even nature's clinging to life! How does the heart warm to it, and recognise the universal brotherhood! (Walshe, 1865: 203–4)

The maternal instinct transcends 'death', is 'more imperative than even nature's clinging to life', so the narrator's apostrophe declaims. The 'universal brotherhood' thus asserted is one which all observers, most particularly Walshe's readers, are required to recognize.

In many portrayals of female victims, the mother's breast is the focus of the narrative gaze, either as source of continuing nourishment, or, most affectingly, a source which is exhausted. One such example occurs in William Carleton's famine novel *The Black Prophet*, published in 1847 and narrating the experiences of earlier famines in Ireland: towards the end of the novel, the inversion of forces of life and death is eloquently portrayed in the description of the 'dying struggles' of an infant 'fast perishing at the now exhausted fountain of its life' (Carleton, 1847: 345). Applying Kristeva's terms, this recalls for readers both a 'primal shelter' (Kristeva, 1977: 176) and the threat of its breakdown, milk being as Marina Warner suggests 'a crucial metaphor of the gift of life' (1976: 192). These symbolic formulations reveal a deep ambivalence at the heart of the maternal figure: on the one hand, a mother's love may signal some transcendence of the horrific reality at hand; yet, on the other, it is the constant reminder that, in Kristeva's words, 'the mother gives life but not infinity' (Kristeva, 1980: 158).

A contemporary illustration from the 1840s demonstrates the affecting power of the maternal image, and also the symbolic translations so often made by writers and artists. In February 1847, James Mahony, a Cork artist employed by the *Illustrated London News*, visited famine-stricken areas in West Cork and supplied a series of engravings, now some of the most famous visual sketches of the famine, to the London paper. On 13 February 1847, a number of engravings appeared with accompanying textual commentary by Mahony during which he describes how his carriage was surrounded by a crowd of 'famished poor'. Amongst them was

a woman carrying in her arms the corpse of a fine child, and making the most distressing appeal to the passengers for aid to enable her to purchase a coffin and bury her dear little baby. This horrible spectacle induced me to make some inquiry about her, when I learned from the people of the hotel that each day brings dozens of such applicants into the town. (Mahony, 1847)

Mahony's comments are quite detailed and realistic; what is most striking is the transition from this verbal report to his engraving of the woman and child, entitled 'Woman Begging at Clonakilty'. The iconic image is of Madonna and child, the drooping lip and frozen eye of the Irish Madonna indicate famine's traces while the woman, holding to her breast the corpse of her dead child, stretches out one hand in supplication to her observers.

The difficulties of representing what is seen and its overwhelming effects are emphasized by almost every commentator of the time: Society of Friends correspondents, government officials, visitors to Ireland. A now famous testimony, written on 24 December 1846, comes from Captain Wynne, a government employee based in West Clare. Writing to his superior in the Board of Works, in a letter reproduced in the Correspondence relating to measures adopted for the relief of distress in Ireland, Wynne reported:

> I ventured through that parish [Clare Abbey] this day, to ascertain the condition of the inhabitants, and although a man not easily moved, I confess I found myself unmanned by the extent and intensity of suffering I witnessed, more especially amongst the women and little children, crowds of whom were to be seen scattered over the turnip fields, like a flock of famishing crows, devouring the raw turnips, mothers half naked, shivering in the snow and sleet, uttering exclamations of despair, whilst their children were screaming with hunger; I am a match for any thing else I may meet with here, but this I cannot stand. (Correspondence, 1846: 434–5)

Wynne's words bear eloquent witness to the unsettling and threatening effects of what he has seen. The scenes of victimization which he describes, while representing the limits of understanding and of representation, also constitute, in his case and in so many other famine narratives, an attempt towards depicting famine. Similarly, the prefacing comments by observers that the events are 'past the power of words' should not distract attention from the representations which they ultimately produce and the strategies employed in this endeavour. Within these famine narratives, the use of female images thus serves as one of the most frequent means of transcending, or avoiding, the feared crisis in representation.

The particular association of the female with the unspeakable is the subject of much comment in psychoanalytical feminist theory. Jacqueline Rose, for example, identifies the gendered nature of what she calls the 'pas tout' or 'not all' which characterizes any system of representation, the 'point of impossibility' which it seeks to refuse: 'And in so far as the system closes over that moment of difference or impossibility, what gets set up in its place is essentially an image of the woman' (Rose, 1986: 219). Similarly, African-American novelist and critic Toni Morrison (1987) has highlighted the ways in which women's experience of slavery has been seen as 'unspeakable' and has remained 'unspoken', covered by a veil of silence and evasion. The female figure becomes the figure of silence and nonspeech, associated, as Rose shows, with 'impossibility'. It is, as Kristeva writes, the 'strange fold that changes culture into nature and speaking into biology' (1977: 182). Yet, through the woman's body, others' words take flesh.

The symbolic uses of the female figure, the 'tradition of ascribing meaning more readily to the female form than the male', have been well addressed by Marina Warner, in her study of the figure of Mary, *Alone of All Her Sex* (1976) and *Monuments and Maidens* (1985), her reading of female allegories. The female form thus possesses an important doubleness: both vehicle of 'attributed meaning' (Warner 1985: 225) and figure of the unspeakable, bearing 'the word' yet also spelling its failure. This ambivalence underlies the use of the female figure in famine representations, a tradition memorably acknowledged by the novelist John Banville in his parodic Big House novel, *Birchwood*. Describing the famine face which Sybil, a central character, has developed, Banville echoes the details of James Mahony's *Illustrated London News* sketch: 'Something had happened to her face, a minute but devastating change. Her left eye seemed to droop a fraction lower than the right, and this imbalance gave to what had been her cool measured gaze, a querulous, faintly crazed cast' (1973: 142). Musing on this scene, Gabriel, the narrator, yields the following, quite extraordinary, meditation:

> I hardly dare to voice the notion which, if it did not come to me then comes to me now, the insane notion that perhaps it was on her, on Sybil, our bright bitch, that the sorrow of the country, of those baffled people in the rotting fields, of the stricken eyes staring out of hovels, was visited against her will and even without her knowledge so that tears might be shed, and the inexpressible expressed. Does that seem a ridiculous suggestion? But I do not suggest, I only wonder. (Banville, 1973: 143)

Banville's formulation is a very seductive one, recognizing both the affective and representational dimensions to the female figure outlined here. Similarly, Kristeva's 'strange fold' captures a central aspect of the female figure: its access to a world of non-speech, from culture to nature. But this latter shift is, in the specific context of famine representations, a very troubling one and relates to the third and last centre of investigation, the social and political dimensions of famine's female figures.

Social and Political Dimensions

Throughout representations of disaster, whether journalistic, visual or literary, the breakdown in the maternal relationship, such as a mother's inability to feed her child, or her rejection of her child, is used to spell the ultimate catastrophe, a collapse in the natural order. Associations of the female with nature and domesticity are more than familiar, but their use within famine representations runs the risk of suggesting that famine too is a breakdown in nature rather than a political and social crisis. The real crisis of authority which constitutes famine, its economic manifestations and political implications, can, consequently, be fatally obscured. Adorno's warning, cited by Warner in her opposition to 'this conflation of nature and woman' (1985: 34) is particularly relevant here: 'Whatever is in the context of bourgeois delusion called nature, is merely the scar of social mutilation.' This danger recurs throughout contemporary media: images of starving mothers and children spell famine's worst horrors, but the affective response thus generated may also involve a passivity and fatalism which works against real understanding. As Maud Ellmann notes, the photographs of famine victims used throughout daily newspapers carry a deeply ambivalent message: 'they flatter our delusions of cultural superiority at the same time that they appeal to our forgotten past, to the famished and abandoned infant in ourselves' (1993: 54). The very frequency of these images has further implications, causing a familiarity and fatigue with such images, and characterizing as somehow inevitable the hunger and starvation which they portray.

The resulting separation of effect from causation is a particular danger in female images of catastrophe, from historiography of the Irish famine to contemporary depictions of disaster. One example from 1840s representations provides a salutary conclusion to this essay. On 18 February 1847, the Cork *Southern Reporter* published a letter from Reverend Richard Francis Webb, rector of Caheragh, which included the following graphic description from one of Webb's parishioners, commissioned by Webb to inspect conditions in a nearby townland.

> The following is a statement of what I *saw* yesterday evening on the lands of Toureen. In a cabbage garden I saw (as I was informed) the bodies of Kate Barry and her two children very lightly covered with earth, the hands and legs of her large body entirely exposed, the flesh completely eaten off by the dogs, the skin and hair of the head lying within a couple of yards to the skull, which, when I first threw my eyes on it, I thought to be part of a horse's tail. (Reproduced from *Correspondence*, 1847: 164–5)

This description is one of the most horrific of the time and has understandably been quite frequently cited by historians (see Ó Gráda, 1989: 42–3). Webb's letter ends with the rector's own ringing condemnation: 'I need make no comment on this, but ask, *are we living in a portion of the United Kingdom?*'

The parliamentary papers of the time, specifically the official correspondence relating to the relief of distress (1847: 164–5), however, yield a further context to the deaths of Kate Barry and her children, one not explored by historians who reproduce the passage above. They show that a copy of Webb's article, as published by the *Southern Reporter*, was sent by Assistant Commissary-General Bishop, a government official based in

Gender and Catastrophe

Skibbereen, to Charles Treveylan, the Treasury Under-Secretary, in London. Bishop's sending of the article, the day after it appeared, is an interesting indication of the importance of media representations to the makers of public policy. Two enclosures accompanied the article, one Bishop's accompanying note and the other a copy of a letter received by Bishop a few days earlier from 'the principal miller in that part of the country', offering for purchase nearly two hundred tons of Indian and other meal – food which, as Bishop reminded Treveylan, was 'within two miles of the parish of Caheragh' (1847: 164–5). Bishop's anger and frustration in being unable to procure this food is tangible. Writing to Treveylan, he bitterly notes that the 'natural inference' from the *Southern Reporter* article was that 'food could not be obtained', a conclusion shown to be patently untrue by the enclosed letter. Knowledge as to the supplies available nearby, and his own powerlessness regarding the procurement of such food, led Bishop to echo to his superior, with devastating irony, Webb's closing words: 'May we not ask, with the rector, "Are we not living in a portion of the United Kingdom?"' (1847: 164).

This correspondence provides some provocative insights into the provision of relief, the operation of relief systems, and the role of media representations, topics of obvious continuing relevance. Furthermore, it generates central questions regarding the distribution of food in Ireland in February 1847, the responsibility for that distribution and what determined, in Amartya Sen's term, people's entitlement to food. It also restores, I would argue, the proper context for the story of Kate Barry's death. The figure of woman may, as a result, stand not only as a horrific image of famine's effects, but as a key indicator of the inequalities which cause individual hunger and large-scale starvation.

Notes

1. For a fuller exploration of the questions raised by this article, see Kelleher, 1997.

2. The three different methods used by Boyle and Ó Gráda to estimate famine mortality yield differentials between male and female deaths of 29,000, 16,000 and 37,000 respectively, based on excess mortality of one million (1986: 554–5). The higher mortality among males from ages 10 to 45 is also, they suggest, a reversal of pre-famine patterns (1986: 554).

3. Webb's comment on this occurrence is of interest: 'Poor things! I can wonder at nothing I hear, after what I have seen of their fearful wretchedness and destitution. None of us can imagine what change would be wrought in ourselves if we had the same shocking experience' (1847: 199). The census of Ireland for 1851, however, recorded a 'considerable decrease' in rates of infanticide, 'so far at least as these records show' during the decade 1841–1851: from 620 in 1841 to 340 in 1851 (part v: 407). The figures for the desertion or exposure of infants during the same period, in contrast, had risen considerably: from 314 in 1841 to 508 in 1851 – 1842, 1843, 1844 and 1847 being the years in which such deaths were 'particu-

larly numerous'. Fitzpatrick shows that crime records for 1844 to 1847 also show a fall in the number of reported infanticides from 1844 to 1846, but a significant increase in 1847 (1995: 29, n.54).

References

Arnold, David. 1988. *Famine: Social Crisis and Historical Change.* London: Blackwell.
Banville, John. 1973. *Birchwood.* (New edition 1987). London: Paladin.
Bennett, William. 1847. *Narrative of a journey of six weeks in Ireland ...* London and Dublin: privately published.
Boyle, Phelim and Ó Gráda, Cormac. 1986. 'Fertility trends, excess mortality, and the Great Irish Famine.' *Demography,* vol. 23, no. 4, November.
Carleton, William. 1847. *The Black Prophet.* Facsimile of 1899 edition, 1972. Shannon: Irish University Press.
Census of Ireland for the Year 1851, V, part 1, House of Commons Papers. 1856 [2087–I] xxix.
Central Relief Committee, *Transactions of the Central Relief Committee of the Society of Friends during the Famine in Ireland, in 1846 and 1847.* Dublin, 1852.
Correspondence from July 1846 to January 1847, relative to the Measures adopted for the Relief of Distress in Ireland (London, 1847), reprinted in *Irish Parliamentary Papers: Famine Series,* vols 6 and 7 (8 vols; 1970). Shannon: Irish University Press.
Crawford, E. Margaret (ed.). 1989. *Famine: the Irish Experience 900–1900: Subsistence Crises and Famine in Ireland.* Edinburgh: John Donald.
Daly, Mary. 1986. *The Great Famine in Ireland,* Dublin: Dublin Historical Association.
Donovan, Daniel. 1848. 'Observations on the peculiar diseases to which the famine of the last year gave origin ...' *Dublin Medical Press,* vol. XXIX.
Drèze, Jean and Sen, Amartya. 1989 *Hunger and Public Action,* WIDER Studies in Development Economics. Oxford: Clarendon.
Ellmann, Maud. 1993. *The Hunger-Artists: Starving, Writing and Imprisonment.* London: Virago.
Fitzpatrick, David. 1997. 'Women and the Great Famine.' In Margaret Kelleher and James H. Murphy (eds), *Separate Spheres? Gender and Nineteenth-Century Ireland.* Dublin: Irish Academic Press.
Greenough, Paul. 1982. *Prosperity and Misery in Modern Bengal.* New York and Oxford: Oxford University Press.
Kelleher, Margaret. 1997. *The Feminization of Famine.* Cork: Cork University Press.
Kristeva, Julia. 1977. 'Stabat Mater.' In Toril Moi (ed.), 1986, *The Kristeva Reader.* Oxford: Blackwell.
Kristeva, Julia. 1980. *Powers of Horror: An Essay on Abjection.* Translated L.S. Roudiez (1982). New York: Columbia.
Luddy, Maria. 1989. 'Prostitution and rescue work in nineteenth-century Ireland.' In Maria Luddy and Cliona Murphy (eds), *Women Surviving: Studies in Irish Women's History in the Nineteenth and Twentieth Centuries.* Dublin: Poolbeg.
McLoughlin, Dympna. 1989. 'Workhouses and Irish female paupers, 1840–1870.' In Maria Luddy and Cliona Murphy (eds), *Women Surviving: Studies in Irish Women's History in the Nineteenth and Twentieth Centuries.* Dublin: Poolbeg.
Mahony, James. 1847. Engravings. *Illustrated London News.* 13 February 1847.
Morrison, Toni. 1987. 'Site of memory.' In William Zinsser (ed.), *Inventing the Truth:*

The Art and Craft of Memoir. Boston: Houghton Mifflin.

Nicholson, Asenath. 1851. *Lights and Shades of Ireland*, 3 vols. London: Gilpin.

Ó Gráda, Cormac. 1989. *The Great Irish Famine, Studies in Economic and Social History*. London: Macmillan.

Ó Gráda, Cormac. 1993. *Ireland Before and After the Famine: Explorations in Economic History, 1800–1925*. Manchester: Manchester University Press.

Osborne, Sidney Godolphin. 1850. *Gleanings in the West of Ireland*. London: Boone.

Ringelheim, Joan M. 1993. 'Women and the Holocaust: a reconsideration of research.' In Carol Rittner and John K. Roth (eds), *Different Voices: Women and the Holocaust*. New York: Paragon House.

Rivers, J.P.W. 1988. 'The nutritional biology of famine.' In G. Harrison (ed.), *Famine*. Oxford: Oxford University Press.

Rose, Jacqueline. 1986. *Sexuality and the Field of Vision*. London and New York: Verso.

Scally, Robert. 1995. *The End of Hidden Ireland*. New York and Oxford: Oxford University Press.

Sen, Amartya. 1981. *Poverty and Famines: An Essay on Entitlement and Deprivation*. Oxford: Oxford University Press.

Southern Reporter, 18 February 1847.

The Times, 9 July 1847.

Walshe, Elizabeth Hely. 1865. *Golden Hills: A Tale of the Irish Famine*. London: Religious Tract Society.

Warner, Marina. 1976. *Alone of All Her Sex: the Myth and Cult of the Virgin Mary*. London: Weidenfeld and Nicolson.

Warner, Marina. 1985. *Monuments and Maidens: the Allegory of the Female Form*. London: Picador.

Webb, R.D. 1847. Letter to the Central Relief Committee, in Central Relief Committee, *Transactions of the Central Relief Committee of the Society of Friends*, Appendix III, p. 199.

19

'Disasters' and Bangladeshi Women
Santi Rozario

Bangladesh has been hit by disaster after disaster since its formation in 1971. The devastating cyclone of 1970 and the 1971 War of Independence, both of which cost countless lives and destroyed vast amounts of property, were just the beginning of a series of calamities and catastrophes which Bangladeshis were to face over the following 25 years. The general consequences of these for the Bangladeshi population, the poor in particular, are well known, if only through the activities of donor agencies responding to each successive crisis. Not much is known, however, about the specific ways these 'disasters' have affected women, poor women in particular. This chapter examines the impact of these ongoing crises, including recent social and political upheavals, on Bangladeshi women.

In particular, this chapter argues that disasters have differential effects on women and men because of the way women's lives are affected by Bengali cultural and gender ideologies. Of most significance here is the culturally prescribed moral and economic dependency of women throughout their lives on their parents, brothers, husbands or sons (Khan, 1992; Lindenbaum, 1974; White, 1992). Other aspects of Bangladeshi culture that affect women are the preference for sons, the ideological principles of purity, *parda*, shame and pollution, and the consequent restrictions on mobility and outside paid work for women.

A central aspect of the deterioration of women's status in rural Bangladesh has been the emergence of substantial numbers of mature unmarried women, either women who have been married and are now divorced or widowed, or women who have never been married. Since mature women, by Bengali cultural definition, should be married, these women are in an anomalous and problematic situation. The first section of this chapter looks at the increased number of women in rural society who fail to find husbands. Their plight is closely linked to the changes in recent decades

to the economic basis of Bangladeshi marriage, which have made it increasingly difficult for parents in poor families to afford to arrange
marriages for their daughters. These developments have been associated
with a growth in low-paid urban female employment, which is also discussed. The second section looks at rural impoverishment, which has led
to a growth in the numbers of women who are divorced or abandoned
by their husbands, and examines the fate of these women.

The remaining two sections of this chapter look at two more specific
situations: the impact of floods on women, and the treatment of the
birangana, women raped by Pakistani soldiers during the war of liberation.
Apart from affecting substantial numbers of women in their own right,
these situations illustrate with particular clarity the way in which the
impact of disastrous situations on women has been affected for the worse
by Bangladeshi cultural norms.

It would be possible to look at a variety of other issues and find
similar problems, almost all traceable in one way or another to the
generally disastrous overall situation of the country, coupled with the
continuing strength of traditional Bangladeshi expectations about women's
proper place and behaviour, and of the consequent restrictions on women's
freedom of action. These issues include, for example, that of family
planning in Bangladesh, where pressure from Western governments and
aid agencies to restrict Bangladeshi population growth has led to the
widespread use of hazardous and inappropriate contraceptive techniques
(Akhter, 1992; Kabeer, 1994a; Hartmann, 1987; Hartmann and Standing,
1989; Reysoo and Huq, 1995; Rozario, 1996). They also include the growth
of more conservative forms of Islam, typically associated with demands
for women to return to traditional roles in a society where these roles are
increasingly unavailable to them. It is hoped that the material presented
here will give a general picture of how poorer rural women have fared
within Bangladeshi society over the last 25 years.

Dowry, Unmarried Women and Factory Work

The gradual transformation of the economic basis of marriage in Bangladeshi society has been a critical factor in changing women's status in
society, since it has meant that marriage has become increasingly difficult
for many young women from poor families. Single women are anomalous
in Bengali society, and in the past marriage was almost universal in rural
Bangladesh. (See Rozario, 1986, 1992; Aziz, 1979; Fruzzetti, 1982;
Blanchet, 1984; Kotalová, 1993 about the ideological basis of marriage in
Bengali society.) A mature woman must be married and her sexuality
must be under the control of her husband. This, along with the related
notions of purity and honour, underlies the anxiety of Bangladeshi families
about sexually fertile single women (including the divorced, widowed and

abandoned women considered in the following section, as well as those who have never been married). Such women should not really be there in the first place, and if they are, they should be kept at home under proper male control. Despite such concerns, the number of mature single women who never achieve marriage continues to increase.

This process has been associated with a transition in the payments made at marriage, from relatively small amounts paid mainly by the groom's family to the bride's (*pon*), to typically much larger payments from the bride's family to the groom's (*dabi*, usually referred to in English as 'dowry'; see Lindenbaum, 1981, Hartmann and Boyce, 1983; Ahmed and Naher, 1987; Rozario, 1992). Dowry in the past was practised in Bangladesh only amongst the Hindu population, and the amounts involved were in most cases quite small. The recent preoccupation with dowry among all Bangladeshis, whether Muslim, Hindu or Christian, is integrally linked to the new phenomenon of the surplus of unmarried women.

In fact, as the overall Bangladeshi data shows, the number of unmarried mature women is lower rather than higher than that of unmarried men. The 'surplus' is a social construction (Rozario, 1992), and the shift from *pon* to *dabi* is directly linked to recent socio-economic changes. With increased urbanization and the increased availability of education, men began to postpone marriage until a much later age, preferring to spend time acquiring education, wealth and status. Men in their late twenties and thirties now prefer to marry women between the ages of 15 and 19. For every man who marries a much younger woman, there is a corresponding unmarried woman of his own age, and it is this which creates the 'surplus' of unmarried women.

While a man can remain unmarried until he is 30 or even 40, a woman not married by the time she is 20 is labelled as unmarriageable. Therefore families are under great pressure to marry off their daughters as soon as possible, even at considerable expense, and parents of desirable grooms were able to demand increasingly substantial payments for their sons. The new inflated *dabi* payments were phrased, as elsewhere in South Asia, as a return on the groom's parents' investment in their son's education (Tambiah et al., 1973; Hartmann and Boyce, 1983).

While dowry was initiated amongst the middle and upper classes, the lower middle classes also began to emulate these practices. Dowry has now become a common phenomenon in all classes in rural Bangladesh, even though the amount of goods and cash transferred amongst the poorer groups is much lower than in the higher classes. This new demand system places the poor parents of mature daughters in almost impossible situations.

The burden of dowry means many parents in poor families fail to find husbands for their daughters. Many of these unmarried women head for the garment factories in the cities and similar sources of urban employment.

Indeed most rural single women go for urban jobs in order to avoid being a burden on their families. Those women I knew who came to the city of Dhaka to work in the garment factories all did so after their parents had given up hope of finding a suitable husband for them, and because they did not want to be economically dependent on their families.

While many of the women in the garment factories come from very poor backgrounds, there is an increasing number for whom this is not true. My brief field research in this area, like Naila Kabeer's work (1994b), indicated that an increasing number of the garment workers, especially those holding supervisory positions, come from lower-middle-class to middle-class backgrounds. Nursing is another profession which in the past attracted only a limited number of women, primarily those from Christian backgrounds. Because nurses' pay is considered very good compared to other available female jobs, nursing is now perceived as a reasonable career option for middle-class women.

Since both rural and urban women who work can no longer be regularly escorted to their workplace, they are forced to negotiate the public space, traditionally essentially a 'male' space, on their own. While these working women are clearly seen to be breaking the traditional norm of *parda* or female seclusion, it would be a mistake to conclude that the ideologies of *parda* and purity are fading into insignificance. What has happened is that women have modified and renegotiated these values to fit their present needs and situation.

In this new situation, women are eager to be seen as respectable and 'good' (*bhalo*) in the eye of *samaj* (community). Thus the ideologies of *parda* and purity have become all the more important as a means of regulating the women's own behaviour. While these women can no longer afford to remain within the four walls of the house, or may not be able to wear a veil, they say that they retain their modesty in other ways: by lowering their gaze, covering themselves well with the end of their saris or scarves, avoiding eye contact with men in the streets and generally not mixing with unrelated men except when it absolutely cannot be avoided. Thus while these women have become spatially much more mobile, the emphasis is more on the way they handle their body: when they are at home, at work, and on the streets. They internalize the values of purity and *parda* and at the same time police each other's behaviour (Siddiqi, 1991).

In the case of girls coming from poor backgrounds, their earnings often become an important source of income for their families back in the village. They typically may support their younger siblings' education or contribute to the family's day-to-day living expenses. There are also stories of some women from poor backgrounds saving their income in order to buy a piece of land for their families. They keep very little of this income for their personal use. However, as Kabeer (1994b) and

Siddiqi (1991) report, and as my interviewees confirmed, many girls also save some of their income to be used as dowry for their marriage. Often, when the parents have given up trying to arrange a marriage for their daughters, the girls find partners themselves in the urban centres.[1] Their source of income in the garment factories, for instance, is attractive to poor and semi-employed men like rickshaw-pullers, or day labourers.

One of my informants commented that these poor Muslim girls are 'getting married all the time, but they are also getting divorced all the time'. These girls are themselves from poor backgrounds and have little or no education; many of them are unable even to sign their names. They marry labourers, rickshaw-pullers and others from similarly poor backgrounds. It would seem that these men marry factory girls because of the girls' income, and in this sense their income can be seen as a form of dowry in these girls' marriages. As my informant added, however, it is very common in such marriages for a girl to discover that her husband has another wife or two (with children) somewhere else, perhaps back in his village of origin. In such cases, girls apparently divorce their husbands 'immediately'. My informant added, *bhalo ghar ei meyeder ashe na* ('good' men do not marry these girls).

Most of these rural single women who migrate to cities live frugally, with distant relatives, or more often in slum areas sharing small rooms with other girls in similar situations. The small salary they receive means that they cannot afford to rent anything better, and in any case landlords are unwilling to let out rooms to single women as they see them as 'more trouble than they are worth'. Without male guardians, single women are perceived as a liability, since they may 'misbehave' by bringing male guests home and even if they do not, their mere presence will attract attention from 'bad' (*kharap*) boys in the neighbourhood.

Thus although the factory girls are exercising some agency in their choice of marriage and divorce, their status continues to be defined by the wider society through the ideologies of purity and marriage and they still occupy a marginal position within it. We may be witnessing the preliminary signs of 'protest' against middle-class gender values with the actions of these women. But until and unless a substantial number of middle-class women also begin to challenge these values, the elite will succeed in maintaining its position at the top of the hierarchy through use of notions of purity, honour and related gender values which are not only disadvantageous, but have disastrous implications for poor women.

Thus the new circumstances have led to the growth of a new low-paid female employment sector, primarily within the cities, which I shall discuss in more detail below. Well-off sections of rural society can afford to keep their women from joining the new lowly paid female employment sector, and continue to use the ideologies of purity and seclusion as a way of legitimizing their honourable position (cf. Rozario, 1992).

The Growth of Rural Poverty: Divorced and Abandoned Women

A second major contributor to the increase in the number of mature women without husbands is the ongoing pauperization of the rural economy. This process began with the British colonial impact, with its systematic destruction of local industries (in particular, textiles) in order to provide markets for British exports. This was followed by the exploitation of the Bangladeshi economy by the former West Pakistan from 1947 to 1971. These factors, along with the internal relations of exploitation between rich and poor, and the series of natural and man-made disasters (for example, war, famine, cyclones, floods), and the lack of natural resources have had enormous implications for the rural population in general.

They have been particularly serious for rural women. We have already seen that poor families, even if able to survive economically, are increasingly unable even to arrange marriages for their daughters. The consequences for families who suffer extreme poverty are more devastating again, since women and children from these families may find themselves divorced or abandoned by desperate husbands, and if they have no relatives able to support them, they are simply left to fend for themselves.

While poverty-stricken rural men have had to struggle for their own and their families' survival, they were at least able to do so free from cultural restrictions as to what activities they undertook. Rural women were always perceived, thanks to Bengali cultural values, as dependent, with their work largely confined within the household. This meant both that they typically had fewer marketable skills, and that many possible ways of earning money were closed to them. Many women, such as those who were widowed or divorced, or those who had been abandoned by men who had gone to urban centres in search of employment, found themselves in a terrible predicament, especially if they also had children to care for. The traditional support system for such people within rural society had gradually fallen apart, and they found themselves with nowhere to turn.

While divorce is allowed in Islam, men are allowed to divorce women more easily than women. Moreover, there is no stigma attached to a divorced man, who usually finds a second wife without much delay. Divorced or abandoned Muslim women, on the other hand, cannot find second husbands easily and are subject to social ostracism. Because the sexuality of a mature woman is considered problematic, she is considered a threat to her family's honour. There is always a potential that she may misbehave sexually and bring dishonour to her family and the surrounding community. Thus a divorced woman's family will make every effort to marry her off to a second husband, but after a certain age women are considered 'old' and out of the marriage market. In Bengali there is a saying that 'a woman is "old" after she reaches age 20' (*kuritey buri*). Yet, age is not a bar for men in the same way.

Widowed and divorced women with children cannot leave their children behind in the village to join the single women in garment factories. A limited amount of employment, mostly low-income and low-status, is provided by NGOs in some regions. But even where such employment is available, the most disadvantaged women may lack the education or connections needed to get such work. Instead, they may resort to very low status work like that of *dai* (traditional birth attendant, see Blanchet, 1984; Rozario, 1995a, 1995b). *Dais* do not command a formal salary but rely on the goodwill of the birthing families for some gifts in the form of clothes, food or cash. This job is not acceptable to well-off or educated people because of lack of salary, and more importantly, because of the polluted nature of birth. *Dais* supplement their income from other sources like working in rich households, doing jutecraft work or joining cooperatives.

Despite this, the status of women in Bangladesh continued, and still continues, to be defined in terms of marriage and motherhood. A single woman, unmarried or divorced, is anomalous in Bangladeshi society and is unable to lead an independent life. As Mahmuda Islam (1979: 226) correctly points out, in Bangladeshi society, 'woman is assigned the role of wife and mother; to adjust with this ideal role she is given a position of inferiority, dependence, subjugation' – in relation, that is, to man. She is neither allowed nor expected to be independent, although, as we have seen, increasing numbers of women have had little choice but to become so.

Women and Floods

Everyone in the West is familiar with the regular news reports of floods, cyclones and other 'natural' disasters in Bangladesh, and the appeals by charities for aid for their victims. There have also been some efforts in recent years, both on the part of the Bangladesh government and of international aid organizations, to reduce the danger of floods through afforestation schemes and the building of embankments (Shaw, 1992: 200). However, there has been little attention paid by NGOs or governments to the way in which these calamities particularly affect the poorer sectors of the rural population, or to the especially serious difficulties faced by poor rural women who are flood victims. As Rosalind Shaw has recently argued, these events are 'as much products of human agency and power as of geophysical events'. Rather than speaking of natural disasters, we should see them as social and political disasters (1992: 202). Their effects are socially and politically mediated, and differentially distributed, and poor rural women and their children are those most at risk.

Women who are forced to take refuge in a camp in the aftermath of a disaster are faced with a very difficult situation. In particular, maintaining their *parda* is likely to be impossible. Shaw argues 'for most Bangladeshi women, the experience of the environment is centred upon *purdah* [*parda*], as well as concepts of pollution which have become incorporated into Bengali Islam' (Shaw, 1992: 207). She goes on to argue that 'women's experience of floods ... is shaped by the necessity to maintain purdah [*parda*] and pollution-removal practices' (210). Sharif Kafi of the Bangladesh Development Partnership Centre's Disaster Resource Unit has commented that 'for women and children, disasters cause unbearable social crises and suffering beyond one's imagination' (1992: 9).

Perhaps the worst experience a poor married woman can have in this situation is of giving birth. Birth is considered polluted and certain rituals must be maintained to remove birth pollution (Blanchet, 1984; Jeffery et al., 1988; Rozario, forthcoming) Living in a camp situation or in a shelter on top of one's house roof means that women have to forgo these rituals, endangering the health of the baby and the mother in the process.

The women and children most at risk after natural disasters such as floods and cyclones are those who do not have men around to act as their protectors. Kafi points to the substantial numbers of families headed by women encountered by aid workers in these situations. Some of these women would have been divorced, widowed or abandoned before the disaster took place, while others would have lost their husbands during the disaster. Not surprisingly, most of these families headed by women are from the lowest socio-economic group. In a UNDP/Intertecht report cited by Kafi, the Canadian researcher G.P. Sevenhuysen noted that 'Families headed by women ... have fewer assets than male-headed families. The ability of women to control land, tools or trade is limited by the social expectation of the community ... Both at the time of disaster, as well as during its aftermath, women have less physical protection and fewer resources for recovery than men' (cited in Kafi, 1992: 10–11).

Kafi's report includes a considerable amount of first-hand case material from women without husbands affected by the 1988 flood, 1989 tornado and 1991 cyclone, as well as from 1992 refugees from Myanmar. It is worth quoting some of this material to illustrate the almost impossible situations which these women are confronted with in times of disaster. These case studies also make it evident that many of the problems faced by these women are socio-economic and cultural in origin, rather than the direct result of the natural disaster. Thus Shom Bala of Kutubdia, a widow with four children affected by the 1991 cyclone, had this to say:

> Being refused shelter, we were really in a fix. There were high risks involved in roaming around from place to place searching for shelter. Because there were some anti-social elements haunting around and looking for young girls and women ... There are instances that those bas[tards] went out in gangs just

before the surge and got at frightened and half conscious young women and girls. Kidnapped them and took them to deserted houses or on bushy embankments and finally abused and violated them. (Kafi, 1992: 33–4)[2]

Shamima Akhter of Saturia, whose husband and son were killed in the 1989 tornado, leaving her with two daughters, came from a relatively prosperous background. Her husband was chairman of a district council (union parishad) and had substantial property. However, all the family's valuables and almost all their land was appropriated by her late husband's brothers while she was recovering in hospital. Since there was no surviving son, *shariah* law apparently left her with no claim to her late husband's agricultural land (Kafi, 1992: 63). She had to go heavily into debt to meet the family's day-to-day needs, and commented,

> It became really difficult a struggle for me to keep my 'person' safe. There emerged a number of people always running after me in the guise of well-wishers, but, practically all of them were debouch criminals. Some of them had sent proposals to me to be a second wife, some wanted me as a 'best friend'; or a kept [woman]. (Kafi, 1992: 64)

This lack of support from the husband's family in the event of widowhood is not uncommon. Indeed, most widowed women are likely to be subjected to the same kind of exploitation as Shamima, rather than receiving any real help from their in-laws.

Khodeja Begum, another woman from Kutubdia who was widowed in the 1991 cyclone, came from a much poorer background. Her husband was a landless labourer and neither his surviving brothers nor her own brother, all landless labourers themselves, were able to provide any support for her. She has a seven-year-old son and two daughters, the youngest only eight months. Her only source of income is through her son and elder daughter begging from door to door for salt, which they sell for cash; there would presumably be too much risk for her as a young woman to go begging herself. She comments, 'It is unbearably heart-rendering for me to see my children begging around. I am willing from my heart to work for earning but there is no employment for me as this is a salt-pan area. Women do not get work here' (Kafi, 1992: 29).

Shabmeraj, a 30-year-old woman from Myanmar who fled to Bangladesh with her five surviving children after her husband was killed in an army crackdown, was interviewed in a refugee camp:

> As we do not have a man among the family members, it took time to get our names on the refugee list. Those who have men with their family, they were virtually fortunate to have their names on the official refugee list at the first chance … As a woman, I have problems of movement in the forest as well as other areas outside the camp. For this reason, we could not build a hut (*jhupri*) for us. Each and every family, who have men with them, have built huts for living purpose, while we are living with another family. (Kafi, 1992: 91–2)

While clearly the trauma of the above women was linked to the 'natural' disasters they had undergone (or, in Shabmeraj's case, to her refugee status), the problems they faced in their struggle to survive were a direct consequence of the values assigned to men and women in Bangladeshi society, and other gender values that have adverse effects on women. As I pointed out in earlier sections, women are expected to be dependent either as daughters, sisters or wives; outside of this the society fails to recognize them. Women are subjected to the norms of *parda* and purity, and not expected to work, own land or run business. Under the circumstances arising after floods, cyclones or tornadoes, the predicament of women without husbands or other male guardians is clear.

The Birangana Issue

The last section of this chapter deals with the treatment of the *biranganas*, women raped by Pakistani soldiers during the 1971 war of liberation. This is one of the most telling examples of the social attitude towards women. The war followed on the non-cooperation movement, led by *Bangabandhu* Sheikh Mujibur Rahman, which had created an unprecedented sense of unity among the Bengali population of what was then East Pakistan, united on the common sentiment of Bengali ethnicity, culture and language. Religious, class or gender divisions within the population seemed insignificant in the face of the crisis they faced in relation to West Pakistan. Sheikh Mujibur Rahman's call for non-cooperation with Pakistanis in an effort to gain sovereignty for Bangladesh was responded to by virtually all Bengalis. Except for the few so-called *rajakars* who supported Pakistani rule and worked as spies for the West Pakistani armies, *joy Bangla* (victory for Bengal) was in everyone's mouth.

The eleven-month-long war took its toll on many Bengalis, but nothing can be compared to the fate of the *biranganas*. These were the 200,000 to 400,000 Bengali women said to have been raped by the Pakistani armies. Many of these raped women later revealed that it was not only the Pakistani armies whom they were raped and tortured by, but also their Bengali 'brothers' who were supposed to be their protectors (Ibrahim, 1994). Sheikh Mujibur Rahman gave these raped women the honorary title of *biranganas* (war heroines), with the intention of giving them a status in society's eyes equivalent to that of the *muktijudhas* (freedom fighters). Rehabilitation centres were opened up for them. However, with few exceptions, neither the Bangladeshi people as a whole, nor their own brothers, fathers or neighbours were prepared to accept them back as members of society. They had lost their virginity and purity and were merely a source of shame.

My account here relies extensively on recent publications on the *biranganas* by Dr Nilima Ibrahim, who worked with many of these women over many years (Ibrahim, 1994, 1995). Their families failed to accept them, husbands refused to take their wives home, and brothers and fathers felt ashamed of taking their sisters or daughters back for fear of losing their face in the community. Husbands and fathers came with presents of saris but said they could not take their wives or daughters back home because, as one of the *birangana* herself said, 'they have *samaj* [community], there are *pachjan* [people] in the *samaj*. One cannot take this fallen and stigmatized woman amongst them' (Ibrahim, 1994: 41). Some men, including those who were freedom fighters, said they would send money every month but still refused to take their wives home (Ibrahim, 1994: 32). In the eyes of society the *biranganas* were whores (*beshha*), even small children used to call them whores *(bebushhey magi)* (Ibrahim, 1994: 65). The few families who did take their women back had to keep a very low profile in the community from then on in order to avoid ridicule. The vast majority of the *biranganas,* however, were not accepted back in the community.

Sheikh Mujibur Rahman again intervened in an effort to find a solution to the challenges faced by the *biranganas*. He realized that in a society where the purity of women was of utmost importance to all social groups, and where women had no status other than through marriage, no Bengali man would accept a *birangana* who had lost her virginity. In a desperate move, the government offered large sums of money to encourage suitable Bengali men to accept the *biranganas* in marriage. Some men did take the offer, but essentially because of the money. They mostly divorced their new wives not long after their marriage.

A significant number of women, realizing the fate that awaited them in Bengali society after liberation, had in fact decided to flee with their Pakistani captors to Pakistan. As one said, in a distant land 'whether I work as a prostitute or sweep roads, people will not recognize me, my husband or child will not ridicule me' (Ibrahim, 1994: 42). Many other *biranganas* committed suicide (Ibrahim, 1994, 1995). The stories of some of the women collected by Ibrahim are heart-rending. For instance, one *birangana* told Ibrahim that she and the other women with her were not forced by the Pakistani soldiers to leave with them:

> We went with them voluntarily because when we were being pulled out from the bunkers by the Indian soldiers, some of us half-clad, others half-dead, the hatred and deceit I saw in the eyes of our countrymen standing by, I could not raise my eyes a second time. They were throwing various dirty words at us … I did not imagine that we would be subjected to so much hatred from our countrymen. Rather, I imagined if the freedom fighters ever find us, they will accept us as their mothers and sisters. Because we did not come into this of our own choice. (Ibrahim, 1994: 59)

The hypocrisy of Bengali society and of Bengali men was underlined in various ways by all the women with whom Dr Ibrahim was able to speak. As one woman said: 'The father and brother who could not protect me from the hands of the wicked enemy, sat in judgement and left me on the grounds of my impurity. What a *beautiful* social system. I feel hatred when I think about it.'

Another *birangana* woman said to Dr Ibrahim: 'I have not given my body like Joan of Arc, but I have dedicated my greatest treasure, my womanhood for my country. Yet nobody inscribed our name on any of the *minars* [monuments]. Possibly because of shame. How can they applaud us when they could not protect us from total destruction' (Ibrahim, 1994: 34). In the same vein, another *birangana* said, 'Today there are so many memorials to martyrs along the various roads. So many roads and bridges are being named after the martyrs. The fathers, mothers, wives and children of the martyrs are not only getting plenty of assistance from the state but also much honour from the society. But where are we?' (Ibrahim, 1994: 69). Male Bengali society could not protect them, and yet when they were tortured and raped by the Pakistani army, presumably as an insult to Bengali men, those men could only blame and ostracize their sisters, wives and daughters for being victims.

Conclusion

The *birangana* issue again makes it clear how far Bangladeshi society continues to be dominated by traditional attitudes to women, based on the norms and values of *parda*, purity, honour and shame. One might think that in the aftermath of the war of liberation by which Bangladesh itself came into being, an exception might have been made for these 'war heroines'. But it is apparent from their treatment that considerations of purity, honour and shame once again took precedence over any sympathy for the plight of these women.

We have seen much the same in the previous sections of this chapter. In each case, through no fault of their own, Bangladeshi women have been forced to transgress the culturally prescribed limits for their gender. Many of the large new group of unmarried women without husbands were forced to enter paid employment in the city, but the limited degree of independence this allowed them brought them no respect from Bengali society. As we have seen, respectable men will not marry these women, who have been polluted by their supposedly free life away from male guardianship. The increasing number of destitute village women, widowed or abandoned by their husbands, find no willingness on society's part to support them or provide them with new social roles. Indeed, as Kafi's case studies of victims of floods and other natural disasters illustrate, such women are likely to find themselves victimized, cheated and exploited by the men of their community. As the *birangana* episode demonstrates very clearly, once women transgress their prescribed roles, however unwillingly, male society is unforgiving.

Bangladeshi society has undoubtedly changed in many ways over the years since liberation. The presence of a large number of Bangladeshi women in the public domain, traditionally the world of men, is one of the most noticeable of those changes. Yet it is evident that this increased public presence of women is hardly a gain for women as a whole. It is primarily a result of the man-made and natural disasters Bangladesh has been facing through this period. Each new crisis pushes more rural people towards the urban centres. As more and more rural poor families become landless, it becomes increasingly vital for their women to work to keep the family alive. Yet we have seen that while the new economic situation has opened up new employment opportunities for some women, and thus allowed them a degree of independence previously unavailable, these transformations in Bangladeshi society have not led to any real change in the fundamental gender ideology of Bangladeshi society. This ideology continues to define women in terms of marriage and motherhood, and to justify their inferior and subordinated condition.

Notes

1. Hilary Standing (1991) found from her research with middle-class Hindu women in Calcutta that parents often refrained from trying to find husbands for their daughters as they became indispensable to their family's economic well-being. When this happened, women often took it upon themselves to find suitable partners.
2. The non-standard language and punctuation are in the original text.

References

Ahmed, Rahnuma and Milu Shamsun Naher. 1987. *Brides and the Demand System in Bangladesh*, Centre for Social Studies, Dhaka University.

Akhter, Farida. 1992. *Depopulating Bangladesh: Essays on the Politics of Fertility.* Dhaka: Narigrantha Prabartana.

Aziz, K.M. Ashraful. 1979. *Kinship in Bangladesh.* Dhaka: International Centre for Diarrhoeal Disease Research.

Blanchet, Thérèse. 1984. *Meanings and Rituals of Birth in Rural Bangladesh.* Dhaka: Dhaka University Press.

Fruzzetti, Lina M. 1982. *The Gift of a Virgin: Women, Marriage, and Ritual in a Bengali Society.* New Jersey: Rutgers University Press.

Hartmann, Betsy and James K. Boyce. 1983. *A Quiet Violence: View from a Bangladeshi Village.* London: Zed Books.

Hartmann, Betsy. 1987. *Reproductive Rights and Wrongs: The Global Politics of Population Control and Contraceptive Choice.* New York: Harper & Row.

Hartmann, Betsy and Hilary Standing. 1989. *The Poverty of Population Control: Family Planning and Health Policy in Bangladesh.* London: Bangladesh International Action Group.

Ibrahim, Nilima. 1994. *Ami Birangana Balchi,* Part I. Dhaka: Jagriti Prashani.

Ibrahim, Nilima. 1995. *Ami Birangana Balchi,* Part II. Dhaka: Jagriti Prashani.

Islam, Mahmuda. 1979. 'Social norms and institutions.' In *The Situation of Women in Bangladesh.* Dhaka: UNICEF.

Jeffery, Patricia, Roger Jeffery and Andrew Lyon. 1988. *Labour Pains and Labour Power: Women and Childbearing in India*. London: Zed Books.

Kabeer, Naila. 1994a. 'Implementing the right to choose: women, motherhood and population policy.' In Naila Kabir, *Reversed Realities: Gender Hierarchies in Development Thought*. New Delhi: Kali for Women.

Kabeer, Naila. 1994b. 'Women's labour in the Bangladesh garment industry: choice and constraints.' In Camilla Fawzi El-Solh and Judy Mabro (eds), *Muslim Women's Choices: Religious Belief and Social Reality*. Oxford: Berg.

Kafi, Sharif A. 1992. *Disaster and Destitute Women: Twelve Case Studies*. Dhaka: Bangladesh Development Partnership Centre.

Khan, Zarina Rahman. 1992. *Women, Work and Values: Contradictions in the Prevailing Notions and the Realities of Women's Lives in Rural Bangladesh*. Centre for Social Studies, Dhaka University.

Kotalová, Jitká. 1993. *Belonging to Others: Cultural Construction of Womanhood Among Muslims in a Village in Bangladesh*. Uppsala: Uppsala University, Sweden.

Lindenbaum, Shirley. 1974. *The Social and Economic Status of Women in Bangladesh*. Dhaka: Ford Foundation.

Lindenbaum, Shirley. 1981. 'Implications for women of changing marriage transactions in Bangladesh', *Studies in Family Planning*, vol. 12, no. 11: 394–401.

Reysoo, F. van der Kwaak and Nasreen Huq. 1995. *The Incentive Trap: A Study of Coercion, Reproductive Rights and Women's Autonomy in Bangladesh*. Leiden: Leiden University

Rozario, Santi. 1986. 'Marginality and the case of unmarried Christian women in a Bangladeshi village', *Contributions to Indian Sociology* (n.s) 20, 2: 261–78.

Rozario, Santi. 1992. *Purity and Communal Boundaries: Women and Social Change in a Bangladeshi Village*. London: Zed Books.

Rozario, Santi. 1995a. 'TBAs (Traditional Birth Attendants) and birth in Bangladeshi villages: cultural and sociological factors', *International Journal of Gynaecology and Obstetrics*, vol. 50, no. 2: 145–52.

Rozario, Santi. 1995b. '*Dai* and midwives: the renegotiation of the status of birth attendants in contemporary Bangladesh.' In J. H. Roberts and C. Vlassoff (eds), *The Female Client and the Health-Care Provider*. Ottawa: International Development Research Centre, pp. 91–112.

Rozario, Santi. 1996. 'Population control and reproductive rights: contraception in Bangladesh and the feminist response.' A paper for the 6th International Interdisciplinary Women's Congress, Adelaide, April 1996.

Rozario, Santi. Forthcoming. 'The Dai and the doctor: discourses on women's reproductive health in rural Bangladesh.' In K. Ram and M. Jolly (eds), *Modernities and Maternities: Colonial and Post-colonial Experiences in Asia and the Pacific*. Cambridge: Cambridge University Press.

Shaw, Rosalind. 1992. '"Nature", "culture" and disasters: floods and gender in Bangladesh.' In E. Croll and D. Parkin (eds), *Bush Base: Forest Farm – Culture, Environment and Development*. London and New York: Routledge.

Siddiqi, Dina M. 1991. 'Discipline and protect: women factory workers in Bangladesh', *Grass Roots*, vol. 1, no. 2: 42–50.

Standing, Hilary. 1991. *Dependence and Autonomy: Women's Employment and the Family in Calcutta*. London and New York: Routledge.

Tambiah, Stanley Jeyaraja and Jack Goody. 1973. *Bridewealth and Dowry*. Cambridge: Cambridge University Press.

White, Sarah C. 1992. *Arguing with the Crocodile: Class and Gender in Bangladesh*. London: Zed Books.

About the Contributors

Bibi Bakare-Yusuf was educated at Goldsmith's College and Warwick University, and has worked as a researcher for BBC Radio 4. Her work on black women and subcultures was published in *Black British Feminist Thought: A Reader* (ed. Heidi Mirza, 1997).

Rada Boric, coordinator of the Zagreb Centre for Women War Victims, is a scholar in Croatian language and literature of the Southern Slavs. She has taught in the Slavic Department at the University of Zagreb, the University of Helsinki and Indiana University, and is a co-founder of the Zagreb independent women's studies course, where she teaches gender and language.

Urvashi Butalia, co-founder of the Indian feminist publishing house Kali for Women, is an Indian feminist activist and writer. She writes on media, communications, publishing and is involved in the Indian women's movement. She is currently working on an oral history of Partition.

Yvonne Corcoran-Nantes is a lecturer in women's studies and politics at the Flinders University of South Australia. She has researched and published on women of the popular classes in Brazil, and women in Central Asia in the post-Soviet era. Two books on Central Asian women and on women and grassroots protest politics in Brazil are in preparation.

Lorraine Dowler completed her Ph.D. in the Department of Geography at Syracuse University. She is assistant professor at Pennsylvania State University and her areas of interest are feminist, cultural and political geography.

Tovi Fenster is a lecturer at the Department of Geography in Tel Aviv University, Israel. She specializes in the fields of ethnicity, citizenship and gender and their relevance to planning. She is a professional consultant to government and non-governmental organizations.

Euan Hague is a part-time instructor in the Geography Department at Syracuse University, New York, and is completing a Ph.D. on 'Geographical Memories: Scotland, Place and People'. His research interests include nationalism and national identity, in particular issues of gender and memory.

Zohl dé Ishtar, an Irish-Australian lesbian, has spent her life campaigning for a nuclear-free and independent Pacific. In 1983 she left Australia with the World Bike Ride for Peace, and has since visited over thirty countries talking about nuclear colonization in the Pacific and Australia. Zohl lived at Greenham Common Women's Peace Camp for five years, where she founded the national network Women Working for a Nuclear Free and Independent Pacific. A journey through the Pacific in 1986–7 led to her book *Daughters of the Pacific* (Spinifex Press, 1994), containing interviews with over one hundred indigenous women. In 1995 she sailed across the Pacific to Moruroa Atoll to protest against the resumption of nuclear testing by the French government.

Roberta Julian (BA, Ph.D. Tas) is a lecturer at the Department of Sociology at the University of Tasmania. Her research interests focus on the social construction of identity, immigration and multiculturalism in the Australian context. She is currently engaged in a research project on refugee settlement experiences funded by the Bureau of Immigration, Multiculturalism and Population Research in Australia, which focuses on refugees in Tasmania. In 1995 she received a University Supplementary Research Grant to engage in research on migrant women in Australia. She has co-authored (with Gary Easthorpe) two chapters on ethnicity and health (both in press).

Margaret Kelleher lectures in English literature at the National University of Ireland, Maynooth. She has published a number of articles on Irish famine literature. Her book *The Feminisation of Famine* is published by Cork University Press (1997).

Yangchen Kikhang, whose family came from U-Tsang, central Tibet, lives in London. Since 1992 she has been working with the Women's Section of Campaign Free Tibet. She has given talks and written articles on the plight of women in Tibet and China, and has been active within the Boycott Beijing Campaign. She has contributed to *Women and Violence* (Zed Books, 1994), *Women Against Fundamentalism* (vol. 1, 1994) and *Feminist Review* (Spring 1994).

Natalya Kosmarskaya trained in the Faculty of Economics, Moscow State University, where she completed her doctorate on the socio-economic profile of traditional rural societies. Currently employed by the Moscow Centre for Gender Studies, a non-governmental public and research organization, her research covers the social anthropology of traditional societies, gender and ethnicity, migration and resettlement, and has taken her to Kirghizia and Oryol region, Central Russia. She has published extensively on women's roles in different socio-cultural milieux, ethnic-national-gender identities and cross-cultural adaptation of migrants.

Ronit Lentin is course coordinator of the M.Phil. in Ethnic and Racial Studies at Trinity College, Dublin, where she lectures in sociology and Women's Studies and where she has researched the gendered relations between Israel and the Shoah. She is an active anti-racism campaigner and has published several novels, as well as articles on feminist research methodologies, daughters of Shoah survivors, women's peace activism, and gender and racism in Ireland. She is the editor of *In from the Shadows: The University of Limerick Women's Studies Collection*, Vols I and II (Limerick, 1995, 1996), and has contributed chapters to several books, including *Jewish-American Women Writers* (ed. Shapiro, 1994), *Women and Social Class* (ed. Zmroczek and O'Mahony, 1998), *Women, Citizenship and Difference* (ed. Yuval-Davis and Werbner, 1998), *Women and War Reader* (ed. Lorentzen and Turpin, 1998), and *Voices of the Second Generation* (ed. Berger and Berger, 1998).

Haideh Moghissi is the author of *Populism and Feminism in Iran: Women's Struggle in a Male-Defined Revolutionary Movement* (Macmillan, 1994). She is assistant professor of Sociology at Atkinson College, York University, Canada. Haideh Moghissi completed her Ph.D. in Political Studies at Queen's University in Canada. Before leaving Iran in 1984, she was a senior researcher with the Iran National Archives; she was a founder of the National Union of Women and member of its first executive board and of the editorial boards of *Barbari* (Equality) and *Zanan Dar Mobnarezeh* (Women in Struggle).

Joan Ringelheim, a philosopher and historian, pioneered research on gender and the Holocaust. She has organized conferences, written essays and set the agenda for research on women and the Holocaust, often in the face of criticism by traditional Holocaust scholars. She is director of education at the Holocaust Memorial Museum in Washington DC.

Santi Rozario was born and brought up in Bangladesh. She lectures in sociology and anthropology at the University of Newcastle, Australia. Her teaching and research encompasses women's studies, the sociology of religion and community and development studies. She is the author of *Purity and Communal Boundaries: Women and Social Change in a Bangladeshi Village* (Zed Books and Allen & Unwin, 1992).

Nelia Sancho is the regional coordinator of Asian Women's Human Rights Council, an Asia-wide network of women's human rights centres, organizations and individuals. She organized public hearings on human rights in Tokyo and in Cairo in 1994, on issues of traffic in women, war crimes against women, and crimes against women related to population policies. A graduate of the University of the Philippines in Diliman, she is involved in Lila-Filipina, an organization of comfort women survivors, Defence for Children International, Gabriela, an alliance of feminist organizations in the Philippines, Streetchildren and Child Workers Support Centre, and others. She has participated in UN human rights meetings and parallel NGO forums in Vienna, Cairo and Copenhagen.

Helen Thomas is a lecturer in English Studies at Oxford Brookes University. Her research interests include black literature and post-colonial theory. She is currently working on a book on eighteenth-century slave narratives.

Judith Zur is a clinical psychologist, family therapist and social anthropologist. Her paper is based on doctoral fieldwork carried out in Guatemala in 1988–90. She has subsequently returned to Guatemala on human rights missions, and recently directed a project running workshops for rural health workers, funded by the Medical Foundation for the Care of Victims of Torture. She is currently managing a project on refugee mental health for the Northwest London Mental Health Trust and is an honorary research fellow in the department of Anthropology at University College London.

Index

blood), 110; women's lives as, 80, 84

prison camps, Serbian, 55–6, 57

professions: women banned from, in Iran, 132; women in, 168

prostitution, 99, 124, 125, 159, 165; rescue work, 245

protection of women, 82; by killing them, 106

Protestantism, 67, 74, 78, 88; espoused in Guatemala, 65

public space, women's negotiation of, 258, 267

public/private dichotomy, 229–30; for women migrants, 219–21; pure and impure spaces, 234, 238

Purea, Queen, 124

purity, 255, 256, 258, 259; of body, 234; of community, dilution of, 103; of family, 232, 233, 236; of race, 95; of women, 105, 108, 139, 264, 266

Quiche Maya women, 64–76

quilimbo settlements, 165

race struggle (*Rassenkampf*), 21, 22

racism, 2, 3, 5, 22, 23, 111, 115, 173

Rafsanjani, Hojatolislam Hashemi, 135

Rahman, Sheikh Mujibur, 264, 265

Rajaii, Aateghe, 135

rape, 10, 24, 25, 28, 39, 43, 44, 50–63, 65, 92, 93, 95, 99, 125, 126, 147, 148, 153, 185, 187, 190; as method of subduing women, 186, 187; as torture, 55; by Pakistani soldiers, 264; committed by UNPROFOR soldiers, 58; definition of, 51; feminization of victim, 55; gang-, 56–8, 65; genocidal, 7, 10, 12 (as military policy, 53; in Bosnia, Herzegovina, 50–63; masculinity and, 53–6); homosexual, 55, 56; in context of Holocaust, 25; in German camps, 26, 27; mass, 2, 5, 10, 41, 144–54; multiple, 56–8; of black women, 190; of boys, 53; of Croatian women, 39; of men, 53, 56; of nuns in Davao, 149; power relations in, 51; prisoner-to-prisoner, 56; psychological, 191; refusal to engage in, 57; structured by power relations, 59; traditional feminist view of, 52, 53

refugee camps, 43, 205, 207, 262, 263

refugee women, 42, 43, 48, 100, 264; collective strategies of, 207; construction of experience, 208; essentializing of, 197; exile of, 205–6; experiences of, 202–8; flight of, 205; health problems of, 206; in Australia, 196–210; invisibility of, 196; resettlement of, 206–8; resistance of, 201; statistics for, 199; victimization of, 196, 200, 201, 208; working with, 41–2

refugees, 2, 4, 6, 7, 44, 92, 101, 104; causes of movement of, 198; formal status of, 48; homogenizing of, 198; integration, in

Holland, 222; movements of (types of, 198; uniqueness of, 198); sponsorship of, 203; the decision to leave, 202–4 (mother's role in, 203)

re-Islamization policy in Iran, 130–4; changes in, 134–6

religion, meaning for women, 108

religious dogma, gendered, 129

remarriage, 138

reparations in war, 150, 152

repatriation: of refugees, 202; resulting from collapse of empire, 212

reproduction: of slaves, as reproduction of property, 181; politics of, 184–93; role of women, elevation of, 79

reputation, importance of, 70

resettlement: in Central Russia, 214–15; in rural areas, 214; resistance to, 107; women's fears of, 102

resistance of women, 164, 166, 173; in Iran, 130, 132, 134; of refugees, 201; of slaves, 188–92

Retchitsa village, 215; questionnaires used in, 216

Return to the Dying Rooms, 113

Ridd, Rosemary, 85

Riefenstahl, Leni, 29

rights of women: in Israel, 233; in slavocratic societies, 162

Ringelheim, Joan, 10, 13, 14, 245

Roma people, killing of, 3

Rongelap atoll, nuclear pollution of, 118

rootlessness, 22

Rosa House, Zagreb, 37, 44

Rose, Jacqueline, 249

Royal African Company, 184

Royal Ulster Constabulary (RUC), 85; women officers carrying arms, 84

Rozario, Santi, 8

Rufina, a 'comfort woman', 144

Russia: backwardness of everyday culture, 215; Central, women migrants in, 211–24; migrants, nature of, 213–14

Russian immigrants in Israel, 231

'Russians in the Orient', 213–14

Russians, killed by Nazis, 3

Rutherford, Jonathan, 58

Rwanda, 12, 13

Rwanda/Tutsi genocide, 4

Ryutaro Hashimoto, 151

Sahgal, Damyanti, 101, 103, 108

Salas, Estelita, 148

Salinog, Tomasa, a 'comfort woman', 144, 145

Sancho, Nelia, 10, 12

Sandercock, L., 227

Sarabhai, Mridula, 101

Saway, Jane, 186